Caribbean Migration
Globalised Identities

'The multidisciplinary perspective of *Caribbean Migration* makes it outstanding.'

> Dr R. Mallet, *Social Psychiatry Section, Medical Research Council Centre, UK*

'*Caribbean Migration* provides, in one place, a variety of important pieces of contemporary research on this area of international migration . . . by noted scholars in the field.'

> Professor Carole Boyce Davis, *Binghamton University*

The Caribbean is characterised by the transnational and migratory nature of its people. The reasons for this and the fundamental historical, cultural and political issues migration raises are the themes of *Caribbean Migration: Globalised Identities*.

This anthology represents important and original directions in the study of Caribbean migration. It takes a comparative perspective on the Caribbean people's migratory experiences within the Caribbean to North America and to Britain, France and the Netherlands. Although the book discusses the causes of migration, its emphasis is on the nature and meaning of the migration experience and on migration as a continuing historical process informed by a vibrant culture.

In addition this volume incorporates new analytical insights such as issues of gender, and new methodologies including the use of life stories and oral history. It explores themes from citizenship and imperialism, the globalisation of both capital and social space to the contemporary problems of the nation-state.

Caribbean Migration: Globalised Identities, edited by Mary Chamberlain, brings together a fresh multi-disciplinary approach to the literature on Caribbean migration from both young and established historians, anthropologists, sociologists, political scientists and geographers from North America, Europe and the Caribbean.

Caribbean Migration

Globalised Identities

Edited by

Mary Chamberlain

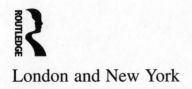

London and New York

First published 1998
by Routledge
11 New Fetter Lane, London EC4P 4EE

Simultaneously published in the USA and Canada
by Routledge
29 West 35th Street, New York, NY 10001

Typeset in Times by Keystroke, Jacaranda Lodge, Wolverhampton
Printed and bound in Great Britain by TJ International Ltd., Padstow, Cornwall

British Library Cataloguing in Publication Data
A catalogue record for this book is available from the British Library

Library of Congress Cataloguing in Publication Data
Chamberlain, Mary, 1947–
    Caribbean migration : globalised identities / Mary Chamberlain.
        p. cm.
    Includes bibliographical references (p.) and index.
    ISBN 0–415–16580–6 (hardcover)
    1. Caribbean Area—Emigration and immigration. 2. West Indians—
Migrations. 3. Identity (Psychology)—Caribbean Area. 4. Family—
Caribbean Area. 5. West Indians—Foreign countries—Social
conditions. I. Title.
JV7321.C48 1998
325.729—dc21   97–45099
                                                                     CIP

ISBN 0–415–16580–6

Contents

Figures and tables

FIGURES

TABLES

Contributors

Margaret Byron lectures in Human Geography in the department of Geography at King's College, University of London. Her research interests include labour migration and development with a particular focus on the Caribbean and migration outcomes for minorities in Europe. Publications include *Post-war Caribbean Migration to Britain: The Unfinished Cycle*. She is currently researching return migration to the Caribbean. This work includes collaboration with Stephanie Condon of INED, Paris on a comparative analysis of return from Britain and France.

Mary Chamberlain is Professor of Modern Social History at Oxford Brookes University. She is the author of *Fenwomen* (1983), *Old Wives' Tales* (1981), *Growing Up In Lambeth* (1989), *Narratives of Exile and Return* (1997), the editor of *Writing Lives: Conversations with Women Writers* (1988) and (with Paul Thompson) *Narrative and Genre* (1997) for the Routledge series *Memory and Narrative: International Debates*, of which she is a principal editor. She is currently working with Harry Goulbourne on Caribbean families in Britain, within the ESRC Programme on Population and Household Change.

Robin Cohen is Professor of Sociology at the University of Warwick. His recent publications include *Frontiers of Identity: The British and the Others* (1994), *Global Diasporas: An Introduction* (1997) and he is editor of *The Cambridge Survey of World Migration* (1995). He was Professor of Sociology at the University of the West Indies, Trinidad, in the late 1970s.

Stephanie Condon is a full-time researcher at the Institut National d'Etudes Demographiques (National Demographic Research Institute) in Paris. After initial studies in modern languages and geography at Salford University, she trained as a geographer at Queen Mary College, University of London, completing her doctoral research on Italian migration to Lyon, France from 1896–1954 in 1987. Her research interests have focused on the theme of migration, international and internal, and more specifically on the history and determinants of Caribbean migration to France.

Nancy Foner, Professor of Anthropology at the State University of New York at Purchase, received her Ph.D. from the University of Chicago. She has done research among Jamaicans in rural Jamaica as well as in London and New York. Her books include *Jamaica Farewell: Jamaican Migrants in London* (1978) and *New Immigrants in New York* (1987). Her latest book, *The Caregiving Dilemma* (1994), is a study of workers in a New York nursing home. She is currently editor of Allyn and Bacon's *New Immigrant Series* and is writing a book that compares immigrants in New York today with immigrants at the turn of the century.

Ramón Grosfoguel is a Senior Research Associate of the Fernand Braudel Center and an Assistant Professor in the Department of Sociology at the State University of New York, Binghamton. He has published articles on Caribbean migration, global cities and international development. He is co-editor of *Puerto Rico Jam: Rethinking Colonialism and Nationalism* and is currently completing a book on colonial Caribbean migrations to France, the Netherlands, England and the United States.

Howard Johnson is Professor of Black American Studies and History at the University of Delaware. He is the author of *The Bahamas in Slavery and Freedom* (1991), *The Bahamas from Slavery to Servitude* (1996) and editor of *After the Crossing: Immigrants and Minorities in Caribbean Creole Society* (1988).

Yvette Kopijn was born in Aruba, Dutch Antilles. In 1994 she graduated in multicultural women's studies and started working on her dissertation at the Belle van Zuylen Instituut, Graduate Centre for Comparative and Multicultural Women's Studies, University of Amsterdam. Her dissertation is concerned with the transmission and transformation of the experience of double migration among three generations of Surinamese-Javanese women in the Netherlands.

Selma Leydesdorff is Chair of Women's Studies and Women's History at the Belle van Zuylen Instituut, Graduate Centre for Comparative and Multicultural Gender Studies at the University of Amsterdam. She has published extensively in women's history, oral history and Jewish history. Recent major books include *We Lived with Dignity: The Jewish Proletariat of Amsterdam 1900–1940* (1994). She is supervising a research project on the comparison of the stories of three generations of migrant women, in which she interviews Antillean women and is a principal editor of the Routledge series Memory and Narrative: International Debates.

Helma Lutz is a sociologist and is currently Professor of General Education and Women's Studies at the Johann Wolfgang Goethe University, Frankfurt. She has carried out research in Germany and the Netherlands, where she is also an associate member of the Amsterdam School for Social Science Research. She has published extensively on issues of gender, migration and the links between them. She is co-editor (with Ann Phoenix and Nira Yuval-Davis) of *Crossfires: Nationalism, Racism and Gender in Europe* (1995) and (with Khalid Koser) of *The New Migration in Europe. Social Constructions and Social Realities* (1997).

Karen Fog Olwig is Senior Lecturer at the Institute of Anthropology at the University of Copenhagen and has written and published extensively on Caribbean migration and migrant communities.

Gert Oostindie directs the Department of Caribbean Studies at the KITLV/Royal Institute of Linguistics and Anthropology in Leiden and holds a chair as Professor of Caribbean Studies at Utrecht University. He is managing editor of *New West Indies Guide* and editor of the KITLV/Royal Institute's Caribbean Series and the *Revista Europea de Estudios Latinoamericanos y del Caribe*. He has served on various scholarly and governmental commissions dealing with the study of the Caribbean, has published widely on history, migration, ethnicity and the Caribbean. He is editor of *Ethnicity in the Caribbean* (1996), *Fifty Years Later. Capitalism, Modernity and Anti-slavery in the Dutch Orbit* (1995), *Caraïbische dilemma's in een 'stagnerend' dekolonisatieproces* (1994), (with Michiel Baud *et al.*), *Etnicidad como estrategia en América Latina y el Caribe* (1996) and *Roosenburg en Mon Bijou: Twee Surinaamse plantages 1720–1870* (1989).

Ceri Peach is Professor of Social Geography and Head of Department at Oxford University. He has held visiting fellowships at ANU, Berkeley and Yale. His research interests are in patterns of migration, settlement and segregation. Books include *West Indian Migration to Britain*, *Urban Social Segregation*, *Ethnic Segregation in Cities* (with Vaughan Robinson and Susan Smith), *Geography and Ethnic Pluralism* (with Colin Clarke and David Ley) and *The Ethnic Minority Population of Great Britain*.

Dwaine Plaza is currently an Assistant Professor at Oregon State University in the Sociology Department. His teaching interests are in race and ethnic relations, migration and refugee issues and research methods. His research focuses on Caribbean migration in the international diaspora. He is currently co-investigator on a research project which examines the life history and employment trajectory of university schooled Indo- and Afro-Caribbean origin men living in Toronto for a co-authored book on the hopes, dreams, aspirations and achievements of second generation Indo- and Afro-Caribbean origin males living in Canada.

Verene Shepherd lectures in the Department of History at the University of the West Indies, Mona, Jamaica. She is the author of *Transients to Settlers: The Experience of Indians in Jamaica 1845–1950* (1993) and co-editor of *Caribbean Slave Society and Economy* (1991) and *Caribbean Freedom* (1993).

Elizabeth Thomas-Hope is the James Seivright Moss-Solomon (Snr) Professor of Environmental Management at the University of the West Indies. She is the author of *Explanation in Caribbean Migration: Perception and the Image* (1992) and *Immigration in the Receiving Countries: the United Kingdom* (1994).

Acknowledgements

'Family and identity: Barbadian migrants to Britain' by Mary Chamberlain was first published in 1994 in *The International Yearbook of Oral History and Life Stories*, Vol. III, Rina Benmayor and Andor Skotnes (eds) *Migration and Identity*, Oxford, Oxford University Press.

'The legacy of migration: immigrant mothers and daughters and the process of intergenerational transmission' by Helma Lutz was first published in Dutch in 1995 in *COMENIUS* 15 (3).

A Dutch version of 'The delusive continuities of the Dutch Caribbean diaspora' by Gert Oostindie was published in Gert Oostindie *Het paradijs overzee. De 'Nederlandse' Caraïben en Nederland* (1997), Amsterdam: Bert Bakker.

Introduction

Mary Chamberlain

International migration strikes at the heart of nationhood and the nation-state, questioning the civic virtue of loyalty, the political certainty of citizenship, the patriotic basis of identity and the geographic security of the border. International migrants are by definition global people whose horizons and allegiances, education and enterprise, family and friendship are both portable and elastic. What, finally, unsettles about international migration is that it internationalizes the nation-state and globalizes identity. Fluidity, not fixity, characterizes the migrant, contemporary nomads and cultural gypsies. And few, if any, people are more global and more migratory than those from the Caribbean. For them, the nation is 'unbound' (Basch *et al.* 1994) and the city, 'boundless' (Chamoiseau 1997).

The idea of globalization is not, of course, new – neither is migration. Both lie at the centre of modernity, were indeed midwives to its birth. But thinking about them is relatively recent. It is as if the post-modern world has permitted them to 'come out', to declare an existence which hitherto dared not speak its name, although in various linguistic guises it has dominated the post Second World War debate. That war, embroiling every continent, left its legacy in the geopolitics of the Cold War which carved up most of the world into incompatible ideological spheres while the remaindered globe formed itself into spheres of non-alignment, a position fully endorsed by (at least) the United States. 'Your cause', as Henry Kissinger (in an address in Zambia during his 1976 tour of black African states) argued:

> is too compatible with our principles for you to need to pursue it by tactics of confrontation with the United States; our self-respect is too strong to let ourselves be pressured either directly or by outside powers.
>
> (Kissinger 1976)

Newly emerging states had to make political choices upon which all aspects of national and economic survival depended and to position their autonomy not merely within a regional perspective, but a global one. Within this new global order, trade emerged not as a precursor to territorial and imperial expansion, or as an economic lubricant but as a display of ideological finery, to sell and seduce. Products became adorned in ideological meaning, and trade in things became replaced by trade in the signs of things (Yurick 1995: 205). Multinational enterprise became the human face of global defence (Vernon 1971). Aid, too, became part of the international political armoury, and the language spoken, in politics or economics, was that of globalization, the global world system, the global economy. The actors were the free-range multinational corporations of the capitalized world, or their battery-farmed counterparts in the Communist world, the state and defence departments, the security and trade departments. The United Nations, a product of the time, was designed to secure and maintain global peace and ensure that a global concept of human rights and basic principles prevailed in all its signatory states.

Such globalization thinly disguised what many saw as neo-colonialism, witnessing that the new world order emerged not only out of the ashes of the Second World War, but also from those of the old empires, who, for the most part, were ideologically, if not strategically, allied to America. And America, along with the Soviet Union and later China, became the new post-war empires who needed the raw materials, trade and strategic support of the new colonies as much as the those new 'colonies' needed the 'empires'. With strategic weapons, strategic capital, global politics, the world had shrunk to a 'global village', aided by the revolution in communications, travel and the media. The media, the new cultural empire, promised to unite the world in the image of itself as much as it threatened to destroy global diversity.

Notwithstanding the revolution in the quieter aspects of globalization, telecommunications, international air travel, satellite TV (in themselves spin-offs from the wider political endeavour), the globalization of world politics and the world economy was, paradoxically, a last attempt by the old nation-states of the old world order to preserve and maintain their autonomies. The threat of communism or of capitalism was not just a threat to world peace, but to the specific order of each nation-state. However disingenuous the rhetoric of NATO or the Warsaw Pact, couched as it was in terms of a moral order, it was the fear of being conquered, militarily, politically and ideologically which drove those alliances, the fear of losing sovereignty and nationhood.

Ironically, in the global post-modern, post-colonial world the political boundaries of nation-states appear increasingly archaic. The much-remarked and publicized focus on ethnicity, on the small and large separatist movements, in both Western and Eastern Europe, Africa and Asia, the emphasis on multiculturalism and redefinitions of ethno-cultural identities in Europe, North America, and Australia have challenged, sometimes brutally, notions of homogeneity which lay, often mythologically, at the core of the old nation-states. Conversely, the debate on federation, whether in Europe or the Caribbean, emphasizes the communality and common cause, within regions hitherto defined by sovereign states, a communality which paradoxically permits and encourages greater diversity. Within a wider geopolitical context, it is possible for ever smaller constituencies to be viable, or to permit the movement of peoples within a vast region contained only by a common passport.

But only so far. The free movement of peoples anywhere contains the threat of chaos, as it always did. It was out of a kind of chaos of the sixteenth and seventeenth centuries (Hobbes' allegorical 'state of nature') that the global, political world as we know it emerged. It was precisely the movement of peoples, from the old world to the new, that vast early modern migration that forged our modern world of empires and nation-states. But ideas of allegiance and loyalties, of patrimony and patrilocality, of kith and kin, of commanding membership or protection, dues due and dues given die hard. Global and local migration destablized the early modern social order (as much as it does the post-modern one), but the predominant response then was to settle the un-settlers, through disguise and division. Undesirable migrants became vagrants, the desirable became citizens.

Thus it was that the Old (and New) Poor Law in Britain and her Empire, including America, stamped hard on vagrants. Locality and fixity conferred rights as well as responsibilities, on the Poor Law Guardians as much as the supplicants. Vagrancy and migration were antithetical notions and yet the two emerged side by side, conferring legitimacy and illegitimacy. Vagrants became migrants through labour, through productivity and migrants became vagrants through non-productivity, through poverty. Migrants became citizens, through ownership, through holding a stake in the land driven by possession and labour. Vagrants had no such claim to citizenship. Indeed, it was this concept of citizen-ship – this Lockean principle based on the pivot of possession and labour – which dominated the debate on membership and citizenship. Citizenship defined not only what you were, but who you were.

The struggle for universal franchise in nineteenth-century Britain was fought precisely around the nature and power of ownership, of property or labour. It was property not labour which was considered the necessary and sufficient claim to citizenship. Property implied fixity, a stake in the land, and the principles at least of local taxation in Britain still rely on notions of fixity, locality as well as property occupation, even though such principles have been partially abandoned in the issue of franchise. In the United States, the first nation-state created out of migration in the modern era, ownership of property defined who had claims to early citizenship – not the native Americans who roamed the land, nor African slaves who laboured on it. Both became, in principle and in practice, vagrants. Their claims to citizenship continue to resonate.

It was not just America which turned the base chaos of migration into the gold of citizenship. Europe's empires, too, tamed the threat of vagrancy into that of permanence and homogeneity. Those who conquered and settled established outposts of Europe elsewhere, little Britains, little Frances, across the seas, claiming the colonies as property by dint of their labour. Yet from the early days of these Empires, there was a hierarchy, the Plimsol line of which was race. Enforced migration, of Africans, and later Asians, did not qualify in the grand enterprise of citizenship or conquest. Their migration was simply the relocation of labour, functional vagrancy devoid of the grandeur of pioneer or enterprise. They were, simply, the spoils of Empire.

In many ways the narrative of America and Empire set the tone for the debates on international migration and globalization. In many ways, they were its prototypes. It was the go-getters who went and got, but it was a one-way movement, an assumption of dominance, a movement of visionaries to America, of missionaries (trading in goods and politics as much as souls) to empire. In much the same way, the contemporary debate on globalization has focused on the international go-getters, the economic and political trend setters, who convert the world and prepare it for international citizenship. Even the critics of globalization begin from a similar premise, that conversion means subversion and submersion of indigeneous custom and practice, that globalization sounds the death knell of cultural diversity at best, self-determination at worst.

The prosecution and defence in the trial of globalization have dazzled its international jury, while the real subversives have been steadily and stealthily undermining its basic assumptions, its old-world premise of *realpolitik*. Moving and manoeuvring, ducking and weaving in the narratives and debates on globalization are, and have been, actual or potential international migrants, slipping through the one-way traffic of globalization by the cultural backroads, absorbing and transforming the global agenda into that of their own, at the same time transforming the cultures and societies into which they enter, momentarily or for ever. A form, as Vertovec observes, of 'globalization from below' (Vertovec 1997).

From the start, the Caribbean emerged as a counter-narrative to the modern narrative of nomad capital which accompanied colonization, and preceded the growth of empire and the formation of nation-states. Even before the Europeans arrived, native Indians had established settlements and trade routes within the islands of the Caribbean and to and from the mainlands of North, Central and South America. Another site, another world, is never far from view within the Caribbean. By definition, islands look out as well as are looked in at, a point well taken by the Europeans who later came to dominate the region, as much as by the African slaves imported to labour there (Equiano 1814). There was always a world beyond, as well as a world left behind. For all the diversity which eventually emerged in the histories and cultures of those islands, there was a commonality in the potential of the far horizon. From the start, the Caribbean was global, linking as it did Europe and the Americas, Africa and Asia. It was diasporic, both the resting place and the launch pad for migrants. Preceding by at least a hundred years any notion of citizenship, of the vision or mission which came, and continues, to dominate debate on globalization, the particular experience of the Caribbean was deemed irrelevant to either grand global cause, and continues to defy the scholarly narratives which attempt to describe the social and cultural formations of the region (Trouillaut 1992; Benítez-Rojo 1996).

Caribbean culture itself is global, a mélange of European, and native Indian, African and Asian. Elements of each, old and new, have forged, and continue to forge, a unique syncretic cultural form (Harney 1996; Benítez-Rojo 1996) which continues to adapt, incorporate and transform the local with the global. Where once the global and the local interchanged with fresh arrivals from Africa or Europe, India or China, Syria or the Lebanon, now the global influences come from satellite TV, or in the hand-luggage of family visiting – or returning – from sojourns elsewhere. For one of the features of Caribbean migration is not only its historical longevity, but its impermanence, what Conway (1988) calls its circularity, and the informal contacts maintained with 'home' by generations of migrants.

The economic and political importance of these features are now readily acknowledged by Caribbean governments in the recognition of foreign exchange earnings sent through remittances and through the spending power of both returnees and the visits home of its citizens, in provisions made for returnees (Chamberlain and Goulbourne, forthcoming) and in, for instance, the consultations made by the Barbadian Commission for Constitutional Reform with Barbadians abroad. Less recognized, perhaps, is how the experience of migration itself developed, paradoxically, a consciousness of the Caribbean, and an awareness of its unique placement and position (Craig 1992), translated at times into direct political action, within the Caribbean (Richardson 1985; Hassankhan 1995) and equally, without; some examples of which Robin Cohen usefully summarizes in this volume. The culture of the Caribbean continues its globalizing mission in the person of its migrants, its transnationals (Basch *et al.* 1994), who traffic freely in and through the culture of the Caribbean, as they have done for five hundred years or so, absorbing what they encounter as much as being absorbed by it, changing and being changed, indigenizing the new as well as the old.

Yet this two-way traffic in migration, and its history, has been relatively neglected in the scholarly literature on Caribbean migration. The grand narratives of migration which accompanied modernity assumed an historic permanence and purpose in migration. These grand narratives, the heroic narrative of America, the homogenizing narrative of empire shaped the nation-state and captured the modern imagination, elaborate unifying metaphors which inverted and subsumed the destabilizing diasporic heart of migration, and which centred, settled and domesticated the nomadic essence of capital and labour which gave rise to it. It is these narratives which have shaped modern and contemporary thinking about citizenship, nationhood, race and migration.

The mythologies of citizenship and mobility, of heroism, exploitation and conquest which glorified and justified European migrations have been deemed irrelevant to the migrations from Africa and India and, more recently, from other locations in what has been significantly called the 'Third World'. Refugees have replaced vagrants, a designation (like vagrancy) of non-status, disqualifying the bearer, but on a global scale, from any claim to citizenship and nationhood and, in its further qualifier of 'economic' refugee, from any hope of labour. Migration and modernity was a one-way traffic, of Europeans to empire, of Africans and Asians within it. Caribbean migration was never viewed as a narrative of statehood or citizenship or loyalty, most particularly and most recently when the destination was not some other colony, but the mother country or the metropole itself. It was viewed as an altogether more iconoclastic movement, unprincipled, untrustworthy and potentially disruptive. The contemporary debate on multiculturalism, located as it is in the politics of post-war, post-colonial and,

I suppose, post-modern societies, has its origins in this colonial, 'modern' past and as such has a long, if often submerged, history (Goulbourne 1991: 87–125; Harris 1993).

The concept of citizenship enabled issues of loyalty, identity and membership to be foregrounded. But it did so in a particular way. It converted migration – in everyway its antonym – to a rational, non-random, irrevocable act of choice. Migrants were *im*migrants. In the United States – the first modern nation grounded in and forged out of migration – the 'melting pot' would cook (almost) everyone alike to a unique American identity, through the promise of economic and social advancement, ensuring in the process their unfailing loyalty. It excluded, significantly, those whose route in was other than by migration. Yet scholarly studies of migration contributed to its vindication; economics explained causation, sociology explained settlement, politics explained citizenship.

This assumption of rationality travelled well and accorded easily with explanations for the migrations into Europe which followed in the wake of the Second World War. The post-war reconstruction of Europe was a rational, planned response not only to the devastation of industry and homes caused by the war, but to the post-war enterprise of constructing a new domestic order, far removed from the class-torn clutter and international anarchy which had characterized the early half of the twentieth century. In Europe the Common Market would rationalize trade and diplomacy, the burgeoning welfare states would rationalize inequality, as much as contemporary design in the home would rationalize the antimacassars in favour of easy-clean Formica chairs. And into this post-war world entered the first phase of Caribbean migrants, coinciding with the labour shortage which Britain's reconstruction programme had created (Peach 1968), while elsewhere in Europe other migrants from the East and South similarly entered into the labour market.

Why did they come? They came to find work, a rational explanation for a seemingly aberrant event. The equation of migrant with worker has continued to dominate the economic and sociological models of migration (Todaro 1976; Wallerstein 1979; Cohen 1987). But it dovetailed with older narratives of race, gender and dependency. The new migrants were seen to be primarily black and colonial, poor and dependent (Huxley 1964). They had always (and only) been seen as labour and often, in the eyes of the colonial authorities, as trouble as well. Their arrival coincided with the contraction of the British Empire and the attempt to redefine Britain's global role in the new world order. Home and abroad, British society (and similar observations may also be made of those other European imperial states, France and the Netherlands) was busy redefining and reconstructing the material and the symbolic fabric of its nation-state (Schwarz 1996). West Indian migrants were seen as a new permanent addition to British society, into which, rationally, they should assimilate and integrate and thus prove worthy of citizenship. They were, first and foremost, *im*migrants.

Between 1948 and 1973 approximately 550,000 people of Caribbean birth arrived in Britain. Large-scale Caribbean migration to France and Holland began a decade or so after that to Britain. By 1982 there were approximately 266,000 people of Caribbean origin in France and by 1988 approximately 308,000 in the Netherlands (Peach 1991). Economic necessity was assumed to be the engine of migration, and assimilation – homogeneity – both the goal and the yardstick of migrant success. Assimilation was possible for, as one anthropologist confidently asserted, 'The West Indian lacks any distinctive and exclusive social organisation' (Patterson 1964).

The response to colonial migration and, by implication, principles of assimilation was, however, in Britain at least, a populist vilification of the migrant which erupted in 1958 in the violence of riots in Notting Hill, and attempted to be calmed by the Immigration Acts of 1962 and 1965 which effectively closed the door on further immigration and by the 1965 and 1968 Race Relations Acts which sought to outlaw racial discrimination. Within twenty years of the arrival of the post-war colonial migrants, assimilation had been replaced by reactive policies designed to control the potential for racial tension. In particular, the Immigration Acts and the 1965 Race Relations Act enshrined ethnicity and race as a political and judicial principle (Goulbourne forthcoming), while fostering at the social level a proactive programme of tolerance. By 1968 the then Home Secretary Roy (now Lord) Jenkins stated that assimilation was neither possible nor desirable and that, instead, Britain should recognize 'cultural diversity' and encourage 'mutual tolerance'. In new, multiracial Britain, the appropriate response was not to change the migrants, but to understand them and to create a society which was, in the words of the Swann Committee Report of 1985 (which sought to enshrine multiculturalism into the education system), 'socially cohesive and culturally diverse' (Swann 1985).

These policy shifts were paralleled in the academy as scholars moved their attention away from charting migrant settlement profiles (Glass 1961; Peach 1968; Foner 1979) and hypothesizing on the nature and practice of racial prejudice and discrimination (Banton 1967) to its impact, teasing out social, cultural and historical explanations of, for instance, underachievement by, in particular, West Indians (Rex and Tomlinson 1979). Since the late 1980s, as class (which always elided racial and ethnic distinction in a broader schema) has lost its analytic and political force, attention has focused on ethnicity, on its impact on politics, on nationhood, on new cultural – hybrid – formations and finally on the meanings of identity and the nature(s) of subjectivities (Hall 1990; Gilroy 1993; Bhabha 1994, 1996), where it has linked arms with prior feminist concerns around subjectivity and gender (Phizlacea 1983; Hall 1992; hooks 1993). In fifty years the debate on 'immigration' (more or less synonymous with race) has moved from homogeniety to fragmentation, from society to culture, from impact to meaning, from migration to diaspora, from modernity to post-modernity.

On the ground, migration continues and, like all cultural forms, it absorbs new dimensions. The revolution in transport and communications has eased the way for many migrants, including those from the Caribbean, to retain their links 'back home'. There is nothing new in this. Such retentions build on well-established historical precedents (Richardson 1983; Chamberlain 1997). More particularly, the pattern of continuing contact with those 'back home' has not only been a central feature of Caribbean migration, but has provided it with its particular and peculiar global flavour, permitting Caribbean retentions in the new creole cultures of the migrant destinations, as much as transmitting and transporting new elements back home. Regular visits, return and re-migration, bi-furcated migration, circular migration have all become part of the lexicon of Caribbean migration, while telecommunications and increasingly the Internet have eased the way for more regular and innovative forms of contact and renewal. Indeed, as Nancy Foner shows, the ease and relative cheapness of travel from North America to the Caribbean has obviated the need for permanent return. There is no longer a need to renounce natality in favour of the 'new' country, to prove to be worthy of 'citizenship' by denying the migratory route. Similar features can also be observed increasingly in other Caribbean destinations. In Britain, while return is now a significant and remarkable feature of the Caribbean migrant communities (the Jamaican and Barbadian communites have declined by 17 per cent between 1981 and 1991, much of it the result of return migration to the Caribbean), continuing contact has reduced the need to return permanently for some, and for others has enabled contact to be retained with children and grandchildren left behind in Britain. Communication has eased the pain and reduced the loss involved in both migration and its return. Both grandmothers and grandchildren cross the ocean frequently and, in the process, not only strengthen family ties but also Caribbean contacts and culture (Chamberlain and Goulbourne forthcoming; Plaza 1997). It is possible to be both Trinidadian and American, Jamaican and British, to be an African-American or to be black British, to be a transnational, the bearer of a global identity. It is possible also to imagine further migrations, to perceive of a national allegiance as a temporary expedient, a pit-stop in a wider migratory endeavour for historically any one destination was but part of a continuum of actual and potential migrant destinations. Caribbean culture engages necessarily with migration and with a migratory imagination. 'I have no nation now,' Derek Walcott (born in St Lucia, cultured in Trinidad, living in America, laureled by the world) wrote, 'but the imagination' (Walcott 1977).

Yet on the ground, migrant lives are also quite prosaic, concerned with the daily round of work, home and family, as well as developing and adapting older cultural patterns and social formations, creating a new syncretic Caribbean culture abroad. Perhaps it is precisely in the mundane that the process of what Craig (1992) calls the 'indigenization' of those diasporic Caribbean communities can be observed, for it is within the family, and the workplace, that the points of similarity and difference, conformity and conflict are negotiated and resolved, where family values and cultural practices are transmitted, contested and transformed, and where identities evolve. One pertinent feature of those families is precisely their international dimension, which extends even beyond the two-way 'transnational' family to incorporate family members beyond the Caribbean, in North America, Australia and elsewhere (Goulbourne and Chamberlain 1997).

And one of the most salient features of Caribbean identities involves, as Stuart Hall (1996: 4) reminds us, 'not the so-called return to roots but a coming-to-terms-with our "routes".'

Such routes involve those passed as well as those to be passed, both metaphorically and literally. To be black and British, African American, Dutch-Javanese-Surinamese, Martiniquian, pays homage to such routes; the terminology alone qualifies any apparent resolution or fixity in identity and incorporates not only history, but its future. But at a more domestic level, so does aunty in America, the cousin in Canada, the brother or sister or grandparent in the Caribbean, the great-grandparent who went to Panama or Cuba, or cut cane in Florida, or came from Venezuela, or commuted between Grenada and Trinidad, family members and relationships whose memories are played out in the conversation over the kitchen table, through the telephone in the hall, the letters on the doormat, or through family friendships formed in the village back home, or on the passage over, and retained in the host country, through the migrant networks, through jug-jug at Christmas, salt fish and ackies, mawby, ginger beer and Red Stripe, through weddings, funerals, christenings and graduations, family albums and tailor-made dresses, the Notting Hill Carnival, the meeting turn, Saturday Schools, the various Caribbean Island Associations, and Yellow Man or Gabby in concert. Indeed, the strength and importance of the family and of family support at both ends of the migration endeavour make migration a family enterprise which, as Plaza reveals, is being given a modern face-lift as small but international family businesses update the old remittances.

For those born in Europe, or North America, the sense of the Caribbean within remains strong, 'When I go *back* to the West Indies' one young black British woman remarked:

> even my accent changes . . . people ask me . . . like in Jamaica, they'll ask me if I'm from East Kingston. In Barbados, they'll ask me if I'm from a certain part of Barbados . . . *you can just be at home in all of these things. I'm not confused about my identity . . . I'm equally at home anywhere.*
>
> (quoted in Chamberlain 1997: 126 emphasis added)

This sense contributes significantly to the indigenization of Caribbean communities – what Kasinitz (1992) calls the 'creolization' of Caribbean communities abroad. But more than the sense of the Caribbean is the sense of the world which the Caribbean gives, an essentially global perspective and global identity. Such identities remain not merely relational, but mobile, unfixed. 'I'm who wants me' one young British-born Barbadian man remarked. 'If the Chinese want me, I'll be Chinese' (quoted in Chamberlain 1997: 120). If modernity was concerned with fixing and locating, post-modernity scrambles such certainties. International migration not only flaunts the old, modern certainties of the borders of the nation-state and challenges concepts of citizenship by insisting on their contingency; it celebrates that uncertainty, that contingency, precisely (in the case of the Caribbean) by being Jamaican and American, Trinidadian and Canadian, Barbadian and British, Dutch and Javanese and Surinamese.

This anthology brings together a multidisciplinary approach to Caribbean migration from historians, anthropologists, sociologists and geographers. It takes a comparative perspective on the migration experiences of Caribbeans not only within the Caribbean, but to North America and to the European metropoles of Britain, France and the Netherlands. It shifts the focus away from the causes of migration, towards the nature and meaning of the migration experience, a shift which has radical implications for those concerned with the consequences of migration and its future. It investigates migration as a continuing historical event which has been informed by, and continues to inform, a vibrant culture of transnational and circular migration, in the 'home' and in the 'host' countries.

Thus Robin Cohen's contribution intervenes in the burgeoning debate on 'diaspora'. He reminds us of the historical uniqueness of the Caribbean both as a region and as a diaspora, and how its unique culture of hybridity has continued to retain aesthetic, political and intellectual links between Africa and New World Africans, and between Caribbean peoples both at home and abroad. More tellingly, Caribbean peoples in the diaspora itself – whether in Europe or North America – have contributed to a transformation of those societies much as their presence in those societies has in turn transformed the Caribbean and contributed to a sense not only of West Indian-ness but within that of a specific cultural consciousness.

Grosfoguel offers an overview of Caribbean communities in Paris, Amsterdam, London and New York. He reminds us that the social, economic and political conditions not only at the time and place of leaving but also at the time and place of arrival have profound implications for the success of labour incorporation. The varying experiences of Caribbean migrants in their respective metropoles need to be seen comparatively before any understanding can be reached; attention must be focused on the peculiarity of local conditions as well as on the profile of the migrants themselves. This perspective is developed further by Foner in her detailed comparison between Jamaicans in London and New York, and Haitians in New York and Miami. She adds the further variable of race relations and time (the 'period effect') to those identified by Grosfoguel and warns against assuming homogeniety in migrant experience, not only across but also within the same country.

But comparisons, as Foner shows, perhaps work most fruitfully when comparing similar or same groups in different locations, where the receiving environment will produce very different experiences. This theme is taken up by Olwig in her study of Nevisians in the US Virgin Island of St John and in Leeds in the United Kingdom. Interviews, she argues, reveal valuable data on migration, in this case on two very different expectations and experiences of Nevisian migrants. But, equally important, is the way in which this experience is related and represented and the process by which it is seen to fit within the life stories and life cycles of the migrants themselves. Interviews, therefore, need to be interpreted at a range of levels if the nuances of migrant experience, which includes the continuing interplay between the local and the global, are to be appreciated.

The emphasis on labour as the principal propeller of migration has necessarily led to a male bias in migration studies. Men, it is assumed, are the pioneer migrants, sending later for their wives and children. This bias reflects as much the epistemological roots of scholarly disciplines as historical precedent. As my own study of Barbadian migrants revealed (Chamberlain 1997), women as well as men migrated, and have done so historically. It is only recently that scholars have begun to look at gender for insights into migration, and within that to focus on the particular experiences of women. But, as Leydesdorff argues, the continuing focus on men, at least in the Netherlands, and men as a particular kind of problem, has dominated the data and obscured the issues which women have encountered as migrants. In order to find out about the daily lives of women as migrants, it is necessary to turn to a life-story approach. This, however, is not without its pitfalls. Picking up on some of the themes raised by Olwig, she alerts us to the difficulties of representation, and the dangers of misrepresentation.

The experience of women as migrants, their capacity to adapt and change, and their role in the transmission of culture are themes developed by Lutz and Kopijn. Using life-story interviews across two generations of Surinamese women, Lutz explores the mental and emotional context of migration. For her, life stories can illuminate the links between subjectivity and material life. She highlights how 'social capital' has been transmitted and transformed across generations and across the oceans, arguing that it is this which enables successful adaptation for successive generations, as well as a continuing sense of Caribbean identity. Kopijn also uses a life-story approach but in this case to explore the double migration of Javanese-Surinamese migrants, and to look at ways in which a Javanese ethnicity was constructed in Surinam and reconstructed in Holland. Migration, she argues, does not stop at the moment of relocation, but continues in its adjustments across generations. In this, women as 'cultural entrepreneurs' play a pivotal role within their families.

The theme of intergenerational transmission is investigated, but in very different ways, by Oostindie and in my own chapter. Oostindie explores the attitudes of young, contemporary Surinamese and Antilleans towards the history of migration to the Netherlands. He looks at the experiences of those (relatively few) Caribbean migrants who arrived in Holland pre and post the Second World War. Then, the overwhelming Dutch response was of benign curiosity. For the most part these early migrants were regarded as exotic and heroic. By comparison, the later immigration which began in the 1960s is qualitatively different. Numerically it is larger. It is more ethnically diverse. The motivations for migration are equally diverse, as were the beliefs in what Holland offered and migrant attitudes towards and relations with the Caribbean. In many ways, the history of Dutch Caribbean migration is very different from that of the British or French Caribbean, and significantly different from its own early history. Echoing Foner's warning, there is nothing constant in Caribbean migration, there are no natural continuities. By contrast, my own chapter, using life-story interviews across generations, picks up on some of the themes opened by Lutz and explores the continuities of values and attitudes within families of Barbadian migrants. It argues for the importance of family histories in understanding migration, and shows how those histories, or salient elements of them, are transmitted and transformed across generations and play a powerful role in the formation of identities and the representations of self.

The continuing vitality of the Caribbean in the life and culture of its peoples abroad is one of the central features of Caribbean migrants. While many of the chapters in this book have explored this dimension and drawn attention to the essential elasticity of the Caribbean as a region, whose frontiers as Susan Craig reminds us 'are not geographical, but living ones' (Craig 1992: 218), it is vital to explore why and how this feature has become so central a characteristic of the Caribbean and its migrations. Migration has often been viewed and analysed from the perspective of the metropole, and its assumptions that migration is both permanent and aberrant, based (as argued earlier) on the need to fix the vagrants and their loyalties. Yet, from the perspective of the Caribbean, migration to, from and within the region has been central to its political creation, its economic sustenance and its cultural core. The first Europeans migrated freely within the region, the Americas and Europe, taking and depositing their capital, their labour (and their labourers) and gobbits of culture. After Emancipation, exercizing freedom for the former slaves more often than not assumed the form of migration – either off the plantations, or off the island altogether. Indeed, so great was the potential exodus from Barbados in 1838 that the House of Assembly passed legislation effectively prohibiting it (Beckles 1990: 112; Chamberlain 1997: 20). Notwithstanding that, migration not only from Barbados but from all the islands in the Caribbean, with destinations in North, South and Central America as well as the Caribbean, continued throughout the nineteenth century and was a well-established feature by the twentieth (Roberts 1955; Ebanks *et al.* 1979; Richardson 1985; Kasinitz 1992). It was not only the former slaves who migrated. Some of the Chinese and Indian indentured labourers who were imported into the region after emancipation either returned to India after their indentureship, or migrated on, to South and Central America (Look Lai 1993; Shepherd 1994; Laurence 1994). Any attempt to understand the complexity of Caribbean migration must take into account its long migratory history and begin to explore some of its lesser-known facets. Thus Shepherd explores one aspect of the Caribbean's migration history in her study of Indian migrants to Jamaica. Brought in to help solve the perceived shortage of labour after the former slaves' migration off the plantations, the Indian labourers, on expiry of their indentureship, then absorbed what was an already established culture of migration and themselves migrated, some back to India, some to the cities, and some further afield, to Cuba, to Panama, and to North and South America, despite opposition, and at times prohibition, from the Jamaican government.

A very different aspect of migration is evoked in Johnson's article on Barbadians who migrated to the Putomayo District of the Amazon in 1904–11. Reminding us of the multidirectional flow and multifaceted dimension of Caribbean migration, Johnson explores the fate and experiences of a small group of Barbadians who migrated to this region to work in the rubber industry with the promise of high wages, free passage, housing and medical expenses, but who found themselves as unwitting accomplices to a highly exploitative labour system where they themselves were the victims of a system of debt peonage. Far from transforming their material circumstances, or escaping the rigid strictures of Barbadian society, these migrants ended their employment contracts often heavily in debt, deeply exploited and morally compromised by their part in the subjugation and virtual enslavement of the native Indians.

Although this may represent one of the lesser-known and least successful components in the history of Caribbean migration, it manifests nevertheless an important dimension of what Thomas-Hope (1992) calls the 'migration tradition'. Returning to the theoretical theme of globalization, she reminds us not only of the centrality of the Caribbean to the global enterprise of modernity, but also how migration has influenced the development of the institutional structures of the Caribbean, and of a culture which supports and encourages the process. In so doing, Caribbean societies, at every level, have been shaped by the continuing interplay between the local and the global, a perspective which was and remains a central dynamic of Caribbean migration culture.

The final essays in this anthology look in some detail at the settlement profile and survival strategies of Caribbean migrants in Britain, France and Canada. Peach's meticulous analysis of the 1991 UK census indicates that, contrary to popular perceptions of the Caribbean population in Britain becoming increasingly segregated socially and ghettoized demographically, there is a considerable degree of geographic dispersal of the population, and a notable movement of Caribbean people (by descent or birth) out from the main cities of earlier concentration. As a result, he argues, there are far higher levels of social interaction than among, for instance, African-Americans in the United States and a significant degree of ethnic mixing.

The issue of gender in settlement and survival is raised by Byron, Condon and Plaza. Whereas, as Peach observes, there is a high concentration of low-skilled work or unemployment among male Caribbeans in Britain, for women the situation is rather different. As Byron shows, black women in Britain have, and have had, a high rate of participation in the labour force in Britain, reflecting the long history of participation in the formal (and informal) economy by women in the Caribbean. This continuing participation may be seen both as a survival strategy, in the Caribbean and Britain, and as an example of the 'indigenization' of the Caribbean in Britain. In some ways it parallels Lutz's findings with Surinamese women who are able to fit their social practices into those of the Netherlands. Although the meanings and contexts of these practices are different in Surinam and Holland, as they are in St Kitts and Britain, exploitation of their superficial conformity enhances women's successful strategies for survival and helps retain Caribbean cultural practices. At the same time, these women, in Britain, have moved increasingly into the service and professional areas and, unlike their male counterparts, have been less affected by downsizing in the industrial and manufacturing sector. Their continuing contribution to the house-hold economy has increased their status within the household although many believe that their lives, while materially more comfortable, are more difficult than those of their mothers in the Caribbean.

The theme of survival strategies is also highlighted by Condon in her study of migrants from Martinique and Guadaloupe to metropolitan France. Indeed, both Byron and Condon challenge the popular belief of women as 'passive' participants in the migration process, a challenge which accords with the evidence of Lutz, Leydesdorff and Kopijn. Condon, however, argues that while the decision to migrate may be based on a long-term strategy for improvement, the employment profile in both the Caribbean and in France is often more haphazard, linked to family experience, social networks and local opportunity. The need to survive, as Condon elegantly points out, leads to strategies based on compromise and coping.

Finally, Plaza's study of Caribbean males in Canada explores the strategies for upward social mobility among university-educated Caribbean-born men. While the particular expression of upward mobility has been shaped by the cultural values of the Caribbean, the strategies adopted by these men have been sharply modified by the opportunities available to them in Canada, and the levels of discrimination experienced. His article thus accords with many of the insights raised by Grosfoguel and Foner, but he adds a further dimension: while many of the men from his sample were forced to lower their aspirations, they compensated by retaining and nurturing family and other links with the Caribbean. This had a double function. It provided a safety cushion, and at the same time a yardstick by which to measure success in Canada. Indeed, perhaps this is a further example of the 'indigenization' of Caribbean peoples abroad, who have always retained links back home as both an insurance policy in the event of 'failure', and as a foil to their own social mobility. Of vital importance in this is the link with family who often helped support the migrant, as the migrant in turn supported the family back home. This now has been given a modern twist as communications and technology has enabled these trans-national links to be converted into transnational enterprise. Perhaps this offers one explanation for the continuing links between Caribbean people at home and abroad, the essence of international migration and global lives, of the 'indigenization' or 'creolization' of Caribbean communities in exile (Kasinitz 1992; Sutton and Chaney 1994) and of their globalized identities, and also for the retention of the mythology of reward which may be one of the drivers of migration and one vital component of its vibrant culture.

As these chapters demonstrate, there are as many routes to studying international migration as the trajectories of migration itself. Equally, as these chapters remind us, while migration may be observed and monitored on a macro level, the active agents in the process are the migrants themselves, whose agendas and responses are created and resolved through a complex cultural and psychological process which manifests itself at both an individual and at a social level. The vibrancy of Caribbean cultures abroad, whether in Holland, France, Britain or North America is strong evidence of a continuing engagement with both the home and the host societies, a clear indication of the reluctance to, and impossibility of, substituting one for the other, and a powerful reminder of how the Caribbean continues to forge a powerful global identity through and in its peoples.

REFERENCES

Basch, L., Glick Schiller N., Szanton Blanc C. (1994) *Nations Unbound: Transnational Projects, Postcolonial Predicaments and Deterritorialized Nation-States*, Langhorne, PA: Gordon and Breach.

Bhabha, Homi (1994) *The Location of Culture*, London: Routledge.

—— (1996) 'Culture's in-between', in S. Hall and P. du Gay (eds) *Questions of Cultural Identity*, London: Sage.

Banton, Michael (1967) *Race Relations*, London: Tavistock.

Benítez-Rojo, Antonio (1996) *The Repeating Island. The Caribbean and the Postmodern Perspective*, Durham, NC: Duke University Press.

Breckles, Hilary (1990) *A History of Barbados*, Cambridge: Cambridge University Press.

Chamberlain, Mary (1997) *Narratives of Exile and Return*, London, Macmillan.

Chamberlain, M. and Goulbourne, H. (forthcoming) *Caribbean Families in Perspective*.

Chamoiseau, Patrick (1997) *Texaco*, New York: Pantheon.

Cohen, R. (1987) *The New Helots: Migrants in the International Division of Labour*, Aldershot: Gower.

Conway, Denis (1988) 'Conceptualising contemporary patterns of Caribbean international mobility', *Caribbean Geography* 2(3): 145–63.

Craig, Susan (1992) 'Intertwining Roots', *Journal of Caribbean History*, 26: 2.

Davison R.B. (1962) *West Indian Migrants*, Oxford: Oxford University Press.

—— (1966) *Black British*, London: Oxford University Press for the Institute of Race Relations.

Ebanks, G., George, P.M. and Nobbe, C.E. (1979) 'Emigration from Barbados', *Social and Economic Studies*, 28(2): 431–49.

Egginton, Joyce (1957) *They Seek A Living*, London: Hutchinson.

Equiano, Olaudah (1814) *The Interesting Narrative of the Life of Olaudah Equiano or Gustavus Vassa, the African*, reprinted in H.L. Gates (ed.) (1987) *The Classic Slave Narratives*, New York: Mentor Books.

Foner, Nancy (1979) *Jamaica Farewell: Jamaican Migrants in London*, London: Routledge and Kegan Paul.

Gilroy, Paul (1993) *The Black Atlantic: Modernity and Double Consciousness*, London: Verso.

Glass, R. (1961) *London's Newcomers*, Cambridge, MA: Harvard University Press.

Goulbourne, H. (1991) *Ethnicity and Nationalism in Post-Imperial Britain*, Cambridge, Cambridge University Press.

—— (forthcoming) *The Colour Line at Century's End*, London, Macmillan.

—— and Chamberlain, M (1997) 'Caribbean families in their international perspective', (unpublished) paper presented to the ESRC's 'Household and Population Change' programme, London, Policy Studies Institute.

Hall, Catherine (1992) *White, Male and Middle Class*, Cambridge: Polity Press.

Hall, Stuart (1990) 'Cultural identity and diaspora', in J. Rutherford (ed.) *Identity: Community, Culture and Difference*, London: Lawrence and Wishart.

—— (1996) 'Who needs identity?', in S. Hall and P. du Guy (eds) *Questions of Cultural Identity*, London: Sage.

Harney, Stefano (1996) *Nationalism and Identity: Culture and the Imagination in a Caribbean Diaspora*, Kingston: The Press, University of the West Indies/London: Zed Books.

Harris, C. (1993) 'Britishism, racism and migration', paper presented at the 25th Annual Conference of the Association of Caribbean Historians, Mona, Jamaica.

Hassankhan, M (1995) 'The influence of migration on political leadership and movements in Suriname', paper presented to Comparative History of Caribbean Migration, Oxford.

Hiro, D. (1973) *Black British White British: A History of Race Relations in Britain*, London: Penguin.

hooks, bell (1993) 'Postmodern blackness', in P. Williams and L. Chrisman (eds) *Colonial Discourse and Post-Colonial Theory*, London: Harvester/Wheatsheaf.

Huxley, Elspeth (1964) *Back Street New Worlds*, London: Chatto and Windus.

Kasinitz, Philip (1992) *Caribbean New York: Black Immigrants and the Politics of Race*, Ithaca, NY: Cornell University Press.

Kissinger, H. (1976) 'The United States and Africa', speech by Secretary of State Henry Kissinger, 27 April 1976, *Survival* XVIII (4), July/August.

Laurence, K.O. (1994) *A Question of Labour*, Kingston, Jamaica: Ian Randle.

Little, K. (1946) *Negroes in Britain*.

Look Lai, W. (1993) *Indentured Labor, Caribbean Sugar: Chinese and Indian Migrants to the British West Indies, 1838–1918*, Baltimore, MD: Johns Hopkins University Press.

Patterson, Sheila (1964) *Dark Strangers: A Study of West Indians in London*, London: Penguin.

Peach, Ceri (1968) *West Indian Migration to Britain: A Social Geography*, Oxford: Oxford University Press.

—— (1991) *The Caribbean in Europe: Contrasting Patterns of Migration and Settlement in Britain, France and the Netherlands*, Research Paper in Ethnic Relations 15, Centre for Research in Ethnic Relations, University of Warwick.

Phizlacea, A. (ed.) (1983) *One Way Ticket: Migration and Female Labour*, London: Routledge and Kegan Paul.

Plaza, D. (1997) 'Frequent flier grannies', paper presented at the 'History of the Family' Conference, Carlton University, Ottawa, Canada, 15–17 May 1997.

Rex, J. (1988) *The Ghetto and the Underclass: Essays on Race and Social Policy*, Aldershot: Avebury.

Rex, J. and Tomlinson, S. (1979) *Colonial Immigrants in a British City: A Class Analysis*, London: Routledge and Kegan Paul.

Richardson, Bonham (1985) *Panama Money in Barbados, 1900–1920*, Knoxville: University of Tennessee Press.

Roberts, G.W. (1955) 'Emigration from the Island of Barbados', *Social and Economic Studies*, (4) 3.

Schwarz, Bill (1996) 'The expansion and contraction of England', introduction to Bill Schwarz (ed.) *The Expansion of England: Race, Ethnicity and Cultural History*, London: Routledge.

Shepherd, V. (1994) *Transients to Settlers. The Experience of Indians in Jamaica 1845–1950*, Leeds: Peepal Tree Books.

Sutton, Constance and Chaney, Elsa (eds) (1994) *Caribbean Life in New York City: Sociocultural Dimensions*, New York: Center for Migration Studies.

Swann, Lord (1985) *Education for All: The Report of the Committee of Inquiry into the Education of Children from Ethnic Minority Groups*, Cmnd 9453, London: HMSO.

Thomas Hope, E. (1992) *Explanation in Caribbean Migration*, London: Macmillan.

Todaro, M.P. (1976) *International Migration in Developing Countries*, Geneva: International Labour Organization.

Trouillaut, M. (1992) 'The Caribbean region: an open frontier in anthropological theory', *Annual Review of Anthropology*, 21:19–42.

Vernon, Raymond (1971) *Multinational Enterprise and National Security*, Adelphi Papers No.74, London: Institute for Strategic Studies.

Vertovec, S. (1997) 'Transnational Communities', ESRC Programme Development Workshop, University of Warwick, 16 January.

Walcott, D. (1977) 'The Schooner Flight', in *The Star-Apple*, New York: Farrar, Strauss and Giroux.

Wallerstein, I. (1979) *The Capitalist World Economy*, Cambridge, Cambridge University Press.

Yurick, Sol (1995) 'The emerging metastate versus the politics of ethno-nationalist identity', in J. Pieterse and B. Parekh (eds) *The Decolonization of the Imagination: Culture, Knowledge and Power*, London and New Jersey: Zed Books.

Part I
Rethinking diaspora

1 Cultural diaspora

The Caribbean case

Robin Cohen

Migration scholars – normally a rather conservative breed of sociologists, historians demographers and geographers – have recently been bemused to find their subject matter assailed by a bevy of postmodernists, novelists and scholars of cultural studies. A reconstitution of the notion of diaspora has been a central concern of these space invaders. For example, the editor of the US journal *Diaspora*, Khacha Tölölyan, a professor of English at Wesleyan University, announced its birth (1991: 3) with the following statement:

> The conviction underpinning this manifesto disguised as a 'Preface' is that *Diaspora* must pursue, in texts literary and visual, canonical and vernacular, indeed in all cultural productions and throughout history, the traces of struggles over and contradictions within ideas and practices of collective identity, of homeland and nation. *Diaspora* is concerned with the way in which nations, real yet imagined communities, are fabulated, brought into being, made and unmade, in culture and politics, both on the land people call their own and in exile.

For postmodernists the collective identity of homeland and nation is a vibrant and constantly changing set of cultural interactions that fundamentally question the very ideas of 'home' and 'host'. It is demonstrable, for example, that uni-directional – 'migration to' or 'return from' – forms of movement are being replaced by asynchronous, transversal flows that involve visiting, studying, seasonal work, tourism and sojourning, rather than whole-family migration, permanent settlement and the adoption of exclusive citizenships. These changing patterns have important sociological consequences. As Vertovec puts it:

> Aesthetic styles, identifications and affinities, dispositions and behaviours, musical genres, linguistic patterns, moralities, religious practices and other cultural phenomena are more globalized, cosmopolitan and creolized or 'hybrid' than ever before. This is especially the case among youth of trans-national communities, whose initial socialization has taken place within the cross-currents of more than one cultural field, and whose ongoing forms of cultural expression and identity are often self-consciously selected, syncretized and elaborated from more than one cultural heritage.
>
> (Vertovec 1996, private correspondence)

One way of conceptualizing the social and cultural outcomes described is to loosen the historical meanings of the notion of 'diaspora' to encompass the construction of these new identities and subjectivities. Suppose we adopt the expression 'cultural diaspora' to encompass the lineaments of many migration experiences in the late modern world. Can cultures can be thought of as having lost their territorial moorings, to have become in effect 'travelling cultures'? Can migrants of African descent from the Caribbean be considered as one of the paradigmatic cases of a cultural diaspora? Do we need more than postcolonial theory to demonstrate that, in practice, a cultural diaspora has emerged? Do we need instead to explore the common experiences, intellectual and political visions and religious movements that cement Afro-Caribbean cultural and migratory experiences? Is the notion of a 'black Atlantic' adequate to our purposes?

THE CARIBBEAN: MIGRATION AND DIASPORA

I turn now to my case study, the consideration of whether the Caribbean peoples abroad constitute a 'new', 'postcolonial', 'hybrid' cultural diaspora. The first and most evident problem in seeing Caribbean peoples as any kind of diaspora is that they are not native to the area. As is well known, the autochtonous peoples of the Caribbean, the Caribs and Arawaks, failed to survive the glories of Western civilization – nearly all died from conquest, overwork and disease. Virtually everybody in the Caribbean came from somewhere else – the African slaves from West Africa, the white settlers, planters and administrators from Europe, and the indentured workers who arrived after the collapse of slavery, from India. This may in and of itself disqualify any consideration given to the idea of a Caribbean diaspora. Settler and immigrant societies are normally conceived of as points of arrival, not departure, sites of a renewed collectivity, not of dissolution, emigration and dispersion.

Second, the peoples of the Caribbean may be thought of as parts of other diasporas – notably the African victim diaspora, the Indian labour diaspora and the European imperial diasporas.[1] Again, surely it would be expected that, if they are free to migrate, a significant proportion of any diasporic community should wish to return to their real or putative homeland. Yet, while some of European descent have returned 'home' to Europe, Caribbean people of Indian and African origin have in recent years been notably disinterested in returning either to India or Africa.

Despite these considerable conceptual obstacles, Hall (1990: 222–37) none the less is convinced that a distinctive Caribbean diasporic identity can be discerned. Caribbean identity, he argues, cannot be rendered simply as a transposition of an African identity to the New World because the rupture of slavery and the admixture of other peoples built into a Caribbean identity a sense of hybridity, diversity and difference. Hall poses the question, 'What makes African-Caribbean people already people of a diaspora?' and answers as follows:

Diaspora does not refer us to those scattered tribes whose identity can only be secured in relation to some sacred homeland to which they must at all costs return, even if it means pushing other people into the sea. This is the old, the imperializing, the hegemonizing form of 'ethnicity'. We have seen the fate of the people of Palestine at the hands of this backward conception of diaspora (and the complicity of the West with it). The diaspora experience as I intend it here is defined not by essence or purity, but by the recognition of a necessary heterogeneity and diversity; by a conception of identity which lives with and through, not despite, difference; by hybridity. Diaspora identities are those which are constantly producing and reproducing themselves anew, through transformation and difference.

(Hall 1990: 235)

In this excerpt Hall is essentially concerned with the diasporic identity that Caribbean peoples created within the geographical bounds of the Caribbean itself. A much more challenging field of enquiry is the degree to which they affirmed, reproduced and created a diasporic identity in the places to which they subsequently moved. Before discussing the nature of this Caribbean diaspora abroad, it is necessary to provide a quick brush-stroke picture of their migration history over the last century or so.

I have just mentioned that Indo-Caribbeans did not go back to India, nor Afro-Caribbeans to Africa. Strictly speaking, this was not always true. At the end of the period of indenture about a quarter of the Indo-Caribbeans returned to India. In the African case, the British colonialists recruited a few dozen Afro-Caribbean train drivers for Nigeria, the French appointed an Antillean governor, Felix Eboué, in the Cameroons and a remarkable young psychiatrist, Frantz Fanon, who was later to become one of the most prominent of all developing world intellectuals, was assigned to the colonial medical service in Algeria. Some voluntary migration, including Garveyite and Rastafarian (see below) settlements, also occurred.

However, these were mere drops in the ocean of Caribbean people who decided to migrate to Panama, the USA and Europe. When Ferdinand de Lesseps, the famous Suez Canal maker, floated a new Panama Canal Company to link the Pacific Ocean to the Caribbean Sea, the Bourse went crazy with the prospects of great profits. In fact, the venture proved a long-drawn-out financial failure. The canal and railway works were dogged by mismanagement and the workers suffered greatly from malaria, snakebite, swamp fever, industrial accidents and bad treatment. The hands for this operation were drawn from many countries, but predominantly from Jamaica.

The Afro-Caribbean minority located in the strip of slums surrounding the Panama Canal Company area is descended from these workers. They have remained largely poor and underprivileged in the Panamanian context, with the key positions of authority and influence being occupied by Hispanics. Other small enclaves in Central America are drawn from Caribbean peoples brought there to establish banana plantations, or to undertake public works. Honduras and some small enclaves in Nicaragua and Guatemala are inhabited by descendants of archipelago Afro-Caribbeans, often still fiercely resisting the abandonment of the English language, which they value as part of their diasporic identity.

Afro-Caribbeans in the USA

The bulk of migrants, however, went to the USA, perhaps a million from the Anglophone Caribbean alone. They went in so many capacities that it would be impossible in this chapter to describe fully the Caribbean social structure in the USA.[2] Temporary contract workers cut cane in Florida; Cuban exiles went to Miami, Haitians often arrived as illegals or boat people; while many middle-class professional people from the Anglophone Caribbean occupied important roles in medicine, in teaching and in retail services. One of the oft-remarked on, but imperfectly researched, characteristics of the English-speaking Caribbean peoples in the USA is their extraordinary success and prominence, not only in the wider black community, but in American society more generally. Within some parts of the black community, Caribbean people are sometimes referred to, in a not entirely friendly way, as 'Jewmaicans'. The Caribbean community monopolizes the laundries, travel agents and hairdressing shops in several New York districts. Moreover, Caribbean people have played a prominent role in political activity – the Garveyite movement, the civil rights struggles and the Black Power Movement being the most notable.

Afro-Caribbeans in the UK

In contrast to the USA, the fortunes of Caribbean migrants in Europe have been less happy. The possible explanations for this relative lack of success are complex: different groups may have gone to Europe, only largely unskilled positions were on offer there, and some migration (notably to the UK and the Netherlands) was 'panic' migration – with the networks of friends, relations and openings in business and education not fully prefigured or prepared. A number of scholars, as well as Caribbean migrants themselves, insist that the high levels of racial discrimination and disadvantage they experienced seriously jeopardized their chances of success (Solomos 1989; Gilroy 1987).

The bulk of Caribbean migration to the UK occurred in the 1950s, and came to a rapid halt in the early 1960s with the implementation of the Commonwealth Immigrants Act forbidding further unregulated migration. With the exception of 'the rush to beat the ban', the movement of migrants to the UK closely shadowed the ebbs and flows of the job vacancies (Peach 1968). Despite finding unskilled jobs, the early experiences of Caribbean people in the UK were often negative ones. They felt that their wartime loyalty had been unacknowledged and that they were treated as an unwelcome problem rather than as valued citizens of the Empire coming to help the motherland. Besides this psychic shock of rejection, at a more practical level occupational mobility was limited, educational successes were meagre and the second generation showed high rates of crime and unemployment.

It is important, however, not be too mired in the negative images that both racists and anti-racists need for their respective political causes. British girls of Afro-Caribbean origin outperform both black and white British boys in school examinations. As in the USA, there is a disproportionately high representation of black athletes and sports persons in the boxing ring, in track and field events, and in cricket and football.[3] Afro-Caribbeans are also well represented in broadcasting and in literary and artistic pursuits, especially the performing arts. Even though this is a somewhat backhanded compliment, the 1996 British Crime Survey, based on a sample of 10,000 people, showed that in the age group 16–29, whereas 43 per cent of whites claimed to have taken drugs, the figure for their Afro-Caribbean peer group was substantially lower, at 34 per cent (cited in the *Guardian*, 4 May 1996: 5).

Perhaps a more significant finding is that the latest census, 1991, shows that the level of ghettoization is low and has been falling since 1961. Using a sophisticated index of segregation, Peach (1995) shows that the levels of Caribbean segregation in London are about half those of African Americans in New York. Moreover, only 3 per cent of the Afro-Caribbean population lived in 'enumeration districts' (the smallest census unit covering 700 people) in which they formed 30 per cent of the population or more. Taken together, these positive indicators may signify a first stage in a wider and deeper thrust to social mobility – in the third, if not the second, generation.

Caribbean peoples in the Netherlands

The Netherlands received about half as many Caribbean immigrants as the UK – approximately 250,000 compared with Britain's 500,000. The numbers, however, are much more significant when they are considered as a proportion of both the Dutch population and of the Caribbean source populations. Caribbean migrants arrived from all over the Dutch Antilles, but predominantly from the former Dutch colony of Surinam. So large was the departure that the population of Surinam was depleted by about half. In that many people were persuaded to leave because of the prospect of an independence with diminished Dutch support, the Surinamese in the Netherlands can be seen to fit into the category of 'panic migrants' mentioned earlier.

The Surinamese in the Netherlands divide, roughly equally, into two ethnic sections – Afro-Surinamese and Indo-Surinamese. The housing situation for many Surinamese is surprisingly favourable – their arrival in Amsterdam conveniently coincided with the abandonment of a 'white elephant' set of luxury apartments the local Dutch did not wish to inhabit. A comparative study of Caribbean peoples in Britain and the Netherlands (Cross and Entzinger 1988) yielded many similarities. In a more recent study, Cross (1995: 72) maintains that exclusion on the grounds of culture, way of life or newness of incorporation is less salient than the class exclusion that arises from the collapse of blue-collar industries. In this respect, the cutting of welfare benefits in the UK in conformity with the ideology of neo-liberalism contrasts with the greater endurance of welfare provisions in the Netherlands. The circumstances of Caribbean peoples in the Netherlands may improve relatively given their more benign public provision.

Antilleans in France

Caribbean migration to France arises in an apparently different form from the cases just considered. The major source areas are the DOM (*départements d'outre-mer*) territories of Martinique and Guadeloupe. Because of the juridical status of the DOM as organic parts of France, migration to the continent is officially considered as internal migration – simply as if one French citizen were to move from one *département* to another. The numbers involved are thought to be about 200,000; and the urban centres, particularly Paris, are the main destinations.

Of course it is important not to confuse appearance with substance. Again, we notice a high predominance of unskilled, manual and public-sector jobs being held by people from the French Antilles, particularly in the 1970s. However, a significant white-collar salariat (for example in the banks and post office) has been recruited by the quasi-official labour agency in the islands. Because certification and formal qualifications are much more important in France than in either the UK or the Netherlands, French Antilleans with the requisite pieces of paper have been able to benefit from the strong meritocratic tradition.

Unlike the British Caribbean population, which has fallen, the French Caribbean population has moved from 165,945 in 1975, to 265,988 in 1982, to 337,006 in 1990 (Condon and Ogden 1996: 38). Although it is difficult to track movements to and from the Caribbean, given that there are no immigration restrictions, Condon and Ogden find that return, circulatory and retirement migration are common, as are family visits and casual tourism. The younger generation of Caribbeans living in France often talk of returning 'for their children's sake'. They place a high value on what they perceive to be their own culture, shared values and 'roots' (p. 46).[4]

At a deeper level, French Antilleans have always shared a Faustian pact with the French state. Should they choose to abandon their Africanness and embrace mother France, they would become French people, citizens, members of a world culture and civilization. Two possible consequences arise from this pact. The more positive is that the French live up to the revolutionary ideals of liberty, equality and fraternity. The most coherent defence of this position appears in Hintjens's (1995) iconoclastic book, in which she claims that decolonization is possible without formal statehood. She argues that in many cases decolonization can be seen as a form of denial, a shedding of the political and moral responsibilities of the colonial powers, an act of dismissal and disdain. For her, post-colonialism is also a political struggle for equality and recognition. It is even more potent if it can be deterritorialized and taken to the heart of the racist empires. The anti-colonial struggle, in short, is for equality within France.

The more negative outcome, of course, would be if the path of assimilation were to turn out to be an illusion, a trap, ultimately a hoax. This would be the cruellest consequence of all – for the French Antilleans in continental France would become a liminal people, no longer able to express their distinctive ethnic identity or recover a sense of 'home'. Lodged in a state of limbo or liminality (Turner 1969; Al-Rasheed 1993: 91–2), they would experience a crisis of meaning, where institutions, values and norms dissolve and collapse. Their *communitas* would be reduced to a parody of the old ways and would be incapable of reconstituting itself in the new setting.

CARIBBEAN PEOPLES AS A CULTURAL DIASPORA

Despite the different destinations and experiences of Caribbean peoples abroad, they remain an exemplary case of a cultural diaspora. This arises first from their common history of forcible dispersion through the slave trade – still shared by virtually all people of African descent, despite their subsequent liberation, settlement and citizenship in the various countries of the New World. Partly, this is a matter of visibility. Unlike (say) in the cases of Jews or Armenians, where superficial disappearance is possible in Europe and North America if exogamy occurs, in the case of those of African descent skin colour normally remains a marker for two, three or more generations – despite exogamy. The deployment of skin colour in many societies as a signifier of status, power and opportunity makes it impossible for any people of African descent to avoid racial stigmatization. As one black British writer puts it, 'our imaginations are conditioned by an enduring proximity to regimes of racial terror' (Gilroy 1993b: 103).

Though important, being phenotypically African and being conscious of racism are, in themselves, insufficient to assign the label 'cultural diaspora' to Afro-Caribbeans. I would suggest that at least four other elements should be present. First, there should be evidence of cultural retention or affirmations of an African identity. Second, there should be a literal or symbolic interest in 'return'. Third, there should be cultural artefacts, products and expressions that show shared concerns and cross influences between Africa, the Caribbean and the destination countries of Caribbean peoples. Fourth, and often forgotten by the intensely cerebral versions of diaspora presented by cultural studies theorists, there should be indications that ordinary Caribbean peoples abroad – in their attitudes, migration patterns and social conduct – behave in ways consistent with the idea of a cultural diaspora.

Retention and affirmations of African identity

With respect to the issue of retention, there are clear examples of a return to Africanness in the Maroon (runaway slave) communities of Jamaican and the so-called 'Bush Negroes' of Surinam. Other, less dramatic, examples abound. Everything from Brazilian cults, Caribbean savings clubs, folklore, musical rhythms, popular art, Trinidadian 'shouters' and voodoo practices have been minutely recorded by scores of anthropologists (notably Herskovitz 1937, 1961; Herskovitz *et al.* 1947). This evidence of retention must, however, not be narrowly understood as freezing African cultures in aspic. As with other migratory groups, New World Africans took the opportunity to throw off the shackles of their prior social constraints. Thus, the famous founding president of a free Haiti, Toussaint L'Ouverture, was as much Jacobin as African; while, arguably, during the Second World War the French Antilles were more loyal to the idea of the French nation than the metropolis itself. Equally, many Anglophone Caribbeans displayed a remarkable loyalty to Britain in both world wars and showed a fierce adherence to British educational, social and political institutions.[5] Using a reinterpretation of the work of W. E. B. Du Bois, Paul Gilroy (1993a; 1993b) supplies an insightful analysis of how African Americans and Afro-Caribbeans live within a 'double consciousness', stemming both from Africa and Europe.

The links between Africa and New World Africans also took the form of literary, ideological and political movements. The African, African-American and Afro-Caribbean intelligentsia has long sought to define some cultural and historical continuities between Africans on the continent and in the diaspora. This movement has flowed in several directions. Kwame Nkrumah, the Ghanaian president, studied in a black university in the USA and articulated the ideas of an African personality and African unity. Léopold Senghor, the president of Senegal, advanced the idea of Négritude. The Trinidadian revolutionary intellectuals George Padmore and C. L. R. James were partly responsible for convening the watershed Manchester Conference of 1945, when the basic lines of struggle for African self-determination were articulated. In the case of the Francophone Caribbean, Aimé Césaire made his spiritual journey to Africa in *Return to My Native Land* (1956). He and other Caribbean leaders were also an important influence on Négritude and had a continuing dialogue with Africans, and peoples of African descent more generally, in journals such as *Présence Africaine*.

A number of literary figures from Trinidad, whose works are imbricated in the evolution of a Caribbean diasporic consciousness, have been ably analysed by Harney (1996). The creation of a post-colonial identity was the project of novelists Earl Lovelace and Michael Anthony. The complexities of creating a new nationalism from Indo-, Sino- and Afro-Caribbean elements was addressed by Valerie Belgrave and Willi Chen, while the dilemmas of Caribbean migrants moving to Canada, Britain and the USA were depicted in the writings of Samuel Selvon, Neil Bissoondath and V. S. Naipaul.

Return movements, literal and symbolic

Despite the small number of Afro-Caribbeans who actually returned to Africa, Caribbean visionaries were at the forefront of the Back-to-Africa movements and in the articulation of the idea of a common fate of African people at home and abroad. The most flamboyant, and immensely popular, of New World return movements was the Universal Negro Improvement Association (UNIA), founded by the Jamaican, Marcus Garvey. Garveyites were particularly strong in the

USA, and representatives of small but ill-fated colonies were sent to Liberia and elsewhere on the continent. Garvey was born in Jamaica in 1887 and had travelled widely in the West Indies and Central America before starting the UNIA. He drew his inspiration from two main strands – the Maroon revolts, which showed even in the New World, and even after the experience of the Middle Passage and slavery, that blacks could still recover some of their African traditions. Second, he was very influenced by the strength of the British imperial idea that people could bluff their way to political dominance by style, appearance and a belief in their own superiority.

Garvey was particularly unimpressed by what he found in the USA. He saw poor blacks beating their heads against brick-wall situations in which they would never be accepted. This experience provided him with the idea of setting up the Black Star Line, a shipping company owned by blacks with the intention literally of reversing the transatlantic slave trade. Though the line was never a great success, when Kwame Nkrumah came to power in Ghana, he adopted it as the name of Ghana's merchant marine.

Although Garvey had returned to Jamaica, with the exception of one large UNIA rally and a convention in Kingston in 1928, he was largely unsuccessful as a politician. He died in obscurity in London in 1940, but he had succeeded in further promoting the consciousness of Africa that had been well developed in Jamaica since the days of the Maroons. The cultural link with Africa was also enhanced by the deep spirituality that converted Christian Jamaicans acquired. They found in the Bible an identification with the ancient Jews. Like the Jews who were dragged off to Egypt and Babylon to slavery, the Africans had been dragged off to the West Indies as slaves.

This biblical and African consciousness became fused together in November 1930, when a new prince, Ras Tafari, was crowned Emperor of Ethiopia and adopted the name Haile Selassie. Some poor, particularly rural, Jamaicans began to described themselves as 'Ethiopians', or followers of the crowned prince Ras Tafari, namely Rastafarians. The Emperor claimed descent from Solomon and Sheba. The denomination of Christianity dated back to the very foundations of the religion; and the fact that they had seen off an Italian army in 1898 became their symbol of resistance. An article published in the *National Geographic* magazine in January 1931, in which there was a discussion about modern Ethiopia that covered the coronation, was passed from hand to hand. This was no fiction. Here were pictures and an article in a white man's magazine! That the British had taken the coronation seriously enough to send the Duke of Gloucester, the son of King George V, to the event was regarded as further proof. The Jamaican national daily, the *Daily Gleaner* (February 1931), carried this letter.

> The whole Ethiopian race throughout the world, or at least the leaders of thought, should regard with the greatest degree of satisfaction the well considered decision of His Majesty's Government to send a deputation headed by a member of the British Royal Family to represent the great Anglo-Saxon

people at the coronation of the only independent state among the millions of Ham's offspring.

The movement itself rapidly spread from its origins in Jamaica, not least because Bob Marley, the celebrated reggae singer, spread the message through the popularity of his music. Yawney (1995) suggests that there may now be more Rastafari living outside Jamaica than on the island, with many activists in the USA, Canada and Britain, as well as Africa itself.[6] Though the movement has often been dismissed as impractical and chiliastic, as Hall (1995: 14) argues, 'It was not the literal Africa that people wanted to return to, it was the language, the symbolic language for describing what suffering was like, it was a metaphor for where they were . . . a language with a double register, a literal and a symbolic register.'

Shared cultural expressions

The idea that there might be complex connections between Africans at home, in the New World and in Africa has been suggested by black writers and intellectuals for over a century. One poignant exploration of 250 years of the African diaspora is provided by the Caribbean-born writer Caryl Phillips (1993), who chronicles the sense of disconnectedness and homelessness of peoples of African descent abroad and how they sought to reconstitute themselves as acting, thinking, emotionally-intact individuals. The title of his novel, *Crossing the River*, evokes the transatlantic slave trade. The author (1993: 237–7) hears the drum beating on the far bank of the natal land and sees the 'many-tongued chorus of the common memory' in West Indian pubs in England, an addicted mother in Brooklyn, a barefoot boy in São Paulo, the reggae rhythms in the hills and valleys of the Caribbean and the carnivals in Trinidad and Rio. Despite the trauma of the middle passage and the human wreckage that resulted, Phillips concludes his novel on an optimistic note. Beloved children arrived on the far bank of the river. They loved and were loved.

Another novelist shows how language and popular expressions are carried by Caribbean migrants to the UK. In this passage, the protagonist in Samuel Selvon's most famous novel, *The Lonely Londoner* (1985), significantly and ironically called Moses, tries with his friends to recapture life in Trinidad and adjust to their new life, after ten years, in London:

> [They] coming together for oldtalk, to find out the latest gen, what happening, when is the next fête, Bart asking if anybody seen his girl anywhere, Cap recounting an incident he had with a woman by the tube station the night before, Big City want to know why the arse he can't win a pool, Galahad recounting a clash with the colour problem in a restaurant in Piccadilly.
>
> (cited in Harney 1996: 103)

While vernacular language crosses the Atlantic in the way demonstrated by Samuel Selvon, a more popular art form is music. Here, in a persuasive essay,

Gilroy (1993b: 37) argues that, 'The contemporary musical forms of the diaspora work within an aesthetic and political framework which demands that they ceaselessly reconstruct their own histories, folding back on themselves time and again to celebrate and validate the simple, unassailable fact of their survival.' The politics of black music are barely beneath the surface in the calypsos of Trinidad, reggae and ska from Jamaica, samba from Brazil, township jazz from South Africa, Highlife from Nigeria and jazz, hip-hop, soul and rap from the USA. In the expressive title of Gilroy's essay, Africans at home and abroad are 'one nation under a groove'.

The most intellectually ambitious attempt to bring out the cross-currents of cultural expression in Africa and the diaspora is made by Paul Gilroy in *The Black Atlantic* (1993a). He strongly resists any attempt to hijack the experience of New World Africans to those particular to African Americans, a tendency he found in some of the 'Afrocentric' positions of American black intellectuals. Rather, he sees the consciousness of the African diaspora as being formed in a complex cultural and social intermingling between Africa, Europe and the Americas. However, this does not lead to cultural uniformity, but rather to a recognition of 'transnational and intercultural multiplicity'. Of course, some degree of unity must exist in the Atlantic Africans' diasporic culture for it to be deemed a shared impulse and form of consciousness. This emergent culture is characterized as 'the Black Atlantic'. His influential work (which needs much more exegesis that I have space to give it here) is also a comment on the nature of modernity, on the idea of a nationalism without a nation-state (or a territory), and on the idea of a 'double consciousness', prefigured in Hegelian phenomenology and expressed in the New World by the double heritage of Africa and Europe.[7]

Social conduct and popular attitudes

Much of the material on the Caribbean diaspora by writers in the field of cultural studies is both challenging and theoretically sophisticated. But to what extent is a transnational identity a lived experience, demonstrated by migrants' social conduct as well as invented in the minds and emotions of writers, musicians and academics? To this question I do not propose a full reply – for only an extensive research project would yield empirically verifiable answers. However, I thought it might be educative to do what might be called a 'reality check' on the broad thesis.

I did this by carefully examining one issue (1–7 May 1996) of the *Weekly Gleaner*, the self-declared 'top Caribbean newspaper' published in south London and comprising a digest of Jamaica's *Daily Gleaner*, together with local editorial matter and letters. That a newspaper of this type appears and sells is, in a sense, indication enough of the strength of a transnational Caribbean identity. What I thought particularly illustrative of the continuing relationship between the Caribbean communities in the UK and the Caribbean was a letter to the editor from a Mr R. Francis of south London. He complained about the discourtesy he had experienced on his last trip to Jamaica in banks, the customs service and government departments. I add the emphasis on the remaining part of his letter:

> I would like to express my view on the way in which *returnees* to Jamaica are treated *back home*. . . . Like other people, I am definitely homesick, I am scared of going back to Jamaica because of the treatment often meted out to returnees and people on holiday. Although *we are away* it should be understood that we have and will always contribute to the finance and development of Jamaica. *It is our country as much as it is those who have never left.*

When one examines the advertisements, the link with 'our country' becomes much more concrete. The pages are stuffed with advertisements for shipping lines, airlines, freight handlers, money transfer services ('Send your cash in a flash', says one), plots for sale in Jamaica, architects, removal companies, vacation accommodation and export houses selling tropicalized refrigerators 'good with the correct voltage and specification *for your country*'. Readers are offered shares on the Jamaican stock exchange and access via a cable company to 'Black Variety Television'.

CONCLUSION

Theodor Adorno once remarked that 'it is part of morality not to be at home in one's own home' (cited Sanadjian 1996: 5). Certainly this seems to be a recurrent theme in the story of Caribbean peoples abroad. In this chapter I have sought to discover whether the Caribbean peoples constitute a 'new', 'postcolonial', 'hybrid' diaspora of the type envisaged by scholars of cultural studies.

I found the general arguments highly suggestive. They could of course not be *conclusive*, for the resistance to empirical work or to meta-theory on the part of postmodernists, would obviate the possibility of any final argument. However, rather than follow a number of the authors I have cited along an endless roller-coaster of meanings, discourses, representations and narratives, I sought to introduce what I have called 'reality markers' to the argument. What was the history of settlement in the Caribbean and migration from the area? What were the fates and fortunes of Caribbean peoples in the different destination areas? Were there systematic differences between those who went to North America, the UK, the Netherlands or France?

In fact all sorts of cultural and political compromises with a diasporic identity arose, particularly, I would suggest, among the French Antilleans in metropolitan France. For example, if we take the four criteria I suggested for assessing whether a Caribbean cultural diaspora existed, the level of cultural retention and interest in 'return' was lowest among those from the Francophone Caribbean. Not of course that it was absent. For Césaire, as for many in the Anglophone Caribbean, the idea of return was subliminal and symbolic. But there is a significant difference between the two language groups. In the English-speaking Caribbean and in the USA, the idea of return spread beyond the intelligentsia to the masses – through the Garveyite and Rastafarian movements.

In their works previously cited, Hall, Gilroy, Harney and others have been able to show that in music, literature, art and language there was considerable cross-pollination of ideas, images and concepts over the waves and the air waves of the black Atlantic. As someone who lived in the Caribbean for two years and maintains ongoing friendships and academic contacts in the area, I recognize many of the nuances proposed by these commentators, who focus on the Caribbean imagination. However, I remain convinced that a more solid and accurate understanding of the nature of the Caribbean cultural diaspora will only be possible by gathering full historical information and sociological data. I cannot provide these here. But I would like to provide something of a preliminary corrective to the 'black Atlantic thesis'.

I submit, with Craig (1992), that it is not without coincidence that 'the enterprise of the Indies' as it was called in Columbus's time, joined the major continents of the globe (Europe, Africa *and* Asia) to the Americas and that with the help of Caribbean labour, the Panama canal added the Pacific. Thus, whatever the sophistication and complexity of the black Atlantic argument, at root it is a historical simplification, which cannot fully explain the process of indigenization and creolization in the Caribbean, despite the lack of indigenees. Nor can it account for the complexities arising from the large Asian presence in the Caribbean and *its* subsequent diasporization.

The social behaviour of Caribbean people in their places of sojourn and settlement provides telling evidence of the creation of a cultural diaspora, but more sustained empirical work needs to be undertaken on this issue. How, to pick up two of Craig's (1992) examples, did the Caribbean carnival evolve into a circuit, linking the archipelago to the metropolitan cities of New York, Toronto, London and elsewhere? By 'how' I mean, who were the principal social actors and social organizations involved? How were the enterprises financed? What was the role of Caribbean governments in cementing these ties? Again, to take another example, the Hindu festival of Phagwa was celebrated by Caribbean people for the first time on the streets of New York in 1991. How was this culture transmitted and borne by migration? How did it become modified? In short, through their roots and branches, or to be precise through their rooting and branching, the people themselves make their diaspora. The frontiers of the region are beyond the Caribbean – in the consciousness of Caribbean people to be sure, but also in their social conduct, migration patterns and achievements in their places of settlement and sojourn.

NOTES

This chapter is an edited version of Cohen 1997: 127–53.

1 For a discussion of these terms see Cohen (1997).
2 For further information, see DeWind *et al.* (1979) and Palmer (1990). Foner (1979, 1985) and Sutton and Makiesky (1975) produced pioneering work comparing the fates and fortunes of Afro-Caribbean people in the USA and Britain.
3 I am well aware that stereotyping and channelling may produce successes in these

areas and do not, of course, argue that achievement in these fields alone is a remotely adequate measure of social mobility.
4 To be clear here, such is the level of acceptance of French culture that these 'roots' are not regarded as being located in Africa, but in Guadeloupe and Martinique.
5 Thus, for example, it presents no paradox to Trinidadians to boast that Prime Minister Eric Williams's famous exposition (1944) of the link between capitalism in Britain and slavery in the West Indies was presented as a doctorate to the University of Oxford.
6 I do not want to get diverted in my text into a sub-theme, but should mention that Yawney's (1995) main thesis is that with the globalization of Rastafarianism, the conservative dominance of the House of Nyahbinghi in Jamaica is being eroded, particularly in respect of gender relations.
7 The first number of a new journal, *Social Identities*, provided the ultimate accolade to an academic author – publishing extended reviews by three reviewers of Gilroy's *Black Atlantic*. This is a useful source from which to begin an appreciation and critique of Gilroy's work.

REFERENCES

Al-Rasheed, M. (1993) 'The meaning of marriage and status in exile: the experience of Iraqi women', *Journal of Refugee Studies* 6(2): 89–103.
Césaire, Aimé (1956) *Return to my Native Land*, Harmondsworth: Penguin.
Cohen, Robin (1997) *Global Diasporas: An Introduction*, London: UCL Press.
Condon, Stephanie A. and Philip E. Ogden (1996) 'Questions of emigration, circulation and return: mobility between the French Caribbean and France', *International Journal of Population Geography* 2(1): 35–50.
Craig, Susan (1992) ' Intertwining roots', *Journal of Caribbean History* 26(2): 215–27 (review article).
Cross, Malcolm (1995) ' "Race", class formation and political interests: a comparison of Amsterdam and London', in Alec G. Hargreaves and Jeremy Leaman (eds) *Racism, Ethnicity and Politics in Contemporary Europe*, Aldershot: Edward Elgar, pp. 47–78.
Cross, Malcolm and Han Entzinger (eds) (1988) *Lost Illusions: Caribbean Minorities in Britain and the Netherlands*, London: Routledge.
DeWind, Seidel, J. and Sheak, J. (1979) 'Contract labour in US agriculture: the West Indian cane cutters in Florida', in Robin Cohen *et al.* (eds) *Peasants and Proletarians: The Struggles of Third World Workers*, London: Hutchinson, pp. 380–99.
Foner, Nancy (1979) 'West Indians in New York and London: a comparative analysis', *International Migration Review* 13(2): 284–97.
—— (1985) 'Race and colour: Jamaican migrants in London and New York', *International Migration Review*19(4): 708–27.
Gilroy, P. (1987) 'There ain't no Black in the Union Jack: the cultural politics of race and nation', London: Hutchinson.
—— (1993a) *The Black Atlantic: Modernity and Double Consciousness*, London: Verso.
—— (1993b) *Small Acts: Thoughts on the Politics of Black Cultures*, London: Serpent's Tail.
Hall, Stuart (1990) 'Cultural identity and diaspora', in Jonathan Rutherford (ed.) *Identity: Community, Culture, Difference*, London: Lawrence & Wishart.
—— (1995) 'Negotiating Caribbean identities', *New Left Review* 209, January– February: 3–14.
Harney, Stefano (1996) *Nationalism and Identity: Culture and the Imagination in a Caribbean Diaspora*, London: Zed Books.
Herskovits, Melville J. (1937) *Life in a Haitian Valley*, New York: Alfred A. Knopf.
—— (1961) *The New World Negro: Selected Papers in Afro-American Studies*, Bloomington, IN: Indiana University Press.

Herskovits, Melville J. *et al.* (1947) *Trinidad Village*, New York: Alfred A. Knopf.

Hintjens, Helen M. (1995) *Alternatives to Independence: Explorations in Post-Colonial Relations*, Aldershot: Dartmouth.

Palmer, R.W. (ed.) (1990) *In search of a Better Life: Perspectives on Migration from the Caribbean*, New York: Praeger.

Peach, Ceri (1968) *West Indian Migration to Britain: A Social Geography*, London: Oxford University Press.

—— (1995) 'Trends in levels of Caribbean segregation, Great Britain, 1961–91', paper presented at a Conference on Comparative History of Migration within the Caribbean and to Europe, Oxford Brookes University, Oxford, 22–4 September.

Phillips, Caryl (1993) *Crossing the River*, London: Picador.

Sanadjian, Manuchehr (1996) 'An anthology of "the people", place, space and "home": (re)constructing the Lur in south-western Iran', *Social Identities* 2(1): 5–36.

Selvon, Samuel (1985) *The Lonely Londoners*, Harlow: Longman.

Solomos, John (1989) *Race and Racism in Contemporary Britain*, Basingstoke: Macmillan.

Sutton, Constance R. and Susan R. Makiesky (1975) 'Migration and West Indian racial and ethnic consciousness', in Helen I. Safa and Brian M. Du Toit (eds) *Migration and Development: Implications for Ethnic Identity and Political Conflict*, The Hague: Mouton, 113–43.

Tölölyan, Khacha (1991) 'Preface', *Diaspora* 1(1): 3–7.

Turner, Victor (1969) *The Ritual Process, Structure and Anti-structure*, London: Routledge & Kegan Paul.

Weiner, Myron (1986) 'Labour migrations and incipient diasporas', in Gabriel Sheffer (ed.) *Modern Diasporas in International Politics*, London: Croom Helm, pp. 47–74.

Williams, Eric (1964) *Capitalism and Slavery*, London: André Deutsch.

Yawney, C.D. (1995) 'The globalization of Rastafari: methodological and conceptual issues', paper presented at the annual Conference of the Society for Caribbean Studies, London.

2 Modes of incorporation:

Colonial Caribbean migrants in Western Europe and the United States

Ramón Grosfoguel

INTRODUCTION

The spatial/geographical configuration of the Caribbean constrained the possibilities of outmigration. To migrate from an island is in general more difficult than to migrate from a peripheral country that shares a border with a core country (e.g. Mexico). Thus, Caribbean people are more vulnerable to the legal-political institutional context of the inter-state system at the time of migration. Whether a given society's incorporation in the inter-state system is that of a Caribbean modern colony or a Caribbean nation-state has crucial consequences on the specificity of its migration process in terms of quantity and class composition. Those Caribbean societies with a colonial legal-political incorporation (e.g. Puerto Rico, Martinique, Guadaloupe and the Dutch Antilles along with Surinam and Jamaica before independence) have a proportionally larger migration than those societies with a nation-state incorporation (e.g. Dominican Republic, Haiti and Cuba). Colonial Caribbean societies have more than half of their populations in the metropoles.

Moreover, the migration from Caribbean modern colonies has a larger rural and/or lower strata composition than that of Caribbean nation-states which consists mainly of urban-middle sectors. The middle-sector migration from Caribbean nation-states includes mostly educated and skilled workers with household incomes that are higher than the average income of the sending countries (Palmer 1974; Foner 1979, 1983; Koslofsky 1981; Bray 1984, 1987; Pedraza-Bailey 1985; Portes and Bach 1985; Stepick and Portes 1986; DeWind and Kinley 1988; Grasmuck and Pessar 1991). On the other hand, the lower strata migration from Caribbean colonial societies mostly consists of unskilled workers with low educational levels who come from low-income households. For instance, Puerto Rico, Martinique, Guadaloupe, Jamaica (before independence), the Dutch Antilles and Surinam (before independence) not only had the largest numbers of migrants to the metropolitan centres as a percentage of the home population, but also their class composition was more rural and/or lower class (Roberts and Mills 1958; Davison 1962; Bureau pour le développement des migrations intéressant les départements d'outre-mer 1968; Bovenkerk 1979, 1987; Centro de Estudios Puertorriqueños 1979; Koslofsky 1981; Bach 1985;

Freeman 1987; Levine 1987; Falcón 1991; Condon and Ogden 1991). Puerto Rico, Surinam and Martinique are the most extreme cases where the agrarian question became obsolete with the massive exportation of the peasantry to the mainland's urban centres (Grosfoguel 1994).

Another distinct feature of Caribbean colonial migration is that it was organized, to different degrees, by metropolitan and /or local political elites through state institutions as a so-called 'solution' to the unemployment problem or through direct recruitment (Davison 1962; Maldonado-Denis 1976; Maldonado 1979; Bovenkerk 1987; Koot 1988; Condon and Ogden 1991; Harris 1993). For example, the Puerto Rican colonial administration created the Migration Division under the island's Department of Labour. This Division served as an intermediary between US businessmen and Puerto Rican workers. They identified labour shortages and recruited Puerto Rican labour to fill the need. Inspired by the Puerto Rican example, the French state also fostered an organized migration in the French Caribbean (Anselin 1979: 42). They created the BUMIDOM (Bureau pour le développement des migrations intéressant les départements d'outre-mer) which served a similar role to the Migration Division in Puerto Rico. The BUMIDOM hired thousands of Martinican and Guadaloupean workers as cheap labour for the metropolitan labour market. In Curaçao and Barbados, the colonial administration also stimulated the recruitment of workers by metropolitan industries as a 'solution' to unemployment (Davison 1962: 26–30; Koot 1988: 249; Harris 1993: 40, 42–43).

Overall, the emigration processes of colonial peoples such as the Martinicans/ Guadaloupeans, Surinamese/Dutch Antilleans, West Indians and Puerto Ricans have more in common than when compared to the migration processes from Caribbean nation-states. They all share citizenship with the metropole, the migration was more or less organized/stimulated by either the peripheral or the metropolitan state, their class/social origin was more rural/unskilled than migrations from Caribbean nation-states, and they all form part of a world-systemic process of colonial labour migration to serve the needs of cheap labour and menial jobs in the core zones of the world-economy during the post-war economic boom.

Despite the similarities in the socio-economic origin of these Caribbean colonial migrants, there are interesting differences regarding the modes of incorporation to the labour market and the social contexts of reception in the metropoles. This chapter attempts to understand the peculiarities of the migration processes of colonial Caribbean migrations to the metropoles. Specifically, it compares the labour market incorporation of Puerto Ricans to the United States, Martinicans/Guadaloupeans to France, Surinamese/Dutch Antilleans to the Netherlands, and West Indians to England. This broad comparative perspective is important for understanding the peculiar modes of incorporation of these colonial migrations to their respective metropoles. The first part is a brief demographic description of the relative position of each colonial migration in its respective metropole. The second part attempts to understand the different modes of incorporation of each colonial Caribbean migration.

BRIEF COMPARATIVE SOCIO-DEMOGRAPHIC DESCRIPTION

Although all Caribbean colonial migrants are incorporated to their respective metropoles as cheap labour and/or in jobs that the white populations reject, the social and economic conditions are not the same for each of these minorities. The French Caribbeans stand out *vis-à-vis* other groups in terms of unemployment rates. Their unemployment rates are quite similar to the French national average (Marie 1993). The Martinicans unemployment rate is even lower than the French national average. However, this is not the case for the other colonial Caribbean migrants. The Puerto Ricans, Surinamese, Dutch Antilleans and British Afro-Caribbeans have unemployment rates that are twice or more the national average (Office of Population Censuses and Surveys 1993; US Department of Commerce 1993; Penninx *et al.* 1993). The Puerto Ricans' unemployment rate is double the United States' national average while those of the Surinamese, Dutch Antilleans and West Indians are more than double their respective national averages. The labour force participation rates (percentages of population 16 years and over either actively employed or actively seeking a job) show a different pattern. The Puerto Rican and Dutch Antillean participation rate is lower than their respective national averages, while the other ethnic groups have higher participation rates than their respective national averages (US Department of Commerce 1993; Penninx *et al.* 1993). The French Antilleans and British Afro-Caribbeans have a much higher participation rate than the French and British national average (Office of Population Censuses and Surveys 1993; Marie 1993). The Surinamese have a slightly higher participation rate than the Dutch national average. It is important to mention that for 40 per cent of the Surinamese and the Dutch Antilleans in the Netherlands the principal source of income is state assistance as oppose to 19 per cent for the Dutch national average (Penninx, *et al.* 1993: 119). Thus, the Surinamese and Dutch Antillean labour force participation rates might include high numbers of underemployed workers.

In terms of occupational characteristics, the majority of the French Antillean labour force (55 per cent for Martinicans and 53 per cent for Guadaloupeans) are incorporated as public employees and only 12 per cent are in manufacturing. This contrasts strongly with the French national average which is 34 per cent in public employment and 23 per cent in manufacturing jobs. It is important to mention that of the four categories of public employment in France (*agents de la fonction publique*), the French Antilleans are mainly located at the bottom of the ladder in terms of salaries, benefits and working conditions. Around 75 per cent of the French Antillean public workers are classified in the C and D categories as opposed to 46 per cent for the total of French workers in this sector (Marie 1986: 4). French Antilleans are generally clerks, janitors, drivers, auxiliary nurses and post office workers in the French public administration.

The employment level of the British Afro-Caribbean labour force in manufacturing is almost equal to Great Britain's national average. Public employees are a low proportion of the workforce in Britain compared to other Western European countries. There is no national data available for Afro-Caribbean public employees. However, it has been documented that Afro-Caribbeans have made progress in public administration white collar jobs. In Greater London, where the Afro-Caribbean population is concentrated, 18 per cent of their jobs were in public administration, compared to 17 per cent for white workers (Cross and Waldinger 1992: 166). Afro-Caribbean occupational distribution in Britain shows a sharp division between males and females. Around 58 per cent of Afro-Caribbean employed females are concentrated as cheap labour in health, clerical, secretarial and personal service occupations (Office of Population Censuses and Surveys 1993, Table 13). Close to half of the Afro-Caribbean employed males are concentrated as machine operators, assemblers, and skilled trades occupations in the transport, manufacturing, and construction industries (ibid.). The other groups show a different pattern. Puerto Ricans, Dutch Antilleans and Surinamese have a higher concentration in manufacturing jobs compared to their respective national averages. Due to the accelerated deindustrialization of the United States, Puerto Ricans were displaced from their traditional economic niche in the labour-intensive manufacturing industry. Today around 40 per cent of the Puerto Rican labour force is concentrated as cheap labour in retail trade and services such as health, administrative support and educational occupations (US Department of Commerce 1993, Table 4). Puerto Ricans have more public administration jobs than the United States' national average. Similar to the Caribbeans in Britain, this is probably due to their concentration in urban areas. However, relative to other racial groups in urban areas such as African-Americans in New York City, Puerto Ricans have a much lower representation in the public sector (Rodriguez 1991: 87–8; Torres 1995: 87–8).

All Caribbean colonial migrants are geographically concentrated in the metropoles' world cities. The French Antilleans are concentrated (75 per cent) in Ile-de-France, better known as the Parisian region. Most Surinamese and Dutch Antilleans live in the Randstad region which is an urban network connecting the largest four cities of the Netherlands: Amsterdam, Utrecht, Rotterdam and The Hague. The majority of British West Indians are concentrated in Greater London. One-third of Puerto Ricans live in the New York metropolitan region. This demographic aspect is crucial in relation to the modes of incorporation to the labour market. Since cities in the core of the capitalist world-economy were the most affected by processes of industrial mobility to the suburbs and deindustrialization in the last twenty years, those colonial Caribbean migrants incorporated mainly in the manufacturing sector were the most affected in terms of unemployment rates and labour market marginalization. Puerto Ricans and West Indians were the most affected due to their large numbers in unskilled labour and the dramatic deindustrialization in England and the United States. Dutch Antilleans/Surinamese were also affected by these processes although in a lower proportion due to the lower level of deindustrialization experienced by the Netherlands in comparison to the other cases. However, their concentration in the Randstad has affected them as well. As Atzema and De Smidt stated:

> In 1985, 63 per cent of the male working population in the Randstad manu-facturing sector were employed in manual jobs. Five years later this figure had

dropped to 33 per cent. The proportion of executive and specialist professions among the male working population in the Randstad, however, increased from 18 per cent in 1985 to 39 per cent in 1990. A spatial division of labour is developing whereby manual labour jobs are increasingly concentrated outside the Randstad, in the rest of the Netherlands.

(Atzema and De Smidt 1992: 294)

Compared to the white Dutch population, the Dutch Antilleans/Surinamese are under-represented in middle- and high-level jobs and over-represented in long-term unemployment (Roelandt and Veenman 1992: 135–7). Since 1985 unemployment rates have increased for these colonial migrants (Amersfoort 1992: 448; Roelandt and Veenman 1992: 136).

The situation of the Martinicans/Guadaloupeans is different from the rest of the colonial Caribbean migrants. They were not affected by these processes due to their high number of workers concentrated in the relatively more protected public sector. Their economic niche as low-level public employees has insulated them from the private market cycles.

In terms of housing tenure, the French Antilleans, British Afro-Caribbeans, Dutch Antilleans and Surinamese show high percentages of people living in public housing, amounts far above their respective national averages. It is well known that the Netherlands and France have an important social housing programme (Preteceille 1973; Choay *et al.* 1985: 295–304; Dieleman 1994). At least until the late 1970s, before the Thatcher administration, so did Great Britain. The figures for public housing for the United States are not available. However, compared to Western European societies, the United States has never had significant public housing programmes since it has relied on private housing as the main source of housing development. Thus, Puerto Ricans have the worst conditions, being highly dependent on renting dilapidated houses in the low-income housing market.

In terms of residential segregation, the Dutch and French cases more effectively disperse these ethnic populations while Puerto Ricans are highly concentrated in urban ghettos and British Afro-Caribbeans are concentrated in urban slums (Brown 1984; Ratcliffe 1988; Massey and Denton 1989; Amersfoort 1992; Body-Gendrot 1993, 1994; Hamnett 1994). Nevertheless, the communities of Caribbean colonial migrants in France and the Netherlands have the potential of becoming ghettos of non-white immigrant populations. The Parisian '*banlieue*' area called Seine-Saint-Denis and the area called Bijlmermeer in Amsterdam concentrate high numbers of migrant workers. Around 20 per cent of all the French Antilleans living in Paris are concentrated in Seine-Saint-Denis together with North African minorities (Marie 1993). Approximately one-third of all Surinamese living in Amsterdam live in Bijlmermeer together with North Africans (Amersfoort 1992). Recent reforms shifting social regulation in favour of market regulation of housing provisions in the Netherlands and the increased racist demands undermining the situation of immigrants in France could lead to the formation of an underclass and the emergence of ghettos. The more the welfare state becomes inscribed in the 'us and them' racist discourses, the possibility of cuts in welfare programmes increases. Puerto Ricans in cities such as New York, Chicago and Philadelphia live segregated in ghettos (Massey and Denton 1989). Similarly, many West Indians concentrated in Greater London and Birmingham are also segregated but not in zones as devastated as the Puerto Ricans in the United States (Rex and Tomlison 1979; Brown 1984).

What accounts for the differences among the modes of incorporation of Caribbean colonial migrants to their respective metropoles? Why do the French Antilleans have similar unemployment rates and participation rates to the French national average? Why did the Surinamese and Dutch Antilleans show similar or worse economic conditions than the British Afro-Caribbeans and the Puerto Ricans, but do not experience the community deterioration they have? What makes the British and American social systems produce marginalized communities such as the New York's Spanish Harlem, North Philadelphia's Puerto Rican 'barrio' or the inner London boroughs such as Hackney and Lambeth? What are the prospects for the same occurring in France and the Netherlands? What are the differences in the racist discourses of each metropolitan society and how do these differences create important nuances in the peculiar incorporation of each Caribbean ethnic group? These are complex questions that cannot be answered by looking at a single variable, but rather require an inter-disciplinary, world-historical and multi-dimensional approach. Obviously, the answers to these questions are well beyond the scope of a short chapter like this, but I pose them as guiding research questions. In what follows, I will attempt to address the relative situation of each group's incorporation to the metropolitan labour market.

DIFFERENTIAL MODES OF INCORPORATION

As citizens of the metropole, labour from 'modern colonies' had free access to the core labour market. This coincided with the postwar world-economic expansion wherein the upper mobility of white workers to better-paid jobs created a 'labour shortage' at the bottom of the core labour market filled by the colonial subjects. However, the entrance of colonial subjects to the core labour market was not perceived neutrally by the host society (Harris 1993). The history of colonialism preceding the migration from modern colonies marked their racialized and stereotypical representations as criminal, lazy and dumb (Hartmann and Husband 1973; Hall *et al.* 1978; Anselin 1979; Fryer 1984; Essed 1990; Rodriguez 1991).

Given the fact that all Caribbean colonial migrants suffered discrimination, the main difference in the modes of incorporation between the four colonial migrations discussed above lies in the level of development of the welfare state in the metropole and what peculiar public policies the state implemented towards their colonial populations. We can advance the following proposition: the more developed the welfare state and the more the state efforts to develop public policies addressed at the successful labour market incorporation of the colonial populations, the more successful the process of incorporation to the host society.

The relative success of the French Caribbeans' incorporation to French society exemplifies this proposition. The Martinicans and Guadaloupeans show a more successful incorporation to the labour market and the receiving society than the other colonial Caribbean migrants despite the absence of 'positive discrimination' policies in the French system. The number of marginalized populations among the Martinicans and Guadaloupeans is even lower than the French national average. This is the result of an organized migration process with sophisticated public policies to guarantee the relatively successful incorporation of these colonial migrants. The French state fostered the massive migration of the French West Indians to France through the BUMIDOM. Although most of the migrants came from unskilled labour backgrounds, they were directly recruited by the BUMIDOM in the islands, helped with transportation costs, and trained in the metropole (Condon and Ogden 1991). This educational training developed skills proper for the French labour market. The dominant policy was to incorporate them within the French public administration. This privileged incorporation insulated them from the cycles of the private market. Although France suffered from deindustrialization, the French Caribbean population was the least affected ethnic group. Public employees in France enjoy job security as well as many benefits not accessible to the majority of the workers in the private sector. In addition, the BUMIDOM helped with housing, orientation concerning welfare programmes in the metropole, and social work.

The Dutch Antilleans and the Surinamese, despite experiencing a process of marginalization in the labour market close to the Puerto Ricans in the United States, have not experienced a similar process of pauperization in the metropole. This is due to the advanced development of the welfare state in the Netherlands relative to the United States. Social housing, as well as the high welfare benefits for single mothers and unemployed persons, serve as a buffer against discrimination and marginalization in the labour market (Hamnett 1994). They have suffered the impact of deindustrialization more than the 'native' Dutch in the Netherlands. However, this has not led to ghetto formation or extreme levels of poverty (Amersfoort 1992). The main difference between the Dutch Caribbeans in the Netherlands and the French Caribbeans in France is the lack of state policies oriented toward the successful incorporation of the former. There are positive discrimination policies for minorities in the Dutch system, but there are no specific public policies addressing the economic incorporation of the Dutch Caribbean population in the Netherlands as in the French case.

The West Indians in Britain are an interesting case. They had access to a well-developed welfare state before the rise of the Thatcher administration in the late 1970s. During those years the welfare state helped to contain the impact of racism in British society towards West Indians. However, after the dismantling of the welfare state, the West Indians have been vulnerable to the private market cycles, deindustrialization and institutional racism. This led to an increase in the marginalization of the second and third generations of West Indians in Great Britain during the 1980s. Although they are not as marginalized in the labour market as the Dutch Caribbeans are in the Netherlands, they experience segregation and poverty similar to that of Puerto Ricans in the US. The explanation of this lies in the lack of specific policies to address the economic incorporation of this population and the effects of cuts in welfare benefits. However, due to the fact that they enjoyed access to a well-developed welfare state during the 1960s and 1970s, they have not yet deteriorated to the levels of Puerto Ricans in the United States.

The Puerto Rican experience in the metropole is the worst among these colonial migrations. They were recruited as cheap labour for the declining manufacturing sectors of the Northeastern region of the United States. As a result of the deindustrialization process, the number of Puerto Ricans out of the labour force has increased (Torres 1995). Moreover, the United States has an underdeveloped welfare state relative to Western European countries. There is a lack of a national public educational system, national public health system and public policies addressing the marginalization of the Puerto Ricans in the United States. In other words, there are no social buffers for Puerto Ricans as there were for Dutch Caribbeans to contain the experience of deindustrialization. Thus, the deterioration of Puerto Rican communities in the United States has increased dramatically over the past twenty years.

CONCLUSION

Caribbean colonial migrations to the metropoles during the postwar era are very similar. The common legal status as citizens of the metropolitan society, the more organized character of the migration process and the large representation of low-skilled workers are distinct features that differentiate colonial Caribbean migrants from Caribbean nation-state migrants. The main differences among these colonial Caribbean migrations lie in the processes of incorporation to the metropoles. Different types of welfare states make a significant difference in terms of cushioning the relative difficulties confronted by these migrants in the host society. The French Caribbeans in France have a relatively more successful incorporation to the labour market than the other Caribbean colonial migrants. The French state created a state institution to guarantee the successful incorporation of these migrants. The Dutch Antilleans and Surinamese in the Netherlands have experienced a high marginalization in the labour market similar to Puerto Ricans in the United States. But the advanced welfare state in the Netherlands has been crucial in avoiding the formation of ghettos or the dilapidation of the housing conditions experienced by Puerto Ricans in the United States. The Afro-Caribbeans in Britain are in an intermediate position. They had access to an advanced welfare society until the early 1980s when the Thatcher administration dismantled many welfare programmes. Thus, they are now confronting processes similar to those of Puerto Ricans in the United States where marginalization in the labour market has translated into a deterioration of their living conditions.

The comparison of the Caribbean colonial populations in the metropoles provides an opportunity to understand the differences and similarities between France, England, The Netherlands and the United States. Future studies should focus on the different meanings of citizenship, race and national identities in each metropolitan society and how they have affected Caribbean colonial populations. This research agenda is an attempt to break with our parochial approaches and to pursue a more comparative, transnational approach.

REFERENCES

Amersfoort, H. Van (1992) 'Ethnic residential patterns in a welfare state: Lessons from Amsterdam, 1970–1990', *New Community* 18(3): 439–56.

Anselin, Alain (1979) *L'emigration antillaise en France: du bantoustan au ghetto*, Paris: Anthropos.

Atzema, Oedzge and De Smidt, Marc (1992) 'Selection and duality in the employment structure of Randstad', *Tijdschrift voor Economische en Sociale Geografie* 83(4): 289–305.

Bach, Robert (1985) 'Political frameworks for international migration', in Steven S. Sanderson (ed.) *The Americas in the New International Division of Labor*, New York: Holmes and Meier, pp. 95–124.

Body-Gendrot, Sophie (1993) *Ville et violence*, Paris: Presses Universitaires de France.

—— (1994) 'Immigration: la rupture sociale et ses limites', *Le Débat* 80 (May–Aug): 168–74.

Bonilla, Frank and Campos, Ricardo (1985) 'Evolving patterns of Puerto Rican migration', in Steven S. Sanderson (ed.) *The Americas in the New International Division of Labor*, New York: Holmes and Meier, pp. 177–205.

Bovenkerk, Frank (1979) 'The Netherlands', in Ronald E. Krane (ed.) *International Labor Migration in Europe*, New York: Praeger, pp. 118–32.

—— (1987) 'Caribbean migration to the Netherlands: from elite to working class', in Barry B. Levine (ed.) *The Caribbean Exodus*, New York: Praeger, pp. 204–13.

Bray, David (1984) 'Economic development: the middle class and international migration in the Dominican Republic', *International Migration Review* 18(2): 217–36.

—— (1987) 'Industrialization, labor migration and employment crises: a comparison of Jamaica and the Dominican Republic', in Richard Tadarnico (ed.) *Crises in the Caribbean Basin*, Beverly Hills: Sage Publications, pp. 79–93.

Brown, Colin (1984) *Black and White Britain. The Third PSI Survey*, London: Heinemann.

Bureau pour le développement des migrations intéressant les départements d'outre-mer (1968) *Etude des problémes d'adaptation des migrants originaires des départements d'outre-mer aux conditions de vie en France métropolitaine*, vol. I, Paris: BDPA.

Centro de Estudios Puertorriqueños (1979 *Labor Migration under Capitalism: The Puerto Rican Experience*, New York: Monthly Review Press.

Choay, Françoise, Brun, Jacques, and Roncayolo, Marcel (1985) 'Production de la ville', in Georges Duby (ed.) *Histoire de la France urbaine*, Paris: Seuil, pp. 233–329.

Condon, Stephanie and Ogden, Philip E. (1991) 'Emigration from the French Caribbean: the origins of an organized migration', *International Journal of Urban and Regional Research* 15(4): 505–23.

Cross, Malcolm and Waldinger, Roger (1992) 'Migrants, minorities, and the ethnic division of Labour', in Susan S. Fainstein, Ian Gordon, and Michael Harloe (eds) *Divided Cities*, Oxford: Blackwell, pp. 151–74.

Davison, R.B. (1962) *West Indian Migrants*, Oxford University Press: London.

DeWind, Josh and Kinley III, David H. (1988) *Aiding Migration: The Impact of International Development Assistance on Haiti*, Boulder, CO and London: Westview Press.

Dieleman, Frans M. (1994) 'Social rented housing: valuable asset or unsustainable burden?', *Urban Studies* 31(3): 447–63.

Essed, Philomena (1990) *Everyday Racism*, California: Hunter House.

Falcón, Luis M. (1991) 'Migration and development: the case of Puerto Rico', in Sergio Díaz-Briquets and Sidney Weintraub (eds) *Determinants of Emigration from Mexico, Central America and the Caribbean*, Boulder, CO: Westview Press, pp. 146–87.

Foner, Nancy (1979) 'West Indians in New York City and London: a comparative analysis' *International Migration Review* 13(2): 284–97.

—— (1983) 'Jamaican migrants: a comparative analysis of the New York and London experience', Occasional Paper No. 36, Center for Latin American and Caribbean Studies, New York University, pp. 1–48.

Freeman, Gary P. (1987) 'Caribbean migration to Britain and France: from assimilation to selection', in Barry B. Levine (ed.) *The Caribbean Exodus*, New York: Praeger, pp. 185–203.

Fryer, Peter (1984) *Staying Power: The History of Black People in Britain*, London: Pluto Press.

Grasmuck, Sherri and Pessar, Patricia (1991) *Between Two Islands: Dominican International Migration*, Berkeley: University of California Press.

Gray, Lois Spier (1966) 'Economic incentives to labor mobility: the Puerto Rican case', Ph.D. dissertation, Columbia University.

Grosfoguel, Ramón (1994) 'Depeasantization and agrarian decline in the Caribbean', in Philip McMichael (ed.) *Food and Agrarian Orders in the World-Economy*, Westport, CT: Praeger, pp. 233–53.

Hall, Stuart, Critcher, Chas, Jefferson, Tony, Clarke, John, and Roberts, Brian (1978) *Policing the Crisis: Mugging, the State, and Law and Order*, New York: Holmes & Meier Publishers.

Hamnett, Chris (1994) 'Social polarization in global cities: theory and evidence', *Urban Studies* 31(3): 401–23.

Harris, Clive (1993) 'Post-war migration and the industrial reserve army', in Winston James and Clive Harris (eds.) *Inside Babylon: The Caribbean Diaspora in Britain*, London: Verso, pp. 9–54.

Hartmann, Paul and Husband, Charles (1973) *Racism and the Mass Media*, Totowa, NJ: Rowman & Littlefield.

Koot, William (1988) 'Emigración de las Antillas Holandesas hacia los Países Bajos. Relaciones de dependencia', in Gerard Pierre-Charles (ed.) *Capital Transnacional y Trabajo en el Caribe*, Mexico City: Instituto de Investigaciones Sociales, pp. 247–61.

Koslofsky, J. (1981) 'Going foreign: causes of Jamaican migration', *NACLA* 15(1): 2–32.

Levine, Barry B. (1987) 'The Puerto Rican exodus: development of the Puerto Rican circuit', in Barry B. Levine (ed.), *The Caribbean Exodus*, New York: Praeger, pp. 93–105.

Maldonado, Edwin (1979) 'Contract labor and the origins of Puerto Rican communities in the United States', *International Migration Review* 13(1): 103–21.

Maldonado-Denis, Manuel (1976) *Puerto Rico y Estados Unidos: Emigración y Colonialismo*, Mexico City: Siglo XXI.

Marie, Claude-Valentin (1986) 'Les populations des Dom-Tom en métropole', *Ici La-Bas* no. 7 (Jan–Feb): 1–8.

—— (1993) *Les Populations des DOM-TOM nées et originaires, résidant en France métropolitaine, recensement de la population de 1990*, Paris: INSEE.

Massey, Douglas S. and Denton, Nancy A. (1989) 'Residential segregation of Mexicans, Puerto Ricans, and Cubans in US metropolitan areas', *Sociology and Social Research* 73(2): 73–83.

Office of Population Censuses and Surveys of Great Britain (1993) *1991 Census, Ethnic Group and Country of Birth, Great Britain, Volume 2*, London: HMSO.

Palmer, R. W. (1974) 'A decade of West Indian migration to the United States', *Social and Economic Studies* 23(4): 571–87.

Pedraza-Bailey, Silvia (1985) *Political and Economic Immigrants in America: Cubans and Mexicans*, Austin: University of Texas Press.

Penninx, Rinus, Schoorl, Jeannette and Van Praag, Carlo (1993) *The Impact of International Migration on Receiving Countries: The Case of the Netherlands*, Amsterdam: Swets & Zeitlinger.

Portes, Alejandro and Bach, Robert L. (1985) *Latin Journey: Cuban and Mexican Immigrants in the United States*, Berkeley: University of California Press.

Preteceille, Edmond (1973) *La Production des grand ensembles*, Paris: Mouton.

Ratcliffe, Peter (1988) 'Race, class, and residence: Afro-Caribbean households in Britain', in Malcolm Cross and Han Entzinger (eds.) *Lost Illusions*, London: Routledge, pp. 126–46.

Rex, John and Tomlinson, Sally (1979) *Colonial Immigrants in a British City: A Class Analysis*, London: Routledge & Kegan Paul.

Roberts, G.W. and Mills, D.O. (1958) *Study of External Migration Affecting Jamaica; 1953–55*, University College of the West Indies, Jamaica: Institute of Social and Economic Research.

Rodriguez, Clara E. (1991) *Puerto Ricans Born in the U.S.A.*, Boulder, CO: Westview Press.

Roelandt, Theo and Veenman, Justus (1992) 'An emerging ethnic underclass in the Netherlands? Some empirical evidence', *New Community*, 19, 1: 129–141.

Stepick, Alex and Portes, Alejandro (1986) 'Flight into despair: a profile of recent Haitian refugees in South Florida', *International Migration Review* 20(1): 329–50.

Torres, Andres (1995) *Between Melting Pot and Mosaic: African-Americans and Puerto Ricans in the New York Political-Economy*, Philadelphia: Temple University Press.

US Department of Commerce (1993) *Persons of Hispanic Origin in the United States, 1990 Census of Population*, Washington, DC: US Government Printing Office.

3 Towards a comparative perspective on Caribbean migration

Nancy Foner

The Caribbean has been more deeply and continuously affected by international migration than any other region in the world. Emigration has long been a way of life for many Caribbean people as they have searched for opportunities that are not available at home. Today, there are large Caribbean communities in North America as well as Europe, and a significant percentage of the population of every Caribbean society lives abroad. As one observer notes, the second city in population numbers for nearly every Caribbean country is now an overseas community: Miami for Cuba, for example, and New York City for Haiti, Jamaica, and Barbados (Segal 1987). Cities outside the United States, too, have large Caribbean populations, with Toronto, London, Paris, and Amsterdam leading the list.

This chapter begins to elaborate a framework for understanding the Caribbean migrant experience in comparative perspective. It draws heavily on my earlier research on Jamaicans in Britain and the United States. What comes out very clearly is that the responses of West Indians to life abroad are neither inevitable nor 'natural'. Much depends on where they move. Of critical importance are the structures of incorporation in the receiving society, including the structure of race and ethnic relations, political and educational systems, and occupational opportunities. Also relevant is geographical distance from the home society. Who moves – the size as well as gender, class, and age composition of the migration stream – is also critical. Finally, there is the time factor – the historical period of mass migration – which helps to shape West Indians' reactions and adaptations abroad.

Within the *same* country, there are also important regional/urban differences that have not received sufficient attention. Using examples from the United States, the chapter sketches out factors that need to be considered in inter-city comparisons.

THE COMPARATIVE APPROACH

Why compare Caribbean migrants in different countries and cities? Such comparisons, for one thing, highlight processes and dynamics that might well be overlooked or minimized if immigrants in only one place were considered on their own. It was when I compared West Indians' occupational attainments in the United States and Britain that it became patently clear that cultural heritage and immigrant status did not, in themselves, adequately account for West Indians' occupational achievements in America. The comparison highlighted the critical role of West Indians' occupational background in the home society and the presence of a large native black population in America in explaining immigrants' accomplishments in the United States (Foner 1979).

In general, the search for explanations of the differences, and similarities, among West Indians in different national settings forces us to sort and clarify the conditions under which specific social and cultural patterns develop among immigrants. The comparative approach, in other words, points to a number of factors that determine the outcome of the migration experience.

Cross-national comparisons point out that cultural explanations are insufficient in explaining processes of adjustment and adaptation. When West Indians in only one receiving society are studied, what often stands out is their cultural background which marks them off from the 'natives' as well as other immigrant groups. Often, culture is invoked to explain why they behave the way they do in their new home. By holding culture constant, cross-national comparisons offer a different perspective. They allow us to begin to assess the relative weight of cultural baggage, on the one hand, and social and economic factors, on the other. Where strong differences between West Indians in two receiving societies emerge, then clearly we need to look beyond culture to explain the differences.

Two studies of non-Caribbean immigrants illustrate the pitfalls of focusing on only one receiving society.[1] One is a comparison of Irish immigrants in Australia and the United States. Many American historians assume that Irish immigrants' cultural disabilities were primary in explaining their adjustment to the New World. The Irish became an urban people in America, many American historians write, because they were unable to confront life outside the cities after being scarred by the Famine, had rudimentary farming experience, and were unwilling to face the isolation of existence in the vastness of rural America. Had American historians looked beyond the borders of the United States to Australia, Malcolm Campbell (1995) observes, they would have given more weight to the role of socioeconomic conditions in the receiving society. For the Irish in Australia were not an urban people: most were drawn to rural areas and preferred life in small country settlements, farms, or even remote pastoral stations to life in the city.

Another study, of Portuguese immigrants, also shows it can be misleading to generalize from research on immigrants in one country. It was only after anthropologist Caroline Brettell (1981) had studied Portuguese immigrants in Paris that she revised some of her conclusions about Portuguese immigrant communities that she had formulated on the basis of a Toronto study. Whereas she had previously assumed that Portuguese immigrants would inevitably cluster together and form community organizations, she now saw, after her Paris study, that this was not necessarily the case. In Paris, unlike Toronto, Brettell found no 'little Portugal' and few voluntary associations. The cultural-political ideology towards immigrants in France and the proximity of France to Portugal, which sustained an active vision of return, militated against the rise of the kind of community and community organizations that she found in Toronto.

Comparisons of immigrants from one country in different cities have many of the same benefits as cross-national contrasts. Certainly, in the United States, many generalizations about West Indian migration are made on the basis of studies of New York. But the United States is not, of course, New York writ large, and, as we will see, there are striking contrasts in the West Indian experience in different cities that are related to, among other things, the size and composition of the West Indian population in each city as well as the socio-economic context.

WEST INDIANS IN BRITAIN AND THE UNITED STATES

In understanding the West Indian immigrant experience I do not want to suggest that the cultural values and patterns immigrants bring with them are unimportant or irrelevant – far from it. Wherever they go, West Indian immigrants carry with them a 'memory of things past' that operates as a filter through which they view and experience life in their new home. Creole patterns rooted in the Caribbean, Raymond Smith suggests in *Kinship and Class in the West Indies*, continue to have force in the immigrant context. When West Indian migrants meet, he writes, in London, Toronto, or New York 'they experience a feeling of identity that is based not only on race or territorial affiliation, but on the common inheritance of a created, valued way of life that is creole' (1988: 184). The growing literature on transnational linkages among West Indian immigrants also points to the continued importance of premigration cultures, stressing how immigrants keep a foot in both camps, as it were, and maintain crucial ties with their home societies even as they spend most of their lives abroad (see Basch *et al.* 1994).

That West Indians in Britain or the United States are immigrants in a strange land also goes a long way toward explaining similarities that emerge in the two settings. West Indians' immigrant status helps account for the presence of ethnic communities in both London and New York; the practice of sending remittances home; and the development of close social networks among immigrants from the same country.

Yet common cultural background and immigrant status cannot account for the many *differences* between West Indians in New York and London. Being West Indian in New York means something very different than it does in London – to the immigrants themselves as well as to the non-West Indian population among whom they live. Faced with new circumstances in their new homes, a good many 'traditional' West Indian beliefs, values, and cultural symbols as well as 'traditional' behaviour patterns inevitably undergo change. The way they change – and the kinds of new patterns that emerge – are shaped by a complex combination of factors related to the nature of the receiving society, the characteristics of the migrant stream, and the period of migration.

The context of incorporation

What stood out, above all, in my study of Jamaicans in New York and London was the crucial impact of the social, economic, and political context into which migrants moved.[2]

Jamaicans confront particular cultural conceptions, hierarchies, and social institutions in New York and London that determine how they experience and react to life abroad. Take something as basic as food. In both London and New York, first-generation immigrants prefer and continue to cook Jamaican dishes like curried goat and rice and peas. Yet in London, Jamaicans eat fish and chips and drink bitter in pubs; in New York, pizza and bagels (a legacy from turn-of-the century Italian and Jewish immigration) become part of the diet. The educational systems in Britain and the United States provide different kinds of opportunities. New York offers a wider array of college and university options, with its vast network of colleges in the City University of New York and State University of New York systems, and, at least so far, affirmative action programmes designed to assist the native black population. Below the college level, however, the picture in New York is bleaker. Jamaicans have to send their children to ghetto schools that are more racially segregated and plagued by more serious drug and crime problems than is the case in London. Indeed, these problems in New York mean that Jamaicans who can afford it look for alternatives to the public school system, typically to the many parochial schools that developed to service the city's white Catholic immigrants of an earlier era.

This leads to the crucial matter of the structure of race relations.[3] The presence of the American black population in New York has meant that Jamaican New Yorkers are less visible to the native-born white population than their counterparts in London. (Blacks now represent about a quarter of New York City's population.) When I did my study of Jamaicans in London in the early 1970s, Jamaicans were a highly visible minority. They, along with other immigrants from India and Pakistan, moved into a society that in racial terms was homogenous and white. The term 'immigrant' in fact was a code word among the English for the large numbers of non-white immigrants who, for the first time, lived in their midst. In the course of political debate, in the treatment of topics connected with them in the media, and in statements by public officials, black immigrants were stigmatized as an inferior group.

Whereas West Indians in London were constantly in the public eye as a social problem or threat to the English way of life, in New York they are, as black, largely invisible as immigrants to the white population. Large-scale immigration is nothing new in New York and there is a long tradition of ethnic diversity. Far from being the centre of public attention, West Indians are often ignored. To most white New Yorkers, they are largely invisible in a sea of anonymous black faces. Indeed, white New Yorkers are usually surprised when they read about the extent to which the city's black population is becoming 'Caribbeanized'. About a quarter of New York City's non-Hispanic black population is now foreign-born.

When West Indians do come to the attention of white society in New York they are often compared with native blacks rather than with the white immigrant or total population. In England, West Indians as well as the British often measure West Indians' achievements against those of the white majority, and this comparison puts West Indians at a clear disadvantage. In the United States, their achievements are 'viewed by the dominant white majority, and come to be viewed by West Indians themselves, in the context of black America' (Sutton and Makiesky 1975). Such a comparison often puts West Indians in a favourable light.

Unlike in London, where 'West Indianness is seldom affirmative' (Lowenthal 1978), in New York it has advantages. Stressing their distinctness from American blacks, Jamaicans feel, brings advantages. One is a sense of ethnic pride. A common theme among them is that West Indians are more ambitious, harder workers, and greater achievers. Jamaican immigrants feel that they save more and are more likely to buy homes than American blacks – and are less likely to go on welfare or live off government benefits. (In fact, West Indians in New York have higher labour force participation rates and higher household incomes than American blacks. See Kasinitz 1992; Kasinitz and Vickerman 1995; Model 1995).[4] Many Jamaicans say that they are less hostile to whites than American blacks but at the same time have more dignity and greater assurance in dealing with whites. Indeed, they feel that setting themselves apart from African-Americans brings better treatment from whites – that they are more respected and more readily accepted than black Americans. 'You're black, but you're not black,' is how one Jamaican put it.

That New York Jamaicans live out much of their lives apart from the presence of whites actually reduces opportunities for racial tensions and conflicts to develop. Although Jamaicans in New York have varied contacts with whites at work, they live mainly in areas of black residence in the boroughs of Brooklyn, Queens, and the Bronx. Rarely are they found living outside the usual neighbour-hoods of West Indian residence or of the black population. Using 1980 census data, Roger Waldinger (1987) calculated an index of segregation, known as the index of dissimilarity, at the community board level for various immigrant and native-born populations. What he found was that West Indian New Yorkers were just as segregated as their American black counterparts. In New York City 70 per cent of Jamaicans would have had to move to be evenly distributed among whites; similar proportions held for American-born blacks and other West Indians. When Jamaicans in New York walk in the street, go to the shops, talk to neighbours, worship, and send their children to school it is, on the whole, other blacks whom they see and deal with. And when they compete for housing and, especially in the case of service workers, for jobs, their rivals are apt to be blacks and other minorities rather than whites.

Much as Jamaicans in London, too, move in Jamaican (and West Indian) social circles, they are less insulated from contact with whites than Jamaicans in New York. In spite of the fairly dense concentration of West Indians in particular areas and in particular streets, there is not the same pattern of residential segregation found in New York City. Ceri Peach's analysis of the 1991 Census found that the index of dissimilarity for London's black Caribbean population was 49 percent; only 3 percent of the black Caribbean population of London lived in enumeration districts (the smallest census unit of about 700 people) in which they formed 30 percent or more of the population (Peach, Chapter 13 of this volume). In black sections of New York, as one West Indian activist in London pointed out, you can walk through and not see a white face, except passing in a car. 'But that's not the case in Britain. We see them every day. We move with them every day' (quoted in Cockburn and Ridgeway 1982). Many incidents that London migrants told me to illustrate their experiences with racial prejudice involved contacts with whites in the neighbourhood – queuing for buses, for example, buying groceries at the corner shop, speaking to neighbours, or observing fights between local white and black children (Foner 1978).

The presence of the large native black population also affects the way West Indians in New York participate in the political process. Even though most Jamaicans in New York cannot vote because they are not naturalized citizens – Jamaicans in England automatically had the right to vote in England since their arrival – from the very start, they, unlike their English counterparts, tended to live in districts where black voters predominated and where they were represented in city, state, and federal legislative bodies by black politicians who spoke for black interests. Increasingly, West Indian politicians in New York play the ethnic card to appeal to the growing number of West Indian voters, but the fact is that race, not ethnicity, emerges as key in many elections and on many political issues. West Indians in New York often unite with American-born blacks in a 'black bloc', especially when 'black' and 'white' interests are seen as being in conflict (Kasinitz 1992). As political scientist John Mollenkopf (1994) notes, blacks are the most reliably Democratic of any voting group and the largest single racial/ethnic component of the electorate in New York City. Both West Indians and African-Americans enthusiastically responded when Jesse Jackson ran for the presidency in 1988, and the black community united, too, to help elect David Dinkins mayor in 1989.

Broadly speaking, the distance of the receiving society from the immigrant homeland can be conceived of as a feature of the new context. Modern transportation and technology have made the world a smaller place, but it still makes a difference that New York is a lot closer to Jamaica than London. Despite reduced airfares and charter flights, the trip from Kingston to New York is cheaper than to London. Phone calls do not cost as much, either. What this means is that it is easier for Jamaicans in New York to visit home (and phone) with greater frequency and to go back in times of family emergency or for special celebrations.

Clearly, this ease of flying home for a visit facilitates the maintenance of transnational ties. In my research, I found it also coloured immigrants' view of return. One reason the Jamaicans I interviewed in New York were less likely to think of moving home on a permanent basis than those I spoke to in London was precisely because it was possible to visit home from New York with fair regularity. Better yet, some planned to move even closer to home, to Florida, which also has warm 'Jamaica-like' weather and has attracted substantial numbers of Jamaican and other West Indian immigrants. There is another possibility for Jamaicans in the United States. Given the relatively close distance to home, many Jamaicans plan to 'commute back and forth', spending part of the year in Jamaica and part in the United States when they retire. Not one of the people I interviewed in London mentioned this option.

Immigrant Characteristics

It is not just a question of where Jamaicans move, but who moves. There are differences in the immigrant streams to Britain and the United States, perhaps most important, their class composition. Although there has been a tendency for Jamaican immigration to the United States to become less skilled and professional over time, overall the flow to the United States has included a higher percentage of professional and non-manual workers than the immigrant stream to Britain in the 1950s and early 1960s (see Foner 1983).

The class composition of the migrant stream has implications for, among other things, immigrants' occupational placement and success. Clearly, it is an important factor accounting for the relatively high percentage of recent Jamaican immigrants in New York in managerial and professional occupations. According to the 1990 census, 21 percent of Jamaican women and 13 percent of Jamaican men in New York City who had arrived in the 1980s were in managerial and professional occupations (Mollenkopf and Kasinitz 1994). Figures available for Jamaicans (in 1966) who had been in Greater London about the same amount of time show a much smaller proportion in professional and managerial jobs: 2 percent of Jamaican men and 14 percent of Jamaican women (Rose *et al.* 1969).

The sheer size of the immigrant stream is obviously critical since it influences, among other things, whether the Jamaican community can support a significant ethnic employment sector and is a potential political force in its own right. Here, Jamaicans in New York have an edge. Between 1955 to 1968 (after which Jamaican immigration dropped to a mere trickle), close to 200,000 Jamaicans moved to Britain. Official figures for the United States are much higher, mainly because the immigration has continued over a much longer period. Between 1966, when the mass movement started in earnest, to 1992, Immigration and Naturalization Service figures show that more than 400,000 legal immigrants have entered the United States from Jamaica. (In 1990, Jamaica was among the top ten countries sending legal immigrants to the United States.) The US Census reports that in 1990, there were 334,000 foreign-born Jamaicans in the entire country, with about half in the New York region. When other English-speaking West Indians are included, the United States – and New York – also come out ahead of Britain and London.

In terms of gender composition, a major difference in the two streams is the pattern of male–female immigration.[5] In Britain, Jamaican men typically came first, later followed by wives (or common-law wives or girlfriends) and children. In the United States, it was more common for women to migrate first, many times followed by their husbands. This American pattern is linked to occupational patterns for Jamaican women – and the need for immigrant visas ('green cards') to reside legally in the United States.

For many Jamaican women, their first job in the United States was working in a private household, caring for young children, often on a live-in basis. One benefit of babysitting jobs was that they were a good way to qualify for visas, especially in the 1960s and 1970s (see Colen 1990). Once women obtained green cards, they could sponsor the immigration of their spouses and children. The availability of live-in employment as private household workers in New York – and the willingness to hire Jamaicans for these jobs – encouraged many women to move there without their spouses. Jamaicans had the right of free entry to Britain before 1962 so there was no thorny visa question during the period of mass migration there. And Jamaican women in Britain did not move into private household work or live-in employment.

The time factor

Finally, there is the time factor: the historical period in which Jamaicans left the island and arrived abroad. The period of mass Jamaican migration to England began in the early 1950s and ended just after the introduction of immigration controls in 1962. The recent mass movement to the United States dates from 1965 legislation which eliminated Jamaica's small quota and it is still going strong.

The time of emigration makes a difference in a number of ways. How migrants evaluate their new home depends on the basis of their comparison: Jamaica was a different place in the 1950s than in the 1970s or 1980s. Among other things, Jamaican independence in 1962, and subsequent political changes, have brought new leaders, new social programmes, expanded mobility opportunities, and new expectations. There is less stigma attached to being black and more pride in 'things Jamaican'. 'When I left Jamaica in the 1950s', Stuart Hall has written:

> it was a society which did not and could not have acknowledged itself to be largely black. When I went back to Jamaica at the end of the sixties and in the early seventies, it was a society even poorer than when I had left it, in material terms, but it had passed through the most profound cultural revolution. . . . It was not any longer trying to be something else, trying to match up to some other image, trying to become something which it could not . . . You know the biggest shock for me was listening to Jamaican radio. I couldn't believe my ears that anybody would be quite so bold as to speak patois, to read the news in that accent. My entire education, my mother's whole career, had been specifically designed to prevent anybody at all, and me in particular, from reading anything of importance in that language.

(Hall 1995: 12)

At the same time, as Hall also notes, Jamaica has recently experienced devastating economic downturns and crises.

The 'period effect' is relevant in terms of the context provided by the receiving society. The postwar years when Jamaicans arrived in England were, in many ways, a time of optimism and expansion in contrast to the more pessimistic mood that prevails about the economy today in both Britain and the United States; then, the welfare state was growing, now it is being chipped away. Technology and transportation have been revolutionized since the 1950s in ways that make it easier for immigrants to maintain transnational ties. Indeed, Jamaica seemed even further away from Britain in the 1950s than it does today, before the age of cheap airline travel (indeed, most Jamaicans came to England by boat).

Philip Kasinitz's (1992) account of differences between today's West Indian immigrants and cohorts earlier in the century brings out, to paraphrase David Lowenthal (1985), that the past is a foreign country. For the large wave of West Indian immigrants who came to New York in the first few decades of this century,[6] identification with native-born African Americans was the key defining fact of their public activities. West Indians who ran for office or held political roles did not emphasize their West Indianness. Nor did West Indians in New York have a newspaper of their own. Although the *Amsterdam News*, the leading black weekly in New York, was owned by a West Indian, this fact could not be discovered by reading it.

Since the 1980s, ethnicity has played an increasingly public role in the lives of Afro-Caribbean New Yorkers. There is now a viable ethnic press and West Indian politicians appeal to voters on the basis of ethnicity, not just race. The massive growth of the West Indian community – more West Indians migrated to the United States in the 1960s and 1970s than in the previous seven decades – is clearly a reason why immigrants now stress their separate ethnic identity in public affairs. But more than numbers are involved, Kasinitz argues. Race is not the monolithic force it was when the first cohort of West Indian migrants came to political consciousness. New insurgent African-American political leaders have come into power, and white politicians now court the ethnic vote as they respond to ethnic demands and even create ethnic constituencies.

Also part of the 'time factor' is the question of how long the migration lasts. Already, the recent mass migration of Jamaicans to the United States has lasted twice as long as the flow to Britain. And it shows no signs of stopping. That new recruits keep coming to the United States, while the movement to Britain basically stopped about twenty years ago, has important implications for processes of incorporation (for figures on net West Indian migration to Britain between 1948 and 1974, see Peach, Chapter 13 of this volume). Recent immigrants bring a continual infusion of people steeped in Jamaican ways and culture. Compared to Britain, perpetual immigration in the United States may well expand the relative influence of the first generation in creating an 'ethnic culture'.

THE CITY AS CONTEXT

London and New York may have the largest concentrations of Jamaicans in Britain and the United States but they are not the only places where they settle. Reading what is written on West Indians in the United States one might not know this, however. Most research on West Indians in the United States has been done in New York, and there is a tendency to assume that the findings and analyses of New York-based studies hold true for West Indians throughout the country. Such assumptions are often not warranted. As the media constantly remind us, New York is special in many ways. West Indians are bound to have different experiences when they settle in other cities like Hartford and Miami, both places with substantial West Indian populations. As Jack Rollwagen (1975) points out in his introduction to a symposium on 'The City as Context', it is wrong to implicitly assume that the life of an immigrant group will be exactly the same regardless of the city in which they live – the city as constant argument, he calls it. Rather, he suggests, there will be noticeable contrasts between immigrant groups from the same cultural background who settle in different American cities, if only because the size of the immigrant group and available opportunities in various cities diverge. Also important, I would add, are other structural features in the cities such as ethnic composition and the historical pattern of West Indian settlement as well as characteristics of the immigrants themselves.

Although there are no detailed studies of English-speaking West Indians in cities outside of New York, research on Haitians in New York and Miami dramatically brings out ways that the city context, and nature of immigration to each city, can affect the immigrant experience. Wherever Haitians go in the United States, they suffer the disabilities that come with being black in a racially divided society. Yet there are striking contrasts between Haitians in Miami and New York. In south Florida, they confront anti-Haitian prejudice that is more intense and widespread than in New York. Haitians who have lived elsewhere in America are struck by this when they move to Florida. Virtually all Haitians who have moved to Miami from northern cities, Alex Stepick (1992) reports, claim that anti-Haitian prejudice is greater in Miami.

The key factor in the different image – and visibility – of Haitians is that most Miami Haitians entered as 'boat people' between 1977 and 1981, arriving after a 720-mile trip, crammed into barely seaworthy vessels. (Some 50,000–70,000 Haitian boat people arrived at this time.) If their manner of arrival was not enough, in the 1970s, a hysterical scare swept through south Florida that tuberculosis was endemic among Haitians. Although this belief proved unfounded and hysteria subsided, 'the damage had been done. . . . Many lost their jobs . . . [and] negative stereotypes and fears of Haitians became firmly embedded in the general south Florida population.' Haitians were perceived by many to be 'disease ridden . . . uneducated, unskilled peasants who could only be a burden to the community' (Stepick 1992: 58). To make matters worse, in the early 1980s the Centers for Disease Control announced that Haitians were one of the prime at risk groups for AIDS; widespread negative stereotypes of Haitians stretched even more deeply and broadly (Stepick 1992: 65).

Although the AIDS scare affected New York Haitians, there was no equivalent tuberculosis hysteria. In New York, Haitian does not mean (and has not meant) 'boat people'. Indeed, those boat people who eventually made their way to New York were a very small proportion of the New York Haitian community. Haitians stand out more in Miami, too, because they are (along with Cubans) one of the two main new immigrant groups. In New York City, Haitians are one of a large variety of recent immigrants; in terms of numbers, they ranked sixth among the newcomers in 1990, coming after Dominicans, Chinese, Jamaicans, Russians, and Guyanese (Mollenkopf and Kasinitz 1994).

Whereas most Haitians in Miami live in a distinct neighbourhood known as Little Haiti, New York Haitians have no such equivalent. This contributes to their relatively low profile in New York as well. Most Haitians live in New York City sections where they are intermingled with English-speaking West Indians and native-born blacks. As a group, New York Haitians are better educated. An analysis of 1990 census data shows that only 7 per cent of New York City area Haitians had an eighth grade education or less compared to 25 per cent of southeast Florida Haitians. In the New York City area 44 per cent had some college education, but only 20 percent in southeast Florida (*Migration World* 1994).

Like other West Indians in New York, Haitians are often invisible, as blacks, to the white population. Indeed, most New Yorkers thought of the 1990–91 black boycott of a Korean grocery store in Brooklyn as a black–Korean conflict and were probably not even aware, from the way the incident was reported in the media, that a Haitian woman was involved and that the store was in a West Indian neighbourhood. (The boycott began when the Haitian woman claimed she was beaten by the Korean greengrocer; her cause was taken up by the wider black community.) Had a similar incident occurred in Miami, my guess is that the woman's Haitian identity would have loomed much larger.

The 'pariah status of Haitian boat people' and the visible manner of their arrival have led to a situation in Miami where Haitians are looked down upon by all segments of the local community, including native blacks (Portes and Stepick 1993). It is not surprising that some middle-class Haitians try to hide their Haitian identity; most live outside of Little Haiti and, if they admit they are Haitian, they are careful to distinguish themselves from the 'boat people' (Stepick 1992). In New York, middle-class Haitians seem more intent on making sure that white Americans know they are Haitian as a way to set themselves apart from, and claim superiority to, American blacks (see Stafford 1987).

The particular ethnic mix in New York and Miami also influences the Haitian immigrant experience. Miami Haitians live in what Portes and Stepick (1993) call a Cuban-American dominated world city. Cubans, the other new immigrant group, now make up about half of metropolitan Miami's population. They have had extraordinary economic success and play a pivotal political role. Indeed, by the late 1980s, Miami's mayor was Cuban. In New York, no other recent immigrant group has this kind of influence or numerical dominance. The New York black population has more political clout than Miami's, and in the early 1990s, Haitians in New York lived in a city with a black American mayor (David

Dinkins). The nature of the ethnic hierarchy in the two cities affects Haitians' view of and relations with the Hispanic population. Miami Cubans are clearly on top in terms of colour and class. In New York, Puerto Ricans and Dominicans, the two largest Hispanic groups (together, nearly three-quarters of New York City's Hispanic population), are much less successful – indeed they have higher poverty and public assistance rates than Haitians. New York Haitians often emphasize their superiority to Puerto Ricans and Dominicans and say these groups are lackadaisical, unambitious, and content to live on welfare (Stafford 1987).

CONCLUSION

From Haitians in two different American cities to Jamaicans in London and New York, I have tried to show that where Caribbean immigrants move determines the way they view life in their new home and the kinds of social and cultural patterns that develop among them there. The social and cultural context of incorporation is undoubtedly the most important factor accounting for differences in the Caribbean immigrant experience across nations and cities. It is also important to consider who moves – in terms of the characteristics of the immigrants – as well as the period in which the immigration takes place.

Although I have focused here on the differences among Caribbean immigrants across nations and cities, there are obviously many similarities as well. A full-scale comparison needs to give these similarities equal weight.[7] And there is the question of what happens to the second generation. My remarks here have to do with first-generation immigrants who have made the move from the Caribbean to the United States or Britain. Clearly, the presence of the American black population has far-reaching effects for the children of Jamaican immigrants in New York, making their experiences much different from those of their counterparts in London. Likewise, children of Haitian 'boat people' in Florida are bound to face different problems than second-generation Haitians in New York.

Whether we look at first- or second-generation Caribbean migrants, let me stress again that we need to go beyond analyses in just one setting. Comparative studies bring out, in a dramatic way, aspects of the immigrant experience that we may take for granted and, in a larger sense, help us to understand the dynamics and processes in the enormous Caribbean diaspora that is a feature of today's world.

NOTES

1 For another call for comparative analysis by a historian see Green (1994). Selma Berrol's (1994) historical comparison of Eastern European Jews in London and New York also brings out the importance of the context of incorporation. Among the reasons why access to the middle class came sooner to New York Jews than Jews in London were the greater opportunities provided by New York public schools and the presence of a larger host community of German Jews. The relative size of the Jewish

communities in London and New York also made a difference; the larger Jewish community in New York provided more jobs and a bigger consumer market and was a stronger bulwark against anti-Semitism. See also Truzzi's (1997) historical comparison, which points to the role of socioeconomic characteristics and the state of inter-ethnic relations in Brazil and the United States in explaining the different patterns of economic incorporation of Syrians and Lebanese in the two countries.

2 My research among Jamaican immigrants in New York in the early 1980s, based on in-depth interviews with forty immigrants and participant observation, is fully reported elsewhere (Foner 1983, 1985, 1986, 1987). In the late 1980s, I also conducted research among health care workers, largely Jamaican immigrants, in a New York nursing home (Foner 1994). The London study, conducted in 1973, included in-depth interviews with 110 respondents, follow-up interviews with twenty people from the original sample, and participant observation (see Foner 1978).

3 The structure of race relations in the receiving society also emerges as key in understanding the different experiences of Nevisian migrants in England (Leeds) and the US Virgin Islands (see Olwig, Chapter 4 of this volume).

4 In 1990, the median West Indian household income in New York was $37,000 compared to $34,939 for native blacks (Kasinitz and Vickerman 1995). As for labour force participation rates, they were 89 percent for foreign-born West Indian men in the New York area (compared to 77 percent for African-American men) and 83 percent for foreign-born West Indian women (compared to 69 percent for African-American women) (Model 1995).

5 See Foner (1986) for a detailed analysis, including explicit comparisons, of the experiences of Jamaican women in New York and London.

6 Thousands of West Indians came early in the century, before 1924 restrictive immigration legislation; some 50,000 from Jamaica alone.

7 See Foner (1983) where I give equal weight to the similarities and differences among Jamaicans in London and New York.

REFERENCES

Basch, L., Glick Schiller, N., and Szanton Blanc, C. (1994) *Nations Unbound: Transnational Projects, Postcolonial Predicaments, and Deterritorialized Nation-States*, Langhorne, PA: Gordon and Breach.

Berrol, S (1994) *East Side/East End: Eastern European Jews in London and New York, 1870–1920*, Westport, CT: Praeger.

Brettell, C. (1981) 'Is the ethnic community inevitable? a comparison of the settlement patterns of Portuguese immigrants in Toronto and Paris', *Journal of Ethnic Studies* 9: 1–17.

Campbell, M. (1995) 'The other immigrants: comparing the Irish in Australia and the United States', *Journal of American Ethnic History* 14: 3–22.

Cockburn, A. and Ridgeway, J. (1982) 'The revolt of the underclass', *Village Voice*, 6–12 January.

Colen, S. (1990) '"Housekeeping" for the Green Card: West Indian household workers, the state and stratified reproduction in New York', in R. Sanjek and S. Colen (eds) *At Work in Homes*, Washington, DC: American Anthropological Association.

Foner, N. (1978) *Jamaica Farewell: Jamaican Migrants in London*, Berkeley: University of California Press; London: Routledge and Kegan Paul.

—— (1979) 'West Indians in New York City and London: a comparative analysis', *International Migration Review* 13: 284–97.

—— (1983) 'Jamaican Migrants: A Comparative Analysis of the New York and London Experience', Occasional Paper No. 36, Center for Latin American and Caribbean Studies, New York University, pp. 1–48.

—— (1985) 'Sex Roles and sensibilities: Jamaican women in New York and London', in R. Simon and C. Brettell (eds) *International Migration: The Female Experience*, Totowa, NJ: Rowman and Allenheld.

—— (1986) 'Race and Color: Jamaican migrants in London and New York', *International Migration Review* 19: 708–27.

—— (1987) 'The Jamaicans: race and ethnicity among migrants in New York', in N. Foner (ed.) *New Immigrants in New York*, New York: Columbia University Press.

—— (1994) *The Caregiving Dilemma: Work in an American Nursing Home*, Berkeley: University of California Press.

Green, N. (1994) 'The comparative method and poststructural structuralism – new perspectives for migration studies', *Journal of American Ethnic History* 13: 3–22.

Hall, S. (1995) 'Negotiating Caribbean identities', *New Left Review* 218: 3–14.

Kasinitz, P. (1992) *Caribbean New York*, Ithaca, NY: Cornell University Press.

Kasinitz, P. and Vickerman, M. (1995) 'Ethnic niches and racial traps: Jamaicans in the New York regional economy', paper presented at the Social Science History Association annual conference, Chicago.

Lowenthal, D. (1978) 'West Indian emigrants overseas', in C. Clarke (ed.) *Caribbean Social Relations*, Monograph No. 8, Centre for Latin American Studies, University of Liverpool.

—— (1985) *The Past is a Foreign Country*, Cambridge: Cambridge University Press.

Migration World (1994) 'Haitians in the US', *Migration World* 22: 8.

Model, S. (1995) 'West Indian prosperity: fact or fiction?', *Social Problems* 42: 501–19.

Mollenkopf, J. (1994) *A Phoenix in the Ashes: The Rise and Fall of the Koch Coalition in New York City Politics*, Princeton, NJ: Princeton University Press.

Mollenkopf, J. and Kasinitz, P. (1994) 'Chancellor's Report on the CUNY Student of the Year 2000', City University of New York.

Portes, A. and Stepick, A. (1993) *City on the Edge: The Transformation of Miami*, Berkeley: University of California Press.

Rollwagen, J. (1975) 'The city as context: the Puerto Ricans of Rochester, New York', *Urban Anthropology* 4: 53–60.

Rose, E.J.B. *et al.* (1969) *Colour and Citizenship*, London: Oxford University Press.

Segal, A. (1987). 'The Caribbean Exodus in a Global Context', in B. Levine (ed.) *Caribbean Exodus*, New York: Praeger.

Smith, R. (1988) *Kinship and Class in the West Indies*, Cambridge: Cambridge University Press.

Stafford, S.B. (1987) 'The Haitians: the cultural meaning of race and ethnicity', in N. Foner (ed.) *New Immigrants in New York*, New York: Columbia University Press.

Stepick, A. (1992) 'The refugees nobody wants: Haitians in Miami', in G. Grenier and A. Stepick (eds.) *Miami Now*, Gainesville: University of Florida Press.

Sutton, C. and Makiesky, S. (1975). 'Migration and West Indian racial and ethnic consciousness,' in H. Safa and B. du Toit (eds) *Migration and Development: Implications for Ethnic Identity and Political Conflict*, The Hague: Mouton, pp. 113–43.

Truzzi, O. (1997) 'The right place at the right time: Syrians and Lebanese in Brazil and the United States, a comparative approach', *Journal of American Ethnic History* 16: 3–34.

Waldinger, R. (1987) 'Beyond nostalgia: the old neighborhood revisited', *New York Affairs* 10: 1–12.

Part II
Migration narratives

4 Constructing lives

Migration narratives and life stories among Nevisians

Karen Fog Olwig

The complexity of Caribbean migration has become increasingly apparent with the recognition of the transnational character and long historical past of Caribbean population movements. A useful approach to the understanding of this complexity will undoubtedly be found in collaborative and comparative research endeavours linking existent case studies of migration and elucidating important overarching themes. In comparative studies, however, the framework of analysis adopted will determine the sort of comparison which is undertaken and hence, to a great extent, the conclusions which may be drawn from it. A framework which singles out for comparison the disparate experiences of migrating from a variety of Caribbean places of origin to their different respective (neo-)colonial metropoles leads to quite different conclusions than one which takes its point of departure in the multifaceted experiences of people who move from a single island society to a multiplicity of metropoles. The former form of comparison can have the effect of privileging the perspective of the metropoles. The metropolitan perspective will thus tend to view migration primarily in terms of unilateral movements, where people travel from areas belonging to their own cultural sphere to the metropole in order to settle there. If, however, one takes as one's point of departure a particular island society, or even a particular family, one will see that there is a long heritage of moving to different migration destinations and that migration to colonial, or neo-colonial, metropoles constitutes only a more recent example of Caribbean population movements. A comparison of the varied experiences of moving from one point of origin to different destinations may therefore show that the common denominators behind migration are not necessarily the sorts of factors which appear to predominate in the interaction between a colonial or neo-colonial metropole and its (former) colonies. We might equally discover factors associated with concerns rooted in the migrants' natal community. This, in any case, is my conclusion after carrying out two decades of research on people from the Leeward Island of Nevis who have moved to destinations in the Caribbean, in North America and Great Britain.

In this chapter I will compare the migration experiences of Nevisians in the US Virgin Island of St John and Leeds in Great Britain on the basis of interviews which I carried out with Nevisians in these places. My interviews suggested that comparison of the experience of migrating to different destinations, as related by the migrants, should be carried out at several different levels of analysis. By combining different readings of migration interviews, which incorporate their various perspectives on migration, it is possible to reach a more comprehensive understanding of the complexity of Caribbean migration and its central importance to the Caribbean people themselves.

The Caribbean has been described as having developed a migration tradition (Thomas-Hope 1978, 1992, 1995) or a migration culture (Richardson 1983, 1989) which revolves around the desire to gain a form of economic and social improvement unattainable within the local societies which emerged after the abolition of slavery. Caribbean people have migrated to whatever areas of economic opportunity were open to them. In the case of Nevis, this includes such different destinations as Trinidad, Cuba, Venezuela, Panama, Curaçao, the Bahamas, Great Britain, the American and British Virgin Islands, St Martin, the United States, and Canada. The migratory movements to Great Britain and the American Virgin Islands (and thereby also the United States) have been particularly massive, and Leeds and St John constitute, today, important points in the global network of social and economic relations which constitute the Nevisian community (Olwig 1993a).[1]

Interviews with migrants, and the writing down of their migration stories, have been used as important data in the study of this community. I would argue that these interviews can be used most fruitfully, if we do not regard them merely as 'a quarry' which can be mined for raw data on the migration process (Tonkin 1990: 33), but also as 'arguments created by people in particular conditions' (ibid.: 29). By elucidating the interrelationship between the 'arguments' presented by migrants and the 'conditions' under which they are offered we may be able to understand a great deal about the way in which people construct their lives, and thereby themselves as persons with a specific social and cultural identity, and the particular circumstances of life, including those related to migration, which led them to relate these stories. The life stories, in other words, will constitute both 'a window' on the 'historical and ethnographic events' which make up what we might call the migration process, and 'a view of the subjective experience of the narrator' (Peacock and Holland 1993: 369).[2]

The stories which were related to me by Nevisians on St John and in Leeds[3] can be read in at least three different ways which complement and supplement each other. They can, of course, be read for different kinds of information on the experiences which the Nevisians have had moving from a small island in the Caribbean to destinations abroad. They can also be read in terms of the way in which these experiences are represented by the Nevisians and what this may tell us about the historical and cultural contexts in which these movements have taken place. And, finally, the narratives can be read as life stories about individuals who have engaged in movements and the significance of these movements to these people as persons with their own life project.

THE MIGRATION EXPERIENCE

Nevisians both on St John and in Leeds were able to give detailed accounts of the events of leaving Nevis, travelling to an unknown destination and looking for a place to live and work. Although the stories varied, all migrants explained having left with a general desire 'for a better life', a desire often nurtured by parents, who had helped finance the trip, together with close relatives at home or abroad. Leaving Nevis therefore often was more of a family endeavour than an individual project, as is the case in this account by a woman in Leeds:

> I came to England, because my parents suggested it. I had no work, and my parents didn't want their children to work as hard in the blazing sun as they had done. They wanted better for their children. They also told us that we should 'broaden our outlook on life and make ourselves better'. I was the first one to leave in the family, and my family got the £65 together for my passage: sold some sheep, borrowed from an uncle, and friends and family gave a little. My auntie in America sent me clothes.

The sort of experiences which Nevisians in St John and Leeds chose to emphasize in their stories about this pursuit of a better life both differed and shared a number of similarities. They differed to a great extent because the social, cultural and physical environments of the two places were quite dissimilar, and they were alike because the process of arriving as an outsider in an unknown place involves many parallel conditions, despite the dissimilarity of the migration destinations.

Migrating to the Virgin Islands

Those who travelled to the American Virgin Islands found a physical and cultural environment much like that of Nevis.[4] Indeed, many emphasized that they particularly liked St John because it reminded them of their home island, being a small West Indian island with a great deal of vegetation. The economic conditions in the Virgin Islands were much better than those on Nevis and other smaller British West Indian islands, however, with many job opportunities in the flourishing tourist industry, particularly within domestic service and construction work. A great number of people from the nearby British West Indies therefore were attracted to the American territory and arrived on a short-term visitors' visa hoping that they might be able to find employment before it expired, and hence qualify for a labour certificate and a more long-term visa. Many employers took advantage of this and offered work below minimum wages. Although this practice was illegal the would-be immigrants could do little about it, being dependent upon the goodwill of their employers for their visas. Caneel Bay Plantation, the only major hotel on the island until the mid 1980s, offered the absolute minimal of legal wages and yet succeeded in maintaining a viable labour force by providing the employees with cheap meals and housing in barracks. Compared with what they had been used to on Nevis, the working conditions at Caneel Bay seemed good to the Nevisians:

When I started at Caneel Bay 16 years ago I got 63¢ an hour. This was in 1962, and I thought that it was a lot of money. In Nevis I had received 50 British West Indian dollars a month, and so I was making about four times as much on St John. I lived at Caneel Bay and paid $4 in rent per month. They took it out of my salary. I also ate all my meals there: breakfast for 30¢, lunch and dinner at 50¢ per meal. We were four in a room, all single men and living in bunk beds. It was a fairly small room, but we were satisfied with what we had.

The obtainment of a permanent immigrant visa was, understandably, a major concern for all Nevisians. This was not just because it would allow a more secure life in the American territory, but also because it would grant greater choice of employment, including the possibility of self-employment, which was illegal under the terms of the temporary labour certificates. A number of Nevisian women who married St Johnians received permanent immigrant status and succeeded in filing for their Nevisian family so that they all obtained permanent visas within a few years. Several of them have even become American citizens, and are holding jobs with public works or the local utility companies. A few of the women have also passed the American high school equivalency examination and become teachers' aides or secretaries. Many of the Nevisians whom I interviewed in the late 1970s, fifteen to twenty years after they had moved to St John, had still not succeeded in acquiring permanent visas, however, largely because Nevis, being a British dependency, had a very small quota within the American immigration system. It was not before the end of my study, around 1980, that the last Nevisians were, finally, being processed for immigrant status.

Nevisians on St John also related having experienced problems finding satisfactory and affordable accommodation in the highly inflated tourist industry on a small island with limited housing. Many of those who were not living at the Caneel Bay barracks had initially been forced to rent small wooden houses, or rather shacks, with no running water at exorbitant prices. When I did my field-work, however, many Nevisians were renting small apartments situated next to the water cistern below the main living quarters of a family residence – owned by either a St Johnian or, more rarely, a Nevisian who had lived longer on the island. A growing number were also purchasing land and building their own houses. This included even a few who had only temporary visas. Some of the houses which these Nevisians built were rather simple wooden structures which had been constructed by the occupants themselves. One Nevisian had even succeeded in purchasing an old dilapidated wooden house for $100, which he repaired so that it was habitable though still rather primitive. A growing number, however, were living in large concrete houses which were clearly an improvement over the housing they had known on Nevis.

The Nevisians on St John emphasized that they maintained close ties with their families on Nevis, and those whose parents were still living on Nevis sent money to them about once a month. They also sent boxes of food, clothing and groceries to Nevis on *The Effort*, a Nevisian boat which plied the waters between Nevis and many of the islands which had attracted Nevisians such as the American and the British Virgin Islands and St Martin. The continued importance of maintaining good relations with the family by offering economic support was of particular urgency for those who did not have a permanent visa and who therefore might have to return to Nevis, should they become incapable of working or lose their job. As one woman explained:

> Some people go away, and they never send anything, letters or money, and yet they return to live in Nevis when they are sick and in need of help. That is wrong, they should not expect that. But by sending money regularly, just by keeping in contact regularly, I am always assured of having a place to go, when I am in need. So it is a form of security, though I don't think of it this way. I just send, because it is natural to me.

Most Nevisians on St John were of the opinion that they had done rather well there, and much better than had been possible had they stayed on Nevis. They emphasized that they had wage employment which paid well compared with what they had received on Nevis. A number of those who had permanent visas had opted to work on their own as, for example, taxi drivers or artisans, and felt that they earned more money and were more independent in this way. Several families were sending their children to college, either at the College of the Virgin Islands on St Thomas, or in the United States. One family, still on temporary visas, somehow managed to pay more than $1,000 per semester for tuition, room and board to keep their oldest daughter in college on St Thomas, even though both parents worked for minimum wages at $2.65 an hour. They had to pay more than twice as much as local residents for their daughter's education because of their continued temporary legal residence in the American territory after having lived and worked for fifteen years on St John.

Some Nevisians were clearly struggling to make a living, however, and they just barely earned enough to pay for food, lodging and necessary clothing, not to speak of the remittances their family on Nevis expected. Some of the single mothers who had children to support on their own found it exceedingly difficult to manage on the slim wages from the domestic work which they usually performed, and they also missed the extended natal family which offered a social context of life and helped with the care of children, giving the women a greater amount of freedom. Many of them had joined fundamentalistic churches such as the Seventh Day Adventist, the Pentecostal and the Baptist Churches, and found in them some of the warmth and support which they were lacking on St John, but also religious bodies which expected considerable economic support in the form of tithing.

Despite the various problems which they had encountered, all Nevisians saw their stay in St John as a good opportunity which they should make the most of. None had immediate plans to move back to Nevis, but many hoped to retire on Nevis and some had built homes there. Most visited Nevis once a year or every few years, in order to see parents and other close relatives there. They regarded Nevis as their home and St John as their place of work and residence for the time being. The main exception to this was found among those who had married St Johnians and started a family on St John with them. The general attitude of the Nevisians toward life on St John was a rather positive and pragmatic one:

> You get a faster dollar here, this being an American territory. The American government finds work for the people, and there are a lot of investments in American territories, which lead to jobs. So this is much better than a British territory. I love Nevis, because I was born there. But to keep up with the rising cost of living I would rather be here.

Migrating to Leeds

The Nevisians in Leeds described quite different migration experiences.[5] The very encounter with Great Britain involved an entirely new environment which had no parallel on Nevis, or the West Indies in general. Many were entirely unprepared for it and described their reaction to arriving in Great Britain as that of receiving a shock. This was the case for this young child who travelled from Nevis to join his parents in Leeds:

> I arrived in short pants and a short sleeved shirt and met this white stuff on the ground that was snow. It was freezing cold . . . I hated it, and I cried for days, I just wanted to go back to those I knew.

> I remember the grey buildings, the smoke that came out of the chimneys, the cold, grey environment. . . .

> I got to like TV, and it became one of my means of escape. I could relate to the TV with the kiddies' things and puppet shows, anything that was sunny and bright in the strange environment I had been placed in. Until I left school at 16–17 years of age I would have gone back to Nevis, if I had had the chance.

Many older Nevisians similarly related that they wished they could have left the strange and seemingly inhospitable environment, and returned to Nevis. They did not have the funds to do so, however, having arrived on one-way tickets, and they had to look for work immediately after arrival. Most found work in a day or two, jobs being plentiful during the 1950s and early 1960s, when they arrived. During the 1970s, some did experience periods of unemployment, where they had lived on support from the government, but none had remained unemployed, in that they had either found another job or been old enough to retire.[6]

Many Nevisians in Leeds expressed dissatisfaction with the kind of work which they were able to obtain. One man described his work for a gas board as 'hot, dusty, dirty and hard'; a woman, who worked in a factory, complained that she found it difficult to perform the same kind of work in the same place for the entire day, being used to doing different kinds of jobs on Nevis during the course of a day; another woman who found her first employment doing domestic work at a college in Oxford left it, because: 'Why leave home to do domestic work for others? I will do it for my parents, but not for others.' The fact that most were hired to do unskilled labour should not have surprised Nevisians, because most had 'nothing to offer but their muscles', as one Nevisian expressed it. But they clearly had expected that better jobs would be available to them, and that they would be paid higher wages:

> We got the worst, though we had come to the country to build it up. We met the chicken in the shops with nobody to buy them and cook them, and we did all that. We came here to open the way, and we got the worst.

The most skilled occupation held by the Nevisians that I interviewed was that of nursing. Yet, all but one of these nurses had taken a two-year course, which did not qualify them to become fully trained nurses:

> I wanted to be a nurse since childhood, I just liked to be with people. When I came to England I knew little about the training available for nurses, and I got two years' training to be a state enrolled nurse. . . . I now regret that I did not take further training, and if I had had proper advice, I would not have succumbed to the two-year training course. Most West Indians have succumbed to it, not for lack of abilities, but because they didn't get proper advice. The hospitals just needed workers, more than full nurses, so they weren't interested in encouraging them to be staff nurses or sisters, as are the nurses who have had the three-year training course. As West Indians we were not aware of the limitations of the two-year course, we were ignorant.

The lack of encouragement to pursue a proper education was experienced even more strongly by the Nevisians' children who went to school in Leeds. They were placed in the lower streams, as compared with English school children, and recommended for CSE exams, rather than O-levels. Instead they were encouraged to do sports and compete in sports events organized by the school, being regarded as physically strong and athletic. Those few who succeeded in taking O-levels described it as one long battle against teachers and the school system:

> A lot of blacks didn't progress, because the teachers subtly suggested certain fields. . . . I wanted to do all O-levels, but because of the teachers, I had to do CSE. But I got a first in three of them, and therefore they count as O-levels. I could have insisted on doing more O-levels, but I didn't know any better. I thought that the teachers were right.

Many, however, had been able to further their education at local colleges, and had received either vocational training as cooks, secretaries or technical assistants of various sorts, or, more rarely, they had succeeded in pursuing university level education. The Nevisian quoted above was one of the latter, and when I interviewed him he had just received his degree in electrical engineering after many years of night school.

Racism was emphasized by the Nevisians as the main problem behind the difficulties which they experienced on the job market and in the educational institutions. As long as they were content to perform the more menial jobs, attend the lowest streams in school and win trophies for the schools at athletic contests, the Nevisians had a place in British society. Their attempts to break out of this role met with many obstacles, however. One woman of Nevisian descent, born and raised in a white neighbourhood in Leeds, remembers the humiliation she experienced when she dared express any ambition at the school:

I remember once a person came from outside the school and asked everybody what they would like to do for a career. I replied: 'nurse' and the older children laughed, saying: 'you don't have black nurses at the hospital!'

The Nevisians explained becoming aware of the limited place accorded them in British society immediately upon arrival in Great Britain. Thus when they began looking for a place to live they realized that they were confined to living in those immigrant ghettoes which were in the process of turning into black neighbourhoods. Such areas, where the houses had been subdivided into bed-sits which could accommodate as many as possible, were anyway the only ones where they could afford to live on the wages which they received. In Leeds they found such an area in Chapeltown, which soon turned into a predominantly West Indian community.

Living in bed-sits, where kitchen and bathroom facilities had to be shared, involved a drastic change in home life for the Nevisians who were used to living with their family in houses of their own:

We stayed in rooms, where we had to share the kitchen. We must work there at the same time. I did not like that so I waited until late at night. I hated sharing the kitchen. They would wait for you to put money in for the gas, and then use it. My parents had their own house with no one talking, spitting into your pot. I used to cry over it.

When I did fieldwork in Leeds during the summers of 1987–89 – twenty-five to thirty years after the Nevisians had moved to Leeds – I only met two older men still living in bed-sits. Some were living in rented apartments, but most had succeeded in purchasing their own house, also in the Chapeltown area. The houses in Chapeltown were relatively inexpensive during the early 1970s, having been run-down by being occupied by so many persons living in bed-sits. Many Nevisian men were able to make good use of the training as carpenters and masons which they had received before leaving for England, and they had turned their houses into attractive family homes. The acquisition of a house also meant the possibility of creating a domestic sphere similar to the one they had known from Nevis. This project had been facilitated by the fact that most had married a Nevisian spouse, either one they knew from home, or one they had met in the West Indian community in Leeds.

Nevisians offered varying opinions on life in England, but most of them were rather negative. They ranged from the pragmatic but entirely negative statement by an elderly retired man still living in a bed-sit who had scraped by on an assortment of jobs until he qualified for retirement: 'I like living in England for one reason: I can't get out, I am stuck and have no choice!' to the more positive statement by a middle-aged woman who had worked as a nurse, having completed the two-year course. She was in the middle of a three-year course as a deacon for the Episcopal church when I interviewed her:

I am glad that I came to England. I learned a lot, I knew nothing in the West Indies. I am glad for where I am. I would not have been there unless I came to England. This has broadened my mind.

Despite the fact that Nevisians described their life in Leeds in rather critical terms, in my eyes they actually seemed to have been rather successful, or at least as successful as the Nevisians on St John. Certainly their standard of living, judged by the houses in which they lived and the kinds of jobs which they held, did not seem markedly different from that of the Nevisians on St John. Furthermore, the British welfare state had provided unemployment benefits and free medical care to those in need as well as free education. While some Nevisians on St John may have had a higher income than those in Leeds, they also have had a great number of expenses to contend with. The Nevisians in Leeds, like those on St John, have been able to send considerable support to their families on Nevis, and a few of them have built houses on Nevis and plan to return there upon retirement.

The tone of the migrant stories told in Leeds was radically different from that of the stories related on St John, however. The former revealed a great deal of bitterness towards the way in which West Indians were being treated in Great Britain, the latter reflected rather an idea of personal struggle, sacrifice or adventure, as the case might be. I shall argue, below, that this difference in the way in which the migrant stories were presented is related to the different ways in which Great Britain and the United States have been perceived by the Nevisians, and probably by West Indians in general.

REPRESENTING THE MIGRATION EXPERIENCE

The interviews with migrants which I collected during research reflected not just historical and ethnographic 'facts' on migration, but also different sorts of arguments offered by the migrants about their experience of migrating. These arguments, and the way in which they were presented, naturally reflected the historical circumstances in which migration took place. A closer examination of the migrants' arguments and the context in which they were generated therefore will grant us another perspective on Caribbean migration.

The Nevisians who had gone to St John could not claim a 'natural' right to live and work in the Virgin Islands. It was quite clear that they had arrived as foreigners on visitors' visas, and that they knew that they would only be eligible for more extended visas if they obtained work for an American employer or an employer with immigrant status. The right to stay on St John which the Nevisians claimed for themselves was based on their willingness to work hard and hence contribute to the well-being of the American territory. The Nevisians also emphasized that since there were plenty of jobs to go around, they did not take away anything from the local population:

> The natives like to complain about the down islanders, but they will not do the work that the aliens do. There are many young fellows doing nothing. . . . I don't think that the St Johnians can blame the aliens for having taken advantage of the working possibilities at Caneel, when they wouldn't do it themselves.

Much of the criticism against the position of 'bonding' which some Nevisians had endured for a great number of years was not directed against the American immigration system as such, but rather against specific employers who were seen to abuse this system:

> [This American woman] was a real devil. She expected me to stay there all the time, thinking that she had acquired a slave, not a bonded maid. . . . After 9 months I decided to leave the job, and I told so to the woman. She then threatened to send me back to Nevis. I said that she could not do this, because I had come on my own, and she had nothing to do with this. . . .

The failure to obtain immigrant status was likewise often couched in terms of accusations of employers who had not helped individual Nevisians acquire permanent visas, because it was advantageous for them to maintain their employees on temporary visas:

> I filed in 1967, when I worked at . . . [a restaurant]. Then I changed job, and when I went to my old employer [a North American woman] to get the papers, which were in her possession, she said that she had thrown them all out. Therefore I have no proof of having filed in 1967, and I had to refile in 1973. . . . I lost my seniority and was set back. . . .

These stories about the problems which Nevisian had encountered in the American immigration system seemed to serve different purposes when related by women and men. For the women, especially the single mothers, the stories illustrated the hardship which they had suffered in order to help their families; for the men, the stories rather served to demonstrate that they had managed to beat the troublesome migration system by displaying a great deal of personal stamina and determination.

Nevisians also justified their presence on St John by reference to the fact that they were not the first to leave their home island to look for economic opportunities abroad. It had been a tradition for Nevisians to travel abroad for work as far back as they could remember; indeed this was a common practice throughout the West Indies. Several Nevisians pointed out that some of the people who were living on St John when they arrived had come themselves a few years before, or were of mixed West Indian background. This was the case for the British Virgin Islanders, for example, and yet some of these people had been the first to call the newly arrived bad names:

> When I first came in 1967, down islanders were not very popular. I remember especially at . . . [a house where she stayed] the granddaughters [whose grandmother was from Tortola] were very quick to use the term 'garret'. . . . Even on Tortola, which is a British territory, they use it for other British islanders. I think it is ridiculous, because they are no better than the rest of us, and they also need a visa to work on the American islands. Even though the granddaughters were so critical of aliens, they still laid with the men, and so I really was glad, when one of the granddaughters had a child for a person that they would call a garret.[7]

In essence, the fact that many West Indians wanted to live and work on St John with its plethora of opportunities in the tourist industry required little explanation, and most Nevisians found that their relations with the St Johnian population were amiable, after the tension of the first years of massive immigration in the early 1960s had subsided. A Nevisian woman explained:

> When I first came the locals were very reserved, but I was gradually accepted, and now I feel that I am generally speaking treated well. It was as if the locals sized you up, and if you were judged to be all right – as you would be, if you were friendly and nice – then they would accept you.

The Nevisians in Leeds were much keener to explain why they had moved to Great Britain. Their stories followed pretty much the same pattern of having been misled by their expectations of going to the mighty and rich mother country of the United Kingdom where their fortune would be made. The disappointment felt when Great Britain could not live up to these expectations was described with a great deal of bitterness in a joint interview with a mother and daughter:

> There were rumours that Britain had opened the gates, the streets were paved with gold, and one could come there to make one's life. . . .

> We expected better, and considering how St Kitts-Nevis were bled by England, we should have been given better conditions, but we were just boxed in by the low wages and the high cost of living. At the very least we should have been paid living wages.

Great Britain was not just perceived to have cheated them out of decent wages and living conditions, but, perhaps more importantly, to have let down their very belief in the colonial institutions of the church and the school. These institutions, which had imparted the importance of leading respectable and upright lives if one were to have any standing in society (Olwig 1990, 1993a), turned out to be of little consequence in British society. Thus it became apparent that the education which they had received in the West Indies prepared them inadequately for good jobs in Great Britain, and that the churches either did not care, or were not able to help them progress in society:

I thought I was coming to my mother country, and that I would be welcomed as one, as we welcomed white persons to the West Indies. I had to recognize prejudice and racism. The church didn't give strong support. In the West Indies, if you wanted a job the church helped you and sought for you. In England, I thought that I would benefit likewise, but it didn't happen. Perhaps I had expected too much, we were a new people coming to a new culture, although we were from a British colony. We were viewed from half opened doors, half drawn curtains, people were sceptical. . . . I had heard so much about 'Rule Britannia', Union Jack, mother of Commonwealth, and I was curious and wanted to see for myself. Some gave a terribly difficult time, but I determined to hold on, fight through, fight for the children. . . .

The only interest the British had in us was as labourers on the sugar plantations to produce sugar and cotton for the British Empire. There was no general education for the people, only for those who were to work in the administration. The missionaries did a good job, but they did it single-handedly. The government was not interested in individuals, but rather in the masses and their service on the plantations.

The way in which the Nevisians in Leeds related their migration experiences reflected the deeply felt sense they had developed of not belonging in Great Britain, except as an underclass of cheap labourers at the bottom of society:

In my opinion we never should have come here. Where I work now I get in contact with all walks of life, and all look like they are saying, 'what are you doing here?' This is especially because I have a decent job and English people are unemployed, and my type of job usually isn't held by black people. When white people see me in the job, they wonder about it, I can see they wonder.

Compared with Leeds, St John seemed to offer the advantage of being part of both the 'home' environment of the West Indies and a Western metropole, which had little cultural connection with the old imperial system. As part of the West Indies, St John offered a familiar cultural, social and physical environment; as part of the United States, the island offered employment opportunities and high wages, which were inconceivable on Nevis, and the ideology of living in a free society with equality for all:

I like it here. I like the many trees here and the nature and scenery. Besides, in Nevis the people are very prejudiced as far as class is concerned. Nevis was very bad formerly, I think it is better now. . . . It is better now in Nevis, but I prefer St John because people are more equal here.

Furthermore, migration in search of better opportunities is regarded as an accepted life strategy on St John, both as a West Indian island and as an American territory. This is not the case in Great Britain, which may be open as far as extending economic and social relations out to the empire is concerned, but extremely closed when it comes to incorporating people from that empire into the local British society. Perhaps this has been the most devastating aspect of the migrant experience in Great Britain.

LIFE STORIES

The interviews which I carried out with the Nevisians focused on their migration experience, and it may therefore seem most correct to describe them as 'migration stories'. I shall here suggest, however, that they were not primarily stories about migration, but rather life stories about the people interviewed. This is because the primary meaning of migration did not seem to be that of leaving Nevis and travelling out to settle in a foreign location, but rather that of becoming an adult and assuming responsibility for one's own life.

Many Nevisians explained that it would have been extremely difficult for them to have become real adults if they had stayed on Nevis. Most were staying with their parents when they left Nevis, and whatever earnings they had made they had given to their parents. They had, in other words, been part of their natal household and under the authority of their parents. It was extremely difficult for them to acquire their own home on Nevis with the limited funds available to them – funds which they moreover turned over to their parents – and hence become independent adults. Furthermore, if they had acquired their own home on Nevis they would have been expected to manage on their own. By leaving Nevis, they could attain a great deal of independence in relation to their parents. At the same time, however, they could maintain close ties and win recognition as adults in relation to their natal home by assuming responsibility for its well-being through remittances. The importance of gaining freedom from parents was noted by many as something which they looked forward to when leaving Nevis:

> The West Indian culture is so rigid at home, and I had thought that it would be good to get away from my parents, I would be free.

This freedom was rather curtailed in England by the landlords who owned the houses where Nevisians rented bed-sits; indeed, an important aspect of the problem of living in rented rooms was the dissatisfaction of living under someone's authority. In some cases these landlords were Nevisians who had arrived earlier on:

> Children were never free to do as they liked, the parents made all the decisions. So when we came here, we thought that we could make our own decisions, but we had to live in other people's houses, which meant other restrictions. . . . I think they imposed the restrictions, partly because they had to pay the bills, partly because they had to show their authority. They had achieved what the new ones had not.

Perhaps the primary importance of becoming independent from parental authorities also partly explains the indifference which many Nevisians expressed towards living in what might look like a rather primitive shack on St John – this house was no worse than what they were used to on Nevis, and they had gained what they wanted, at least for the time being: a place of their own.

The custom of leaving the home in order to get away from parents' authority had been adopted by some of the young Nevisians before leaving Nevis. Thus a number of men related having left their home as children because of some disagreement with parents and moving in with other relatives or friends:

> When I was 12 I left to live with my aunt, because I fell out with my mother. I was not treated fairly by her present husband, and as a kid I was a bit obstinate. So my aunt took me to help them with the domestic work – look after animals, pick grass, look for firewood.

> When I was about 16 I went to St Kitts, where I worked on an estate which was privately owned. Two cousins of mine had cousins on St Kitts who were not related to me, and I lived with them. I could live there as family and paid no rent. But they were glad to have me there, because I helped with errands.

The early short move to a relative on Nevis thus was often followed by a more distant move to St Kitts which offered work at better wages in sugar plantations. Moving to St Kitts was also a fairly common pattern among young women who had had children out of wedlock and found their parents' anger about their 'misfortune' too difficult to live with. By moving to St Kitts they would also be better able to help support the family and the baby, who was often left behind with their mother on Nevis.

Moving away from Nevis was not just a display of independence in relation to parents but also a demonstration of filial duty to them, because the move would enable the youngsters to send remittances to their family back home. Thus, many Nevisians emphasized that they had left Nevis in order to help support their family back home:

> My father died, and since I was the eldest of the lot, I left to earn my own living and help support my mother and siblings. I had a cousin in St Thomas who thought that since I was the eldest, she would send for me. I was 16 when I came here, and I had just finished school at the seventh standard . . .

> When I worked on St Thomas at first I made $10 a month. Still I managed to send things back, because I had no expenses myself. . . .

> Most Nevisians here take care of their people back home. They feel obligated to take care of them. They were brought up with a closeness of ties, so that they feel they should help. They know that their parents worked for them, and so they feel they must help the parents.

Such help gives the children a respected position in the natal community on Nevis; indeed, for some the pressure of maintaining this status is an important motivating factor for the sending of remittances. Apparently some parents in Nevis are aware of this and know how to use it to their own advantage:

I send £20–35 for my parents every month. My two brothers also send. The other month I sent £130, when they asked for the fridge. . . . I feel that we must support the parents. If we didn't send money, we would have a bad name in the village, and I am happy that the villagers see that they have a five-bedroom house with TV, telephone and a fridge. A couple of months ago, I had tough times, and I sent nothing for my parents. My mother then went to the welfare department to beg for money. She was told that she couldn't get anything with so many children abroad to support her. I got very upset about it and told her off for her greed. I told her to get food on credit in the shop, if she has no money, because she will know that money is coming later. But after my mother carried on like that I have made sure that I send every month, and I have told my father to be sure that he saves. . . . My mother now is very proud of her daughter who sends so much and says , 'It's mi pickney in England.'

The great importance for Nevisians of leaving as a way of coming of age was summed up nicely by one young Nevisian on St John who explained his move to St John simply by saying: 'After you grow up you want to take up responsibilities, and this is easier outside.' Another way of interrelating maturing with leaving is found in this explication by a woman of why St John to her was preferable to Nevis:

It is better on St John than on Nevis. I became a woman here. I lived at home in Nevis, and so all my adult life has been here. I was 18 when I settled here. . . . As long as you live in your parents' house on Nevis, you are regarded by them as a child, and so it was not before coming here that I became a grown woman.

This close linkage between movement and growing up raises the question of whether, to a Nevisian way of thinking, it makes sense to single out 'migration' as a specially designated activity which is set apart from the normal course of settled life. Leaving the parents' authority for the more independent space in the house of an aunt for economic independence in the sugar plantations on St Kitts, or for greater economic opportunities and freedom on St John or Leeds, can be regarded as a long chain of movements which allow a gradual process of assuming responsibility and hence becoming a respected adult member of the community. For many Nevisians leaving the island therefore is not a matter of taking a grave decision about emigration, but a natural part of the process of growing up, as explained by this woman on St John:

When you grow up on Nevis you wait for your turn to leave the island. It is usually the oldest one who leaves first, and then the next ones, according to their age.

St John with its 'faster dollar' and ideology of independence and equality suited the Nevisians, even though many of them had to suffer long years of migration problems which kept them all but free and independent. Leeds with its old class system which became translated into a hierarchy of race did not, because it kept Nevisians under the authority of those who were placed in positions of power in the social structure. In this way, the British experience made it much more difficult for the Nevisians to become responsible adults. Furthermore, Nevisians on St John were able to return to Nevis frequently, living just a short plane trip away, and thus enjoy the high social standing they had in their native community by virtue of having left it. One Nevisian on St John, who provided regular support to the wife and children he had left on Nevis, and who visited them several times a year, thus was able to claim:

> I am better respected when I come home, because I have been outside the island and made it there.

The fact that he shared a tiny downstairs apartment with several other Nevisians, earned minimum wages at Caneel Bay Plantation and still was on a temporary visa apparently had little significance. The Nevisians in Leeds were not similarly able to enjoy a position of respect on frequent visits to their natal community, trips to the West Indies being costly and long. They had to seek this respect in the British society where they lived, and many felt they did this in vain.

CONCLUSION

In this chapter I have argued that by reading the interviews which I carried out among Nevisians on St John and Leeds from several different points of view, it is possible to attain a more complex understanding of the phenomenon which we have chosen to designate as 'migration' in anthropology and other social sciences. I have shown that the interviews contain a wealth of information on the experience of leaving the home island and settling in a strange place. The manner of representing this information in and of itself also offers important insights into the historical and cultural context within which this movement took place and the way in which it influenced the perception of this movement by those involved in it. Finally, the personal lives, which were implicated in this movement, provided a framework of analysis which is sensitive to the basic significance of moving in the life-cycle of Nevisians. It suggests that the interplay between local loyalties and increasingly global relations may provide an important key to understanding the transnational Nevisian community.

NOTES

1 For a more detailed analysis of these two migration communities, see my longer study, *Global Culture, Local Identity: Continuity and Change in the Afro-Caribbean Community of Nevis* (Olwig 1993a) which analyses the significance of migration in Nevisian society from a historical anthropological point of view. This work also includes a study of New Haven, Connecticut, an important American migration destination for Nevisians during the first two decades of this century. A briefer analysis of the Nevisian migration experiences, which focuses on women, can be found in Olwig (1993b).

2 The methodological and theoretical significance of 'life history' or 'life story' interviews has been subject to a great deal of discussion in anthropology. See, for example, Watson (1976), Langness and Frank (1981), Little (1980), Watson and Watson-Franke (1985), Peacock and Holland (1993), Gullestad (1996).

3 In the period from 1977 to 1980, twenty-one men and 29 women were interviewed on St John. All had been born on Nevis although a few had come to St John as children to stay with family there. Fifteen men and twenty-six women were interviewed in Leeds during the summers of 1987–89. All but seven of them had been born on Nevis and had, with one exception, arrived in Great Britain in the period from the mid-1950s to the early 1960s. The seven who were not born on Nevis had been born in Leeds of Nevisian parents. The questions which I asked in Leeds and on St John had a slightly different focus. On St John the interviews were primarily concerned with documenting the nature of the network of relations which tied Nevisians on Nevis and the Virgin Islands together in trans-local families, and the way in which this network of ties influenced the Nevisians' adaptation in their migration destination. These interviews were structured largely in the light of interviews with nine Nevisians, eight women and one man, which focused on the life story of the interviewees with a view to eliciting their 'migration stories'. The interviews in Leeds primarily took the form of 'migration stories', although they also included a number of questions on the importance of the Nevis-based family networks to these interviewees.

4 West Indian migration to the American Virgin Islands has been documented in a number of works; see, for example, Green (1972), Lewis (1972), Olwig (1985).

5 This description of the Nevisian migration experiences in Leeds finds many parallels in other works on West Indian migration to Great Britain; see, for example, Philpott (1973), Foner (1979), Gilroy (1987), Gmelch (1992), Byron (1994).

6 This does not mean, of course, that unemployment has not been a problem to West Indians in Great Britain in general.

7 'Garret' refers to a bird that steals from other birds' nests.

REFERENCES

Byron, Margaret (1994) *Post-war Caribbean Migration to Britain: The Unfinished Cycle*, Aldershot: Avebury.

Foner, Nancy (1979) *Jamaica Farewell: Jamaican Migrants in London*, London: Routledge and Kegan Paul.

Gilroy, Paul (1987) *"There ain't No Black in the Union Jack." The Cultural Politics of Race and Nation*, London: Hutchinson.

Gmelch, George (1992) *Double Passage: The Lives of Caribbean Migrants Abroad and Back Home*, Ann Arbor: University of Michigan Press.

Green, James W. (1972) 'Social Networks in St Croix, United States Virgin Islands', Ph.D. dissertation, University of Washington, Seattle.

Gullestad, Marianne (1996) *Everyday Life Philosophers, Modernity, Morality and Autobiography in Norway*, Oslo: Scandinavian University Press.

Langness, Lewis and Gelya Frank (1981) *Lives: An Anthropological Approach to Biography*, Novato, CA: Chandler and Sharp.

Lewis, Gordon K. (1972) *The Virgin Islands. A Caribbean Lilliput*, Evanston, IL: Northwestern University Press.

Little, Kenneth (1980) 'Explanation and individual lives: a reconsideration of life writing in anthropology'. *Dialectical Anthropology* 5 215–26.

Olwig, Karen Fog (1985) *Cultural Adaptation and Resistance: Three Centuries of Afro-Caribbean Life on St John*, Gainesville: University of Florida Press.

—— (1990) 'The struggle for respectability: Methodism and Afro-Caribbean culture in 19th century Nevis', *Nieuwe West-Indische Gids/New West Indies Guide* 64(3, 4): 93–114.

—— (1993a) *Global Culture, Island Identity. Continuity and Change in the Afro-Caribbean Community of Nevis*, Reading: Harwood Academic Publishers.

—— (1993b) 'The Migration Experience: Nevisian Women at Home and Abroad', in J. Momsen (ed.) *Women and Change in the Caribbean*, London: James Currey, pp. 159–66.

Peacock, James L. and Dorothy C. Holland (1993) 'The narrated self: life stories in process', *Ethos* 21(4): 367–83.

Philpott, Stuart B. (1973) *West Indian Migration: The Montserrat Case*, London: Athlone Press.

Richardson, Bonham (1983) *Caribbean Migrants. Environment and Human Survival on St Kitts and Nevis*, Knoxville: University of Tennessee Press.

—— (1989) 'Caribbean migrations, 1838–1985, in F.W. Knight and C.A. Palmer (eds) *The Modern Caribbean*, Chapel Hill: University of North Carolina Press, pp. 203–28.

Thomas-Hope, E. (1978) 'The establishment of a migration tradition: British West Indian movements to the Hispanic Caribbean in the century after Emancipation', in C.G. Clarke (ed.) *Caribbean Social Relations*, Liverpool: Centre for Latin American Studies, Monograph Series No. 8, pp. 66–81.

—— (1992) *Explanation in Caribbean Migration*, London: Macmillan.

—— (1995) 'Island systems and the paradox of freedom: migration in the post-emancipation Leeward Islands', in K.F. Olwig (ed.) *Small Islands, Large Questions. Society, Culture and Resistance in the Post-Emancipation Caribbean*, London: Frank Cass, pp. 161–75.

Tonkin, Elizabeth (1990) 'History and the myth of realism' in R. Samuel and P. Thompson (eds) *The Myths We Live By*, London: Routledge, pp. 25–35.

Watson, Lawrence C. (1976) 'Understanding a life history as a subjective document: hermeneutical and phenomenological perspectives, *Ethos* 4(1): 95–131.

Waston, Lawrence C. and Watson-Franke, M.B. (1985) *Interpreting Life Histories*, New Brunswick: Rutgers University Press.

5 Genres of migration

Selma Leydesdorff

For the most part, studies of migrants from the Dutch Antilles to the Netherlands have focused on the group considered to be the most problematic, male adolescents (Fridus 1988; Amesz *et al.* 1989; Hulst 1997). Very little empirical work has been done with women from the Antilles, although stereotypes and mythologies (of Antillean women not fitting in with 'normal' Dutch patterns, or how they are subject to male abuse) abound. Statistics (Olton 1994) indicate that most women from the Antilles live in single-parent families, but this reveals little about the day-to-day experiences of these women as migrants, about what it was like for them to leave one country for another, or, indeed, how their assumption that life in the new country would be better has subsequently influenced their attitudes and behaviour.[1] For this kind of detail and information, it is necessary to use interviews.[2]

Interviews are not, however, innocent. They give subjective information, and produce a narrative from the interaction between the storyteller and the interviewer (or listener). This narrative will then address a collective listening and reading audience who will hear or read the story in its next phase. The process of interview blends the autobiographical and the collective into a written text, which then becomes an objectified source for academic research. In the process, the interaction between two persons often becomes hidden, and left to interpretation. But the interest of an interview rests as much on the empirical data revealed, as in the process of its manufacture. Interviews are sometimes further complicated by a cultural and social disjunction between the position and expectations of the interviewer and the interviewee, between (in this case) my position as a white Dutch professor and these often reluctant storytellers. What kind of knowledge could, therefore, be created, and how would this help us to gain an understanding of the lives of Antillean women in Holland?

Elizabeth Tonkin (1992) alerted us to the importance of genre in oral (as well as literary) narratives, and to its role in the analysis and interpretation of text. Narratives are not spontaneous, but are constructed according to a way of talking about the past, and crystallized into a formalized method of recounting history that dominates the personal story. Tonkin's suggestion has shifted the focus of research on oral narrative to the character of genre itself. In this sense, oral histories themselves produce a new kind of genre, the modifier 'oral' reflects its foundation as a spoken text. It is, however, a text told to someone. Although the interaction between listener and narrator has vanished into the silence of the text (in the same measure as the silences we usually allude to when we mean hidden and untold stories), its essential property (and its possibilities) as genre should not be forgotten.

This chapter presents a close reading of two interviews with women who migrated to Holland during the 1980s. It focuses, however, on a reinterpretation of the meaning of text as a new form of intercultural genre, a genre which, I would argue, arose in the course of the large migration from people from the former Dutch colonies to the 'mother country'. This genre is redolent with references to race, sexuality and despair, told by women who are clearly reluctant to deal with a society which expects them to adapt to a culture which is not their own. The stories are not, of course, neutral. Rather, they reflect an ideological and political bias in their efforts to deal with me, the representative of this alien culture.

The narrators of my interviews were women from Curaçao. The context is the migration of people from the Antilles to Holland during the economic crisis of the 1980s. Although the Antilles are part of the Dutch Empire, they have a quasi-independent status. As a result of this, the frontiers of Holland are open to migration. This has always been the case, but it is only in the last twenty years that migration to the Netherlands on a large scale has taken place.[3] There is a myth in the Antilles that life in Europe is better.

Let us take a close look at these Antillean newcomers: why did they migrate? One explanation is that they expected to improve their economic fortunes. The departure of the Dutch oil company Shell sent the region into an economic tailspin: it affected industry and small shopkeepers alike. Life appeared hopeless, and migration offered a way out of this deprivation. All the women with whom I spoke had the impression that the welfare system in Holland was sufficiently well organized to enable some quality of life. From the perspective of the Caribbean, the amount of welfare in guilders had seemed enormous. Only after their arrival in the Netherlands did they realize that expenses were so high that living off social security allowed for very few comforts. Prior to that, little or no thought had been given to the social position awaiting them, and many have yet to understand the administrative intricacies of the system. For instance, it is often hard to understand why it is not possible to take a small job if in receipt of social aid. As one woman observed, 'It is unfair. People who work can have two jobs, but people living off social security are not allowed to do a thing.' She did not mean that it was unfair that some people had two jobs while others were unemployed, but deplored the lack of any means for doubling her income. Equally, social security is paid per family unit, depending on the size of the household. But if a male lover moves in with you, it is considered as a single household and both partners lose their individual benefits. Jointly, therefore, they will receive considerably less than the benefits paid to single individuals.

People arriving in Holland from the Antilles are not considered aliens. They are nationals of the Kingdom of the Netherlands and require no permit or citizenship application. While most attended primary education in Dutch, their version of the Dutch language is characterized by its formal mode and its literary vocabulary. One might expect them to integrate smoothly into Dutch society (Koot and Ringeling 1984).[4] Immigrants from the Antilles, however, are viewed as a highly problematic group. The adult males, in particular, are considered potentially dangerous and have a reputation for abusing and selling drugs. The women are regarded as bad mothers. By Dutch standards, they are permissive, especially toward the male adolescents in the households. The common denominator is, however, poverty, and there are few available alternative options. Some of the second generation are building a new life, but the majority, especially the later migrants, belong to the lower strata of Dutch society.[5]

Many Antilleans live in Bijlmermeer, one of the suburbs of Amsterdam, where the initial interviews were conducted. There is a subculture of migrant life, where the boys risk turning into delinquents and many of the men are absent, thus confirming stereotypes about Caribbean male behaviour. The world of women appeared to operate separately from the male world. Even though men may be physically present in the family or household, women organize daily life. Many of these women do not accept the pattern of the Western nuclear family in which – and this is especially the case in the Netherlands – the man takes care of the finances. In the Antilles, many of these women used to work or at least look for work: earning a living through paid work or peddling was considered a normal part of a woman's life. After their arrival in the Netherlands, their economic circumstances deteriorated progressively, and the women became isolated in their responsibility. Many of these women have remained single or unmarried mothers and although they receive enough money to survive, it is not more than this. As soon as men stay or move in, however, the Antillean women run into financial trouble.[6]

Despite the bad economic consequences of sharing their household with a man, many of these women still believed in marriage and were torn between their actual circumstances and the old moral standards. 'It is a better life without a man,' said one of them 'but it is better for a girl to find a husband.' Most would also insist that the aim of educating a daughter was to marry her to a good and, if possible, wealthier husband. An added complication involves the deceptive compatibility between their old morals and traditional Dutch values. In the Antilles, the 'other' woman and the 'other' children (the husband's children with another woman) are tolerated, a tolerance which coexists with beliefs in the importance of marriage. Such an attitude is inconceivable in other parts of Dutch society. The women are well aware of this, and this led to confusion, almost riddles, in the interviews. For instance, although I would start by asking how large the family had been, during interviews more members of the family and more brothers and sisters would turn up, who had not been mentioned before. These family members, born out of wedlock, proved essential to the narrative, such as an hitherto unmentioned sister who had taken care of the migration or who had looked after the children when the mother had left Curaçao.

In addition to the reluctance to describe family structures for fear of a possibile misunderstanding, or disapproval, problems in cross-cultural interviewing arise elsewhere in the methodology. Life stories assume a chronology. The interview opens with the story of childhood. This is, however, a Western pattern and the notion of chronology is not suited to interviews within this part of Antillean culture. Stories are told in a circular manner, from which I the Western researcher, attempt to extract a chronology, aware that in the process my pattern is imposed on a narrative, either in the course of the interview or in the interpretation after-wards. In either case, it is almost a form of violation. Other narrative structures, in their turn, create a speech pattern which is highly associative and has become the language of the subculture.[7]

The suburbs of Amsterdam and its Antillean community seemed optimally suited for creating the subculture I found there. This is a quarter with huge apart-ment buildings, within which are small ghettos of different migrant populations. It is possible to live there without having much to do with the host society. It is only through the education of children that some links are made with the host society. Some of my interviews were conducted among the poorest residents of the local community, the group who were perhaps the most estranged from Dutch society, but who also had the most realistic assessments of it. 'They will never accept or hire us,' said one young woman, and without any hesitation her friend added, 'they despise us'. People living there appeared to lack expectations, and the interviews were virtually devoid of evidence of interaction with their surroundings. The genre of these residents could be seen to be a total rejection of Dutch culture, regrets about their migration, and grief, with little hope of improvement. Women bore the burden of this, since they were responsible for the children and the elderly. They were the ultimate sources of protection in a society experienced as unwelcoming and hostile.

This sentiment influenced their behaviour towards me. They would, for instance, often make themselves unavailable when I wanted to interview them, or they said they could not find the time or, in the course of the interview, would be interrupted: someone would enter, a child required care, food had to be served. Nevertheless, so long as I refrained from formal interviews, participated through adapted cultural behaviour and did not concentrate on specific interviews, they grew to trust me and confide in me their negative opinions and experiences of Dutch society. They considered me a representative of that hostile society, but sympathetic to their lives. If we created a genre at all, one could say that we formalized their complaints about Dutch society and their deep regrets over their decision to migrate.

There were few differences between different generations, although the older women tended to present an even rosier picture about life on the old island. They also complained more about having nothing to do in Holland and the lack of respect from the younger generation. Indeed, there was not very much they could do. Their daughters (on welfare) spent their time caring for their children, but as soon as they got older there was an emptiness. I was saddened by the importance of television in their lives. Soap operas were one of the few reasons they got up in the morning. The women lived in a social void, filled by their clinging together. The language heard, never reflected by indigeneous Dutch public opinion, was of despair and hatred. If this research had been presented at that stage, it would only have told you about this dismal existence, a genre of regret.

Fortunately, the horizons available to Antilleans extend beyond the suburban ghetto of the big city. In the hope of integration, some people have left for smaller communities; others arrived there on migration joining, in many cases, a member of the family who was already living there. In addition to those interviews in the ghettoes of Amsterdam, sixteen life-story interviews with Antillean women were carried out in the smaller towns of Hoorn, Medemblik, Alkmaar, Enkhuizen and Purmerend, north of Amsterdam, the contacts mediated through a Centre for Women and other cultural institutions. The fact that women attended the cultural institutions makes clear that the sample was relatively self-selecting. In contrast to the earlier sets of interviews, however, these interviews were conducted with a part of the Antillean community which was willing and able to adapt to the new conditions or to integrate and seek employment in Dutch society. Nevertheless, some of the problems of interpersonal relations and cross-cultural interviewing remained relevant to this group. Let me now focus on two of these interviews and consider their narratives.

Jenny has lived in the Netherlands for more than nine years. Jenny still thinks about returning. She has failed to find permanent employment and lives on welfare in a poor neighbourhood where other Antilleans live. Jenny reproaches her Antillean neighbours for being immoral, an accusation similar to those made against the group in Amsterdam. Jenny was raised in Curaçao in a strict Catholic family and had few opportunities to leave home unchaperoned. Although she had some secondary education she never completed it, not recognising the importance of passing the final examinations in order to progress in life. She had a very high opinion of her devout Catholic family. Her upbringing was strict and her family upheld high moral standards. Her mother peddled goods, while her older sister took care of the family. In her lifestory, her father remained hidden for a long time. She told me nothing of his activities except that he came home at night. He was the strictest; in particular, he forbade his daughters to go out unchaperoned. Both his sternness and the prevailing unemployment figured among Jenny's reasons for coming to Holland. Nevertheless:

My father was a devout Catholic and had a love child (*buitenkind*), as is often the case on the islands. Men have children out of wedlock with their mistresses. My father was very worried that we would deviate [from respectable behaviour] and was therefore terribly strict.

Jenny knew the child, who came to live in their house. Her father had an obligation to take care of her, since the child's mother was unable to do so.

This fact was integrated in the story of her father being so religious. Indeed, it was her father's religious beliefs which forced him to take care of the child. This child went to Church with the rest of her family every Sunday. In the Caribbean, this story was not unusual and fitted into a more general cultural pattern. Sharing the story with me, however, was another matter. Jenny assumed that I would not understand the easy acceptance of love children, although she knew that I was neither Catholic nor imbued with rigid Catholic principles.

She started out by omitting the incident. Since this illegitimate 'sister' is essential to her story after migration, helping Jenny to settle where she is now, she eventually had to tell me about her. Jenny began with a tirade against the way her strict father treated her mother. In the process, the sister came up. Initially, her rage seemed directed against this child as well. During the interview, however, she made clear that she accepted her father's sexual behaviour and lifestyle. This conduct did not affect her respect for him and was apparently expected behaviour. To minimize the possibility that I, like all Dutch people, would construe his acts as a lack of morality, she shared some stories about men with me.

Men were important in her life, but as players in a secret game of seduction in which her respectability remained intact. Jenny talked about sex openly with me, but her sexual discourse served to conceal her sadness about the different cultural environment in Holland. Dutch men and women collaborate, according to Jenny. In Antillean households, women do all the work.

> Antillean women accept everything [from their men]. If he sleeps around, she accepts it. If he does not do the housework, she does not seem to care. They pamper their husbands. The men have their meals cooked for them and come home to find the house clean and their clothes washed and ironed.

Despite that, she argued that would never marry a Dutch man. Life here was so different, and back 'home' she would have been married to an Antillean man and would either have moved in with her in-laws or he would have moved in with her. The storytelling ended as an effort to share with me ideas on sexual liberalisms through which she tried not to offend me. In order to share she praised the freedom of Dutch women. Superfically, one was not aware how big the problem of men was in her life.

This coding of sexuality and respectability were not the only reasons for Jenny's mistrust of Dutch society. Again, she had difficulty explaining this sense to me. As one of the few Dutch people she had an opportunity to talk to, she felt I might be able to help her by, for instance, serving as a referee when she applied for a job. She decided to migrate to the Netherlands in the early 1980s, which at the time seemed the only option available. She failed from the beginning and spent two years in a state of severe depression watching television. She still has to overcome her anxiety of the small town where she lives and can hardly find her way around. During her brief periods of employment or adult education, she has failed to live up to the punctuality of Dutch Protestant bureaucratic society. She has a different understanding about time. Still, life was much better now, she told me. In Holland, a woman was free, even though life was far from pleasant. But it was impossible for her to express the ambivalence and be honest with me about the fact that this new freedom goes with poverty and despair.

Jenny felt that she would never get a fair chance. Nevertheless, she tried to cling to her hope of eventual success.

I have applied everywhere. You feel like you are not wanted. I am not angry, but it is depressing. How can one make ends meet? In Curaçao, your family supports you, unlike here. Still, it is very depressing. My motivation is less, I am reluctant to do things and keep postponing them. If I take a course, I don't see the purpose.

She attributed the use of drugs in the community to unemployment and explained that the problem affected, and stigmatised, the whole community. She was scared of drug abuse and hoped she would stay away from it. But life had been so hard that she lacked self-confidence. 'You see, in Curaçao I was different, . . . I was self-assured, arrogant. I had to change.' She blamed herself for her misfortune, since she did not want to criticize Dutch society. Yet the paratext of the interview could be interpreted as praise of migration, combined with a kind of nostalgia toward the future. In this future, the values of life are at peace, and the happiness of her childhood in the country she has lost returns.

My brief interviews with Jenny's mother conveyed the same impression. Her mother felt free now, unlike in the old days back in Curaçao. True, she had a small shop and earned money in the market there and has very little to do now. Though welfare has ensured her economic independence, she no longer felt the pride of owning a small business. But she took it for granted that her pride will return some day. Jenny and her mother both praised their migration, but suffered from isolation, unemployment, the poverty of welfare, and a lack of things to do in their lives. They expressed themselves exclusively through a positive story, a rationale. At certain points, however, the other story trickled through and offered a glimpse of the ambivalence that characterizes the migrant identity.

Charlotte's story was also a result of my interaction with her. She came to Holland to join her fiancé who was already here. She did not know that he had another woman, who had accepted her existence as the real wife. He picked Charlotte up at the airport with two of her children and took her to a remote provincial town. He did not tell her about the other woman but invented a story that he had to work and left. She was alone in an unknown society in a town where she knew no one. In the beginning, she did not know where to go. All the streets seemed so large, and it was only because of hunger that she dared to enter a shop. Her fiancé visited twice a week. Several months passed before she ventured further in the street, where she met by accident another woman from the Antilles. With her help she managed to contact the rest of her family and was able to escape to the little town where she is now living. Until then she (and probably also her fiancé's other woman) had given a large part of the social security money to him. The story stands out for its sadness, but it is not exceptional. Family reunification (family is also your fiancé with whom you have children) has contributed to the abuse she experienced. For her fiancé it meant another source of money from the social security.

I interviewed Charlotte when she was in trouble with the police about her children and with the social security administration. Her respectability was very different from Jenny's. It mostly consisted of her absolute refusal to use drugs and the way she kept her home clean and neat. She also lived in a small town, in a modest but respectable home in a white neighbourhood. Before she agreed to an interview, she wanted to know my opinion of the things that had happened to her. Her Dutch was very poor, although back home she had been a good student. Her speech was a clear indication of her background, of poverty within the confines of Caribbean Catholicism.

Charlotte's story was more rooted in Caribbean culture, especially with respect to female–male relationships. Her world consisted almost exclusively of women. The man in her life entered at odd moments when it suited him or when he thought she could give him some money, which she usually did. Charlotte was, however, unable to explain to me that parts of her story were perfectly normal from her perspective. Like her mother and even her grandmother, in fact like many women of their class, she never knew the stable nuclear family life she saw all around her. She was aware, however, that most Dutch people do not understand her way of life.

How did Charlotte impart to me that she is at odds with the world around her? She tried to convey this sense by telling me the story about the system and her victimization. She told me she did not understand why the Dutch have so many rules. She talked about rules to express the local racism that hurt her.

> You know my neighbours, their house is like mine. But I live in this one here. What happens in this house is my business. My sister moved in with me. She has five children, who walk in and out of the house. Sometimes children make noise, they listen to the radio or watch television. The neighbours started to argue with me. People who came to visit me were not allowed to park in front of my neighbours' houses.

I pointed out that the house might indeed have been small for two sisters and eight children. Nevertheless, I understood perfectly that where Charlotte comes from in Curaçao, it was not uncommon for large families to live in two or three rooms. She would never understand that the house in Holland was too small for such a large family. 'No,' she answered, 'all their regulations and rules are the problem: they want me to wash my clothes in the morning and not at night.' It emerged that there had been a fight with the neighbours when her noisy washing machine and dryer were on at night. The children were growing so fast she had not been able to buy enough clothes to fit them and she would have to wash and dry their clothes overnight. By the end of the story, a neighbour called them dirty niggers and assaulted them.

Charlotte wanted me to sympathize with her. While not wishing to imply that Dutch society was racist, nevertheless she suggested that even though Dutch society does not tolerate overt racism, many incidents occurred anyway. For instance, all black children in the school her children used to attend were branded as 'slow learners', which, in her view, served to separate the whites from the blacks and resulted in the blacks attending a special school. Indeed, official discussions on the subject failed to consider the cultural differences, and subsumed it under a discourse of educational difference, in the process failing to come to terms wth issues of identity and reinforcing the rigid white culture of that part of the country.

According to her, ridiculous as the rules were, they extended to her private life as well. She was allowed to have a boyfriend, she could make love with him, but she could not live with him. In our contact after the interview, I was unable to explain that as long as she is legally married (she subsequently married the father of her children) and her husband gets his welfare through her bank account, she will be unable to move on with her life. The underlying rationale was that whenever he was around, the money was spent on drugs and clothes. Charlotte knew she had to deal with the Dutch, and she knows she cannot blame the fact that her life is at odds with the system on racism alone. Thus, she referred to and focused on the system and its regulations. This picture tied in perfectly with the discourse broadcast on television about 'other' people with the same problem. Social security was unfair to all who collect welfare benefits, as the system seemed irrational and unnecessarily strict to the people who depend upon it.

Welfare recipients are not the only people who resort to this genre of blaming the system. Politicians employ the same rhetoric when they accuse the system of being irrational, which, in their case, means it is too permissive. Both sides use their strategy of blaming the system as a genre for expressing disagreement. It reveals that Dutch society is struggling with the migrants and has by no means resolved the problem of cultural and economic differences. To talk about the inadequate system is the universal genre here, and the story is permeated by the polarization between its 'victims' and its 'perpetrators'.

Can experiences possibly be transmitted and communicated in this context where the representation of power is so clearly on one side? I would answer the question by pointing out that while experiences are *always* transmitted and communicated by the act of interviewing, many layers come into play here. They obscure the interview. Both women have assumed that they will be unable to convey their true feeling about their migration, their despair, their anxiety, and their anger. They have chosen their stories with care and fitted them into narratives and genres which might be acceptable to what they perceive as the average Dutch opinion. These stories conceal a world of depression, sadness, and anger thereby covering up ambivalence and uprootedness.

The history of experience can only be traced through interviews. The historian must, however, be aware of both the interaction and the cultural conflict inherent between interviewer and narrator. This tension becomes visible through an analysis of the transcripts which not only express feelings and personal histories, but reveal ways to represent, or attempt to represent, other worlds – the one left behind in the past, the one encountered in the present, and the one in which the old and the new are in the process of being negotiated. Essentially, it is a context and experience of ambivalence which is being articulated. That ambivalence is both painful and often lacks an expressive form. As such, it inhibits looking at their own culture, for that might challenge not only what is certain, but also what provides them with an identity, as well as, paradoxically, the rationale for migrating. At the same time, it inhibits looking at their place and role within

Dutch society, for to do so would make them either complicit in a rhetoric of racism, or appear duped by the promises of improvement. There is an ambivalence, too, for women in particular, between the financial independence which was possible in the Antilles, and the ideological independence expected of them in the Netherlands, and a tension between the ways in which both these forms of independence could be married in their minds, but not within the constrained circumstances in which they find themselves in the Netherlands. Indeed, the lifestyle on welfare in which many find themselves in Holland is profoundly at variance with their notion of their role and status as women, as mothers and grandmothers, wives and lovers with which they grew up in Curaçao. Not only is the ambivalence and tension difficult to articulate; equally inhibiting is the sense that to do so confirms their subordinate relation to power, and has the potential to be misunderstood, and misjudged.

However trusted and accepted the interviewer, he or she, by their very position, is perceived as part of a relation to power which is denied to these women. This is itself part of the structure of ambivalence, and part of its resolution is to create a lifestory couched in the genres of migration, of disappointment and regret, of a nostalgia for what the future could hold and a critique of the rules and regulations which restrain and prevent this, or, equally, of praise for the independence of Dutch women, of the tolerance of Dutch society. It is the function of the historian to recognize it as genre, to recognize therefore its social origins in shaping personal accounts of the past and the present, and to begin to unravel the meanings and the codes, as well as the denials and the exclusions, inherent in it. It is the function of the historian also to recognize its context, that this genre is also the product of the interview, that it (and not some other) has been chosen and employed, by the interviewee (who after all has the power to provide or withhold information), to guarantee its meaning for the interview, and to continue to guarantee that meaning as it is disseminated.

NOTES

All names which appear in this chapter are pseudonyms.

1 There are some literary sources, see, for instance, Beaujon 1957; Lebacs 1971; Blinder 1973. See also Hoving (1995) and Rutgers (1994) for references to female Dutch writers who express their experience as migrants.
2 For the methodological approach see the essays in *International Yearbook of Oral History and Life Stories*, vol. iii, *Migration and Identity*, Oxford, 1995.
3 For recent data see: B.T.J. Hooghoemstra, M. Niphuis-Nell (1995) *Allochtone Vrouwen*, Rapport Sociaal en Cultureel Planbureau, Rijswijk.
4 In the early 1970s most Antilleans who migrated were the better educated. It was assumed, therefore, that easy integration was a general pattern.
5 See also *Met het oog op mei 1997*, 1994, The Hague: Adviesraad van de regering voor het emancipatiebeleid.
6 I am aware that there is a discussion on the place of women in Caribbean culture and that any generalization stigmatizes. See, for instance, the introduction to Shepherd *et al.* (1995)

7   This makes the relation between an oral and written text such a challenge especially in Antillean culture, see Glaser and Pausch (1994).

BIBLIOGRAPHY

Amesz, Jeneke, Fridus, Steijlen and Vermeulen, Hans (1989) *Andere Antillianen: carrieres van laaggeschoolde Antilliaanse jongeren in een grote stad*, Amsterdam: Het Spinhuis.
Beaujon, A. (1957) *Gedichten aan de Baaj en elders*, Amsterdam: Bezige Bij.
Blinder, O. (1973) *Incognito*, Rotterdam: Flamboyant.
Fridus, Steijlen (1988) *Gemiste kansen: een onderzoek naar randgroepvorming-sprocessen onder Antilliaanse jongeren in Amsterdam Zuid-Oost*, Amsterdam: University of Amsterdam and Gemeente Amsterdam.
Glaser, M. and Pausch, M. (1994) *Between Orality and Writing*, Amsterdam: Atlanta.
Hoving, I (1995) *The Castration of Livingstone and Other Stories, Reading African and Caribbean Migrant Women's Writing*, Amsterdam.
Hulst, Hans van (1997) *Morgen bloeit het diabaas: de Antilliaanse volksklasse in de Nederlandse samenleving*, Amsterdam: Het Spinhuis.
Koot, W. and Ringeling, A. (1984) *De Antillianen*, Muiderberg: Coutinho.
Lebacs, D. (1971) *Sherry* (s.n./s.j).
Olton, T.P. (1994) *Minderheidsstatus of stijgingsdrang, Antilliaanse/Arubaanse vrouwen in Amsterdam en hun gezinsvorming*, Delft: Eburton.
Rutgers, W. (1994) *Beneden en boven de wind: literatuur van de Nederlandse Antillen en Aruba*, Amsterdam: Bezige Bij.
Shepherd, V., Brereton, B. and Bailey, B. (1995) *Engendering History, Caribbean Women in Historical Perspective*, Kingston: Ian Randle Publishers/London: James Currey Publishers.
Tonkin, Elizabeth (1992) *Narrating Our Past, The Social Construction of Oral History*, Cambridge: Cambridge University Press.

Part III
Ethnicity and identity

6 The legacy of migration:

Immigrant mothers and daughters and the process of intergenerational transmission

Helma Lutz

INTRODUCTION

Migration studies are a rapidly growing research area, in which a wide range of very different empirical and theoretical approaches have been developed in recent years. While macro-approaches are mainly used by economists, sociologists and political scientists, micro-approaches to migration studies can be found in psychology, pedagogy and cultural anthropology. One of the dominant models which is frequently applied in both micro- and macro-approaches is the 'push-pull' model. This model proposes that structural push-factors like (relative) poverty, political instability and social disintegration in the country of origin in combination with pull-factors like labour shortage and good economic conditions in the country of destiny, lead to migration movements from under-developed to highly industrialized societies. Both micro- and macro-level research follow the pattern of a schematic 'before and after' analysis, assuming that the country of origin and the country of destiny are worlds apart. In migration studies, the before is mainly defined in terms of traditional, rural, and even archaic while the after is seen as quite the opposite: modern, urban and individualized.[1] In the application of this model, the individual migrant becomes invisible in the overall structure or she/he is defined as victim of these structures, struggling to cope with the personal consequences of the physical move, torn between irreconcilable cultures, flung into an identity crisis (see Lutz 1991: Chapter 1).

According to this view, migrants, especially females, appear to be 'puppets on a string', doomed to follow a pre-written script, dependent on the help and leadership from others in search of a new identity.[2] This perception of migration as a cause of identity deterioration is not new. It was already put forward by one of the founding fathers of the sociology of knowledge, Alfred Schütz, in his famous essay 'The stranger' (Schütz, 1972).

In the sociology of knowledge, *intergenerational transmission* is the key element in the 'creation of the social' (Mannheim, 1927). The knowledge of standardized cultural prescriptions is unquestioningly handed down from generation to generation as model for the 'normal' situation. Schütz analysed the psychological problems caused by migration as automatically resulting in a loss of orientation and personal crisis, not only for the first generation but also for migrants' children and even grandchildren. Where people's life-course and their perception of collective belonging and destiny are interrupted, intergenerational transmission is thrown into crisis, thereby becoming an identity issue. Contrary to these perceptions of migration as an anomaly, I argue that this view does not take into account people's ability to deal with a changing environment by using their *social capital*, that is, their cultural resources.[3] I want to show that, by making migrants' reactions to structural changes the focus of research, a much more dynamic picture unfolds. Migration can be perceived as an intermediary in a person's life-course by which cultural schemes and patterns are changed, reformulated and reproduced. Migration becomes a 'rite of passage' and mental travelling between different locales, a more or less stable basis for conceiving one's own belonging.

The intergenerational transmission of cultural knowledge among immigrant mothers and daughters is the starting point for this argument. Intergenerational transference involves the study of *continuity and change* in the cultural knowledge of migrant groups. As women have been (and still are) seen as the main cultural transmitters, the study of female migrants takes into account their key role in the socialization process. The processes of *intergenerational continuity and discontinuity* can be understood by looking at the life-stories of mothers and their daughters and reconstructing cultural patterns. By focusing on immigrant women's *accounts*, a more dynamic understanding of the mental and emotional changes migrants undergo in the aftermath of their physical move, can be obtained. Instead of a 'before and after'perception which treats migration as the missing link, the individual is seen as one who has lived through the changes, adapted to them or not, and created strategies of resistance. The life-story includes gains and losses, hopes and betrayals, successes and failures, trials and errors, interpreted and told from the perspective of today. Life-stories contain transgenerational experiences: over and above individual life-course experience they are shaped by the processing of family stories. The messages of former generations are mirrored in storytelling and exemplified in (moral) guidelines. As Elisabeth Stone (1988) has shown in her study of the meaning of family storytelling, in practically every family stories are the way by which families distinguish themselves from others. The stories 'sponsor and mirror the aspiration of a family' (ibid., p.6). Hidden 'under the skin', they tend to be of persistent importance, even where they are painful enough to be rejected. Children may loathe their families and leave home, but the stories persist as a prologue in further life. This is not to say that there are no conflicts involved in the process of transmission, but it is this process which is in charge of 'cultural changes'. Through the life-stories of immigrant mothers and daughters I try to illuminate the aftermath of migration as an identity issue.

SURINAMESE MOTHERS AND DAUGHTERS

My research was conducted between 1992 and 1993. I carried out biographical interviews with forty immigrant women, twenty mother–daughter couples. Half of my respondents were of Creole and the other half of Hindustani background (see also Lutz, 1994a).[4] By choosing Creole and Hindustani women I have selected the two largest groups of Surinamese immigrants in the Netherlands, making up a population of 220,000 in 1993. Surinam (the former Dutch Guyana) is a country of multi-ethnic and multi-religious composition. This was the result of the Dutch colonial policy of transferring workers to the plantations of the South American continent, first slaves from Africa, then, after the abolition of slavery, contract workers from India and finally from another Dutch colony, Indonesia. As a consequence of the decolonization process this mixture of ethnicities, backgrounds and religious beliefs is also found among the Surinamese immigrants in the Netherlands.[5]

The Surinamese immigrant community is found throughout the Netherlands, but is concentrated in the cities of Amsterdam, The Hague, Utrecht and Rotterdam. This community is not homogenous and includes all social classes. The average level of education is almost comparable with the indigenous Dutch population and Surinamese women and men can now be found in the professions and in almost every sector of social life. Nevertheless, unemployment is much higher among the Surinamese population; and housing, discrimination and the future of the next generation are still serious problems for this group (see also Essed, 1991; Lutz 1994a; Sansone, 1992).

The study of this group is of particular interest not only because Surinamese immigrants make up the largest ethnic minority group in the Netherlands, but also because of the intrinsic colonial linkages between Surinam and the Netherlands. Contrary to other immigrant groups like the Turks or Moroccans, the Surinamese arrived in the Netherlands with the 'cultural capital' of a Dutch education, coming from a society which was shaped by the colonizer according to their Dutch model. Thus, analysing the intergenerational transmission of this group also reflects the transmission of a knowledge shaped by colonial history.

In the following sections I will present the account of one case of a Creole mother and daughter. This case exemplifies the mother–daughter-relation of other black interviewees with respect to the particular cultural 'heritage' of the 'black' history of the Caribbean. After elaborating this case by analysing continuity and discontinuity in the family history, I focus on the moral messages ('respectability' and the 'economy of kin') which are transmitted and trans-formed. And, finally, I show how the legacy of migration becomes an issue of 'generational work'.[6]

THE CASUAL MIGRATION OF MRS GRANT

Mrs Grant is a 50-year-old woman who is presently working as a social worker in a multi-ethnic neighbourhood in a borough of Amsterdam. She left Surinam together with her husband and her three children in 1973 and has stayed in the Netherlands ever since. Mrs Grant was born in the capital of Surinam, Paramaribo, as the oldest child of a large family of seven children. Her father, who had migrated from French Guyana to Surinam as a young man, was mostly absent from family life as he worked in the jungle and in the goldmines while her mother ran the extended family, helping and being helped by female kin. Mrs Grant calls herself a member of the Creole '*volksklasse*', referring to the low educational status of her family and to a certain lifestyle of mutual (material and emotional) support.[7] Mrs Grant first left school at the age of 14 because her family could not afford the school fees and started to work in a cloth shop. Later, her mother succeeded in finding other family members to support her daughter's education at a teacher training college which she left and became a substitute teacher. After having worked for several years at an elementary school, she found a better job as secretary at one of the ministries and became a civil servant. At the age of 23 she gave birth to her first son, three years later her second son was born, and, finally, her daughter. She ultimately married the father of her children with whom she had lived together in concubinage, a very common and legally acceptable substitute for marriage in Surinam and the rest of the Caribbean. Mrs Grant continued to work, leaving her children in the care of female family members. Though she lost her whole network of childcare support when the family moved to the Netherlands, Mrs Grant's narrative hardly indicates that emigration had changed her life significantly. She explained the decision for migration by saying that she and her husband had never intended to emigrate. Rather they had made use of an opportunity, legally guaranteed by the Dutch state to every civil servant 'on duty' in the colonies, of taking a one-year sabbatical leave to the 'motherland'. With a somewhat mischievous smile, Mrs Grant remarked that this law had not been intended for the black colonial subjects, but rather for white civil servants who wanted to be sent home from the tropics.

The Grant family did not return to Surinam. Both partners asked their employer in Surinam for a prolongation of their status of absence and, in the meantime, Surinam was declared independent in 1975. In the words of Mrs Grant, 'national independence was pushed down our throats', indicating that she did not approve of the Dutch government's act.[8] There are many indications in Mrs Grant's narrative that the Grants had decided to stay in the Netherlands for good because of the declaration of independence. Mrs Grant and her husband had found jobs and her husband had started studying economics which he could not have done in Surinam. The children went to school and the family moved to the suburbs, even buying a house. However, it was not until 1982 that Mrs Grant realized that her dream of return had become unrealistic and that her emigration had turned out to be permanent. As the turning point, Mrs Grant mentioned the 'December-murders', referring to the murder of the political Surinamese elite in Paramaribo in December 1982. This event has become a collective justification for many Surinamese (middle-class) migrants of their final decision to stay in the Netherlands. Mrs Grant now dismisses the idea of returning to Surinam as unrealistic, although she has kept close contact over the years with family members who stayed. Her account clearly shows how a deep identification and engagement with her society of origin can go hand in hand with her integration in Dutch society.

The experience of migration has not led to drastic changes in Mrs Grant's life. After arriving in Holland, she continued to combine working and mothering. Since the daily support of her female kin was missing, she had to manage family-life in a nuclear family setting with the support of her husband. Over the years she became an activist in the Dutch black women's movement and, at the same time, she was committed to the amelioration of the socio-economical situation in Surinam. She and her husband are active members of a lodge of Freemasonry which enables them to combine their commitment to their country with their everyday life in Holland. While (mentally) travelling between her two homes does not seem to be a problem for her, she is very much aware of the fact that her children are subjected to problems because of their skin colour. This unforeseen consequence of her and her husband's decision to move to a society where immigrants from Surinam are discriminated against was not intended by her and may be one reason why she presents her migration as a casual event – something that just happened. In order to compensate for the unexpected, she has tried to make her children less vulnerable by providing them with an excellent education and – through her activism in the black women's movement – becoming a role model with a fighting spirit. At the same time she took pains to ensure that her children would not despise their 'roots' or their family background. Thus, Mrs Grant, as any other migrant mother, had to perform a balancing act: she had to make sure that the family rules, norms and values were continued without losing sight of the actual changes in their lives.

CONTINUITY AND CHANGE: THE MORAL ECONOMY OF THE *VOLKSKLASSE*

Mrs Grant repeatedly presented herself as a member of the Creole *volksklasse*, thereby implicitly referring to the moral economy of this class.[9] In the literature on the Caribbean, the family-structure of the *volksklasse* is described as matrifocal or latent matrifocal.[10] As result of the slave economy and possibly in combination with matriarchal heritage of African cultures, black working class families have developed a form of matriarchal family structure. This family structure displays several legitimate variations, as for example concubinage or 'visiting relationship', where the women's role is differentiated in accordance to their sexual relationship with a man, whether they are the 'interior' woman (*binnenvrouw*) or the 'exterior' woman (*buitenvrouw*). According to these rules, men are generally not expected to be monogamous, but they do have certain (financial and emotional) responsibilities towards the mother of their children. A 'respectable woman' is judged by her care for her mother and her children as well as by her ability to generate a family income through working or more or less regular financial contributions from her 'man'. Although Surinamese family life has been subject to rapid changes for centuries, particularly under the tutelage of Christian churches and schools which have done their best to direct this life-style toward a 'decent' Christian patriarchal marriage, the life-style of the *volksklasse* has survived.[11] So have the moral guidelines of this class. It is very likely that Mrs Grant had a hard time sticking to her intention to continue working when she came to the Netherlands, since the average Dutch woman in 1973 was a housewife and only 28 per cent of the women worked outside the house. But it is also very likely that her attitude was reconfirmed later in the 1980s through her activities in the black women's movement. In contemporary Dutch society her attitude is in accordance with the official Dutch emancipation ideology: a woman has to be (economically) independent and work for a salary.

Thus, a moral rule which originates in a particular (colonial) historical context can fit quite nicely into a different social environment. The moral rules of the (slave) economy, which made family life unavailable for black women and taught women to be ready to support their children by themselves, seem perfectly in accordance with the ideologies of autonomy and self-sufficiency of contemporary Dutch society. In fact, it is the discontinuity of gender relations and the individ-ualization processes in the Netherlands which guarantee the continuity of Mrs Grant's (personal and collective) moral rules.

Respectability: 'Surinamese women teach you that these two hands are your husband, your real husband'

Part of the moral rules of her class is the issue of respectability and the duty to be(come) a respectable person. It is noticeable how Mrs Grant (re)constructs and thereby legitimizes her own actions. Most of her guidelines come from her mother as the person who seems to be the most 'significant other' in her account. Mrs Grant refers alternately to her mother's guidelines or to 'what Surinamese women do in general'. It was her mother who instructed her about her 'natural' duties (material and immaterial support) towards her female kin and her mother-in-law, thereby transferring generations-old rules. 'What Surinamese women do in general' is a code for a moral rule of their class: a rule which survives actual life changes. Mrs Grant had followed her mother's precepts without grumbling and has passed them on to her own daughter. She used her mother's decisive authority in moral judgement as a source of legitimation for her own actions, thereby emphasizing her mother's role as the most respected and the most 'credible person'.[12] Along these lines, Mrs Grant draws the picture of a strong bond between herself and her mother: even her own 'stubborn character' is presented as a family feature, a social heritage from her mother. Although she would not like her daughter Amalia to feel as responsible for her as she was for her mother, the moral rule that a mother is to be respected by her daughter is strong and consistent.

There is no indication in Mrs Grant's account that the moral judgements of her father, her husband or other male kin make any difference to her. They either do not occur or remain well in the background of her account – a phenomenon which is clarified by the following quote:

> Well, it's not meant to be negative, but I have been educated like this . . . that I have to be able to care for myself, that I better not count on a man. Surinamese mothers teach you that: do not count on a man. 'Cause your mother teaches you. She says: 'these two hands, that is your man. That is your *real* man'. . . . Yes, and I thought, with three children and if the man left, well, then I could do it if I keep my job.

With an obvious nod in my direction, Mrs Grant provides a slight excuse for her non-Western view and then proceeds to explain the rules of her kin which are also the rules of her class by situating herself in relation to them. It was striking that the life rules which Mrs Grant has successfully transferred to her children have not been transformed by the reality of her own life. She has been married to her husband for more than twenty-five years. Her husband, who is reported to be monogamous, has never left her and after the migration to Holland has taken over a considerable amount of household tasks and childcare. Yet, in her account as well as in the narrative of her daughter, Mr Grant was almost invisible. A possible explanation for why Mrs Grant has not corrected her rules into the direction of her lived reality might be found in the fact that she and her husband are the only stable couple in her vast kinship network. This means that Mrs Grant would have had to present herself as an exception in a sea of broken relationships. Thus, by admitting and associating herself with divergent norms, she would have implicitly separated herself from her kin and her class. As she has already moved away from her class background through education and lifestyle, particularly after she emigrated to Holland, she may prefer to protect the emotional links with her kin.

AMALIA GRANT: THE LEGACY OF MIGRATION

Her daughter Amalia has learned her mother's lesson on the importance of kinship bonds. Though the high investment of time sometimes interferes with her other activities like studying and working, Amalia acknowledges that 'as years go by your friends change, but your family stays forever'. Moreover, as her 'real family is her mother', the main (emotional) investment invariably resides in that direction. While Amalia Grant's account tends to be a hymn of praise to her mother – in which she is typical of the majority of my daughter-respondents – there is one exception: she disapproves of her parents' decision to move to Holland. Contrary to what she had always thought, namely, that her parents had left Surinam for economic reasons, when visiting Surinam recently, she learned that her father had a good position there before the family left. Amalia came to realize that 'if we would have stayed there we would not have belonged to the lowest status group either. This is why I do not understand why it was necessary to go to The Netherlands.' What for her parents was a challenge, an adventure, a temporary solution for problems at work, or a combination of all this together, became a matter of serious doubt for Amalia. It was, however, never a subject for family debate and probably never will be. Like the avoidance of stories about the Holocaust experience in many Jewish families (see Inowlocki, 1993), arguing about their parents' migration decision is a painful emotional issue for migrant children – an area of potential family conflict.

Amalia Grant at the age of 24 is about to graduate with a degree in international and European civil law which will enable her to work outside the Netherlands. In the future, she confesses, she would rather go to Surinam than stay in Holland. Considering the tremendous economic and political problems that make contemporary life in Surinam almost as difficult as life in Third World countries, her plans sound rather peculiar. Given her recent six-week visit to Surinam, she had an excellent knowledge of the country's situation and her ambitions can, therefore, hardly be dismissed as unrealistic or utopian. Amalia sums up the advantages of her education, a Western diploma, and her personal capacities acquired through her upbringing in the West which have provided her with an analytical framework for expressing her opinions. While rational assessments overlay her reflections, she also draws upon the underlying emotional reasons in her explanation:

> It is so much nicer there. The food is good and the weather is much nicer and . . . the chance to feel at home is so much greater there. I mean that I can blend in with the crowd. Do you understand? I mean, I do feel at home here [in The Netherlands], . . . I grew up here . . . but, it's just different.

Considering her statement that she has hardly ever had personal experiences with racism and her own domestic sphere of 'black pride', this comment comes as a surprise. Amalia's parents have equipped their children with the best education, a capacity to speak Dutch perfectly without any trace of dialect (which is even rare for the majority of indigenous Dutch) and many other requirements for successful integration in Dutch society. In the terminology of Pierre Bourdieu, Amalia Grant seems to have a high amount of social and cultural capital at her disposal and would be predetermined for a career in Holland. Nevertheless, Amalia's life-story reflects the dilemmas of the 'unauthorized existence' – dilemmas which mark the lives of the vast majority of second-generation migrants. These young people express feelings of not 'really' belonging to the Dutch people and the Dutch nation and not being in accordance with the contemporary symbolism of nationality and its boundaries.[13] Amalia is very aware of the fact that the paradox of 'not belonging' is true for both countries: her physical appearance makes her noticeable in Holland, while her behaviour and her language, her perfect Dutch, make her stand out in Surinam. This leads to a situation which sometimes 'drives her crazy'. Amalia would rather conceive of herself as a cosmopolitan, but in the face of the political unlikeliness of this option, her choice for Surinam becomes a much more realistic and rational solution to her dilemma than might be assumed at first sight. She is prepared to invest energy into assimilation into Surinamese society. She would change her perfect Dutch into the Surinamese Dutch dialect; she would learn the Sranantongo, the

Surinamese-Creole language, and she would adapt to Surinamese habits of dress. She obviously assumes that an attempt 'to blend into the crowd' of a multi-ethnic Surinamese society is more promising than waiting for a radical change in the Dutch perception of black people. Amalia Grant has not (yet) adopted her mother's fighting spirit and despite her mother's efforts to convince her to join a black women's group, she has resisted. However, her attitude is not passive either. A plausible interpretation might be that rather than fighting on two frontlines, Amalia tries to do something about her situation by choosing the Surinam option first.

A second interpretation which combines well with the above, is that Amalia's choice can be seen as a solution to her ambivalent feelings towards her strong mother. In search of authenticity, Amalia's emigration to Surinam would be a legitimate escape which at the same time avoided arguments or clashes. As in many other mother–daughter relationships, in the case of the Grant mother and daughter the difficult process of a daughter's detachment can be identified. Amalia regards her mother as a very strong, rational and intelligent person, who is widely respected and is successful in everything she does. Mrs Grant is simultaneously a model, an idol and a source of inspiration. For Amalia, becoming like her mother is a heavy burden. She confesses that, for a long time, she has perceived of herself as a 'poor imitation' of her mother. Through emigration and the (physical) distance from her mother, Amalia may hope to develop independently. Rather than accusing or confronting her parents with her disapproval of their decision to migrate, she tries to find an acceptable solution for the dilemmas in which she feels caught. By loosening physical proximity she tightens emotional connections, combining her search for authenticity with a strong family loyalty. Emigrating to the country where her parents come from is a challenge *and* a legacy for her. Amalia continues the family theme of migration – a chain initiated by her grandfather who migrated from French to Dutch Guyana. As the daughter, she picks up where her parents gave up and continues the family history.

However, Amalia's solution is also a silent act of aggression against her parents, an act of revenge. Implicitly she realizes her protest and her disapproval of her parents' migration. Beneath the surface of harmony, the intergenerational consensus is beginning to crack.

Thus, there are both diffences and commonalities in the meaning of migration for mother and daughter. Where Mrs Grant is able to easily bridge the gap between the two societies, for Amalia this combination seems to be slightly different, much more ambivalent, and sometimes even problematic. Nevertheless, she is prepared to retrace the itineraries of her parents, albeit, in her case, in the opposite direction. Like her parents, she is confident that her 'social and cultural' capital is sufficient to make a living in Surinam. Her legacy of migration consists of the coping strategies acquired by her family over three generations.

GENERATIONAL WORK

The legacy of migration is an instance of 'generational work'. Generational work entails the constructive efforts of parents and children to deal with the consequences of severe changes in their social environment through the course of life-events (here, migration) for their sense of being at home and their definition of self. The creation of a sense of belonging is the primary task of mothers who are usually (made) responsible for the well-being of their children. They are expected to equip their children with the necessary tools to prepare them for life in a new environment. At the same time, they have to assure the stability of kinship-bonding. Giving their children a home under circumstances of displacement is a difficult task, but one which is achieved by the majority of migrant mothers. As traditional gate-keepers and protectors of (female) respectability, mothers have to make sure that daughters lead a life in accordance with the moral judgement of their kin. However, making sure their children are happy and raising them to agree with their personal and collective moral rules can become a double burden.

Mrs Grant's reaction to Amalia's decision to go to Surinam indicates just such a mixed feeling: on the one hand she would rather have her daughter stay in physical proximity, but, on the other hand, she approves of Amalia's choice. Mrs Grant expresses her happiness with her daughter's decision, because 'my upbringing would have failed if my children had despised Surinam'. This quotation illuminates the constant doubts which Mrs Grant entertains about the success of her upbringing. Of all her children, she says that her daughter had always seemed to be most adapted to the Dutch way of living. She mentions Amalia's preference for sleeping with an open window in the winter and her love for skating as indicators of her 'Dutchness'. This quotation provides a glimpse of the uneasiness and fear of alienation which migrant mothers encounter. Where should they draw the line between new and old habits? How can they make sure that their daughters do not become estranged from them? How can they safeguard the respectability of their daughters in order not to be accused by kinship members of having failed to provide a proper education?

These are questions relevant to the upbringing of children under all diasporic conditions. The fear and uneasiness of mothers could lead to authoritarian or arrogant reactions. However, in my study I found indications of quite a different response: namely a process of ongoing negotiation and reformulation of a shared 'cultural heritage'. The answer to the question what is *our* way of doing, thinking, acting is not fixed but constantly redefined by both parents and children.

In the case of mother and daughter Grant, it is obvious that Amalia subscribes to many of her mother's habits and values, but is also subject to her mother's disapproval from time to time. Amalia's decision to emigrate releases her mother from these doubts. Although Amalia may have acquired Dutch habits and a different life-style, by choosing the 'road to Surinam' she confirms her affinity with her 'roots'. Mrs Grant, with hardly restrained pride, tells me that Amalia, during her stay in Surinam, never complained about mosquito bites. That makes her a true 'child of the tropics'. While Amalia may never actually take the step and emigrate to Surinam, nevertheless, the fact that she has developed these plans is sufficient for understanding the dynamics of intergenerational continuity and discontinuity. Continuity in the strengthening of family ties can be reached through an act of imagination as well.

In conclusion, I have emphasized the impact of migration on migrants of two generations. The vast majority of first-generation migrants cannot foresee or prepare themselves to handle the personal consequences of migration. In fact, any fear or doubt about the outcome of the migration project has to be subdued in view of the larger interest at stake. For this reason, strategies are essential for managing emigration in everyday life. The biographical approach provides a better understanding of how these strategies are achieved. As Wolfram Fischer-Rosenthal (1995) has argued, 'biography bridges the theoretical gap between an inner and an outer sphere'. In this case, biography provides the link between the migrant agent and the structure of society. It is the life-story which mirrors everything a person has lived through and in which the meaning of migration comes to the fore. The objection could be raised that only the members of the first generation have personally encountered the consequences of migration, having been the ones who actually emigrated. This is certainly the case for the majority of the second-generation children who were not born or raised in their parents' country of origin. However, through family storytelling, (moral) lessons are transferred to the next generation and children learn the lessons and guidelines born of the experiences of their parents and grandparents.

In contrast to classical theories which assume that migration must automatically lead to an identity crisis, I have argued that migrants use their *social capital*, their cultural resources, to adapt to new environments. The analysis of the biographical accounts of a mother and a daughter shows that the assumption that Western and migrant cultures are irreconcilable has to be dismissed. Certain aspects of migrants' social capital, for example the moral rules of the Creole *volksklasse*, can even be endorsed by the dominant culture. However, this does not mean that migrants are accepted easily by the dominant society. Rather, there is reluctance to grant the immigrant a substantial place in society and culture. The study of *continuity and change* in intergenerational transmission is crucial for a better understanding of the emotional consequences of migration and the dynamics involved in life-course changes. Through the analysis of migrant women's narratives, integration into a foreign society becomes viewable as *work* rather than a matter of desire or intent. It is moreover work which is hardly acknowledged by the dominant society, nor rarely appears in studies of migration. Any attempt to understand migrants' life situation must take this intergenerational element into account.

NOTES

This chapter is a revised version of a paper presented at the 'International Conference of Oral History' at Columbia University, New York, October 1994. I want to thank Lena

Inowlocki, Gloria Wekker, Kathy Davis and the members of the text analysis group of the University of Utrecht for their comments on an earlier version of this chapter. (All the names used in this chapter are pseudonyms.)

1 It is noticeable that migration researchers hardly ever consult the historical analysis of nineteenth-century Europe's migration movements from the countryside to industrializing areas for their evaluation of twentieth-century migration phenomena. Whilst in those times societies were divided into modern and traditional parts internally, by now the allocation of 'modern' is reserved for the highly industrialized European or North American societies.

2 One could also use Garfinkel's term of 'cultural dope' (Garfinkel 1967) which refers to the omission of an actor's perspective from functionalist theories.

3 With 'social capital' I refer to one aspect of the French sociologist Bourdieu's concept of 'symbolic capital', comprising the social capacities and the social networks acquired through family socialization.

4 The term 'Creole' derives from the Portugese *crioulo* (*criar* = to educate, to breed). In the colonial societies of South America and the Caribbean the term referred to somebody who, contrary to those who were bought, was born and raised in the house. In the period of slavery the descendants of slaves and imported animals were named Creoles. No earlier than in the twentieth century, with the arrival of contract workers from the Asian sub-continent, were the latter differentiated from the descendants of black and mixed black and white parents by calling these Creole (see Rudolf van Lier, 1971: 2.)

5 On the origins of the multi-ethnic society of Surinam, see also Mies van Niekerk (1993).

6 Lena Inowlocki (1993) developed this concept analogous to that of 'biographical work' (Riemann und Schütze, 1991), which represents a person's altered orientation to her changed personal and social identity through the course of life events. In her study on the intergenerational transmission in displaced families of Jewish communities, she has emphasized the constructive efforts of the younger and the older generation to redefine their identity together. Here, the interruption of the intergenerational continuity of life-course serves as a condition for the communicative (discursive) reproduction of cultural schemes.

7 The English words 'working class' does not cover the meaning of *volksklasse*. *Volksklasse* makes refence to the urban lower class of slave descent in which a certain culture has been developed by preserving elements of the African culture. Members of the *volksklasse* differentiate themselves from middle-class Creoles who are more oriented towards the lifestyle and the value system of the Dutch, also mixing much more with them (see Rudolf van Lier, 1971; Gloria Wekker, 1994). On the phenomenon of colour as a symbol of social status prevailing in the (post)colonial states of the Caribbean, see also Verena Martinez-Alier (1974).

8 The declaration of independence was not expected by the vast majority of the population and though it was welcomed by the middle class and the elite, the timing and the conditions of the declaration were and continue to be the subject of controversy. Some of the political consequences were an outburst of ethnic division and economic and social turmoil, followed by an exodus to the Netherlands. Currently the number of Surinamese immigrants in the Netherlands equals the population of Surinam itself.

9 The term 'moral economy of class' refers to Haleh Afshar's article on three generations of Pakistani women in the United Kingdom (Afshar 1989).

10 For a good overview on Creole working class family structures see Tijno Venema (1992).

11 This was supposedly reified in the Netherlands in the 1980s by the Dutch concept of '*lat-relations*', the 'living-apart together', which nowadays is accepted as a formal relationship which meets the requirements for obtaining social security benefits.

12 This term derives from Kathy Davis's reflections on the moral legitimation of decision making (see: Davis, 1994: Chapter 6).
13 For this paradoxical experience, see also Sawitri Saharso (1992) and the documentary on youth and racism in the Netherlands by Rudolf Leiprecht and Erik Willems (1994).

REFERENCES

Afshar, H. (1989) 'Gender roles and the "moral economy of kin" among Pakistani women in West Yorkshire', *New Community*, 15(2): 211–25.
Davis, K. (1994) *Reshaping the Female Body. The Dilemmas of Cosmetic Surgery*, New York: Routledge.
Essed, Ph. (1991) *Understanding Everyday Racism*, London: Sage.
Fischer-Rosenthal, W. (1995) 'The problem with identity: Biography as solution to some (post)modernist dilemmas', *COMENIUS* (15)3: 250–64.
Garfinkel, H. (1967) *Studies in Ethnomethodology*, Englewood Cliffs NJ: Prentice-Hall, Cambridge: Polity Press.
Inowlocki, L. (1993). 'Grandmothers, mothers and daughters. Intergenerational transmission in displaced families in three Jewish communities', in D. Bertaux and P. Thompson (eds) *International Yearbook of Oral History and Life Stories*, vol. II, *Between Generations*, Oxford: Oxford University Press, pp. 139–53.
Lier, R. Van (1971) *Samenleving in een grensbegied*, Deventer: van Loghum Slaterus (first published 1949).
Leiprecht, R. and Willems, E. (1994) *Het zit toch dichterbij. Jongeren en racisme in Nederland*, Amsterdam: Jobfilm.
Lutz, Helma (1991) *Welten Verbinden. Türkische Sozialarbeiterinnen in den Niederlanden und in der Bundesrepublik Deutschland* Frankfurt am Main: IKO Verlag.
—— (1994a) 'The tension between ethnicity and work. Immigrant women in The Netherlands', in H. Afshar and M. Maynard (eds) *The Dynamics of 'Race' and Gender. Some Feminist Interventions*, Basingstoke: Taylor and Francis, pp. 182–95.
—— (1994b) 'Ik maak geen ruzie en ik ga netjes. Surinaamse moeders en dochters in Nederland', *LOVER* (21)2: 53–5.
Mannheim, K. (1927) 'Das Problem der Generationen', *Kölner Vierteljahreshefte für Soziologie* 7: 157–85, 309–30.
Martinez-Alier, V. (1974) *Marriage, Class and Colour in Nineteenth-Century Cuba*, Cambridge: Cambridge University Press.
Niekerk, M. Van (1993) 'A historical approach to ethnic differences in social mobility: Creoles and Hindustanis in Surinam', paper presented at the conference on The Anthropology of Ethnicity, 15–18 December, Amsterdam.
Riemann, G. and Schütze, F. (1991) 'Trajectory as a basic theoretical concept for suffering and disorderly social processes', in D.R. Maines (ed.) *Social Organization and Social Process. Essays in the Honor of Anselm Strauss*, New York: Aldine de Gruyter, pp. 333–57.
Saharso, S. (1992) *Jan en alleman. Etnische jeugd over etnische identiteit, discriminatie en vriendschap*, Utrecht: Jan van Arkel.
Sansone, L. (1992) *Schitteren in de schaduw. Overlevingsstrategieën, subcultuur en etniciteit van Creoolse jongeren uit de lagere klasse in Amsterdam 1981–1990*, Amsterdam: Het Spinhuis.
Schütz, A. (1972) 'Der Fremde. Ein sozialpsychologischer Versuch', in A. Schütz *Gesammelte Aufsätze. Studien zur soziologischen Theorie*, vol 2. The Hague: Martinus Nijhoff, pp.53–69.
Stone, E. (1988) *Black Sheep and Kissing Cousins. How our Family Stories Shape Us*, New York: Penguin.

108 *Helma Lutz*

Venema, T. (1992) *Famiri Nanga Kulturu. Creoolse sociale verhoudingen en Winti in Amsterdam*, Amsterdam: Het Spinhuis.

Wekker, G. (1994) *Ik ben een gouden munt. Subjectiviteit en seksualiteit van Creoolse volksklasse vrouwen in Paramaribo*, Amsterdam: Vita (English original: 'I am gold money. The contradictions of selves, gender and sexuality in a female working class Afro Surinamese setting', dissertation, UCLA 1992).

7 Constructions of ethnicity in the diaspora

The case of three generations of Surinamese-Javanese women in the Netherlands

Yvette Kopijn

INTRODUCTION

Between the years 1890 and 1939 exactly 32,956 Javanese contract labourers were transferred from the Dutch East Indies (now Indonesia) to Surinam. Although contract migration was not a new phenomenon in Central America and the Caribbean,[1] the abolition of slavery facilitated a large-scale coolie trade in the nineteenth and twentieth century throughout the area (Baud *et al.* 1994: 106). Surinam also participated in this coolie trade. After the emancipation of slaves in 1863, Surinam not only faced relative labour shortages on the plantations,[2] they also had difficulty in dealing with the British and the Indian government to get a continuous supply of contract labourers from India. As the Dutch East Indies coped with a surplus of labour, the Dutch colonial rulers found it reasonable, even humane, to import the Javanese to Surinam in order to provide cheap labour on the plantations (Ismaël 1949: 22). Consent was therefore given in 1890 to the transportation of one hundred Javanese coolies to the plantation Mariënburg (Waal Malefijt 1963: 25).

During the twentieth century, migration gained a new impulse throughout the whole region. Urbanization, transmigration, and migration to the 'mother country' became essential coping strategies. The increased economic activity due to the Second World War, and the need for a higher socio-economic status, had caused many Javanese to seek their fortune in the urban areas (Ramsoedh 1990: 72). In 1975, just before the proclamation of independence several thousands of Surinamese-Javanese considered migration once again. As they feared (like many other Surinamese) ethnic conflicts would arise once the country was independent, migration took the form of a real exodus. Another contributing factor was that in 1980 the military Bouterse temporarily took over power, leading to the so-called 'December-murders' of 1982, in which fifteen prominent Surinamese were killed, also causing many Javanese to leave the country.

It is this history of double migration that this chapter focuses upon. It will analyse how the history of double migration – and the memories and myths attached to it – has shaped and informed the constructions of ethnicity in the diaspora. As my doctoral research project concerns intergenerational transmission and transformation of identity among three generations of Surinamese-Javanese women, the life stories of three generations of women within one family will be used to explore the ways in which (grand)daughters, have – more or less consciously – used the ways that their (grand)mothers responded to migration as a means for coping with their own experience of migration and for formulating an identity that is responsive to this experience. As life stories allow insights into the lived interior of migration processes, oral history seems to be an adequate method of research. As Benmayor and Skotnes (1994: 14–15) put it: 'The personal story . . . speaks precisely to how individual migrants make sense of their experiences, whilst constantly building and reinventing identities from multiple sources, often lacing them with deep ambivalence.' Before discussing the issue it is however appropriate to elaborate on the main concepts that will be used in this chapter.

For a time, migration has been conceived as a disruption in the life-course of people, interrupting perceptions of collective belonging and destiny. Underlying this approach has been the assumption that migration is a single movement in space and a single moment in time, while the focus falls on the act of crossing (Benmayor and Skotnes 1994: 8).

This chapter, however, will argue that migration is more a *process* of discontinuity and continuity, in which cultural schemes and identities are endlessly rearranged for new functions (compare with Eastmond 1993: 36–40). To reconstruct what is familiar is a well-known psychological means by which migrants cope with forced separation and loss. Yet, what appears to be cultural stagnation, as an attempt to replicate the past, in fact conceals a turbulent process of identity construction, in which cultural schemes are continuously redefined and new cultural elements added (Soest and Verdonck 1988: 98–9). Women, for instance, as mothers and daughters, may choose to accept, modify or recreate cultural schemes, according to the circumstances in which they are situated: schemes that are taken from their 'ethnic traditions' and continuously reformulated through the filters of the process of intergenerational transmission and transformation (compare with Bhachu 1993: 99–101; Woollett *et al.* 1994: 126). Consequently, migrants do not undergo a total transformation into newly created persons (Ben-Ezer 194: 115). Likewise, continuity does not so much mean absence of change as the ability to integrate change in culturally meaningful ways.

Focusing on what may be called the *social construction of ethnicity* it may become evident that the effects of migration are long term and critical in shaping and reshaping both collective and individual identities (compare with Benmayor and Skotnes 1994: 8). In this sense, transmission of the experience of migration, and the constructions of ethnicity involved, may serve as *cultural capital*[3] for future generations, a symbolic 'guide' as to how to reconstruct and maintain a 'faith' in the coherence of everyday life to be achieved through providing symbolic interpretations. In this sense, migration is relevant, not only for the first generation, but also for the generations to come (compare with Andezia 1986; Chamberlain 1994: 133).

Second, focusing on the social construction of ethnicity makes us realize that the meaning given to ethnicity is neither fixed, nor natural. Ethnicity is an aspect of identity which produces and reproduces itself through – and not despite – change and difference. It has its origin somewhere; yet, like all that is historical, it undergoes continuous change. Within the construction of ethnic identity the present also constructs the past. In accounting for the past, to either justify or criticize it, the past is often selectively appropriated, invented, remembered or forgotten (Chapman *et al.* 1989). Hence, instead of conceiving ethnicity as a completed historical fact, we now should consider it as a scenario, a circulation of memories, fantasies, and myths[4] about the past that has to be routinely created and sustained in the reflexive activities of the individual. Because new events and experiences must continuously be sorted into the ongoing 'narrative' about the past, the scenario will be accordingly reconstructed, or even receive competition from other scenarios about the past. The study of ethnicity thus implies the study of the problems surrounding the creation, interpretation, and the recollection of competing readings of the past. Moreover, as individuals construct their identity in relation to the different narratives about the past, ethnicity still presumes continuity, but it is such continuity as *interpreted* by the individual (Hall 1991: 177–92; Giddens 1991: 52–4; Chamberlain 1994: 120–1).[5]

CONSTRUCTIONS OF ETHNICITY IN SURINAM

The Javanese came to Surinam as a collection of individuals who had to make the most of it once they arrived. Yet in the beginning, communality was hard to find among them. First of all, the Javanese formed a motley group of individuals. Not only had they been recruited from different parts of the island, they also had different ethnicities: among them were Sundanese, Madurese, and Javanese who had migrated to Sunda. Some were even recruited from Sumatra and the south of Borneo (Grodd 1971: 55; Suparlan 1976: 10–11). Consequently, most people did not know their shipmates, they did not speak a common language, and, more importantly, they had different conceptions about what was meant by 'being Javanese'.

Second, the shortage of women hindered the creation of a collective culture and identity. Initially, the planters only recruited single people, mostly men. They considered women a bad risk because pregnancy and childbearing would make them less productive (Hoefte 1987: 56). Yet, women seem to have played a major role in regulating social relations on Java, being a crucial link in the network of relatives, carrying out the habit of *sambatan* (mutual help between relatives and neighbours), and making the most important (financial) decisions within the household (Geertz 1961: 45–6, 78–9). Consequently, the shortage of women must have been strongly felt within the Javanese community in Surinam. According to Suparlan (1976: 120) concubinage, promiscuity and prostitution were common practices.[6]

The internal heterogeneity, added to their young age and lower class background[7] made it hard to define what was to be understood as 'being Javanese'. As they were the first immigrants, there was no role model for becoming a Javanese in Surinam. Thousands of kilometres away from home, the immigrants from Java, Madura, Sunda, Sumatra, and Borneo therefore had to discover the right 'voice' or 'style' by virtue of what they remembered or imagined to be 'Javanese' (compare with Baud *et al.* 1994: 112–13). Within this invention of 'being Javanese', 'traditions' were given new meaning: that of security and cultural autonomy.

The formation of so-called *djadji-groups* was the first attempt to construct a new system of social relations, out of which a common culture and identity could eventually evolve. As the Javanese had been in the same boat both literally and metaphorically, they considered their shipmates a substitute for the family they had left behind. These *djadji-groups*, which served as a basis for many joint activities, eventually contained several generations.[8]

What made the Javanese actually aspire to a culture and identity of their own? Following Baud *et al.* (1994: 91–7) there are several factors affecting the formation of what he calls an 'ethnic strategy' of creating and emphasizing one's own ethnicity. The first is the nature of migration and the ideas concerning the duration of stay. Contract migration more or less involved a forced migration,[9] which generally leads to the rejection of the receiving society, and the 'development of an ideology of return'. As most Javanese felt 'betrayed', they perceived their stay in Surinam as a life in exile, waiting for return. Java remained alive as a dream, as a point of reference without which life would either be meaningless, or become 'assimilated to the life of the other' (compare with Moutoussamy 1989: 30). From these feelings the Javanese made up several scenarios to return to their place of birth, while never realizing them. Most Javanese kept postponing their return until they finally reached the 'point of no return' (Jordaan 1987: 56–57).[10] As this 'myth of return' had also taken root in the minds of the other ethnic groups in Surinam, the Surinamese-Javanese were seen as unwelcome guests in a society in which their silence and invisibility made up the dimensions of their rejection.[11]

A second factor affecting the formation of an ethnic strategy was the actual possibility of upward social mobility. In the context of contract labour, upward social mobility was only possible *after* termination of the contract. At the plantations however, all Javanese were confronted with the same poverty and misery. Life merely took place on the plantations and although it was recorded that the planters had to take care of free housing, medical care and education, measures were hardly taken (Breunissen and Grasveld 1930: 23). Moreover, the contract placed the workers under stringent social and disciplinary control. The so-called *penal sanction*, for instance, made 'laziness' or unwillingness to work punishable by jail sentences. As they were finally paid per task, only exceptionally good workers were indeed capable of earning the official 60 cents for a man and 40 cents for woman (Hoefte 1987: 62).[12] But after the five-year contract most Javanese remained poor. As they were the last to arrive in Surinam, only the poorest plots of land were available to them, while in Paramaribo they had to compete with Creoles and Hindustani who had already settled their businesses. Their insecure socio-economic position and the lack of any perspective made them stick to their own 'traditions'.

As a third factor affecting the construction of ethnicity, Baud detects the way in which immigrants and their ethnic expressions are represented by the receiving society. In Surinam, the Javanese were merely stigmatized and discriminated against. The planters, for instance, did not attribute the poverty and the 'immoral' conduct of the Javanese to the circumstances in which they kept them, but to their cultural traits and their low kind. As such, uneconomic behaviour was seen as typically Javanese, while their taste for gambling, theft, and prostitution were understood as proof of their inferiority. On account of the negative qualities that were attributed to them, the Javanese were considered suitable for few activities other than plantation work and prostitution (Blanckensteijn 1923: 252). These culturalistic explanations enabled the Surinamese government to justify their 'hands-off policy' of isolating and segregating the Javanese from society.[13]

But also the Creoles (ex-slaves) looked down upon the Javanese. The fact that they came to Surinam to do the plantation work from which they had just been 'freed' in their view reduced them to 'semi-slaves'. 'Kan, sang joe sabi joe kong dja nanga karta na joe neckie' ('Man, you know nothing, you came here with a card around your neck') was an expression with which they showed their disdain. A widespread term of abuse against Javanese women became *mbaju*, which is an abbreviation of 'mbaju, kwatje mek-mek' ('sister, a quarter to make love to you') (Suparlan 1976: 86). Additionally, the British-Indians usually called them *malahi* ('stupid'). The fact that they had arrived before the Javanese, added to the protection they enjoyed from the British consul, made them feel superior to their fellow contractants (Derveld 1982a: 21).

Being caught in a double rejection by both colonial rulers and other ethnic groups, the Javanese were thus forced to live an 'insular existence' (Itwaru 1989: 204). From their position as an 'outcast minority' (Suparlan 1976: 127), they eventually realized that they could only find security among themselves. They would be in a state of *rukun* (living in harmony) among themselves; they would speak *ngoko* (plain Javanese) among themselves and *krama* (high Javanese) towards the elderly to show them their respect; they would not cease to be Muslims, combining Islam with Agama Djawa[14] (Javanese religion): they would give their *slametan* (ritual ceremonies with food-offerings for well-being), put their *sadjen* (burn incense for the well-being of the deceased), and organize their *tajub* feasts (Suparlan 1976: 127).

Their newly created identity was also expressed in their emotional and artistic works. Following Suparlan (1976: 124), the excessive gambling among the Javanese can partly be understood as a manifestation of their frustrations and their deprivation of money. Also the extravagant spending for *slametan* and *tajub* feasts can be viewed as a means of overcoming 'felt threat' from the social environment (Suparlan 1976: 124). 'Being Javanese' was thus used as an adaptive strategy (compare with Thakur 1989: 123). By emphasizing certain cultural traditions that were suitable to their new environment and by ignoring reality, they had a feeling of confidence among themselves (Suparlan 1976: 125).

Yet, the formation of a Javanese culture and identity did not emerge solely out of the psychological need for security. Political-ideological principles were also involved. Over the years both the increasing number of older Javanese who had some experience of life, and women and families, had facilitated refinement of the Javanese culture and identity in Surinam (Breunissen and Grasveld 1990: 44; Suparlan 1976: 144). Soon, however, conflicts arose around the question of what should be meant by 'being Javanese' in Surinam. So-called traditionalists adhered to the 'Javanese' culture and religion as it had developed in Surinam, while trying to refine it by orienting themselves towards Java. The reformists considered the pre-Islamic elements like *slametan, sadjen,* and *tajub* to be the cause of the low morality and 'outcast minority' status of the Javanese in Surinam. As these elements resulted in behaviour that cut across the Islamic teachings, like drinking, gambling, concubinage, and theft, they wanted to expurgate the Islamic practice in Surinam and encourage the Javanese to invest their money in business trade and good education for their children (Suparlan 1976: 317– 21).

When after the Second World War the Javanese were allowed to form their own political parties, the traditionalists were united into the KTPI (Kaoem Tani Persatoean Indonesia). Taking advantage of the prevailing nostalgia for Java, their main slogan was 'mulih nDjowo' (to return to Java). The PBIS (Pergerakan Bangsa Indonesia Surinam), in which reformists and Christian Javanese were united, also propagated the idea of a return to Java, but only after having improved their socio-economic position in Surinam. Only then would the Javanese be able to return back to Java as a respected man (Suparlan 1976: 317–329).

The conflict led to a profound discord within the Javanese community. Wedges were driven between parents and children, between spouses, and between relatives (Ismaël 1954: 261–2). Only when, paradoxically enough, the political leaders and about one thousand of their followers decided to trade Surinam for Java in 1954, did the conflict weaken (Suparlan 1976: 319).[15]

The controversy actually concealed an intergenerational conflict as well as a conflict between rural and urban dwellers. As urbanization and transmigration had helped many Javanese to break out of their isolation and mix with other ethnic groups, children started to blame their parents who, by clinging to a far away past, had not provided them with a perspective in Surinam. Moreover, for the younger generation it sometimes was hard to belong to an ethnic group that was stigmatized as 'outcast minority'. As their ethnicity more or less coincided with a low socio-economic status, 'being Javanese in Surinam' simply meant fewer opportunities.

In reaction to this 'identity trap', some tried to define a Surinamese-Javanese culture and identity. Clearly, social and psychological factors interacted within this definition. They realized that if they wanted to gain a better place in society, they had to pick up some of the Creole-European culture. Consequently, most of them chose to act Creole-European in public, whilst retaining their own culture and identity in private as well as possible (Suparlan 1976: 158–173).[16]

Others tried to reform and refine the Javanese culture as it had evolved within Surinam. Both Christian education[17] and the fact the Indonesians had gained independence in 1949 had caused some Javanese to study and value their own culture and religion more profoundly (Ramsoedh 1990: 100–1). A movement of *cultural renaissance* evolved, in which the Indonesian embassy helped the Surinamese-Javanese to refine their culture by stimulating the correct usage of the Javanese language and etiquette, by providing guidance in the authentic performance of Javanese arts and instruments, and by supporting the reform of Islam (Suparlan 1976: 141–2; 196).[18]

CONSTRUCTIONS OF ETHNICITY IN THE NETHERLANDS

The proclamation of independence of Surinam in 1975 made many Surinamese-Javanese consider migration again. Not only were they afraid ethnic conflicts would arise once the country became independent, some of them also wanted to escape the disdain and abuse of the traditionalists. The elderly, in particular, followed the leader of the PBIS-party who told them that he would take them to the 'promised land'. In Holland, they were sent to a former seminary. Eventually, an old people's home was built for them. Mrs Kidjo, the grandmother of the family, was one of the people who followed Mr Dasiman (the PBIS-leader) to this home. She was born in 1919 at a plantation in Saramacca district when her parents were still under contract. As there were no schools available, she never received any education. After termination of the contract, her parents moved to Lelydorp, an area in which only Javanese live. At the age of 18, she was married off and bore nine children. She and her second husband still live together in a home for the elderly. Mrs Kidjo told me:

> I had heard a call on the radio from Dasiman. He said that we could fly to the Netherlands now, if we wanted to. He said that in Holland we would be taken care of properly. You would get 800 or even one thousand guilders, even if you did not work ... I discussed it with my friends. They said that they too wanted to go to the Netherlands. Then I went up to my husband to see what he felt like. He thought we'd better take the chance ... So, then we left for Holland, together with one of my daughters and her husband ... to the promised land. That was in 1975.

After a life full of hardship, the Javanese in the old people's home now take comfort in an 'imaginary home coming'. As Mrs Kidjo knows that her parents more or less escaped from Java, she has come to realise that she can never actually return to Java. Alternatively, she sees Holland as their final destination, whilst travelling in her mind, and retaining her habits and practices as she knew them in Surinam. While Java still remains a point of reference, she and her friends have found their peace in Holland, where at last they are being taken care of and are given the opportunity to 'be themselves among themselves': having their Javanese meals, going to the mosque five times a day, and attending the gamelan performances that are held occasionally.

Within the second generation, things are more ambiguous. Just like their parents, most of the women I interviewed have chosen the Netherlands as their new home on a more or less voluntary basis. As they had learned already in Surinam that they do not belong to Java, they now want to be where their children are. Moreover, after Bouterse temporarily took over power, most Javanese do not feel like returning to Surinam, although democracy has been re-established since 1987.

Yet, despite their gravitation towards Holland, most women of the second generation realize that they are as invisible within the Dutch society as they were in Surinam. As most Dutch believe that only Creoles and Hindustani come from Surinam, they often mistake the Surinamese-Javanese for Indonesians or Dutch-Indians (people from mixed Indonesian-Dutch descent). Being caught in this persisting invisibility, some seek security in their own Surinamese-Javanese culture and identity, while trying to reformulate them for the Dutch situation. Just as their (grand)parents reacted to their isolated position within Surinam, this generation is establishing their own Surinamese-Javanese associations in the larger cities of Holland, recreating a network of Surinamese-Javanese 'families' on which they hope to depend, persisting in their habit of joint festivities and activities like the celebrating of birthdays, attending gamelan performances, and organizing football tournaments.

Still, just as in Surinam, this does not mean that there are no conflicts involved.[19] Not only does there exist severe competition among Surinamese-Javanese associations, but families are also sometimes divided. Within the family of Mrs Kidjo, for example, the split in the family had already occurred in Surinam. After her husband died, she married off her oldest daughter, who moved to Paramaribo. She later sent the other children to her daughter in order to provide for a good education. She kept two daughters in Lelydorp. As she had insufficient money to pay the school fees, she removed them from school in order to help her earn a living. Mrs Djopawiro, aged 41, married for twenty-three years with three children, is one of these daughters. She remained with her mother all the while, while the other children received a good education. Throughout the years she was ridiculed and belittled by her siblings for not taking up the opportunity for a good education and better material circumstances. This difference in orientation still persisted after most of the family had migrated to the Netherlands.

The invisibility within both Dutch society and her own family, next to the fact that her husband more or less forced her to move to the Netherlands, sometimes gives Mrs Djopawiro the feeling of living in a 'second exile'. As a young girl she had decided to remain faithful to her mother and spend her youth in an area where the Javanese were left to themselves. As she had actually experienced – and partly internalized – the status of 'outcast minority' within the Surinamese society, she feels that she never really belonged to Surinam. Now that she is experiencing the isolation and invisibility once again in Holland, partly because of the misconception of the Dutch, partly because of the continuing isolated position within her own family, migration has now made her look back at her own youth and reflect upon her own identity:

You just fight for your life, you want to have a better life. You just do it for your mother, don't you? Therefore I say . . . a kind of commitment, because you listened too much to your mother [. . .] That's why I tell my children: 'You don't need to feel obliged to me.' We lived very differently, but now they live in modern times. 'Cause then, if you'd not listened to your mother, then they say: 'You're impudent, you're disobedient' . . . She [Mrs Kidjo] had no choice. I'm the one on whom she could count. 'Cause the others say: 'I'm not going to work that hard for mum. I don't have to work hard, I'm well off now: nice clothes, nice shoes when needed, pocket money . . . 'I'm just an old-fashioned Javanese. I am, if you compare it with the other relatives, then I'm very religious . . . and I just don't care about luxury things! Yet, people say: 'You're old-fashioned, you should let it go.' I say: 'No, I just feel it, right?', I said, 'I'm the master of my own body', I said. Yes, one way or the other, those words always come back to me. But it never bothered me.

Yet, although she identifies herself as an 'old-fashioned Javanese', at the same time she is well aware that she has already reformulated her attitude towards life:

When I came here, my sister said: 'People are different down here' . . . Now that I've experienced it myself . . . yes, they're different after all, you have to live differently down here. Of course, that's quite a situation, to cram up this thought, for me it was very . . . different.

Wonny, the daughter of Mrs Djopawiro is 22 and has a two-year-old daughter. She does not want to rely on her boyfriend, but live an independent life, so they live 'together-apart'. As her boyfriend is of Dutch-Indian (of mixed Dutch and Indonesian) descent, Wonny – more or less consciously – has taken the isolation and invisibility of the Surinamese-Javanese in the Netherlands as an opportunity to escape the identity trap in which her mother felt captured in Surinam, and identify as Dutch-Indian. She has learned from her mother that she does not belong in Surinam. Moreover, as the Creole-Surinamese are often discriminated and stigmatized within the Dutch society, whereas the Indonesian culture is viewed as a 'refined' culture – by both Dutch and Surinamese-Javanese themselves – identifying with and being identified as Dutch-Indian and/or Indonesian, enables her to hide her 'true' identity and escape stigmatization.

I do find it a beautiful country, Indonesia . . . One way or the other, there are my roots. And not in Surinam. I mean, I was just born in Surinam, but originally we don't come from there. I'm proud, you know. That I'm Dutch-Indian, that I came from there. And I find it funny as well, because . . . people ask you for instance: 'You must be from Indonesia, mustn't you?' 'No, I was born in Surinam.' 'What? But in Surinam, only Creoles live there?' 'Are you crazy?' 'Not at all! No, I'm just a Javanese-Surinamese, I'm a Surinamese-Javanese.' Oh . . . they don't get it at all. But then again, it's also nice. I mean, strictly speaking, I come from Indonesia, while I was born in Surinam, and raised down here. Yes, that really is something unique.

Moreover, identifying with her Dutch-Indian family-in-law gives her the additional benefit of combining elements of the Dutch way of life with the Surinamese-Javanese identity, as she knows it from her mother:

> I have my own income, I receive social assistance . . . And for me, that means independence . . . In the future, I want to have my own job, but now it's important that there is someone to look after Milou [her daughter] . . . I don't think, I don't I know, those working mothers nowadays . . . Then I think: 'what is more important? You've chosen for your child. Spend those five years on your child, those are the most important years. Then you can go to work. Yes, people think: that's important and I have to earn a lot of money for my child's future. But you only have to give children your love. What's the fuss? . . . No, just let me do it my way. And of course there are people who don't get it: 'Why you're not married?' or 'Isn't Max supposed to take care of you?' Even girls of my own age. But then I think: Just cut it off. No, not at all, I don't want it that way.

Knowing from her own youth how important it is to get the chance to get on with your life your own way, Mrs Djopawiro manages to be at peace with the way in which her daughter has reformulated the Surinamese-Javanese way of life. And maybe just because of that she does not want to impose her way of living upon her daughter. Instead, she tells her daughter to define her own identity:

> I say to her: 'You must see yourself how you live. We live in modern times. But I am and will stay just like I am.' . . . She has a boyfriend, they're living together and still, if I had to say, as a mother: 'This is what you have to do,' that would be difficult . . . and I won't force them. Look, I always say: 'Doesn't matter whom you marry, as long as you're happy.' They're [the 'parents-in-law'] just different people.

Wonny is well aware of the effort it took her mother to help her find a sense of wholeness after migration and to accept her daughter's definition of 'being Surinamese-Javanese' in the Netherlands. She has experienced her mother reformulating her attitude towards life and towards raising her daughter:

> You know what I like about her? That she, in her youth, has experienced it all, and that she then kind of dropped it and then showed me: 'Take care that you're well off; take care that you will be independent and not have to rely on others like me.' Indeed, that's what she taught me. Yet, she was also very strict. She had, she uhm, yes, now and then she was really inconsistent . . . Then she said: 'Take care that your boyfriend takes care of you' and 'It's important that a man supports you.'

However, she also realizes that through her reformulation she also helps her mother to cope with the experience of migration and find a way to reconcile with the Dutch society:

> My parents have become more broad-minded just because of me. . . . when I listen to my mother, when she was only little, she had to work hard and all that,

did not finish her school and . . . ah well, it just couldn't have been different in those times . . . But there are certain habits of which I think: 'Oh please, just look at it differently!' . . . Now, they don't meddle with my affairs anymore and . . . they help me, but not like: 'Do this' and 'Do that' . . . I'm glad that I'm the one who set them thinking. . . . People in those times, they only worked and worked and worked. . . . Now, I have an easier time. I can reflect on those things. And only because they have worked so hard and I'm just grateful. . . . And I just, I just want to give my parents something of the way I feel now.

CONCLUSION

In this chapter, an historical approach to migration is used in order to show that migration does not stop after the moment of relocation, but is more a long-term process that also affects the generations who did not experience the act of crossing themselves. In this sense, transmission of the experience of migration, and the constructions of ethnicity – whether carried out consciously or unconsciously – may serve as a coping strategy for future generations. Learning from the ways their (grand)mothers responded to migration, (grand)daughters are capable of restoring a feeling of belonging and formulating an identity that is responsive to their experience of migration.

Appreciating migration as a process thus leads us automatically to the family as one of the most important media through which transmission and transformation of culture and identity takes place. Women, as grandmothers and mothers, seem to be the main cultural transmitters within the family. Focusing on the family will therefore enable us to acknowledge the role of migrant women as originators and innovators of new cultural forms, as negotiators who are actively engaging with their culture, whilst continuously transforming it. Recognizing the role of migrant women as *cultural entrepreneurs* (Bhachu 1993: 99–101) may enable us to identify representations of migrant women as 'passive' recipients of their culture as a stereotype that really needs to be repudiated.

NOTES

Pseudonyms have been used for all interview-based sources.

1 The first intercontinental flow of contract migration had already taken place in the seventeenth and eighteenth century and involved an outflow from the countries of Western Europe to colonial settlements in the New World (Engerman 1986: 263).
2 I speak of relative labour shortage since in fact there were enough workers. As the planters held the wages artificially low, most ex-slaves settled down in Paramaribo as free labourers or moved to those estates which could afford to pay higher wages. This resulted in a *relative* shortage of labourers, which raised the wages and reduced the profits. Contract labourers were thus recruited to restrain the wages and to assure a reserve of cheap labour (Hassankhan 1993: 11–12).
3 The term 'cultural capital' is derived from the sociologist Pierre Bourdieu (in Pels 1992: 126–7) and refers to a form of capital which serves as symbolic capital and provides the individual with an additional material and symbolic benefit. Cultural capital can, for instance, be a certain mentality, intelligence or skill. It can, to some

extent depending on the specific period, society or social class, be acquired without intentional imprinting. The transmission of cultural capital may thus occur unconsciously.

4 Both Connerton (1989) and Chamberlain (1994) have pointed out that memories – both individually and collectively memorized experiences – play a vital role in the construction of identity: they often serve as imaginative accounts of significations, along which lives are interpreted, constructed and changed. Furthermore, Bhabha (1994: 192–3) has noted that the role of fantasy and myth in the construction of identity could have particular significant implications for a colonial regime that relies for its authority on the projection of 'inferiority' on other races, cultures, and histories.

5 This does not mean hat the construction of ethnicity is always carried out consciously. As Giddens (1991: 35–42) has noted, many of the elements of being able 'to go on' are carried out at the level of what he calls *'practical consciousness'*. This form of consciousness, which often has a 'tacit' or 'taken-for-granted' quality, produces daily routines that help the individual to cultivate a sense of self and a mode of orientation in everyday life. Consequently, social change and continuity seem to be the product of both intended (strategic) and accidental (un-strategic) effects of agency (see also Fischer 1986: 195).

Also Bourdieu has pointed out that individuals often use strategies that are not the result of explicitly or consciously pursued goals. Social agency is often led by a 'feeling for practice' or 'a feeling for the game'. As such, it is often the product of what he calls a *'practical knowledge'* (Bourdieu, in Pels 1992: 64–5).

Both theories are meaningful for our notion of ethnicity, as they realize that migrants not only (re)construct their collective and individual identities through the politics of a conscious confrontation, but also through their natural familiarity with the symbolic and material cultures. From these, they appropriate, transform and reproduce them both unselfconsciously and strategically.

6 In this sense, women took advantage of their rarity. Plagued by a continuous lack of food, women turned to prostitution as a means to earn some extra cash. Moreover, they were in a position to be very selective in choosing their lovers. Consequently, the shortage of women sometimes led to suicide among men and crimes of passion (Ismaël 1949: 127).

7 Gooswit (1994) has noted that most had been poor urban dwellers or landless farmers who had lived with another family where they received food and housing for services rendered. These so-called *pondok* were mostly men who lived outside their parental home not only because of economic reasons, but also because of relational problems (Gooswit 1994: 174).

8 For women, there was also another side to these *djadji-groups*. Women who had just arrived at the plantations were usually divided among single men, while so-called *bandols*, leaders on account of their muscle power, violently took control over the most attractive women. Additionally, the men undertook the task of 'protecting' the women from outsiders which often resulted in brawls between the various *djadji-groups*. Although women had often left Java to escape from an arranged marriage (De Waal Malefijt 1963: 29–30), in Surinam they were again initially appreciated as mere property that could be given away, gambled away or sold (De Waal Malefijt 1963: 86–9; Suparlan 1976: 120; Hoefte 1987: 63–5).

9 The use of deception and coercion to force the Javanese to commit themselves into a five-year contract seems to have been common practice among recruiting agents, especially when female contractants were involved. According to Ranneft Meijer (1914: 1–17), Assistant-Resident of Semarang, 'the recruiting officers lure the women with promises of marriage', they 'depict the future [as] too beautiful', or they 'threaten that the future will be unpleasant for non-contractants'. In addition, Suparlan (1976, appendix I) has found reports of women being lured to Surinam with promises

of wages of one guilder a day, women being 'sold' to the recruiting officer when their husband had found another wife, or women who were simply kidnapped.

10 Another explanation for the small number of repatriants – only 7,697 would actually return – seems to lie in the colonial policy of Surinam. As the Dutch gradually came to realize that Surinam would only flourish if the immigration system also led to the growth of the permanent population, they started offering land while guaranteeing a free return passage (Ismaël 1949: 70–1, 96). In reality, however, the possibility of return was sometimes cut off by not providing a boat (Eimers 1988: 76).

11 Until the 1950s, the 'myth of return' remained to play a major role in the lives of the Javanese. In 1933, for instance, the political activist Anton de Kom, who strove to improve the Surinamese working class, took advantage of their nostalgia. He spread rumours that he would enable them to return to Java if they would report to him. As a result, an increasing flow of Javanese left the plantations without permission for De Kom's residence. When De Kom was arrested again, large groups of Javanese left for Paramaribo. Riots followed and the Surinamese government retaliated by tightening their control over the Javanese associations (Lier 1977: 280–2; Ramsoedh 1990: 34–7).

Another instance in which the 'myth of return' turned up was in the propaganda of the political parties that were founded after the Second World War. Both KTPI and PBIS used the longing for Java among their people to guarantee their own future (Suparlan 1976: 317–29). I will return to this subject later.

12 Not only were women paid less, but by creating sexual divisions between 'heavy' and 'light' tasks, the planters additionally forced women to do the most menial and lowest-paying jobs. Moreover, as most women formerly seem to have been employed as nannies, maids, and batik women, they were less prepared for the fieldwork than men (Hoefte 1990: 12).

13 Surprisingly enough, several contemporary scholars adopted these culturalistic explanations of the miserable socio-economic position of the Javanese in Surinam. Panday (1959), for instance, pointed to the collectivistic tradition of the *dessa* (small Javanese village) society that would have been pursued at the Surinamese plantations, and which would have made it very hard for the Javanese to cultivate a plot of land on an individual basis. In addition, Ismaël (1949) and De Waal Malefijt (1963) believed the behaviour of the Javanese to be not so much a reaction to their environment as the product of their own 'traditional' culture: the egalitarian Javanese culture and the central notion of *rukun* (living in harmony) would not encourage economic activity. Consequently, the economic opportunities which Surinam offered would just not have been used by the Javanese. Unfortunately, these culturalistic explanations leave room for only one conclusion: it is not the socio-economic environment of the Javanese but their own culture that has to change (compare with Kruyer 1968 : 78–9).

14 The *Agama Djawa* refers to the teachings regarding the place of man in the universe and communication with that universe. The basic principle is the notion of *sangkan paraning dumadi* (Where does man come from, what and who is he now, and what and where is his destiny?). This principle refers to two domains of explanation: the activities around the life cycle (*slametans, sadjen*, etc), and the concept of the place of man in the universe and the different powers that animate it (Suparlan 1976: 239).

15 As conflicts remained to play a central role in the Surinamese-Javanese community, the idea of *rukun* was more an ideal than it has ever been reality. As Suparlan put it: 'If indeed the Javanese live in harmony amongst each other, the idiom of *rukun* would not be stressed time after time by the ones in authority in order to maintain the social order' (Suparlan 1976: 19).

16 Most of them knew that the 'Javanese' culture in Surinam gradually had been transformed into a Surinamese-Javanese culture, in which eventually a Surinamese-Javanese way of life (Suparlan 1976), as well as a Surinamese-Javanese language had evolved, in which the Javanese language was supplemented with words derived from

the Creole language, Dutch, and Hindi (Vruggink 1993; Gooswit 1994: 179). This made them realize that their culture and identity already consisted of both Javanese and Surinamese cultural schemes.

17 For long, the Javanese had resisted education for their children. Since it was mostly Christian missionaries who had founded the elementary schools and day-nurseries around the plantations, and boarding schools for children of the districts in Paramaribo, they were afraid their children would become alienated from their own group. Yet, as the resistance against education gradually diminished, the Christian boarding schools enabled higher education for Javanese children. In return, this paved the way for the formation of an intellectual elite and the emancipation of the Javanese within the Surinamese society (Ramsoedh 1990: 101–102).

18 In a sense, the support from the Indonesian embassy met the need for a collective memory, which would provide the Javanese-Surinamese with a historical consciousness. The first generation had to cope with a painful and problematic past, but the younger generations knew little about it. As Leydesdorff (1994) has pointed out, oppressing and dispelling all that is problematic to the realm of the unconscious, causes confusion in the memory and creates uncertainty about one's own identity. As this confusion is transmitted to next generations, it is one of the causes of ambivalent identity. The Indonesian embassy now seemed to have enabled the younger generations to restore, in part, this historical consciousness.

19 According to Gooswit (1994: 180) the conflict between the traditionalists and the reformists still persists within the Surinamese-Javanese community in Holland.

BIBLIOGRAPHY

Anzedia, S. (1986) 'Women's roles in organizing life: Algerian female immigrants in France', in R.J. Simon and C.B. Bretell (eds) *International Migration: The Female Experience*, Totowa, NJ: Rowman and Allenheid.

Baud, M. *et al.* (1994) *Etniciteit als stragie in Latijns-Amerika en de Caraïben*, Amsterdam: Amsterdam University Press.

Ben-Ezer, G. (1994) 'Ethiopian Jews encounter Israel: narratives of migration and the problem of identity', in R. Benmayor and A. Skotnes (eds), *Migration and Identity, International Yearbook of Oral History and Life Stories*, vol.III, Oxford: Oxford University Press.

Benmayor, R. and Skotnes, A. (eds.) (1994), *Migration and Identity, International Yearbook of Oral History and Life Stories*, vol.III, Oxford: Oxford University Press.

Blanckensteijn, M. van (1923) *Suriname*, Rotterdam.

Bhabha, H., interviewed by Paul Thompson (1994), 'Between identities', in R. Benmayor and A. Skotnes (eds) *Migration and Identity, International Yearbook of Oral History and Life Stories*, vol.III, Oxford: Oxford University Press.

Bhachu, P. (1993) 'Identities constructed and reconstructed: representations of Asian women in Britain', in G. Buijs (ed.) *Migrant Women: Crossing Boundaries and Changing Identities*, Oxford: Berg.

Breunissen, K. and Grasveld, F. (1990) *Ik ben een Javaan uit Suriname*, Hilversum: Stichting Ideële Filmprodukties.

Chamberlain, M. (1994) 'Family and identity: Barbadian migrants to Britain', in R. Benmayor and A. Skotnes (eds) *Migration and Identity, International Yearbook of Oral History and Life Stories*', vol. III, Oxford: Oxford University Press.

Chapman, M., McDonald, M. and Tonkin, E. (1989) 'Introduction', in E. Tonkin, M. McDonald and M. Chapman (eds) *History and Ethnicity*, ASA monograph, London: Routledge.

Connerton, P. (1989) *How Societies Remember*, Cambridge: Cambridge University Press.

Derveld, F.E.R. (1982) *De Politieke Mobilisatie en Integratie van de Javanen in Suriname*, Groningen: Bouma's Boekhandel.

—— (1982a) 'Hoe dachten de planters en overige bevolkingsgroepen over de Javanen', OSO, 1(2): 23–43.

Eastmond, M. (1993) 'Reconstructing life: Chilean refugee women and the dilemmas of exile', in G. Buijs (ed.) *Migrant Women: Crossing Boundaries and Changing Identities*, Oxford: Berg.

Eimers, D. (1988) *Enkele reis Semarang-Paramaribo: emigratie van Javaanse kontrakt-arbeidsters naar Suriname 1890–1939*, Utrecht: Rijks Universiteit Utrecht.

Engerman, Stanley L, (1986) 'Servants to slaves to servants: contract labour and European expansion', in P.C. Emmer (ed.) *Colonialism and Migration: Indentured Labour Before and After Slavery*, Dordrecht: Martinus Nijhoff.

Fischer, Michael M.J. (1986) 'Ethnicity and the post-modern arts of memory', in James Clifford and George E. Marcus (eds) *Writing Culture: The Poetics and politics of ethnography*, School of American Research Advanced Seminar, Berkeley, CA: University of California Press, pp. 194–233.

Geertz, H. (1961) *The Javanese Family, a Study of Kinship and Socialization*, New York: Free Press of Glencoe.

Giddens, A. (1991) *Modernity and Self-Identity; Self and Society in Late Modern Age*, Cambridge: Polity Press.

Gooswit, S. (1994) 'Veranderende identificatie bij Javanen in Diaspora', OSO, 13(2): 173–83.

Grodd, G. (1971) *Kulturwandel der Indonesischen Einwanderung in Suriname*, Freiburg.

Hall, S. (1991) *Het minimale Zelf en andere opstellen*, Amsterdam: SUA.

Hassankhan, Maurits S. (1993) 'Inleiding', in L. Gobardhan-Rambocus and Maurits S. Hassankhan (eds) *Immigratie en ontwikkeling: emancipatieproces van contractanten*, Paramaribo: Anton de Kom Universiteit.

Hoefte, R. (1987) 'Female indentured labour in Surinam: for better or worse?, *Boletín de Estudios Latino-Americanos y del Caribe*, no. 42: 55–70.

—— (1990) *De betovering verbroken: de migratie van Javanen naar Suriname en het Rapport van Vleuten*, Dordrecht: Foris.

Ismaël, J. (1949) *De immigratie van Indonesiërs in Suriname*, Amsterdam: Sticusa.

—— (1954) 'De positie van de Indonesiër in het nieuwe Suriname', *Indonesië*, 4(3/4).

Itwaru, A. (1989) 'Exile and Commemoration', in F. Birdalsingh (ed.) *Indenture and Exile: The Indo-Caribbean Experience*, Toronto: Ontario Association for Studies in Indo-Caribbean Culture, pp. 202–6.

Jordaan, H.R. (1987) ' "De weg over den grooten landbouw in dienstbaarheid, naar den kleinen landbouw in eigen doen . . . " ' de invloed van het koloniale bestuursbeleid en de economische omstandigheden op de achtergebleven maatschappelijke positie van de Javaanse immigranten in Suriname 1917–1940, term paper, Rijks Universiteit Leiden.

Kruyer, G.J. (1968) *Suriname en zijn buren, landen in ontwikkeling*, Meppel: Boom.

Leydesdorf, S. (1994) unpublished paper.

Lier, R. van (1977) *Samenleving in een grensgebied. Een sociaal-historische studie van Suriname*, 3rd edn, Amsterdam: Emmergin.

Meyer Ranneft, J.W. (1914) 'De misstanden bij de werving op Java', *Tijdschrift voor Binnenlandsch Bestuur*, 46.

Moutoussay (1989), 'Indianness in the French West Indies', in F. Birdalsingh (ed.), *Indenture and Exile: The Indo-Caribbean Experience*, Toronto: Ontario Association for Studies in Indo-Caribbean Culture, pp. 27–36.

Panday, R.M.N. (1959) *Agriculture in Surinam (1650–1950): an inquiry into the causes of its decline*, Amsterdam.

Pels, D. (ed.) (1989) *Opstellen over smaak, habitus en het veldbegrip gekozen door Dick Pels*, Amsterdam: Van Giennep.

Rarnsoedh, H.K. (1990) *Suriname 1933–1944: Koloniale politiek en beleid onder gouverneur Kielstra*, Delft: Eburon.

Soest, R. van and Verdonk, B. (1988) 'Etnische identiteit: de psychologische betekenis van afkomst', *De Psycholoog*, 23(3): 97–103.

Solors, W. (1989) *The Invention of Ethnicity*, New York: Oxford University Press.

Suparlan, Parsudi (1976) *The Javanese in Surinam: Ethnicity in an Ethnically Plural Society*, Champaign, IL: University of Illinois.

Thakur (1989) 'British and Dutch colonial policies in Guyana and Surinam', in F. Birdalsingh (ed.) *Indenture and Exile: The Indo-Caribbean Experience*, Toronto: Ontario Association for Studies in Indo-Caribbean Culture, pp. 115–25.

Verhey, E. and Van Westerloo, G. (1984) 'Ik heb niet gestolen, ik ben gestolen', *Vrij Nederland*, 24 December 1984.

Vruggink, H. (1993) 'Het Javaans-Surinaams', in L. Gobardhan-Rambocus and Maurits S. Hassankhan (eds), *Immigratie en ontwikkeling: emancipatieproces van contractanten*, Paramaribo: Anton de Kom Universiteit.

Waal Malefijt, A. de (1963) *The Javanese of Surinam. Segment of a Plural Society*, Assen: Van Gorcum and Comp.

Woollett, A., Marschall, H., Nicholson, P. and Dosanjh, N. (1994) 'Asian women's ethnic identity: the impact of gender and context in the accounts of women bringing up children in East London', *Feminism and Psychology*, 4(1): 119–2.

Part IV
Family and identity

8 The delusive continuities of the Dutch Caribbean diaspora

Gert Oostindie

5 May 1995 was a special day: the Germans had capitulated fifty years earlier, putting an end to five years of Nazi occupation of the Netherlands. The Breestraat in Leiden was the scene of brass bands, old Harleys and jeeps against a background of *tableaux vivants* referring to the Occupation. In between marched war veterans: British, American and Canadian.

I thought of Frank Koulen, who could have been walking here too if he had not died ten years earlier. Born in New Nickerie, Surinam in 1922, he died in Terneuzen, Zealand Flanders in 1985. It seems easy enough to outline his biography. He was born into the Creole working class, into a family of absent men – his sons were the first males in four generations to transmit the name of Koulen.[1] He was brought up by his grandmother until she died. Then his mother took over the task of raising him, but she died soon afterwards too. Eleven years old by now, he ended up in the Tilburg Lay Brothers' orphanage. The Brothers thought he showed promise and enabled him to learn a profession after completing full primary school education. He trained in metalwork, but Surinam did not have much to offer. In 1939, at the age of sixteen, he emigrated to Curaçao to work in the Shell refinery there. Like most of his fellow countrymen, he lived in the Suffisant district, better known at the time as 'Surinam village'. It was there, not in the Netherlands, that the first chapters of the modern Dutch Caribbean migration history were written.

In 1943 he signed a five-year contract with the navy.[2] The marines were trained in the United States and England before being deployed in the liberation of the Netherlands. In September 1944 they set out from Normandy for the Netherlands. The offensive was halted in Zealand Flanders and was not completed until the spring of 1945. That winter Koulen met a young woman from Terneuzen, and they married in 1947. When the first of their seven children was born, Koulen was serving in Indonesia – very much against his will, but still under military discipline – where the Dutch were using force to try to avert independence. In 1949, when he was called up again, he asked to be released from service because of his objections of principle. In the end he was granted an honourable discharge. The rest of his story is a modest variation on the rags to riches theme. As a small-scale entrepreneur and especially as the driving force behind a steadily growing jazz centre, Koulen made a name for himself in

Zealand. In terms of education and work, his children reached heights which their father had only dreamed of during his difficult childhood in Surinam. He revisited his country once, in 1980, but despite his pride in his origins and his race, it was a disappointing encounter. The hated colonialism had come to an end, but he noted with regret that he was unable to accept the lethargy and provincialism of life in Surinam.

It is not just my own involvement – Frank Koulen was my father-in-law – which is my reason for telling this story. I have told it here to introduce a reflection on the contrast between early Caribbean Dutch history and today, and the significance of that prehistory for present-day migrants. It would be a good thing if biographical sketches like that of Koulen were typical of Caribbean history in the Netherlands, but that is not the case, as the title of this chapter suggests. Second, more and more I have wondered whether an early history like that of Frank Koulen has any significance at all for the masses of later migrants and their children. I have grown more sceptical about that as well. And finally, the existence of different, often contradictory versions of this very story has gradually helped me to realize how cautious we must be in interpreting all the individual histories.

These reflections are the thread running through this chapter. I have tried to find a solid basis for them by once again outlining the course of the historical events and by testing my ideas against the results of a modest street research among Caribbean Dutch.[3]

PRELUDE: THE SLAVES

But let us start at the beginning of the story. The history of Surinamese and Antilleans[4] in the Netherlands goes back to the earliest years of colonization. It is the same story that can be told for all of the Caribbean colonies and their mother countries. The Indians who were taken to the 'fatherland' as exotic curiosities; the slaves who went too as servants and status symbols; the colonial elites, who tried to find a trace of 'refined' living in the Netherlands; and their children, who went to study there. There were never very many of them; in that respect the history of the Dutch Caribbean differs from that of the neighbouring countries. In eighteenth-century England, the number of blacks, mainly from the West Indian colonies, was estimated to be some tens of thousands. The relatively large-scale migration of both slaves and free persons from the French Caribbean led to far-reaching legal restrictions. The mixture of economic and racist arguments used at the time reads as an *unheimische* prelude to present-day debates. As for Spain and Portugal, large numbers of Africans were living there long before the *conquista*. This black population was constantly supplemented in a roundabout way through the slaving concerns in the New World.

By comparison, the presence of Caribbeans and Africans in the Netherlands was negligible. By far the largest proportion of all blacks who arrived there came from Surinam, followed – though a long way behind – by Curaçao. They were few in number. Even at the peak of the Surinam plantation economy, the third quarter of the eighteenth century, hardly more than twenty slaves and a few free coloureds left for 'patria' each year, and the vast majority of them returned later. These figures were even lower during the preceding and subsequent periods. The conclusion must therefore be that, prior to the twentieth century, the presence of Afro-Caribbeans in the Netherlands was negligible. This is even truer of Africans. The contrast with England, France and the two Iberian countries is clear. It is not difficult to explain. While the centre of gravity of the colonial empires of the other European countries was in the Atlantic world, the Netherlands focused on Asia. The Dutch trading posts in Africa and the slave colonies in the Caribbean were always of secondary importance.

What remains of this period are lost trails and a few nice anecdotes. I have collected and described a lot of them, and enjoyed doing so. Nice anecdotes, even though they are often heart-rending – but it is hard to attach any more importance than that to them. The free Indian Erikeja Jupitor, who made a notarial statement in Amsterdam in 1688 on behalf of a soldier who had served in Surinam as an interpreter. The anonymous slave who was taken to the Netherlands around 1700, joined the Reformed Church there, but seven years later, back in her own country, returned to her own belief that was 'much more pleasing to the senses'. Quasje, banished from Surinam for trading weapons with the maroons, but eventually sent back from the Netherlands by a judge who sympathized with Quasje's regret at having to depart two years earlier, 'leaving behind his wife, children and livelihood'. Free orphans from Paramaribo, who were to receive a Protestant education in the Amsterdam Orphanage and were enabled to learn a craft before embarking on the journey back. John Gabriel Stedman's slave Quaco, with whom Stedman was so contented that he took the youth with him to Europe, only to give him away there as a present to the Countess of Roosendaal. The slave Virginie from Curaçao, who waged a bitter struggle on both sides of the Atlantic for her own freedom and that of her children. J.J. Jonas, born a slave, who, 'despite her black colour', developed in the Netherlands to become a 'well-educated Lady, who spoke French as purely and fluently as the best Parisienne and was as fluent in German and English as in Dutch'. The black man skating over the frozen Amsterdam canals, immortalized by the German poet Freiligrath in his poem 'Der Schlittschuh-laufende Neger' (1833).

The transience of these fragments of the past is in sharp contrast to comparable events elsewhere. The English experience is particularly interesting in this connection. The massive presence of West Indian slaves there repeatedly raised the question of whether slavery was acceptable on British soil. This question was answered in the negative in a test trial in 1772. Although this verdict turned out not to have a definitive character, the Somerset case is still regarded as a milestone on the road towards the abolition of slavery in the British West Indies. Moreover, several race riots occurred in this period in British cities. The simple fact that there were so many West Indians in England made it impossible to forget or ignore the slavery issue.

In the Netherlands, on the other hand, the presence of Caribbean slaves was so limited that a clear policy on their status was never formulated. Right up to the last day before the abolition of slavery on 1 July 1863, the few slaves who had been taken to the Netherlands with their masters had no secure basis on which to claim their freedom. Their almost invisible presence meant that the Dutch were confronted even less with the facts of slavery in the Caribbean colonies. Unlike the English situation, the presence of blacks in the Netherlands was hardly visible, devoid of political or social significance, and did not hasten the abolition of slavery.

THE EXODUS AND THE ILLUSION OF CONTINUITY

While the arrival of slaves ended by definition after 1863, there was continuity in a different type of migration: that of the colonial elite. In the search for expansion of the colonial horizon, and especially for good education, the better-off Surinamese and Antilleans kept on travelling to the Netherlands. The motive remains unchanged today, and is one of the few continuities in three centuries of migration history. The difference lies in what came afterwards; the return that used to be taken for granted at one time gradually became a receding horizon.

Statistically, this Caribbean history in the Netherlands hardly looks any more than a footnote to a larger story. The number of West Indian students who studied in the Netherlands in previous centuries was rarely more than a handful at any one time. The situation did not change until after the Second World War. By the end of the 1950s there were a few hundred Antillean and particularly Surinam students, and their numbers multiplied in the course of the following decades. All the same, they remained on a modest scale, and the percentage of students among the Caribbean population in the Netherlands actually declined. Seen from a wider perspective, however, the presence of Caribbean students in the Netherlands acquired an enormous importance. By means of their Dutch education, the orientation of the colonial elites was unambiguously attached to 'Patria'. Moreover, paradoxically, the experience of a period of study in Europe was eventually to play a decisive role in the development of postwar Surinam nationalism (the same is true, though to a lesser degree, of Antillean nationalism). More than the awareness of economic and perhaps even constitutional dependence, the inevitability of a period of study in the mother country has left its mark on practically every Dutch Caribbean intellectual. Even the Surinam nationalism of the 1950s and 1960s, and independence in the 1970s, are unthinkable without the Dutch intermezzo that the protagonists once went through.

During the first half of this century 'other' Surinamese and Antilleans found their way to the Netherlands too on an incidental basis. Enterprising individuals, mainly men, most of them from the Afro-Surinam working class. They too are a source of wonderful anecdotes. The 'professional Negroes', especially musicians, who skilfully exploited the exoticism of their appearance and their artistic talents, had come a long way since the end of the nineteenth century, when Surinamese could literally be put on display without benefiting from it themselves at all. There were also a few sailors, labourers and clerks. The best known of the migrants is the Afro-Surinamese Anton de Kom. De Kom (b. 1898) went to the Netherlands in 1922. He soon became active in the anti-colonial movement and – in secret – in the Communist Party. As such he was a source of concern to the Dutch authorities. After returning to Surinam in 1932, he was at the centre of serious riots which earned him a compulsory 'repatriation' to the land of the ruler. In 1934 he published *We Slaves of Surinam*. This book made De Kom one of the first in the Caribbean – leaving aside Haiti and the Spanish-speaking Caribbean – to rewrite the history of his country in an anti-colonial manner. A German translation was published almost immediately in Moscow. During the war he was a member of the Resistance, was arrested and deported to Germany. This remarkable Surinamese died in the Neuengamme concentration camp on 24 April 1945. Most of his relatives – his wife was Dutch – live in the Netherlands, but it is the university of Surinam which bears his name, a heritage of the period of military rule under Desi Bouterse.

These migrants remained isolated cases with a high curiosity value until the 1960s. Frank Koulen was known as 'the Negro' in the harbour town of Terneuzen – he was the only one. In 1946 the total size of the Surinam community in the Netherlands was estimated at 3,000, and in 1966 at 13,000. The Antillean component accounted for no more than a few thousand persons. Compared with the next stage, but also compared with what had already been a dramatic emigration from other parts of the Caribbean towards the United States and Britain, the exodus from the Dutch Caribbean was thus still modest in scale. This can largely be explained by the spectacular economic growth of Curaçao and Aruba from the late 1920s on. The oil refineries and all the sectors expanding around them provided a lot of jobs, both for the local population and for immigrants; those with the status of fellow citizens (from Surinam and the Windward Islands) received preferential treatment. The oil boom did not really die out until the late 1960s. Besides, the Surinam economy went through a strong growth period from the 1940s as a result of the bauxite. Furthermore, there was a weak labour market in the Netherlands. There was even a clear emigration surplus after 1945. This only changed in the 1960s, but this was the time when the specific recruitment of labourers from the Mediterranean countries started. Unlike the situation in England and France, in the Netherlands hardly any labourers were recruited from the Caribbean.

So when an exodus did get under way in the late 1960s, first and above all in Surinam, and later in Curaçao as well, there was not only a change in numbers but a qualitative change. For the first time, emigration to the Netherlands outstripped migration within the Caribbean parts of the Kingdom. From now on Dutch Caribbean migration was to be extremely conservative; the goal is practically always the relatively safe mother country. As for the situation in the Netherlands, the exoticism disappeared, and in a certain sense too the heroism of the prehistory of courageous individuals, musicians, nationalists. The new migrants represented for the first time a cross-section of the societies from which they came. The surplus of men disappeared; the ethnic diversity of Surinam displaced the former Afro-Surinam preponderance; and most of the migrants were now from the lower classes. Education and work were still a motive for migration. Yet while the chance of success in those sectors fell, the orientation towards Dutch welfare state provisions grew. These provisions were and still are relatively favourable; this, however, soon turned out to be not entirely positive. A part of the current Dutch Caribbean population is dependent on them, which keeps them in a paralysing stranglehold. A comparable ambivalent blessing lay in the continuing growth of the Caribbean Dutch population. The increasing numbers and concentration created the condition for the emergence of 'ethnic' enclaves which functioned as havens in a heartless world. However, precisely this new security may have hindered integration and social mobility.[5]

In the meantime the Caribbean community in the Netherlands has continued to grow. The Surinam community today is estimated at over 275,000. The Antillean community, mainly from Curaçao, has increased to the present figure of 90,000.[6] It is typical that the statistics have become not only more refined, but also more problematical in a number of ways. The current practice of classifying the second generation in the statistics as Surinamese or Antillean may correspond more closely to the ideas of their parents and to that of white Dutch than to the feelings of many members of the younger generation themselves.

The growth of the Surinamese population in the Netherlands was most spectacular around the time of independence (1975). Settlement and naturalization in the Netherlands have become considerably harder since 1980, but illegal immigration continues. Furthermore, the share of the second generation is growing fast, and the third will soon be on the way. The Antillean group, mainly from Curaçao, still consists mainly of the first generation. Finally, the constitutional situation has contributed to the negative phenomenon that, while the migration between Curaçao and the Netherlands is two-directional, the one between Surinam and its former mother country is in fact only a one-way traffic. This is another depressing result of decolonization, which has not failed to have an impact on Surinam nationalism.[7]

The notion of 'delusive continuity' will now be clearer. There are a number of constants in Caribbean migration to the Netherlands. People from the Caribbean came to 'patria' from the earliest days of colonization. There was always a strong orientation towards the mother country. The Dutch reactions to the predominantly coloured migrants – a subject not yet discussed here – were never free of problems. However, it is the fault lines which are more significant. The number of migrants has become incomparably larger and their presence is permanent. This has given the diaspora a significance of an entirely different kind, both in the Netherlands and in the Caribbean. The latter point is clear; the failure of the independence of Surinam is closely connected with the exodus, and the island communities of the Antilles too have been profoundly affected by the scale of the emigration. The former, the relatively large-scale and far-reaching effects of the Caribbean diaspora in 'patria', was often expressed in a more reserved attitude towards Caribbean migrants on the part of the Dutch. The question of race relations gradually lost its former relatively easy-going character.

Events could hardly have proceeded differently, given the rather profound changes which the Netherlands underwent in the postwar period. The first wave of immigration from Indonesia was followed in the 1960s by the predominantly spontaneous influx of migrants from the Caribbean and the migration from the Mediterranean, which was initially organized from the Netherlands. More recently, the 'foreign' population has been enlarged with refugees and people seeking asylum. Now that these 'newcomers' account for around 7 per cent of the population, the Netherlands has been forced to become a multi-ethnic society, whether it likes it or not. This is particularly true of the large cities; more than 25 per cent of the population in Amsterdam is classified as of foreign extraction, and the corresponding percentage for young people is twice as high.

There are now good grounds for speaking of the emergence of an ethnic under-class. In terms of a number of socio-economic criteria, the 'foreign' population lags far behind the 'native' population, and although there are large differences within the various ethnic groups, generally speaking the gap between 'foreigners' and 'natives' is widening. The fact that this assumes less dramatic forms in the Netherlands than in many other immigration countries is closely connected with the social safety-net which still covers all aspects of life. However, state intervention of this kind has tended to disguise rather than prevent the marginal-ization of a very large number of new Dutch. With the ongoing contraction of the welfare state during the last few years, they too are beginning to experience how precarious it is to depend on a hand which can take as well as give.

In relative terms, the situation of the Dutch Caribbean diaspora is not so bad. There is a fairly large middle class, and according to the main socioeconomic indicators the position of Dutch citizens of (partly) Caribbean extraction is more favourable than that of the migrants from the Mediterranean. Understandably, however, the Surinamese and Antilleans do not compare their situation with that of other immigrants, but with that of the 'native' Dutch – and that picture is not so rosy. In addition, there is a degree of xenophobia and racism among the 'native' population; although its actual scale is the subject of debate, it is undeniably more pronounced than it was a few decades ago. This is the background against which one should view the concern and often anger or disenchantment of Caribbean Dutch at life in the capital. Materially it may be a better life than in the Caribbean, but by now it is by no means satisfying in terms of the new local standards which they have appropriated – to pass over the satisfaction, appreciation and happiness that many are unable to find here.

The new situation which arose as a result of the recent large-scale immigra-tion confronted the Netherlands with 'others' in an unprecedented way. While Italians were still considered pretty exotic around 1960, since then the borders have been extended (for 'Europeans'), but on the other hand it has become more difficult for outsiders to become 'Dutch'. Once again, this is much easier for someone from the Antilles or Surinam than for a Turk or Moroccan – as is clearly shown by interethnic relations and marriages – but it has indisputably become more difficult than it used to be. It is this trend which sometimes makes the older Caribbean migrants so bitter about the present-day situation, and which makes it virtually impossible for black youths to believe that things really were better 'in the old days' than they are now.

INTERPRETATIONS

If the fault lines are clearer than the continuity of the migration history, it is natural to ask what that early history still means for the present-day generations of Caribbean Dutch. There is not much point in raising this question for the more distant past; the answers are hidden too far back in time. We can ask ourselves what the experiences were of the earlier migrants who lived in a 'different' era. One wonders how did they feel in 'patria', that Surinam slave, that Curaçaoan child of a *shon* and his slave girl, those children from the colonial elites? How were they treated there? It is substance for speculation, but hardly anything serious can be said. Travellers from the elites have scarcely left any testimony. All that is left of the others are some scattered anecdotes and the occasional testimony. Only recent history has left a wide trail of bureaucratic and personal papers in its wake. In addition, the fact that it is in the imperfect tense means that those involved can still have their say.

Some ten years ago I carried out research on the history of Surinamese in the Netherlands. My research stopped at 1954 – an arbitrary limit except in a constitutional sense.[8] However, it was possible to have conversations with many older Surinamese who had already been in the Netherlands for years. At the same time my colleague Emy Maduro held interviews with older generations of Antilleans. The results of all these interviews did provide some contours of Caribbean life in the Netherlands between the 1930s and the 1960s. In brief, it was a period in which the Dutch hardly came into contact with West Indians or other non-whites. The rarity of such encounters usually had favourable results. It may be true that European culture was permeated by ethnocentrism and a feeling of superiority to the non-West; The Netherlands was no exception in this respect, and this had an effect on the attitude towards coloured migrants. All the same, if encounters took place at all, they were dominated by naivety and curiosity rather than hostility. Additional research in press and government archives introduced some clouds to this relatively untroubled sky, but did not substantially alter the picture. The same was true of remarks by the various interviewees themselves. 'In general we were treated well, though I can mention some annoying incidents as well. Fortunately they were not very common. In the last instance, it was easier for Surinamese then than nowadays.' And so on, often followed by a tirade against 'some Surinamese' who 'today spoil it for the rest'. My Curaçaoan colleague was told similar stories by her interviewees.

What were the contours? What comes over to us today is the indescribable shelteredness of the Netherlands in the middle decades of the century (the period of the German occupation was an altogether different story). The related lack of familiarity on the part of the Dutch with 'foreigners', especially if their skin was dark. The continual confusion of East Indians and West Indians. The idea that blacks only lived in Africa and the United States, not in the Dutch colonial empire. The myths and expectations regarding typical black characteristics, from a feeling for music to sexual prowess. The naïve remarks on skin pigmentation ('is it colourfast?'), hair, teeth. And, beside that lack of familiarity, a wide range of attitudes, from quiet fascination to undisguised irritation – though there was more of the former than of the latter, most of the interviewees stressed. 'Well-intentioned curiosity?' I sometimes asked, and the interviewee usually agreed.

In retrospect, I have come to realize that it is precisely the sheltered quality of life in the Netherlands at that time – incidentally, it should not be taken to imply that present-day Dutch culture is all that cosmopolitan either – which helps to explain the predominantly positive tone of the memories. It was apparently fairly easy for a lack of familiarity to make way for acceptance, once the other was recognized as 'one of us'. Despite all the external differences, this was an easy step to take in the case of the migrants from the Dutch Caribbean colonies. They spoke Dutch, the Surinamese remarkably well. They generally belonged to the colonial middle class, with its strongly Dutch-oriented culture. And they could often join subcultures with a certain sense of security. The Catholics from Curaçao picked up the thread again with the Lay Brothers and the Catholic universities in the South, while the Moravian background of the Surinam students made it easier for them to relate to the Protestant Free University. Likewise, Anton de Kom found a setting in the Communist movement which immediately recognized him as being 'one of us'. It was just as natural for the marines stationed in Terneuzen to be assisted by the villagers whom they had just liberated. One of the friendships that it provided in the case of the black but Catholic corporal Frank Koulen was that of the butcher. With winter approaching, he got a girl who lived nearby to knit the corporal a jumper; she later became his wife. Shelteredness implied a tendency to accept people in the same social situation, or like-minded people in a religious or ideological sense, despite what were initially such dominant differences. This openness created the conditions for a certain security.

This almost idyllic picture has to be taken with a pinch of salt. First, it has to be stated that, no matter how well-intentioned the surroundings may have been, isolation was almost always one of the factors which determined the experience. It was not until the 1950s that the Surinam associations gradually began to achieve something of the importance that they had had back in Surinam. In fact, however, it was not until the 1970s in the case of the Surinamese, and the 1980s in the case of the Curaçaoans, that they could boast something of a culture of their own on Dutch soil. It may be supposed that the earlier isolation created a sense of loneliness, and many of the interviewees confirmed this supposition. This is not everything, and perhaps not even the most difficult part. Isolation and loneliness cannot usually be reconstructed from the archives, and the same is true of the feelings of being accepted or not. Interviews with Surinamese or Antilleans can provide some further information on this point, but how much are they prepared to tell a (white Dutch) interviewer, how reliable are their memories, and, depending on the positions they adopt today, how willing are they to suppress or magnify their recollections?

My own experiences with this set of problems have made me more sceptical, not so much about the possibility of reconstructing events, nor even about the recording of emotions, but about how to assess them. Every individual life-story, every individual description of what took place or was experienced at some point in time is a construction which not only varies from one individual to another, but is equally dependent on the context in which the recollection is retold, the distance in time from the original event, and the audience that one hopes to reach (or not to reach). Let me try to make this clear with a few remarks on the stories about Frank Koulen. When I was recording his life story in 1984 and 1985, I had conversations mainly with him and with one of his three daughters. After his death in 1985, when I got to know the family better, I was surprised at the divergences between the stories, and started asking myself different questions. I offer them for consideration.

The degree of acceptance by the Dutch is always a key issue, even more than the feelings which are so hard to discuss which this evokes in the 'object'. Nothing seems to be a foregone conclusion. A nickname like 'the Negro' immediately underscores that the white environment could hardly forget about the difference in physical appearance. But hardly is not the same as never. And was 'the Negro' merely a neutral statement, like 'redhead' or 'longlegs', or was it a denigrating or affectionate term? What was more characteristic: the fact that the white woman wanted to marry this black man, and was allowed to do so, or the fact that various members of her family objected to it? Is it significant that some of the latter soon changed their minds completely? How is one to explain the fact that the various children from this one, tight-knit family – all coloured, something else that was seen in Terneuzen for the first time – have such different ideas about these questions, and have such different memories of their childhood? What is the relation between the development of their memory and their own later experiences, for some in the Netherlands, for others also or predominantly in the highly colour-sensitive Caribbean and the United States? And why does their white mother sometimes tell such different stories? Sometimes I can answer these questions, but I am simply raising them here to emphasize how careful we must be in interpreting all those individual migration stories. It is patently obvious that there is no single story, but an enormous collection of stories, and that the quest for the 'typical' story is only meaningful in a limited way. Perhaps we may succeed in reconstructing something of a lowest common denominator of experiences; but the feelings which go along with them cannot be reduced to a meaningful collection of experiences of the same kind. What we can and should do, however, is to reflect on ways of doing justice to the highly divergent stories. A first prerequisite in this respect is the recording and analysis of large collections of data and interviews. In turn, this calls for learning to scrutinize those stories for such obvious variables as ethnicity, nationality, gender, generation, class, kinship, length of stay, and degree of success in the new environment. Even then, the most difficult task is still probably that of searching for the space between what is told and what is felt.

One further remark in this connection. Researchers on Caribbean migration tend to concentrate on the migrants, but in the last resort to write an account in which their experiences and feelings are set within a broader framework. By now we have become aware of the fact that the migrants have their own story. At the same time, however, there is often a tendency to think in classic bipolar terms when it comes to tackling the question of where the 'real' stories are to be found. In this sense the research approach I once adopted now strikes me as naïve. It is a particularly inappropriate approach when we are writing about the early migrants, who in the Netherlands at least (characteristically!) chose white partners almost by definition – were able to choose them more easily than in England and in sharp contrast to the United States – and thus had racially mixed children.[9] It seems advisable to be less doctrinaire than our statisticians in this field, who in their quantifying wisdom polish the racist US principle that white plus black equals black. The statisticians decided on their classification on the basis of honourable considerations, but as historians it is better for us to try to represent life in its actual diversity. This implies, among other things, that we should talk more seriously with the white partners and surroundings, and not be too eager to represent the children as Caribbean while they might feel more British, French or Dutch.

'CIRCUS FIGURES'

In 1986 the Curaçaoan historian Emy Maduro and myself published the first book on Caribbean history in the Netherlands. Published simultaneously with a volume on the history of Indonesians in the metropolis,[10] *In het land van de overheerser II: Antillianen en Surinamers in Nederland, 1634/1667–1954* received a relatively large amount of publicity. Some two thousand copies were sold – a large figure for the Dutch-language market. The reviews, largely by outsiders, and personal reactions, mainly from those involved, were predominantly friendly. Ten years ago that all gave the idea of having made a substantial contribution not only to historiography but even to the awareness and to improving the image of the groups involved.

Nowadays it is easier to question the mildly euphoric mood of the time. Who read the book and was satisfied with it apart from a Dutch reading public that had not known anything about this history before? Mainly, I now believe, relatively small groups of Surinamese and Antilleans. First of all, those directly involved, who could now read and get others to read their forgotten history in terms which, despite the necessary academic distance, were still quite flattering. The image in which the older generations recognized themselves was that of serious students, hard workers, who were generally well treated but did not offer the slightest provocation not to be. They were also satisfied because they were not described as white Dutch, but as people who were proud of their origins and who at the same time could cope perfectly with the modernity of the Netherlands.

More politically oriented, nationalistic Surinamese and Antilleans could also feel well served by the book. Of course, the title helped, and the book devoted considerable attention to the nationalist victories of the diaspora: the pre-war agitation against racism and fascism, the spectacular career of Anton de Kom, suffering and resistance during the German occupation, and the postwar political and cultural nationalism. And then there were the sections on the period of accursed slavery, of course, which once again showed how dependent the slaves were on their masters, but also included stories of clever male and female slaves who, like genuine Anansis/Nanzis,[11] despite all opposition, obtained their freedom.

Once you are out of the warm shower, you begin to realize that not only the distribution of *In het land van de overheerser*, but in a general sense the interest in the subject, has nevertheless mainly been a matter for a small group of those directly involved, younger intellectuals, and a very limited Dutch public. The absence of any broader or more in-depth follow-up to the book by others is an indication of this. The themes of the few larger publications which did appear suggest the same: a collection of recollections of Anton de Kom, another with fragments from the history of Surinam nationalism in the Netherlands, a work of journalism full of anecdotes on 'the first Negro' in all kinds of obscure parts of the Netherlands, a biography of a Surinam jazz musician who preferred to be presented as a black *American* (even more exotic).[12] Then there was a catalogue of a controversial exhibition on Western images of blacks, in which that theme from *In het land van de overheerser* was treated in more detail and in a consid-erably more assertive tone, and the much more distanced treatment of the same subject by Blakely, *Blacks in the Dutch World*. The last two studies raise in particular the question of to what extent the cultural expressions analysed in them really reflect the development of (monolithic?) Dutch culture, and whether it is reasonable to speak about national reactions to a phenomenon (the presence of blacks, or images of blacks) that was completely marginal in the Netherlands until a few decades ago.[13]

The small number of the other publications and their apparently modest impact confirmed my doubts about the importance of publications of this kind, my own included. What do present-day Caribbean Dutch know about their 'prehistory'? What importance do they attach to it? As part of a larger survey, a non-select group of Dutch of Surinam or Antillean origin were asked what they knew about that early history.[14] The results confirmed my doubts resoundingly. The vast majority of the interviewees thought that Caribbean history in the Netherlands did not begin until the postwar period. Only a tiny minority knew that Surinam and Antillean slaves had been taken to the Netherlands in the past. Precisely a small number of highly engaged Surinamese described the early generation as 'a handful of circus figures', a reference to the late nineteenth-century colonial exhibitions with their areas for 'natives', or to the twentieth-century 'professional Negroes'. The prehistory has no point of reference at all to offer for Surinamese of British Indian or Javanese extraction: the diaspora of 'their' group began in the 1970s, and they hardly relate at all to the themes of Creole nationalism. Furthermore, there is no organized transfer of the history of the migrants. In so far as stories are told at all, this is done within a small circle, which is usually ethnically homogeneous. There have not been many attempts to place the story of the migrants in historical perspective through local television or radio programmes to date.

A conclusion is hard to avoid. You are not dead until you are forgotten. The history of Frank Koulen and all the other early migrants who remain anonymous here continues as long as their immediate relatives and friends still talk about them. But at the same time their stories – and this is even truer of the stories about the eighteenth-century slaves or nineteenth-century students – no longer appear to hold any interest at all for most Caribbean Dutch. The actual rupture in the migration history which can be situated around 1970 has also left its mark in the memory of the diaspora.

A MULTI-FACETED DIASPORA

So if the roots of the diaspora only reach back a couple of decades – two generations at most – in the experience of most Caribbean Dutch, can we speak of history at all? I am not arguing for a pointless internecine warfare between historians and (other) social scientists on who the legitimate 'owner' of the research object is. Still, we cannot entirely ignore the conclusion that we are addressing a history that is only just beginning, and that it is by no means clear what direction it is heading in. What is studied in a British Caribbean context is a story covering many generations, a history whose contours have gradually crystallized: the bifurcation towards England and the United States/Canada, the varying degrees of success in both directions, the degree of circularity of the migration, and the differences in behaviour and experiences of the various generations involved.

The Dutch Caribbean diaspora is still lacking in clear-cut contours. There is some clarity as regards which topics are analysed to death by social scientists, such as social mobility, position on the labour market, and participation in education. The picture that emerges from this research gives grounds for concern in some respects, but at the same time bears witness to large differences within the by no means uniform Caribbean Dutch population group. The ethnicity factor seems – justifiably – to be receiving more and more attention in these analyses. How could it be otherwise? Even where it is possible to carry out more historically oriented research, we cannot get around the fact that the Caribbean Dutch diaspora actually breaks down into widely divergent groups: the Curaçaoans and the Surinamese of Creole, British Indian and Javanese origin live in social spheres which are to a large extent different from one another. In this respect the British West Indian diaspora is considerably more homogeneous, despite the differences in island characters which are so often pinpointed.

A ready illustration of the importance of these ethnic contrasts is furnished by the indications that the Hindustani Surinam group is more successful in social terms than its Creole Surinam counterpart. Moreover, with respect to the use of leisure time and affective relations, the disparity which was so typical of Surinam is continued, or even reinforced, in the Netherlands. 'Race' is certainly not the only factor in this process. There is still an enormous gap separating the Afro-Surinam world from the Afro-Curaçaoan one. The cultural differences between the two groups were traditionally expressed most clearly in the mutual unintelligibility of their individual languages, i.e. Sranan Tongo and Papiamentu. The linguistic choice made in the diaspora could eventually diminish this cleavage, though, ironically enough, as a result of the 'colonial' language. For the time being this process is proceeding at a snail's pace. While Dutch – with all of its variations of Surinam-Dutch – is gradually gaining ground at the expense of Sranan Tongo among Afro-Surinamese, between themselves Curaçaoans in the Netherlands cling to Papiamentu, that unmistakable mark of their own culture.

In other respects too it is futile to imagine the Caribbean Dutch diaspora in uniform terms. The shorter duration of Antillean history in the Netherlands increases the orientation towards 'there'. The divergent paths followed by constitutional developments have also had a direct, painful effect on the migration. The continuing 'post-colonial' status of the Netherlands Antilles – a relatively autonomous part of the Kingdom of the Netherlands – guarantees Antilleans both a comparatively high standard of living on the islands and the right to freedom of movement between the two parts of the Kingdom and to settle in either of them. It is therefore hardly surprising that there is a large degree of two-way traffic in the case of Curaçaoan migrants. The contrast with Surinam is stark. Not only have the standard of living and the economic prospects there fallen dramatically in the two decades since independence, at the same time independence heralded the end of the possibility of settling freely in either country. The protracted crisis has meant a virtual drying up of the return migration to Surinam. The new constitutional relation also made it more and more difficult to follow the legal route to the Netherlands; hence an increasing number of Surinamese left illegally for the former mother country.

WHERE IS HOME?

How important is 'there' today for Caribbean Dutch, and to what extent do Surinamese differ from Antilleans in the way they think and talk? I have tried to obtain some insight into these questions by means of street research. When asked where their close relatives lived, more than half replied that they lived mainly in the Netherlands; only half that number replied that most of their relatives lived 'there'. As one would expect, the latter figure was appreciably higher for the Antilleans than for the Surinamese – twice as high, in fact. For these Antilleans, then, the word 'family' still refers primarily to 'there', a stage which the Surinam interviewees passed long ago (Table 8.1).

Of course, the place of residence of the close relatives elicits a natural affinity, and in this sense it is striking to what extent the Surinam Dutch we interviewed in the Netherlands are rooted there. However, this does not mean that they have forgotten their overseas relatives and friends. There were no significant differences between the various groups in the frequency of telephone calls;

Table 8.1 Domicile of close relatives, related to ethnic background of respondents

| | Ethnic background | | | | | Total |
	C	H	M	J	A	
In the Netherlands	37	9	3	1	4	54
In country of origin	10	5	4	1	9	29
Evenly distributed	8	5	1	1	4	19
Elsewhere	–	1	–	–	–	1
Total	55	20	8	3	17	103

Abbreviations: C, Creole Surinamese; H, Hindustani Surinamese; M, Surinamese of mixed origins; J, Javanese Surinamese; A, Antilleans.

Table 8.2 Dispatch of parcels and/or money remittance to the country of origin, related to ethnic background of respondents

| | Ethnic background | | | | | Total |
	C	H	M	J	A	
Yes, ships parcels/sends money	41	11	4	1	2	59
No, does not send anything	13	9	4	2	14	42
No reply	1	–	–	–	1	2
Total	55	20	8	3	17	103

Abbreviations: C, Creole Surinamese; H, Hindustani Surinamese; M, Surinamese of mixed origins; J, Javanese Surinamese; A, Antilleans.

though the number of Surinamese who hardly correspond any more was high, at least in this sample. Nor were there significant differences in the frequency of visits. On the other hand, the majority of Creole Surinamese in particular indicated that they regularly sent food parcels or money (Table 8.2). The considerably better economic situation on Curaçao probably explains why this direct support does not play any significant part in the Antillean Dutch circuit.

Another question is that of the affinity which Caribbean Dutch feel with 'here' and 'there'. Once again, the sample suggests that the Surinamese, especially the younger generation, identify more closely with their new home country than the Antilleans do; but in both cases this orientation remains ambivalent (Table 8.3). Further questioning confirmed the natural supposition that most of them also feel a close affinity with 'fellow countrymen or countrywomen'. In general, they also feel a close affinity with 'fellow countrymen' in the Netherlands; this affinity extends to a lesser extent to Caribbean Dutch from elsewhere. At the same time, however, the orientation of Surinamese and Antilleans in an intimate sphere like that of choice of partner shifts towards Dutch partners alongside or even in preference to 'fellow countrymen or countrywomen', a shift which is confirmed by the impressions one gets from walking down the street today.

Table 8.3 Affinity with the country of origin and/or the Netherlands, related to age and ethnic background of respondents

	Age					Ethnic background					Total
	I	II	III	IV	V	C	H	M	J	A	
Mainly with the Netherlands	1	13	11	6	3	18	8	4	–	4	34
Mainly with c.o.o.	3	11	10	11	7	21	7	3	2	9	42
With both	–	4	11	1	4	13	5	–	–	2	20
Declines choice	1	1	–	–	1	1	–	–	1	1	3
No reply	–	–	2	1	1	2	–	1	–	1	4
Total	5	29	34	19	16	55	20	8	3	17	103

Abbreviations: I = < 20 years; II, 20–29 years; III, 30–39 years; IV, 40–49 years; V, ≥ 50 years; c.o.o., country of origin; C, Creole Surinamese; H, Hindustani Surinamese; M, Surinamese of mixed origins; J, Javanese Surinamese; A, Antilleans.

Table 8.4 Desire to remigrate eventually to country of origin, related to ethnic background and sex of respondents.

	Ethnic background					Sex		Total
	C	H	M	J	A	Female	Male	
Will return	14	1	2	–	10	14	13	27
Conditionally positive	22	11	3	1	2	22	17	39
Will stay in the Netherlands	18	7	3	2	3	16	17	33
No reply	1	1	–	–	2	4	–	4
Total	55	20	8	3	17	56	47	103

Abbreviations: C, Creole Surinamese; H, Hindustani Surinamese; M, Surinamese of mixed origins; J, Javanese Surinamese; A, Antilleans.

Note: Category of 'conditionally positive': respondent expresses intention to remigrate, but makes return conditional upon significant improval of the situation in the country of origin.

Finally, the bitter reality of the differences in the standard of living 'there' is directly expressed in the prospects of ever going back (Table 8.4). Most of the Antilleans assumed that they would return. This was appreciably more complex for Surinamese. A large majority responded that they would (re)settle in Surinam at some point in the future, but most of the members of this group tied this wish to a number of conditions. The reality of the migration statistics suggests that they were expressing a wish or a socially desirable reply rather than a genuine option.

The results of this modest sample suggest a clear-cut difference between Curaçaoans and Surinamese; on the other hand, neither gender nor generation seem to play an important role in this sample, nor does the ethnic background of the Surinamese. While both groups retain a sense of affinity with the country of birth and with fellow countrymen both in the Netherlands and in the Caribbean, there is much less likelihood that the Surinamese desire to return expresses a real option. This difference cannot be explained in terms of a significantly better position of the Surinamese in the Netherlands, but is connected with the troubled situation in Surinam itself. One might expect that the orientation towards 'there' will decrease further among later generations. The fact that this does not emerge from the statistics indicates that the younger Dutch generation of Surinam origin still feels a certain involvement with that country, but also that among the older generation of Surinamese too, the orientation has shifted, in the direction of *Bakrakondre*. The fact that this is apparently much less true of the Antilleans is partly due to the more favourable situation on their island. In addition, it is relevant that the Antillean migration to *Ulanda* started up later and was on a smaller scale – the island still exists for them as the paradise overseas, while the Surinamese lost their Eldorado long ago.

In all kinds of gradations, the lives of these migrants, and especially of their children, are still firmly orientated on 'here' and 'there', on a Caribbean background and on the mother country that never had such a direct significance before. One might be tempted to forget that this orientation has remained remarkably limited. Despite the fact that many have found their feet in the Netherlands, for many others *Bakrakondre* or *Ulanda* has completely failed to offer the opening to social success or personal development. The statistics on the labour market, education, housing, etc. point in the same direction as those on medical consumption or crime: there is still a long way to go, and many will deny that the right route has been chosen. All the same, the option of a different destination is hardly of any importance; the rather worn metaphor of the umbilical cord linking the mother country with the former colonies is more relevant than ever. This is striking, and is evidence not just of the time-hallowed intertwining of interests which is so often cited, but equally of the postcolonial 'trap': although the Netherlands may not be an easy destination, it is still the country where there is the best chance of success, and where failure can be concealed the longest.

The Dutch Caribbean case is not an isolated one. Generally speaking, the Caribbean migration to Europe is much more heavily influenced by the attractiveness of what by Caribbean and American standards is an extremely extended welfare state – a magnet which turns out to be a trap now that many of these facilities are being curtailed. This is as true of the West Indians in England and of the *négropolitains* in France as it is of the Caribbeans in the Netherlands. These former subjects enjoy more privileges than other groups of immigrants, such as unconditional citizenship and access to social services. All the same, their situation is sometimes even less favourable than that of other immigrants. In the case of the USA, the parallel contrast can be drawn between what were generally characterized – until recently – as successful West Indians, on the one hand, and the Puerto Ricans in New York and its vicinity who are often regarded as losers.

The awkward question rears it head: are (post)colonial traumatization and patronizing perhaps factors which make it difficult for the *nuyoricans* in the USA, the Jamaicans in England and the Martiniquans in France to make full use of what is in theory a relatively favourable starting position? Might the same apply to migrants from the Antilles and Surinam in the Netherlands? Might the frustration of many Caribbean Dutch about the lack of success be connected with unrealistic expectations, the result of a feeling cultivated for generations that everything is better there, and a feeling which became attached to this later on that *Ulanda* or *Bakrakondre* is obliged to give after having taken for so long? There seems to be a lot to be said for such a hypothesis, and for the conclusion that this attitude not only increases frustration but also has a paralysing effect; not just because the discontented stop believing in their own ability, but also in the sense that the number of those who decide to seek their fortune outside the Netherlands is still negligible.[15] For those who fail to seize the opportunities, the protection afforded by the mother country can imperceptibly be transformed into a stranglehold.

OLD STORIES AND A NEW FUTURE

The history of Dutch Caribbean migration is marked, not by continuities, but by a fault line which has emerged in the last decades. Furthermore, there is no single history which unites Surinam and the Antilles. Finally, while the Dutch Caribbean migrants are part of a much larger story about Caribbean migrations, there are hardly any traces of an awareness of this fact. No matter how much has been said about a shared fate, the Caribbean diaspora is still essentially divided, ignorant and uninterested in the parallel histories.

What does all this mean for the historiography of the Dutch Caribbean diaspora? First of all, it would be incorrect not to differentiate between Antilleans and Surinamese. In fact, it even seems misguided to attribute a single past to the different ethnic groups from Surinam. Another point which should be borne in mind is that the circularity of the migration currents, the continuous come and go of migrants which is so often assumed in studies of the Caribbean diaspora must be investigated and not taken as given. In view of the fact that the gap between the Netherlands and Surinam seems to be growing, it is no longer so natural that historians of the diaspora should continue to let themselves be guided by the ever more mythical idea of the first generations of migrants, as if the transatlantic crossing were to remain a constant two-way traffic. The Antillean migration history seems to fit the standard Caribbean pattern better than the Surinam one-way traffic. But perhaps it is sensible not to accept the cherished ideas on a Caribbean migration movement, which is always two-directional, too readily.

The Dutch Caribbean population numbers 365,000, and will continue to grow. However, it is bound to become increasingly Dutch, although at the same time it is creating it own niches in a dominant culture which, in turn, partly as a result of the spectrum of migrations, is also continuously caught up in a process of relatively profound change. All the same, it is obvious that Caribbean culture in exile is under much heavier pressure than the culture of the 'mother country', no matter how much globalization embraces all cultures. In this sense the commonly voiced belief in the resilience of those Caribbean cultures which even flourish in the relative isolation of the diaspora seems to be overoptimistic. Similar caution should be exercised regarding the belief in the 'transnational family networks' which are supposed to link the Caribbean diaspora with what is perhaps too readily labelled 'home'. The prehistory of the current diaspora may go back a long way, but it took a decisive new turn a couple of decades ago. Historians will increasingly have to write a story of detachment from 'there' and the often difficult, often discouraged attachment to 'here'. A lot of this work is already being done by an army of social scientists, but the fact that even the liveliest studies lack a sense of history would appear to say something, not only about the researchers and their interests, but also about the low level of interest in the history of the migration on the part of their interviewees.

Still, there are wonderful tales to be told, and they *are* told. When I first recorded stories of this kind more than ten years ago, I had hardly any idea of their depth and scope, nor of the inevitable, almost systematic distortions, repetitions and clichés they contain. The challenge is undoubtedly to search further for stories, and in the process to raise different, less obvious questions and to make connections. The stories are there, even though the earliest, from before the exodus, are growing more and more scarce. Particularly the older generation of Surinamese and Antilleans from the single round of street interviews indicated that they passed on the stories of their own histories, stories which are certainly given a hearing. Historians can help to preserve those stories, but they should do so without romanticizing them. The 'old' stories of isolated migrants in an almost 100 per cent white world belong definitively to the past.

Surinam war veterans have often complained bitterly that their role in the Second World War was never noticed. It is a justifiable complaint, but at the same time this will never change: they were simply a minimal group. Their stories run into the dozens only. They are no match for the stories of millions of others. Only now has that all changed, only now are the Caribbean Dutch a visible group in Dutch society. But it does not matter to the veterans any more. Their history remains an early footnote to the exodus. A few observers of the 5 May parade may be reminded of touching memories of a Caribbean migrant, but that history is not the same as the history which is being written today.

NOTES

1 The surname was taken to Surinam around the turn of the century by another migrant worker. *Balata bleeder* Samuel Frederik Koulen, born in Berbice in 1881, was recorded as living at Achterstraat 5 in Nieuw Nickerie, although at the time of the census he was 'away (in the forest)', *1921 Census, Nickerie District*. (Balata is a rubberlike substance produced from the latex of the balata tree; the labourers who worked in the interior of the Guyanas to extract latex from the trees were called balata bleeders.)

2   After the German occupation of the Netherlands and the Japanese occupation of Indonesia, these two Caribbean colonies were the only 'free' Dutch territories.

3   The survey of Dutch Caribbean history is mainly taken from Gert Oostindie and Emy Maduro, *In het land van de overheerser II: Antillianen en Surinamers in Nederland, 1634/1667–1954* (Dordrecht: Foris, 1986); and my articles, 'Caribbean migration to the Netherlands: a journey to disappointment?', in Malcolm Cross and Han Entzinger (eds), *Lost Illusions: Caribbean Minorities in Britain and the Netherlands* (London: Routledge, 1988, pp. 54–72); 'Preludes to the exodus: Surinamers in the Netherlands, 1667–1960s', in Gary Brana-Shute (ed.), *Resistance and Rebellion in Surinam: Old and New* (Williamsburg: College of William and Mary, 1990, pp. 231–58); and 'Migrations et identités des populations Caribéennes aux Pays-Bas', in Fred Reno (ed.), *Identité et politique de la Caraïbe et de l'Europe multiculturelles* (Paris: Economica, 1995, pp. 59–80); plus the literature cited there. For present purposes, I have refrained from giving detailed refererences.

4   The Netherlands Antilles consisted of six islands until the separation of Aruba (1986). The migrants are predominantly from the main island, Curaçao. Therefore, in this text 'Antilleans' and 'Curaçaoans' are generally used interchangeably.

5   Cf. Livio Sansone, *Schitteren in de schaduw: Overlevingsstrategieën, subcultuur en etniciteit van Creoolse jongeren uit de lagere klasse in Amsterdam 1981–1990* (Amsterdam: Het Spinhuis, 1992).

6   The population in Surinam itself is estimated at less than 400,000, that from the Netherlands Antilles at 215,000 (160,000 of them on Curaçao), and that of Aruba at 85,000. More than half of the interviewees in the street survey were unable to provide a reasonable estimate of the number of people 'there', or of the number of their fellow countrymen in the Netherlands.

7   See my 'Ethnicity, nationalism, and the exodus: the Dutch Caribbean predicament', in Gert Oostindie (ed.), *Ethnicity in the Caribbean* (London: Macmillan, 1996, pp. 206–31).

8   In 1954, the *Statuut* or Charter of the Kingdom of the Netherlands was promulgated, granting for the first time a high degree of domestic autonomy to the two Caribbean partners in what then became the tripartite Kingdom. Whereas Surinam became independent in 1975, the Netherlands Antilles and (since its secession from The Netherlands Antilles in 1986) Aruba still function within the same regime, and have repeatedly declined to move from their present semi-autonomy to full independence.

9   Scholars like Chamberlain and Olwig, despite their correct and theoretically interesting emphasis on the importance of family networks in the migration process, do not pay much attention to the consequences of interracial relations for the family network, which is then by definition no longer exclusively Caribbean (in terms of origin or orientation). This approach may be justified to a large extent in the US or British context, but it is clearly too restrictive for dealing with the French Caribbean and Dutch Caribbean migration history. Cf. Mary Chamberlain, 'Family narratives and migration dynamics: Barbadians to Britain', *New West Indian Guide* 69 (1995), pp. 253–75; and 'Absence and the "Consolation of Freedom": British-Barbadian identities' (unpublished paper, presented to the International Conference on Oral History, Columbia University, New York, 18–23 October 1994). Karen Fog Olwig, *Global Culture, Island Identity: Continuity and Change in the Afro-Caribbean Community of Nevis* (Reading: Harwood Academic Publishers, 1993); and 'Life stories: individual and family in the migration process' (unpublished paper, presented at the KITLV/Royal Institute of Linguistics and Anthropology, Leiden, 8 May 1996).

10   Harry Poeze *et al.*, *In het land van de overheerser I: Indonesiërs in Nederland, 1600–1950* (Dordrecht: Foris, 1986). In translation, the title would be *In the Land of the Ruler*.

11 Anansi/Anancy/Nanzi/Nancy – a character in African/Caribbean folklore – is a spider who assumes different shapes and forms to escape from numerous scrapes.

12 Cf. Rudie Kagie, *De eerste neger: Herinneringen aan de komst van een nieuwe bevolkingsgroep* (Bussum: Wereldvenster 1989); Herman Oppenneer, *Kid Dynamite: De legende leeft* (Amsterdam: Mets, 1995); *Vereniging Ons Suriname 18 januari 1919–18 januari 1989* . . . (Amsterdam: Ons Suriname), 1990.

13 Blakely has some provocative suggestions in this respect, while Nederveen Pieterse takes it all to be a matter of course, which is hardly very satisfactory: Allison Blakely, *Blacks in the Dutch World: The Evolution of Racial Imagery in a Modern Society* (Bloomington: Indiana University Press, 1993); Jan Nederveen Pieterse, *Wit over Zwart: Beelden van Afrika en zwarten in de Westerse populaire cultuur* (Amsterdam: Koninklijk Instituut voor de Tropen, 1990).

14 The interviews were held in Amsterdam, Rotterdam, The Hague, Leiden and Zoetermeer in the summer of 1995. I would like to thank the interviewees for their willingness to reply to the questions. A total of 103 interviews were conducted and processed. The research findings were processed in forty tables, four of which are reproduced here; the other relevant results are summarized in the text. I would like to thank Ronnie Lemmers, Ineke ten Kate, Paul van de Koevering, Ingrid Koulen, Marco Last and Roselle Servage for the enthusiastic and conscientious assistance that they lent to the research.

15 Though a small tributary of the Surinam diaspora has developed in the United States during the last few decades.

9 Family and identity

Barbadian migrants to Britain

Mary Chamberlain

'Our family love to travel' Olive told me,

> my grandfather was in Cuba and send for my two uncles. . . . He leave the girls
> . . . with his wife. Then after my mother could get grown up, then she went to
> Trinidad . . . and leave me very small, as a baby. . . . [My mother] was working
> in Trinidad. . . . Then she . . . went on to Panama and meet her husband there.
> He took her from Panama to Jamaica. . . . I come up to England, 1958.[1]

Between 1955 and 1966, over 27,000 Barbadians migrated to Britain.[2] It was
the largest mass migration from the island since that to Panama in the first
two decades of the twentieth century, when approximately 45,000 Barbadians
migrated.[3] The decades in between saw a steady flow of Barbadians to destinations within the Caribbean and beyond, to North and South America. Fear of the
consequences of unemployment, and the resulting claims for overpopulation, led
the government of Barbados to play an active role in the twentieth century in
securing outlets for employment abroad. As early as 1905, a recruitment office
was established in Bridgetown to encourage the movement of labour to Panama.
Similar offices were established throughout the 1930s and 1940s to recruit labour
to the United States. In I955 the government began a Sponsored Workers Scheme
and appointed a Liaison Officer in London whose brief was to secure employment for Barbadians in Britain. 'The population pressure in Barbados is such,'
wrote the Liaison Officer in London to the Permanent Secretary of the Ministry
of Transport and Labour 'that migration is the only solution.'[4]

This was in marked contrast to nineteenth-century government policy which,
despite a high population density[5] and widespread poverty, perceived migration
as a threat to the plantation economy and restricted it through legislation. Yet
for the former slaves, independence from plantation discipline was a vital
post-Emancipation goal. Given the shortage of land and opportunity in
nineteenth-century Barbados, migration was seen by them as a route towards
achieving this end. Popular goals and government policy were directly opposed.
Wherever possible, therefore, Barbadians left,[6] and returned. Within popular
perception, such migrations appeared not only as sources of income, but also
as assertions of independence, if not acts of defiance, or heroism (given the
location of the island and the dangers of sea travel).

By the end of the nineteenth century the government reversed its policy and encouraged migration.[7] Throughout the twentieth century Barbadians travelled: Panama and Cuba, Curaçao and Trinidad, America and Britain, each destination coinciding with demands for labour from overseas. Olive's story was one I was to hear repeated many times. Yet the significance of her story lies not in the locations described, nor in the brief history of migration which it encapsulates, but in the simple fact that hers was a *family* which 'love to travel'.

Two major themes – motive and identity – pervade British studies of post-war Caribbean migration. In the first instance, using governmental and official data, the motive is perceived to be rational and economic, driven by a broader dynamic conforming to 'safety valve' policies in the home country, and labour demand in Britain. In the second, the focus has passed beyond an initial concern with problems of adjustment and assimilation in the metropole into investigating alienation, deviance, and/or the development of cultural form. Few academic studies have used oral sources, and none have investigated migration using family histories as primary data. Indeed, most studies written from this metropolitan perspective have perceived migration from the Caribbean as a discrete and aberrant event, rather than part of the Caribbean's continuing history of mobility, and have conflated individual island cultures into a broad Caribbean experience.

Once, however, family histories are taken as a perspective, then the motives for migration, and questions of identity, become more complex, ambiguous, and culturally specific. The significance of the family has long preoccupied the social and behavioural sciences. The family is central in the process of socialization, in the creation of attitudes and culture, and for the understanding of behaviour and relationships. Although some historians have looked to demography to provide clues to shifting family structures over time, or to genealogy for tracing family allegiances and lineage, most historians have been slow to recognize the role of the family in the process of social change or stasis. Even oral historians use family detail as a mirror to reflect the mentalities of a period, rather than the tool to understanding how those mentalities have been constructed and shaped, transmitted and transformed. The emphasis, and the debate, has been around the substance of memory, rather than the historical *context* in which memory is formulated and reformulated.

It is this context which needs now to be examined, for what may appear to be an individual, economic motive in migration often involves a family history of social and geographic mobility; equally, what may appear as a response to structural forces and migration policies may derive from, and conform to, a culture of migration which places not only a material but a symbolic value on the process itself. At the same time, questions of identity are not reduced to forms of cultural expression in the metropole, but shift into a more contradictory, and mobile set of allegiances in which, again, the family, as the generator and reflector of culture, plays a central role. This tips the analytical balance away from the host and into the home society. From this perspective, migration is seen as the norm, not a departure from it, and the image of the migrant searching for an identity – like Peter Pan, chasing a shadow – becomes irrelevant.

This chapter arises from life-story interviews with fifty Barbadians. To date, interviews have been conducted with two generations of family members, though the project will include third-generation family members. I contacted the majority of informants through members of the Barbados Association and conducted nineteen interviews with migrants resident in Britain, sixteen with their parents in Barbados, and fifteen with return migrants. Contact was made with the latter through Barbadian friendship networks in Britain. Of the group of migrants and return migrants, all but two had family members of previous generations migrate. Statistically this is not surprising given the high levels of migration from Barbados throughout the twentieth century.

It becomes immediately apparent, however, that most families will include a model for migration, which suggests that the motivation to move may well originate as much in the family as in the material and structural conditions surrounding departure. In this sample, migration is the rule, rather than the exception. What form the family model assumes may, however, be more ambiguous and will have a bearing on perception and attitudes to migration and identity. This chapter attempts to explore questions of motive and identity by tracing a detailed lineage of migration within three families from the overall sample, and by focusing on two particular themes, the structure of families and models of migration.

One important characteristic of Barbadian families is the generational leap-frogging of childcare. Olive,[8] whose story began this chapter, had been brought up, in her mother's absence (in Trinidad), by her maternal grandmother and great-grandmother. Lola, her great-grandmother, had also raised Olive's mother (whose father was away in Cuba, and whose mother had to work). When Olive migrated to Britain in 1956, she left three of her four children in the care of her mother, and the fourth, her son Jasper, in the care of her grandmother, whom, Jasper recalls, 'I loved . . . dearly . . . she was so much a part of me. . . . I sometimes believe that my great-grandmother is still looking after me.'[9]

'Our family,' Olive insists, was 'very, very close.'[10] 'A big, happy family,' according to Jasper,[11] in which family identity was the primary loyalty and where,

> family meant something. The family relationship was very strong. My grandfather had about three women . . . and this all became part of the family . . . because we all belonged to one person . . . my grandfather. . . . The outside[12] family and the inside family, all were family.[13]

As a result, 'relatives used to travel for miles to bring . . . provisions'[14] to provide continuing support for each other. The family facilitated migration in other ways. Olive's grandfather, who migrated to Cuba, paid for the passage to Cuba for his sons. In the same way, when Olive's husband first went to Britain, it was her mother who provided the money for the passage. Throughout the travels of the family members, close contact and financial support was maintained. When Olive's uncles followed their father to Cuba, 'they send back [remittances] to their mum. [When] my mother went too, my mum send back to her mum, they're always sending. . . . My uncle came from Curaçao . . . and used to send out a lot of clothes . . . and everything you could think of.'[15] In the same way, when Olive's husband migrated, her mother (by then in Jamaica) used, as Jasper recalled, 'to send money for us . . . maybe once every fortnight',[16] until his father was in a position to send money home.

In this family, the pattern of childcare and family support enabled the migration of three generations of its members. At the same time, migration assisted in the maintenance of the family back home It was a reciprocal pattern, ensuring family loyalty and a continuing family identity across the generations and across the seas. It may account for the ultimate return of family members to Barbados, which in turn became a component of this family's model of migration. Olive's grandfather returned from Cuba. Her uncle returned from Curaçao. Olive and Jasper both returned in 1988 from Britain. Jasper's daughter, although born in Britain, has also returned to Barbados.

But there is another script which helps to account for this loyalty and identification. Both Olive and Jasper stress that they were not 'plantation people', that is, agricultural labourers. They may have worked *at* a plantation; they were not *of* the plantation. This pride of independence can be traced to Lola who, in the nineteenth century, succeeded in buying the family an acre of land from the plantation for ten dollars.

Until the twentieth century, the majority of black Barbadians were plantation labourers, governed by the Contract Law of 1840, which bound them to work exclusively for the plantation from whom a 'house spot' was rented. Since most of the land was under white ownership, and since black labourers had little money to buy land, the majority were forced to rent land (a house spot) from the plantation and became liable, therefore, under the Contract Law. The Contract Law, imposed after the abolition of slavery, was perceived as its successor,[17] and one of the major impediments to realizing, in material terms, the freedom promised by the (full) Emancipation of 1838. It was not repealed until 1937. The desire to be independent of the plantation was very strong, although until the first two decades of the twentieth century (and the money generated from the migration to Panama) relatively few could achieve it.[18] Lola, however, had raised sufficient money, by baking and selling bread, to buy the family both land and release from the Contract Law. Although the house no longer exists, Jasper remembers,

> there is a corner . . . known as Lola's Corner . . . where she baked. . . . There's nothing there now, just the piece of land . . . which has been handed down from the family, from Lola to her daughter, which was my great-grandmother, to my grandmother, to my mother, and I suppose my mother pass it on to me.[19]

Lola's independence, of which the land remains a potent symbol, provides a clue to the sense of pride and family identity. It pervades the accounts of her family, whether they were descendants by blood or marriage. Olive's grandfather returned from Cuba 'a wealthy man', a fisherman who owned three boats and was able to support 'his own family at home, plus his outside relationships'.[20] Olive's uncle returned from Curaçao and built a 'lovely bungalow'. It pervades also the choice of occupation. Lola was a baker. Olive's grandmother was a cook; her mother had a restaurant business in Jamaica. Jasper himself made his money from catering. 'Our family,' as Olive says, 'belong to the kitchen'.[21]

The role of Lola was fundamental in the creation of family identity. There is a clear recollection of genealogy and a recognition of her role in differentiating and demarcating the family route away from direct dependence on the plantation. Lola's aspirations had become incorporated into a family dynamic and had generated a family loyalty which was as much a part of the family inheritance as Lola's Corner. Jasper believed his great-grandmother's spirit lived in him. At the same time, the family permitted and encouraged migration, and the model of migration and successful return created in the family was one which supported and enhanced this dynamic. Although the decision to leave, made by different members of this family, may have been prompted by a simple and time-specific economic expedient, the movement contains within it a far more complex history of social mobility, and geographic migration, in which loyalty to and identity with the family and with Barbados were maintained and strengthened.

The model of migration offered in the second family is more ambivalent. Here, the theme which emerges is one of struggle and resistance, and a reshaping of the family migration model. It is a theme consistent through two generations, although it assumes a different form. Charles was born in 1913 in St George, Barbados. He has two children of whom Irene, the eldest, migrated to Britain in 1960.

Charles's father migrated to Panama before he was born. He sent no remittances and made no contact. Charles never knew his father. Although his mother remained in Barbados, Charles was raised by his maternal grandparents. One maternal uncle who had also gone to Panama did, however, send remittances which proved the leitmotif of Charles's life:

> When I were at the age of 12 years old, my uncle . . . said he want me to go to secondary school because the people in Panama who is educated gets the best job. . . . My grandmother had a brother and he worked on an estate as the bookkeeper. The white half could work there.[22] . . . So I was to go to Combermere.[23] I had my money, my books, my khaki suit, everything ready. The money . . . that my uncle send to pay for the school fees, it was eight dollars and eight cents. I will never forget this as long as I live. . . . I was home one evening . . . and my grandmother sister came very dressed. Two sisters came, two aunts, and my grandmother get dress. I saw her boots, her umbrella, and they leave. I do not know where they were going. But the next thing I heard, my uncle that was the bookkeeper . . . they ship him to Canada. . . . My grandmother took the money, with my two aunts, and ship my uncle to Canada.[24]

This uncle had got 'heself in trouble', through gambling with 'all these white fellas'.[25] Unlike Olive's family, this model of migration is confusing. Charles's father migrates and abandons him. One uncle migrates and promises him a better future. Another uncle 'robs' him of that future, by leaving himself on the money destined for Charles's education. The story of the 'robbery' occurred within the first few minutes of the interview. It was all Charles wished to tell. The interview concluded:

> I made a oath. . . . If I walk the road, pick paper bag, bottles and sell, my children got to get a secondary education. . . . I've made that vow, for what my family did me. . . . But my other two friends (who went to Combermere) . . . ent as successful as me. I came out successful. My children will get education. I have a roof over my head and I am not hungry . . . I don't owe nobody nothing. Nothing.[26]

How did that success come about? Charles himself migrated shortly after his marriage to Muriel in 1941. He went first to Trinidad, then to St Lucia. After the war, he migrated to America, then returned to St Lucia where he stayed until 1978 when he retired and came home to Barbados. Charles was a master tailor by trade. He secured work, however, as a clerk on the American bases in St Lucia, even though 'I were not educated . . . I didn't went to Combermere but . . . I was really bright, man.'[27] His wife helped him in his work. 'And I thank she. . . . First thing she made me do, bought a dictionary and I got . . . a small book . . . algebras, different arithmetic . . . how to make up accounts, reports, all different things.'[28]

He worked as a clerk all his life, supplementing his income with tailoring. On each migration, Charles insisted that his family accompany him. 'No where I go to live and . . . there's no way my family can't come. . . . I have seen too many homes broken up.'[29] It was a story which his daughter, Irene, reflected upon:

> My mother said that when my father sent for her, everybody says 'You're not going to St Lucia?' They thought it was bush and forest and snakes and donkeys . . . They said . . . 'That's no place to take a child.' And so my father said, 'But now we're a family' . . . that's as he saw it, that we were a family and you don't split a family up. . . . He's always kept and maintained that . . . They say black men don't have that kind of responsibility, the women are usually left to do everything . . . they blame slavery, they blame the . . . economic set up in the West Indies. Well, it certainly wasn't the case in my family. I don't know where my father got his ideas from.[30]

On one level, Charles's own migration enabled him to fulfil the oath he made for himself when 'robbed' of his education. Throughout his narrative, the notion of being 'robbed' was frequently portrayed. Migration became synonymous with theft and absence. His motivation appeared to be to restore what he perceived as a lost inheritance – of education, success, and family. Charles paid for his two children to go to secondary school. Both now have university degrees.

This was a family that was 'together', but where, because of migration, the extended family did not function in an active or supportive role. In order to understand Irene's motivation for migrating to England in 1960, we need also to look at her mother, Muriel. She came from a family who 'felt we was a different breed, more elaborate in that neighbourhood [in Barbados]'.[31] Muriel's grandfather owned a 'big, upstairs house. Thirty, forty acres of land. He was a rich man.'[32] Like Lola, in the first story, he had amassed his fortune and secured the family's independence. Unlike her, this was the result of remittances sent by his children who had migrated to Panama and the United States.

The family employed servants in the house and hired labour to work the land. Muriel passed through seventh standard at elementary school and was sent to learn dressmaking. She wanted to be a nurse,

> I was very bright too ... [but] I believe my parents were a bit ... backward ... not that they didn't have the money to pay.... They would look out for the boys more than the girls, because [they say] a woman role in the house.... If I had my life to live over ... I would be a brilliant woman some part of the world.[33]

In St Lucia, Muriel and Charles had servants in the house and, like Muriel's mother, hired labour to work the land. She engaged in voluntary work. Her friends were 'doctors and lawyers'. She helped Charles become a white-collar worker. For her, migration created her family's wealth and enabled her to maintain her status. Her only regret was her lack of further education.

For their daughter, Irene, the perspective on migration synthesized the complexities of class and struggle which was her familial inheritance. According to Irene, her father, Charles, migrated 'because he married my mother. It sounds silly, but for some reason he wasn't accepted by the family. Then he thought he was going to ... make a life for himself and come back to Barbados and ... prove his worth, so to speak.'[34] Irene grew up in St Lucia,

> and that was awful.... St Lucians tended not to like the Barbadians very much.... It was always 'You're from Barbados, why don't you go back where you came from?' ... I wanted to belong and to be accepted, so I learned to speak patois.... I joined the Catholic religion, all that.[35]

Irene felt an outsider in St Lucia, distanced by nationality, culture, and by class: 'I wouldn't say that we were wealthy, but ... we had servants ... and the best of everything ... beautiful hand-made leather shoes ... music lessons, all that sort of thing ... and that created a lot of envy in people.'[36] She also felt an outsider in her own family in Barbados, 'I missed out on all this sort of grandma, granddad, aunts, uncles, cousins, all that sort of thing.... When I met them I always felt somehow an outsider.'[37] 'The whole thing came to a head for me,' she explained, in 1956, when

> I won a scholarship to go to Puerto Rico to train as a nurse.... My father ... thought it wasn't good enough ... if you were privileged enough to go to

a grammar school, well, they thought teaching, or working in a bank, anything like that would be better than nursing. Nursing . . . just didn't have that kind of status.[38]

The scholarship was subsequently withdrawn when it was discovered that Irene was not St Lucian. 'I realized, yes, I am a stranger.'[39] According to her father, she was 'robbed'. After this, Irene was sent to stay with an aunt in Barbados. She remained there for two years, then migrated to England, to train as a nurse, this time with her parents' support. Within a year of arriving in England, however, Irene gave up her training to marry. Her husband was Barbadian, but 'life was rough. . . . I was living in a working-class area, being a working-class mum with working-class children and had middle-class values and expectations. . . . That was an awful time in my life . . . a very big mistake.'[40]

At the time, class differences, she felt, were not important. 'This was England, and we were both young. . . . In the West Indies, he didn't have the opportunity.'[41] Migration had been the source of the family's social mobility. For Irene, it resulted in downward mobility. 'I didn't even correspond with my parents. I felt such a failure.'[42] Irene struggled to complete her training and study for a degree. She divorced her husband and remarried. Her second husband had gone to Combermere.

For Charles, migration implied absence. For his wife, it implied mobility. For Irene, it implied class and cultural distance. Paradoxically, however, for all of them it also implied opportunity. Like her father, Irene had to struggle and, like her father, she had won against the odds. Moreover, she had become the professional woman her mother had aspired to. But if the models and, therefore, the motives were mixed, what of identity? Unlike Olive and Jasper, the wider family did not provide a custom-made identity. Education was a dynamic, but it was a recent one. Irene lived her life as an outsider – in St Lucia, with her family in Barbados, with her first husband in England. The identity originates in the act of migration itself, and in the success deriving from that. 'To get here,' Irene says, 'it's not been easy.' 'I have a roof over my head and I am not hungry,' Charles insists, 'I don't owe nobody nothing. Nothing.' Charles and his wife returned to Barbados. Irene and her husband have made plans to return.

The third family investigates the perspective of the young 'non-voluntary' migrant to Britain and the search for identity for her generation of Barbadians in Britain. Beulah came to Britain in 1960 as a child of ten. Her mother had migrated four years previously. Her great-great-uncle had migrated to Cuba in 1920. Beulah recalls how her great-grandmother (born in 1898) 'used to tell me . . . all these stories . . . about her brother who went to Cuba. She never saw him again and I always remember as a little girl thinking how sad this was. It was a memory that stayed with me, how sad it was that he went away and they never saw him again.'[43]

Beulah recounts that story. Her mother, Estella, does not mention it. Why this story assumes a prominence relates to Beulah's use of family and lineage in the formation of identity. Her uncle in Cuba functioned as a metaphor for loss of family and identification. Beulah considers herself to be 'culturally together', in contrast to the confused identities held by her British-born siblings. Unlike her siblings, Beulah's early and formative years were spent in Barbados with her great-grandmother. This provided her with an awareness of family which she considers missing in their childhood. At the same time, however, she has reconstructed her family as a conscious response to growing up black in Britain, and in direct contrast to her siblings who have constructed a 'pseudo-English' identity. As a result, she considers them unable to come to terms with being black in Britain, which has resulted in their alienated and alienating behaviour. Her great-great-uncle's disappearance has become a mechanism by which her position is justified, and that of her siblings explained.[44]

Beulah's mother, Estella, was born in 1930 but raised by her maternal grandmother, a plantation labourer. In 1950 Estella gave birth to Beulah. When she migrated to Britain in 1956, she left Beulah in the care of this grandmother. 'My first image,' Beulah recalls, 'is of my great-grandmother'.

> I went everywhere with [her] . . . to the fields, when she was hoeing. . . . She put me under a guava tree. . . . 'Bo-bo, sit there till I come back.' . . . And bed time . . . I would be washed, night dress on, and then I would sit on her lap . . . and we would talk . . . and as she talked, she would be rocking me and singing . . . she told me Nancy stories, which frightened me to death.[45]

Like Jasper, Beulah 'can feel her presence even now'. By contrast, her mother, 'was this woman who wafted in, smelling of perfume, with nail polish, wide skirts, thin waist, made a lot of noise in the house, laughing, and out she waft again. . . . My great-grandmother was everything to me.' Beulah was an 'outside' child. Her father was,

> what they call the 'village ram'. . . . He was a bus driver and that time, in the fifties, if you were a bus driver, you had all the girls and the prestige. . . . I remember him taking me down to his family . . . and I used to feel like a little treasure. . . . My [paternal] grandmother . . . just showed me off.[47]

Why did Beulah's mother Estella migrate in 1956? She was living 'comfortable' on her earnings (as a dressmaker), her grandmother's support, and with maintenance from Beulah's father. She had no pressing economic motive for moving away. Everybody was leaving so 'I thought I'd go and have a try . . . I was young and free and happy. I was this pretty young girl in this lovely red coat.'[48] When she left Beulah with her grandmother, 'I never bothered about it, because I know she was in good hands, it was Granny who used to do all the work on Beulah. . . . So when I had to leave her, I just kiss her down the water front, I kissed them all and said goodbye, and I weren't no way guilty for leaving.'[49]

Like many, Estella planned to stay for a short time. Shortly after arriving in Britain, however, she married. Four years later, at age 10, Beulah came to Britain to live with her mother, her stepfather, and her British-born siblings. However,

'I've never recovered from the fact that she'd had other children. . . . I feel bereaved since she's had the other four children, and I still can't come to terms with sharing her.'[50]

Her relationship with her stepfather was fraught. Beulah describes him as a violent and selfish man. She had to 'mother her mother', and her half-siblings, protecting them against her stepfather. By contrast, 'I had a charmed upbringing . . . in the Caribbean.' By contrast, also, her own father is 'wonderful . . . I am,' she says, 'eternally grateful to her [mother] for giving me him.'

These are important contrasts, ultimately shaping how she grew up and lived as a black woman, a Barbadian, in Britain. Her family loyalties became orientated towards the great-grandmother in Barbados, and her father, rather than her siblings in Britain, a circumstance which, 'worries me, because culturally the fact that you are all [from] the same mother, in the Caribbean . . . you're all one, doesn't matter who the father is, but I just can't love them.'[51]

Beulah analyses this in terms of her relationship with her stepfather and in terms of culture. The two are inseparable. Her British-born siblings, she argues, 'deny' everything. One sister holds to 'a fairy tale upbringing that she has fabricated for herself . . . to me that's a form of denial', refusing to confront what Beulah perceives to be the truth about their father or her parents' marriage. This same sister married an Englishman, and 'was super English . . . to the point when her first born child would look at my mother and scream. . . . If his white family picked him up, he laughed, and he would look at any of us and he would burst out in tears. . . . I feel that if his mother died, we would never see him again.'[52]

She gives further examples. What worries her, she says, 'is any person with a black skin who says there's no such thing as prejudice or racism. . . . In the Brixton riots, [my sister] blamed everybody with a black skin for the fact that they were rioting. Now, that worried me.'[53] One brother, 'is in many ways pseudo-English. . . . I worry about him because culturally I'm very together and he isn't and I often wonder, if any of that falls apart, what will he have to fall back on?'[54]

Beulah's analysis of both her siblings' response and her own is clear. First, her siblings did not have a Caribbean upbringing, and could not share, therefore, in the experience of family. Beulah says she was her '[great] grandmother's child'; she still feels her 'presence'. Second, and importantly, although her siblings were born in the 1960s, neither her stepfather, nor her mother, were into this 'culture thing'. Beulah, on the other hand, was brought into an early awareness of race by her father who:

> is what you would consider a true black man, black in complexion and black of mind. . . . He would always preach to us that you are as good, if not better, than anybody else you meet. . . . He would tell us that people were racist, but we were not to allow that to get in our way . . . we had to try and overcome whatever in our lives was an obstacle. . . . So consequently I grew up always with this . . . feeling of confidence in myself which the others haven't got, they don't have that at all, so they're not together.[55]

Third, as a result of her father, and his influence, Beulah acquired an awareness of family which articulated and made sense of her own experience.

My father's very strong on family. He would sit and talk to me about his
parents and all my other family that I got in Barbados. . . . [So] . . . I've got
roots that the children [her younger siblings] haven't got. . . . When I went to
school we were taught to assimilate, to blend but because I had my father
. . . I was able to keep my stability, so I can see that the other children are
quite screwed up.[56]

Lineage and family offer scope for forging an identity. She argues it in her
own case and sees a change in one of her sisters,

when we had the Brixton riots . . . it was like a turning-point in her life. She
said to me, 'Do you know what? I was in Asda [a supermarket] yesterday, and
I could feel everybody looking at me, as if to say, "you black bitch".' And I
said , to her, 'Good . . . now you know what it's all about.' . . . From then I've
seen a change in her, in that this girl has since been to Barbados. . . . She'd
turned up at her grandfather, her father's father. He didn't know she was
coming. He recognized her, he embraced her, he kissed her. Everybody in the
village came and they were just pleased that she was theirs. . . . That was one
of the things that, well, be it her blackness, that she felt. She said she felt
as if she belonged to the people of Barbados. . . . She's since applied to be
registered as a citizen. . . . She's teaching black studies, so she's come a
long way. . . . She has taught herself to make sweetbread, black cake, souse,
cou-cou from a book.[57]

Clearly, Beulah's relationship with her stepfather and siblings may have
contributed to a sense of exclusion. Like her great-uncle, though at a metaphoric
level, they 'went away'. As a result, this intensified the need for Beulah to
reconstruct, and emphasize, 'family'. On the other hand, the extended family
commonly incorporates step-parents and half-siblings. Her experience is not
atypical. Her half-sister has now taken a similar route in the construction of
identity.

In many ways, the first-generation migrants to Britain – that of Estella and her
cohort – retained a Barbadian identity. The generation born in Britain, or brought
there as young children, have had to construct theirs. Loss of family, and with
it identity, was the theme behind Beulah's story of her great-great-uncle; the
importance of discovery pervades her narrative. Her two sons travel frequently to
Barbados, as do her young grandsons. They stay with Estella's mother, or with her
father, Conrad, who returned to Barbados in 1992. Beulah intends to return to
Barbados. So do her children. Estella has remigrated to Canada though she, too,
plans to return. Like Jasper's family, there are five clearly defined generations, of
which the last three, reared or born in Britain, see their identity with their family
across the ocean.

These three case-studies have been drawn from a wider sample. Although the details of family histories differ, nevertheless investigating family data across generations may provide new dimensions on migration, revealing the motives as complex, varied, even obscure, and implying that orthodox 'push–pull' explanation for migration, and models of migrant behaviour, may be inadequate in several fundamental ways. It suggests also how cultural values, created, absorbed, transmitted, and transformed at the macro level, may have their origins at a micro level within the family. The data argues strongly for the existence of a migration culture, which in the twentieth century ran parallel with government policy, though it had developed in opposition to it in the nineteenth century. Parallelism should not be confused with conformity. This culture has several features which can be identified through family histories. Thus social and family structures enabled and encouraged migration. In the three studies presented here, the importance of grandparents in the raising of grandchildren is clear. The wider sample confirms the resilience, and the role, of the bifurcated family where examples are presented of first- and second-generation British-born children being sent home to grandparents or family in Barbados. The study also displays a degree of gender equality in terms of migration, often obscured by more conventional approaches to the subject. Moreover, the sense of identity generated by family links is an important determinant in out-and-return migration, and in the perceptions and awareness of the Barbadian community in Britain. It also suggests a link between identity, family, professional success, and migration goals. The motive for migration may therefore have more to do with maintenance of the family livelihood, and with the enhancement of status and experience, within a culture which prizes migration *per se*, and historically has perceived it as a statement of independence, than individual economic self-advancement. Indeed, for the most part in this sample, those who migrated were skilled, employed workers, not economically the most needy, for whom time spent abroad was conceived, and continues to be conceived, as temporary.

This chapter has identified family models as an alternative, and primary, locus of migrant motivation, and transmitter of a migration culture, obscured in metropolitan based, and biased, studies of migration. The existence of such culture, and the importance of family, is supported by research elsewhere in the study, which reveals how this culture then transferred to Britain and enabled the development there of survival strategies, such as social networks ('the grapevine'), cultural tolerance, employment mobility and multiplicity, and exploitation of opportunity and reward. Such behaviour is often perceived as deviant. From a migrant perspective, it is logical and predicated upon an eventual return.

ACKNOWLEDGEMENT

I would like to acknowledge the Nuffield Foundation whose grant enabled me to conduct this research.

NOTES

1 B5/1/A/9,2. All quotations are from the Barbados Migration Project, tapes and transcripts deposited with the National Life Story Collection of the National Sound Archive of the British Library.
2 Compilation figures from the Office of Population Census and Survey of England and Wales.
3 Exact figures are not available. These are quoted by Beckles (1990).
4 22 June 1960. L10/19 Vol.1 Barbados, Department of Archives (hereafter BDA).
5 In 1844 the population of Barbados was 122,200 or 740 per square mile. By 1891 the population had increased to 182,900 or 1,096 per square mile (Roberts 1955). In 1871 the death rate for the Parish of St Philip, Barbados was 44.10 per 1,000: *Report of the Barbados Emigration Commission* (1895), (BDA).
6 Census returns from the British West Indian Territories in the nineteenth century indicate that, despite restrictions on out migration, significant numbers of Barbadians had migrated – 20,000 by 1866, mainly to British Guyana and Trinidad, 30,000 by 1891. The 1891 census for Trinidad records 14,000 resident Barbadians. They also indicate a high level of return migration (BDA).
7 The 1895 Barbados Emigration Commission suggested that willingness to migrate should be made a condition of Parish Relief. Although this was not implemented, the post of Superintendent of Emigration was created and merged with the Clerkship of the Poor Law Board. *Report of the Barbados Emigration Commission.* 1895 (BDA).
8 Pseudonyms have been used throughout this chapter.
9 B9/1/A/12.
10 B5/1/A/3.
11 B9/1/A/2.
12 The terms 'outside' and 'inside' are commonly used to describe extra and intra-marital relationships and family.
13 B9/1/A/9.
14 B9/1/A/9–10.
15 B5/1/A/10–11.
16 B9/1/A/23.
17 See Chamberlain (1990).
18 For a study of the economic and political implications of this, see Richardson (1985).
19 B9/1/A/16.
20 B9/1/A/10.
21 B5/1/A/3.
22 A great-grandparent had been white. At that time, black Barbadians were not given management positions on the plantations. This uncle, however, was sufficiently light skinned to secure work as a plantation bookkeeper.
23 Combermere was one of the leading secondary schools in Barbados. It was fee paying. Free secondary school education was not provided until 1962. Until then, the majority of black Barbadians had an elementary education only.
24 B3/1/A/3.
25 B3/1/A/4.
26 B3/1/B/17.
27 B3/1/A/8.
28 Ibid.
29 B3/1/A/10.
30 BBI/1/A/16.
31 B2/1/A/5.
32 B2/1/A/2.
33 B2/1/A/8–9.
34 BBI/1/A/3.

35 BBI/1/A/5.
36 BBI/1/A/7.
37 BBI/1/A/5.
38 BBI/I/A/10.
39 BBI/1/A/7.
40 BBI/1/B/34–7.
41 Ibid.
42 BBI/1/B/38.
43 BB50/1/B.
44 For an interesting discussion on the role of family myths, see John Byng-Hall (1990).
45 BB50/1/A.
46 BB50/1/A.
47 BB50/1/B.
48 BB49/1/B.
49 Ibid.
50 BB50/1/A.
51 Ibid.
52 BB50/1/B.
53 Ibid.
54 BB50/2/A.
55 BB50/1/B.
56 Ibid.
57 BB50/2/A.

REFERENCES

Beckles, H. (1990) *A History of Barbados*, Cambridge, Cambridge University Press.
Byng-Hall, J. with Thompson P. (1990) 'The power of family myths' in R. Samuel and P. Thompson (eds) *The Myths We Live By*, London, Routledge.
Chamberlain, M. (1990) 'Renters and farmers: the Barbadian plantation tenantry system' *Journal of Caribbean History* 24(2): 195–225.
Richardson, B. (1985) *Panama Money in Barbados. 1900–1920*, Knoxville, University of Tennessee Press.
Roberts, G.W. (1955) 'Emigration from the island of Barbados', *Social and Economic Studies*, 4(3): 245–88.

Part V
Caribbean migration cultures

10 Indians, Jamaica and the emergence of a modern migration culture

Verene A. Shepherd

The Caribbean region has been affected by the international movement of labour since the seventeenth century, participating in the white servant trade from Europe and the forced migration of African captives via the transatlantic slave trade. Other pre-emancipation population movements were the forced relocation of indigenous labour within the Caribbean, the intra-Caribbean slave trade, marronage and the intra-colony re-distribution of slaves, particularly after the abolition of the slave trade. In the post-slavery period, less coercive[1] migration currents developed: migration within individual territories, immigration of indentured servants primarily from Asia, intra-Caribbean population movement and emigration of labourers to countries outside of the region.

It is with the post-slavery population movements that this chapter is concerned. It explores the specific experiences of the [East] Indians in the former British colony of Jamaica, arguing that the importation of Indians between 1845 and 1916 was clearly linked to the emergence of a modern migration culture in Jamaica after the abolition of slavery, involving a complex internal relocation of ex-slave labour and the emigration of African-Jamaicans in the face of deteriorating political and socio-economic conditions in the island. But though imported to compensate for the decrease in the supply of ex-slave labour to the plantations and to build up a reserve of rural agricultural labourers, Indians and their descendants themselves became a part of the island's migration culture, demonstrating that nineteenth-century international population movements did not necessarily involve the permanent relocation of people from one country to another. Indeed, Denis Conway has recently constructed a conceptual distinction between emigration and what he terms 'circulation' – an alternative international mobility pattern involving reciprocal flows of people without the permanent settlement component which characterizes emigration (Conway 1988: 145–63). Certainly the Indians were involved in a complicated pattern of immigration, repatriation, return migration, internal migration, seasonal migration and emigration.

EMANCIPATION, EX-SLAVE MOBILITY AND IMMIGRATION

The immigration of Indians to Jamaica was intimately associated with the new mobility among the labouring class, freed from the legal obligation to remain attached to the properties of their former owners after 1838. In Jamaica, the availability of land for cultivation, the coercive tactics of landholders which made ex-slaves unwilling to continue in a capital–labour relationship with estate owners, the lack of proper remuneration on the estates and technological stagnation on the estates which gave workers no relief from arduous physical labour all combined to motivate ex-slaves to withdraw gradually from the estates and turn instead to petty cash-cropping or subsistence agriculture. A significant number migrated to newly created free villages.[2] Some former female slaves retreated to the so-called 'private sphere' to reconstruct the black family, or abandoned estate labour for subsistence farming, 'higglering', or a variety of non-agricultural occupations in the urban sector. Displaced estate artisans, primarily male, migrated to the urban centres to enter the wage labour market (Roberts 1957: 105–6).

The result of such population movement was unpredictability and instability in the labour supply which did not satisfy the landholders' desire for monopoly control of the labour market. It was within this context that various immigrant groups were brought into Jamaica to supplement the African-Jamaican labour force from the 1830s, but especially after the 1850s and 1880s when, despite planter opposition, ex-slaves, rural and urban-based, emigrated in significant numbers to Panama, Cuba and elsewhere.[3]

Indians comprised the majority of the imported indentured labourers. Landholders hoped that through long contracts, immigrant labourers would be anchored to the estates, thus assuring them of a controllable and reliable nucleus of labourers. They also hoped to use imported labourers to create competition for estate labour and depress wage rates. Between 1838 when the first Indians were landed in Guyana under the 'Gladstone Experiment', and 1917 when the last shipments reached Trinidad and Guyana, just over 500,000 Indians had been imported to the entire Caribbean (Laurence 1971). The largest numbers of Indians were imported by Guyana (238,909) and Trinidad (143,939). Smaller numbers were imported by Guadeloupe (42,000), Jamaica (38,681), Suriname (34,304), Martinique (25,509) and the British Windward Islands (10,026) (Laurence 1971).

FROM INDIA TO JAMAICA

It is difficult to arrive at an accurate importation figure for Jamaica between 1845 and 1916 because of the gaps in the information relating to ship arrivals; but Gisela Eisner's (1974: 144) figure of 38,681 or 7.7 per cent of the total Caribbean importation seems acceptable.[4]

The primarily Hindu contract labourers came from various areas of India. The area of recruitment shifted from year to year depending on social and economic conditions in India and the demands of the landholders. For example, landholders accused 'Madrasis' and Muslims of being rebellious and intractable and did not encourage their recruitment.[5] Prospective emigrants were drawn from all castes – high and low – and were recruited inside and outside of their villages (at times through deception). The majority of recruits were in the age group 10–30. In the period 1867–1916, 88 per cent of males and 82 per cent of females recruited for Jamaica fell into this age group (Roberts 1957: 129). The proportion of males over 30 was less than 5 per cent. After being deemed medically fit for embarkation, they were shipped, either from Calcutta or Madras, to the colonies.

As with most schemes of labour migration, Indian immigration to Jamaica and the rest of the Caribbean was male-dominated. Only 15 per cent of the 261 who arrived on the *Blundell* in 1845 and 15 per cent of the 319 on the *Hyderabad* in 1846 were females. Despite efforts by the British government to get planters to conform to a 40:100 female–male ratio, the sexual disparity in Indian immigration to Jamaica continued to the end of the immigration scheme. There was some improvement by the late nineteenth and early twentieth centuries when females comprised on average 30 per cent on each ship arriving in Jamaica down to 1916.[6]

Indian immigrants served out their indenture primarily on sugar and banana plantations and livestock farms in rural Jamaica. In the 1840s they were required to work under one-year contracts. Large-scale abandonment of estate labour by the Indians at the end of their one-year contract combined with planter agitation for the lengthening of contracts resulted in the introduction of three-year contracts in 1850 and five-year contracts in 1862. Proprietors maintained a gender discriminatory wage policy throughout the operation of the system of Indian indentureship. While all immigrants earned subsistence wages, women, and children up to 16 years, earned just 9*d*. [pence] per day or per task, while adult male labourers over age 16 earned between 1*s*.[shilling] and 1s. 6*d*. In addition to the maintenance of a wage differential according to sex, there was a gender division of labour, with male labourers being assigned the more remunerative tasks. The immigrants were subjected to numerous labour laws, contravention of which fetched punishments ranging from fines to imprisonment. From all indications, the period of indentureship did not result in any great economic gain for the majority of immigrants.

At the expiration of their contracts, Indians became legally free, although they had to remain in the island for another five years before being able to return to India or leave the island for another country. Proprietors did everything in their power to turn the importation of transient labourers into permanent settler migration.

FROM JAMAICA TO INDIA: REPATRIATION SCHEMES

Repatriation was an integral part of the nineteenth-century Indian indenture contract, in strong contrast to the pre-emancipation white and African labour migration schemes. The philosophy underlying the entire Indian indenture system, however, envisaged the immigrant contract labourers as transients within the plantation system, who would spend ten years in the colonies (five years in the case of the French colonies) before returning to India. The safeguard of the free return passage as an indispensable element of the indenture contract was insisted upon by the government of India and concerned liberal-humanitarian elements in Britain who were afraid of being accused of participating in a revived slave trade by the still active anti-slavery society. In addition, as Walton Look Lai (1993: 217–18) observes, the Indians themselves might not have embarked on the long journey to the Caribbean without its inclusion. The rationale for official insistence on repatriation was the belief that it was not enough to rely upon the 'frugality' of the emigrant in saving to return, or on the 'generosity' of the proprietor, without recourse to law.

Repatriation was a contentious issue between Indians and the plantocracy in Jamaica; and ex-indentured immigrants had to be vigilant about their entitlement. Up to the 1860s, return passages became due and claimable after five years in the colony; thereafter they became due after ten years of continuous residence. After 1903, return passages had to be claimed within two years of becoming due (Shepherd 1994: 93).

The repatriation of Indians from Jamaica started late – in 1853 – leading the Colonial Land and Emigration Commission to remark that: 'financial difficulties have rendered Jamaica more tardy than her sister colonies British Guiana and Trinidad in furnishing Indian labourers with the return passage to which they are entitled'.[7] The British government was reluctant to grant a loan for repatriation, and the Jamaican Assembly refused to vote new taxes to cover the cost. As immigration was halted until the obligation to repatriate those imported in the 1840s had been honoured, a portion of the Imperial loan was finally used to pay the return passages in 1853 (Shepherd 1994: 93).

A new Immigration Act of 1858 made firmer provisions for repatriation. It stipulated that the costs were to be met from General Revenue. An 'Immigrants Colonization and Return Passage Fund' was also set up and financed by a per annum contribution of £1 per adult from General Revenue (Shepherd 1994: 94–5). The passing of the new Act did not guarantee the smooth operation of the repatriation scheme; for the proprietors had never supported the idea of repatriation and sought every means to subvert it. The first reason was that, having paid to import the Indians, they wished them to remain in the island and form a surplus labour force as a guarantee against high wages. Another reason for their opposition was the expense of the return journey. Between 1871 and 1897, importers bore the full cost of £6 10s. for each adult who opted to return to India; and they spent a total of £22,710 on return passages from 1891–95. To save themselves the cost of these return passages, up to 1879, they encouraged 'time-expired' immigrants to accept a cash grant of £12 or 10 acres of Crown Land in lieu of repatriation. This offer was a strong incentive for some Indians to remain in Jamaica. Such incentive was accepted by those who had broken ties with India, had no wish to return and saw the prospect of improving their lives with ready cash. While proprietors would have preferred the Indians to accept marginal lands in lieu of repatriation, most of those who opted to waive their right to repatriation chose the cash grant; for their complaint was that the lands being offered were in remote areas and were generally uncultivatable. A cash grant, on the other hand, would enable the Indians to purchase land in more suitable areas. However, in 1879, the option of a cash grant was removed, and only land was offered. By this time, some £32,000 had already been spent on bounties. Land grants were briefly removed as an option in 1897, but were reinstated in 1903. By 1906, however, it was becoming almost as expensive to provide land grants in lieu of repatriation (about £12 per head) as repatriation itself (about £15 per adult); so the offer of land grants in lieu of return passages was withdrawn. The Protector, F.L. Pearce, claimed that a reason for removing land grants in lieu of repatriation was that he had not foreseen the anticipated decline in the number requesting repatriation when land grants were reintroduced in 1903. He could well have added that land grants were being refused by most to whom they were offered because of the marginal nature of the land being offered and their unsuitability for rice, sugar or banana cultivation. Instead he noted in his 1909/10 report that:

> this object [of increasing settlement] has not been achieved for the rate of return passages has remained undiminished while the expense of allotting land to the Coolies [*sic*] who stay . . . has been added to the burden of the Fund.[8]

The decision to discontinue land grants was influenced by changes in the immigration law which, after 1897, introduced a new requirement for immigrants to finance a part of the cost of their return passage. The immigration law of 1897, further amended in 1899, abolished completely free return passages. Up to 1909, each adult male returnee was required to contribute one-quarter, and each adult female returnee one-sixth of the full cost of the return passage. After 1909, the contributions were increased to 50 per cent (or £7 10s. 6d.) for each man and 33 per cent (or £5) for each woman. In addition, each returnee had to pay for warm clothing and blankets for the journey to India at a rate of £1 for each adult, 15s. for children age 4–10 and 5s. for those under 4. Children and the disabled were repatriated at the expense of the colony (minus the cost of warm clothes and blankets).

The new laws immediately caused a decrease in the number requesting repatriation. Whereas 680 had opted for repatriation in 1906, only 111 applied for repatriation in 1909. In fact, after 1897, there was often not a large enough number of Indians requiring repatriation to fill a return ship. Consequently, returnees from Jamaica had to be accommodated on ships from Guyana. This led to frustration for many as the ship from Guyana did not always have space for those from Jamaica who then had to wait for the next ship (Shepherd 1994: 94–7). On account of the fear of a high mortality rate on return ships, Guyana at times refused to carry those considered too old and disabled.

The unsatisfactory repatriation arrangements, the cessation of government-sponsored repatriation after 1929, the opposition to the return of 'dis-Indianized natives' among certain groups in India and the poor economic status of most Indians which made them unable to pay for their own return passages, resulted in just around 38 per cent of Indians from Jamaica returning to India between 1850 and 1930. Of the 16,354 who arrived between 1872 and 1913, some 6.55 per cent returned to India. Some 1,547 returned in the period 1850–54; another

126 returned between 1855–59. There were no further returns to India until 1870–74. In all, up to 1917, 11,959 or 31 per cent of the 38,681 who arrived, returned to India. This percentage was lower than the British Windward Islands' 38 per cent, Suriname's 34 per cent and Guyana's 32 per cent; but it was higher than the return figures for Guadeloupe (approximately 18 per cent); Trinidad (22.4 per cent) and Martinique (20 per cent) (Laurence 1971: 57). There was cessation of repatriation during the years of World War I when, not only was the journey unsafe, but return ships were requisitioned by the Navy. In fact, there was no return ship between 1916 and 1922. The following year, 676 were repatriated. As the last batch of Indian contract workers arrived in Jamaica in 1916, their repatriation was due in 1926. The government gave them two additional years in which to claim and finally provided a ship in 1929. The last 425 returnees went back to India on the overcrowded *Sutlej* in 1929. Thereafter, there was no more government-assisted repatriation from Jamaica, even though requests continued to flood the immigration office.

THE INTERNAL MIGRATION OF INDIANS

From the 1880s Indians migrated to Kingston and St Andrew from the contiguous rural parishes of St Mary, Portland, St Thomas and St Catherine as well as from more distant parishes such as Clarendon and Westmoreland. Successive governors imposed restrictions on rural–urban migration of Indians in the nineteenth century in the belief that the movement of labourers created a drain on the numbers of estate workers. But once they were released from their role as indentured servants in rural agricultural production and became geographically mobile, Indians exercised their right to sell their labour in the urban market where wages were typically higher. The rural to urban movement intensified from the 1920s when increasing urbanization and the creation of a labour surplus, at a time when emigration to either Cuba or Panama was no longer an option, determined the outward movement to the towns.

The period of really significant Indian emigration to Kingston occurred between 1921 and 1943, also a period of great rural to urban migration of African-Jamaicans. In fact, 80 per cent of all internal migration occurred in this period (Roberts 1957: 152). The pre-1921 internal migration had been basically a redistribution of the rural population, not in any way parallel to the urbanward drift of the post-1921 period. In fact, the number of persons living in Kingston and St Andrew grew from 117,000 in 1921 to 237,000 in 1943 – an increase of 101.8 per cent. In 1943, 1,279 Indians resided in Kingston and 2,769 in the peri-urban area of St Andrew, representing 2.6 per cent of the total population of the city and 18.9 per cent of the total Indian population in Jamaica (Shepherd 1986: 131–2). The rural–urban population movement intensified in the 1940s, so that by 1946, Indians in Kingston represented 24 per cent of the city's population (Shepherd 1993: 21).

The number of Indians located in the urban area by the mid-1940s seemed to have been higher in Jamaica than in other British Caribbean territories.

Comparative census data reveal that 9.14 per cent of the total Indian population (and 21.80 per cent of the entire population) in the British Caribbean was to be found in urban areas in 1946. The report of the 1946 census commissioners indicated, however, that 'Jamaica, with 4,052 Indians in urban areas and 17,341 in the rural parishes, appears to have a smaller rural bias among East Indians'.[9] Other Asians were more heavily concentrated in the urban sectors, particularly in Guyana where only just under 33 per cent of the Chinese population was not settled in Georgetown. By 1982, 61 per cent of the total Chinese population in Jamaica were urban dwellers.[10]

While the end of indentured contracts, the difficulty experienced by 'time-expired' Indians in securing jobs and the low estate wages acted as push factors in the trek from rural parishes; other contributing factors were the return of migrants and the discriminatory hiring practices in the 1930s. Employers gave preference to returning male labourers and experienced African-Jamaican workers in the economic turmoil of the early twentieth century. J.D. Tyson, who visited the Caribbean after the labour rebellions of the 1930s, recorded that few Indians, particularly women, could find work (Tyson n.d.: 33). The male as breadwinner ideology which was prevalent at the time determined gender discrimination in job allocation. Not surprisingly, Indian women comprised a significant proportion of those emigrating to Kingston and St Andrew and by 1943 outnumbered their male counterparts. They sought employment as domestic servants and shop assistants. Most domestic jobs were taken by African-Jamaicans, however; and very few Indian women were literate enough to be shop assistants. The avenue they chose was market gardening and the door-to-door peddling of the fruits and vegetables. This was an open area of opportunity, and they sought to fill this niche within an urban context of non-production of foodstuffs.

MIGRATION TO FOREIGN COUNTRIES

As long as new employment opportunities presented themselves and the means of transportation existed, international mobility was viewed as a viable strategy by the working class of all ethnic groups. The activities of the new emergent United States industrial capitalists, the expansion of oceanic passenger transportation especially since 1911, the failure of the USA to fill labour needs with indigenous labourers or US citizens created a new labour opportunity for time-expired Indians. Furthermore, wages in the canal zone ranged from 80 cents to $1.04 compared to from 9*d.* to 1*s.* 6*d.* (roughly 25–70 cents) in Jamaica. Instead of re-indenturing, remaining in the urban core or returning to India, Indians and Indian-Jamaicans joined the trek to Cuba and Central America, with a few going further afield.

From the late nineteenth century, officials in India and Jamaica consistently opposed the re-emigration of Indians and the emigration of Indian-Jamaicans and placed many obstacles in their way (at times in addition to those placed in the way of the general migrating population). The efforts to prevent the re-emigration of 'time-expired' Indians were related to the fear of a further reduction in the island's labour force in the face of the emigration of Jamaicans and the shunning of estate labour by many of those who stayed. The government in India went as far as to rule that, unless it could be substantiated that they had independent means of subsistence, Indians should not be allowed to leave Jamaica except for the purpose of returning to India.[11]

Indians who nevertheless wished to leave the island had to get permission from the governor of Jamaica as well as clearance from the Immigration Department before being issued with passports. Any one who tried to leave without first obtaining a passport was fined £10. Prospective Indian emigrants were told clearly that they should expect no financial assistance from the colony; and that once they had applied for, and received passports to go to a third country, they forfeited any claim for government-assisted repatriation.

Before 1906, Indians were also told that they forfeited any claim to land in lieu of repatriation once they decided to re-emigrate. Certain countries were deemed prohibited destinations for Indians; and it was made illegal for them to sign contracts to work in such countries. Section 44 of Law 23 of 1879 declared that:

> no Indian immigrant in this island shall without permission from the Governor, enter into any contract for industrial service in any prohibited place, or quit this island under any agreement or with any intent to enter into any such contract.

Cuba was one of the earliest prohibited places; though the ban was consistently ignored by the Indians. The prohibition was eventually lifted in 1905 in the face of the need for workers in the sugar mills of the Guantanamo Valley. In 1882, a ban was also placed on the emigration of Indians to Mexico. Other prohibited places were Ecuador and Guatemala. Despite the ban, agents from these countries tried to inveigle Indians to seek jobs abroad. The United Fruit Company, for example, tried to recruit Indians for their plantations in Guatemala. Agents from Mexico recruited Indian labourers for work at Coatzacoalcos, one of the terminal harbours for the proposed Interoceanic railway; and in the early twentieth century, J.P. McDonald, contractor in charge of the Guayaquil to Quito railroad in Ecuador, tried to recruit labourers for this project. The ban on migration to Cuba, Mexico, Ecuador and Guatemala did not apply to African-Jamaicans, deemed free agents. The Indians, however, had been imported at the expense of planters and general revenue. Recruiters claimed, however, that Indians tended to honour their contracts to a greater degree than African-Jamaicans, and so evinced a preference for the former.

Indian emigration declined after 1930 because of restrictive immigration policies in receiving countries, war conditions and the unfavourable economic climate in Cuba, Panama and elsewhere during the post-war depression (Shepherd 1994: 136–40).

On account of the official opposition to the emigration of labourers and the obstacles placed in the way of prospective emigrants, many evaded the official channels and left illegally. This makes it difficult to do any accurate quantitative analysis of Indian migration from Jamaica. Furthermore, it was not until 1882 that some attempt was made to keep separate figures for Indians who left Jamaica for third countries. The Agent-General of Immigration, David Ewart, could only *speculate* that about 500 of those who arrived in Jamaica between 1845 and 1847 left the island in the 1840s, probably for Cuba.[12] Indians were employed only under one-year contracts in the 1840s and could leave the estates after that. Like other post-slavery labourers like the Germans and Liberated Africans, they exercised this mobility after the first year, opting to follow African-Jamaicans to Cuba where wages on sugar plantations were higher. Recruiters from Central America also made forays into the countryside, trying to get Indians to leave Jamaica. Other sources show that between 1882 and 1892, 1,137 Indians re-emigrated.[13] By 1912, the number had increased to 1,512. It is estimated that a further 2,011 left between 1913 and 1930.[14] This was in contrast to the over 50,000 African-Jamaicans who had migrated in the period 1891 to 1916 and who had in fact been leaving the island at a rate of 1,000 per month for Cuba, Mexico, Panama and Yucatan.[15]

The tantalizing 'Passport Registers' found among the Protector of Immigrants' Papers in the Jamaica Archives fail to give the expected definitive figure for Indian outmigration. Admittedly, in contrast to other sources, these records provide the most details on those issued with passports after 1916, listing the emigrant's name, height, colour, distinguishing marks, country of birth, age (of children only), sex and destination;[16] but they carry no entries for the years 1929, 1930, 1931, 1933 and 1934. The entry 'nil' is simply given in the register for these years without any further explanation. For the years for which data are provided, the Registers show that 2,076 Indians left the island between 1916 and 1935.

The overwhelming majority of Indians were issued with passports for Cuba which, by the early twentieth century, was a popular destination for Jamaica migrants. Indeed, in 1919, of thirty-four countries from which emigrants in Cuba originated, Jamaica contributed 29.64 per cent (Knight 1985: 101). As in the case of the general emigrating group, the peak year for Indian emigration to Cuba was 1920 when 725 left (compared to 24,461 African-Jamaicans); but the numbers fell off drastically thereafter, petering out by 1935 when only one passport was issued. Passports were also issued to those going to Panama (Colon), Mexico and other Central American countries. By the 1930s, countries of destination for Indians included Trinidad, Honduras, Guyana, and Puerto Limon in Costa Rica. A small number went to 'America' (probably a reference to the United States of America, though this was not at all significant until much later). The majority who were issued with passports were born in Jamaica. Most of those who left were male, under 10 per cent being female. Only eight of the Indian females who re-emigrated went to countries other than Cuba. The male–female disparity was less pronounced among African-Jamaican emigrants. Franklin Knight records that in the period 1922–33, while males outnumbered females among Jamaican migrants to Cuba, it was only by a small percentage. For example, in 1922, 54.14 per cent were males and 45.82 per cent females. Ten years later 50.63 per cent of the migrants were males compared to 49.37 per cent who were females (Knight 1985: 102). A total of forty-six children ranging in ages from 18 months to 18 years (still considered a minor then) left with their parents.

It is unclear how many Indians returned from foreign countries. A total of 42,042 Jamaicans are said to have returned from Cuba in 1931 (1985: 101); and 11,600 of the 24,300 labourers who left for Panama in the period 1883–84 are said to have returned, even temporarily. But the sources do not distinguish returnees by ethnic groups. What is clear, though, is that after 1921, several factors affected the emigration of Jamaicans/Indian-Jamaicans. The ban imposed on Caribbean migrants by the Congress of the USA in 1921 and 1924, anti-foreign labour laws of the Machado regime in Cuba, and the downturn in the foreign labour needs in Central America – all restricted the outlets for Jamaican emigration. By 1931, a mere fifty-two emigrants went to Cuba from Jamaica (1985: 100).

CONCLUSION

A review of the migration history of Indians reveals certain trends: their entry to the region was primarily voluntary; repatriation was a vital part of the indenture contract, the sexual disparity among the immigrant group was even more pronounced than in the case of the slave trade; there was great sexual disparity among those leaving for seasonal or permanent work outside of Jamaica; repatriation was a contested issue, but about 38 per cent returned to India; immigration developed into permanent settler migration, and obstacles were placed in the way of outmigration – above and beyond those placed in the way of African-Jamaicans. Many had no choice but to adopt Jamaica or a third country as home; for once they emigrated, they forfeited the right to a return passage to India. In other respects, the Indians joined a Caribbean migration culture: the majority settled in the region (like other immigrant groups), despite the existence of the repatriation aspect of the immigration law; there was sexual disparity in migration and outmigration (though exaggerated in the case of the Indians); they joined the urbanward trek in the twentieth century, their mobility became a source of tension with the planter-class and when they chose to emigrate (permanently or temporarily) they chose the same destinations as African-Jamaicans.

NOTES

1 There will always be a debate over how really voluntary were indentured labour migration, the movement of former slaves off the plantation and the outmigration of workers.
2 See Paget (1987) and Satchell (1990) for information on the rise and expansion of free villages in Jamaica.
3 For a full discussion of Jamaican labour migration, see Petras (1988) and Roberts (1957: 133–40).
4 Previous estimates excluded the 615 who arrived in 1916.

5 *Blue Book of Jamaica* 1898–99 (Kingston: Government Printing Office, 1899) and Jamaica Archives, Colonial Secretary's Office (hereafter CSO), 1B/5/18/65, Despatch 352, Governor Olivier to the Earl of Crewe, 27 August 1910.
6 Ships' papers, CGF 1B/9, Jamaica Archives, see also Shepherd (1995: 238).
7 Enclosure in Despatch 16, Bulwer-Lytton to Governor Darling, 7 June 1858, in *Papers Relating to the West Indian Colonies and Mauritius*, 1858.
8 *Protector of Immigrants Report, 1909–1910.*
9 *The West Indian Census of 1946*, p. 14.
10 *Ibid.*
11 Jamaica Archives, CSO 1B/5/18/56, Despatch 433, Governor of Jamaica to Secretary of State Chamberlain, 30 July 1902.
12 Parliamentary Papers (hereafter PP) 1858, Murdoch and Rogers to T.F. Elliot, 25 October 1858.
13 Public Record Office (hereafter PRO), London, CO 571/5, Governor Manning to the Sectretary of States, 3 January 1916.
14 Jamaica Archives, CGF 1B/9/67, Passport Registers, 1916–1935.
15 PRO, CO 571/5, Governor Manning to the Secretary of State, 1916.
16 Jamaica Archives File 1B/9/67. It should be noted that in some years, no destination was indicated, the column for destinations showing only the ship on which the immigrant had arrived in Jamaica. In such cases also, the sex of the person was not specifically indicated as in most years; so that only the names (one Indian name only, e.g. Sarna, Bhagahoo, etc.) provide a clue to the sex of the passport holder. The absence of the usual indication of sex has implications for my calculations of the percentage of females who left. However, I received help from an Indian-Jamaican who gave me advice on which name was male and which female.

REFERENCES

Conway, Denis (1988) 'Conceptualising contemporary patterns of Caribbean international mobility', *Caribbean Geography* 2(3): 145–63.

Eisner, Gisela (1974, reprint) *Jamaica 1830–1930: A Study in Economic Growth*, Westport, CT: Greenwood Press Publishers.

Knight, Franklin (1985) 'Jamaican migrants and the Cuban sugar industry, 1900–1934' in Manuel Moreno Fraginals, Frank Moya Pons and Stanley Engerman (eds) *Between Slavery and Free Labor: the Spanish Speaking Caribbean in the Nineteenth Century*, Baltimore, MD: Johns Hopkins University Press, pp. 94–114.

Laurence, K.O. (1971) *Immigration into the West Indies in the 19th Century*, Barbados: Caribbean Universities Press.

Look Lai, Walton (1993) *Indentured Labor, Caribbean Sugar: Chinese and Indian Migrants to the British West Indies, 1838–1918*, Baltimore, MD: Johns Hopkins University Press.

Paget, H. (1987) 'The free village system in Jamaica', *Apprenticeship and Emancipation*, Special Publication of the Department of Extramural Studies, University of the West Indies, Mona, Jamaica, pp. 45–58.

Petras, Elizabeth McLean (1988) *Jamaican Labour Migration: White Capital and Black Labor, 1850–1930*, London and Boulder, CO: Westview Press.

Roberts, G.W. (1957) *Population of Jamaica*, Cambridge: Cambridge University Press.

Satchell, V. (1990) *From Plots to Plantations: Land Transactions in Jamaica*, Kingston: ISER.

Shepherd, V. (1986) 'From rural plantations to urban slums: the economic status and problems of East Indians in Kingston, Jamaica in the late nineteenth and early twentieth centuries', *Immigrants and Minorities* 5(2): 129–44.

—— (1993) 'Indian females in Jamaica: an analysis of the population censuses, 1861–1943', *Jamaican Historical Review* 18.

—— (1994) *Transients to settlers: the Experience of Indians in Jamaica 1845–1950*, Leeds: Peepal Tree Publishers.

—— (1995) 'Gender, migration and settlement: the indentureship and post-indentureship experience of Indian females in Jamaica, 1845–1943' in V. Shepherd, B. Brereton and B. Bailey (eds) *Engendering history: Caribbean women in Historical Perspective*, Kingston: Ian Randle Publishers/London: James Currey Publishers.

Tyson, J.D. (n.d.) *The conditions of Indians in Jamaica, British Guiana and Trinidad, 1938–39*, Simla: Government of India Press.

11 Barbadian migrants in the Putumayo district of the Amazon, 1904–11

Howard Johnson

The multi-directional nature of the external labour migration, which has been a characteristic feature of British Caribbean societies since Emancipation, has often been obscured by the emphasis placed on the large-scale migratory outflows in the scholarly literature. Scholars of Caribbean migration have generally concentrated on the outward movement of migrants to and experience in Panama, Costa Rica, the United States, and Great Britain (Newton 1984; Lewis 1980; Conniff 1985; Petras 1988; Purcell 1993; Peach 1968; Foner 1978; Chamberlain 1997). Yet it is often the numerically insignificant population movements which best illustrate the desperation of British West Indian migrants as they sought outlets for the sale of their labour power. This chapter examines the experience of a small group of Barbadians who migrated to the Putumayo district of the Amazon, in the first decade of twentieth century, where they worked in the rubber industry. In that context, they operated primarily as enforcers in a coercive and exploitative labour system which kept the indigenous Amazonian population in virtual slavery and were themselves victims of a system of debt peonage. Although the experience of the Indian population has been extensively examined, that of the Barbadian migrants has received little attention.[1]

The 196 labourers who were recruited in Barbados during 1904–5 for work in Putumayo formed an insignificant proportion of the broader Barbadian diaspora of the first two decades of the twentieth century. It has been estimated that 45,000 Barbadians migrated to the Isthmus of Panama in the period 1905–15 from a population of less than 200,000 (Richardson 1985: 3). By the turn of the century, emigration had long been established, among black Barbadians, as a strategy for coping with a quasi-feudal socio-economic system, which had been in place since emancipation, landlessness, and chronic unemployment and underemployment.[2] After 1838, Barbadians had migrated, in large numbers, to Trinidad and British Guiana – the new plantation frontiers – where wage levels were higher than those of Barbados and Crown land was available for squatting and eventually for purchase. By the opening years of the 1870s, the outward movement of Barbadians was further stimulated by population pressures. Colonial officials who had earlier lent their support to planter efforts to restrict labour migration by legislation came increasingly to regard emigration as the solution to the island's problems of overcrowding and unemployment. With the economic depression in the region's sugar industry after 1884, in part a result of European subsidized beet sugar competition, Barbadians sought new emigration outlets in countries in Central and South America where United States invest-ment provided increased employment opportunities.[3]

The group of 196 Barbadian men who were recruited to work in the Putumayo district in 1904–5 was employed by the firm of J. C. Arana y Hermanos, based in Iquitos, Peru, which was later merged into the Peruvian Amazon Rubber Company – a limited company incorporated in England in 1907 (Sawyer 1984: 79).[4] The choice of Barbados for recruiting labour for the Amazon was probably determined by its reputation as a source of exportable unskilled labour and its position as a port of call for the major steamship lines which linked Europe, North America and the Amazon (Greenfield 1983: 49). The male recruits (pre-dominantly but not exclusively Barbadians) were engaged as general labourers for a two-year term. Their contracts, which were signed by Abel Alarco, a partner in the firm, and countersigned by a police magistrate, stipulated that free passages in both directions should be provided by the employer and wages at the rate of £2.1*s*. 8*d*. per month were to be paid, in addition to free meals (three times daily), free medical attention and accommodation. The contracts also specified that there should be six working days weekly, with work commencing at 7 a.m. and ending at sunset, except for one-hour breaks for breakfast and dinner. The recruits were allowed a cash advance of a month's wages, which could be paid prior to departure.[5]

Our knowledge of the subsequent experience of the Barbadian migrants is based primarily on the reports made by Roger Casement, then British Consul-General in Rio de Janeiro, after visiting the Putumayo region late in 1910. In July of that year, Sir Edward Grey, the British Foreign Secretary, had charged Casement with the responsibility for carrying out an independent investigation into the system of rubber collection and the treatment of the native Indians by the employees of the Peruvian Amazon Company.[6] The Foreign Office's interest in conditions in the Putumayo was prompted by the fact that the Peruvian Amazon Company was based in Britain and employed British subjects – the Barbadians – in that area (Sawyer 1984: 82). Casement was expected to accompany the commission of enquiry which the company had appointed after allegations of atrocities perpetrated on the Indians in the Amazon had surfaced in a series of articles published in a London magazine, the *Truth* (Sawyer 1984: 84). The commission's terms of reference were 'to report on the possibilities of commercial development of the company's properties and to enquire into the present relations between the native employees and the agents of the company'. Casement's brief extended to examining 'the relations obtaining between British subjects in those regions and the company's agents'.[7] His account of the Barbadians' role in the existing labour system was based primarily on their personal (and often self-incriminating) testimony.

Although the contract drawn up in Barbados was specific about the obligations of employer and labourer, aspects of the agreement were disregarded by the recruiting company on the arrival of the Barbadians in the Amazon. Early indications of the discontent of Barbadian labourers came in the form of a letter to the *Barbados Advocate*, published in April 1906. Writing from a location somewhere in Peru, a group of four labourers complained:

> Sir – We are sorry to trobble you But pleas to put this in your papers about the labours that left barbadoes on the Second of March 1905 for peru South America they have not delt with us according to the Contract they took us from Barbados as labours, after we reach there they refuse to give us any wages according to the Contract saying they pay to the Government of Barbados a Sum of £15 for each head of us and now we are Suffering day by day as Slaves we thought that we was going there as labours but we found out afterwards there is Slaves where we are. We cannot get away for there is soldiers guarding us. That is because they carry us where there is no Council that we can apply to.
>
> (Richardson 1985: 110)

As the preceding letter indicates, some Barbadian migrants were concerned not only about the failure of their employer to pay the wage rates specified in the contract but also about the nature of the work they were expected to undertake. On their arrival in Manaus, the capital of the state of Amazonas in Brazil, some of the Barbadian labourers were sent to Iquitos and employed on an estate called Nanai, a few miles downstream from that town. Casement discovered that the labourers at Nanai had expressed their dissatisfaction with their wages (which were one-half of the local rate of pay) and the food they received by the terms of their contract. As a result, most of these labourers had left the service of the firm before the completion of their contracts.[8]

The nature of the work in which the 100 labourers, who were sent directly to the Putumayo district, were engaged was vastly different from that of the Nanai group. Recruited as general labourers, these men were, in Casement's words, 'forced to act as armed bullies and terrorists over the surrounding native population', who provided the labour for the extractive activities of the rubber industry.[9] In Manaus, some of the Barbadian labourers had been warned that they would not be employed as general labourers but would be armed and used to coerce the Indians to work for their employers. They were also told that the savage Indians would kill them. Alarmed at these stories, several Barbadians had appealed to the British vice-consul to be released from their contracts. They were told, however, that the contracts had been legally entered into, in a British colony, and were thus binding in Peru. These men had left for the Putumayo district only after they were taken aboard the river steamer under police escort.[10]

The work performed by the Barbadian labourers in the Putumayo district is best understood in the context of a wider discussion of the development of the rubber industry in that area and the way in which labour was organized. The extractive rubber industry in the Putumayo region developed as part of the export boom in that commodity by the closing decades of the nineteenth century as Latin American countries responded to the demand from the industrializing nations of the northern hemisphere for this basic raw material. In the early nineteenth century, European industry had become increasingly aware of the uses for rubber especially for the manufacture of rubberized, waterproofed fabrics. It was not, however, until after 1839 when Charles Goodyear perfected the vulcanization process that there was a sharp increase in the demand for rubber. The export boom in rubber came with the bicycle craze of the 1890s and the increased popularity of the automobile after 1900. Until 1912, the Amazon Valley was the world's main supplier of rubber. This area was the natural habitat of the tree *Hevea brasiliensis* from which a high-quality rubber was produced (Weinstein 1983: 8–10).

Initially, Brazil had benefited primarily from the exploitation of this natural resource of the Amazon Valley as rubber traders used the transportation network provided by the extensive river system which flowed within its borders. By the end of the nineteenth century, however, other Latin American countries which bordered on the Amazon had developed an interest in extracting this form of wealth from the lowland rain forests. One area which attracted this interest was the Putumayo region which consists primarily of the area drained by two tributaries of the Putumayo River, the Igaraparaná and the Caraparaná, of approximately 10,000 square miles. This region borders on the republics of Colombia, Peru, and Ecuador and was, at one time, claimed (in part) by all three. During the rubber boom years, the main claimants to sovereignty over the district were Colombia and Peru. It was, however, Peru which came to exercise control over the disputed area on the basis of its occupation of the territory and the maintenance of a semblance of law and order by powerful Peruvian commercial interests operating in that region (Sawyer 1984: 77–8).

The exploitation of the forest resources of the Putumayo district for rubber production for the export trade had begun in the early 1880s when Colombian rubber traders or '*caucheros*' ventured into that area from the settled regions on the upper waters of the Putumayo. These traders came in search of an 'inferior kind of rubber' known as '*sernambi*' or '*jebe debil*' (weak fine rubber) produced by the indigenous population in that region. The banks of the Igaraparaná and the Caraparaná were stocked with the *Hevea brasiliensis* trees which provided the 'milk' from which this rubber was processed. The main interest of the traders was not, however, in trees scattered throughout the region but in the existence of several tribes – among them the Huitotos, the Boras, the Andokes, and the Ocainas – who inhabited the area. These groups of Indians eventually formed, under compulsion, the labour force for rubber extraction. As Casement observed: 'The rubber trees of themselves were of no value; it was Indians who could be made or induced to tap them and to bring in the rubber on the white man's terms that all the invading "conquistadores" were in search of.'[11]

The Colombian traders capitalized on the Putumayo Indians' production of rubber for their own use. Their technique of rubber extraction and processing was to gash the tree with a knife or machete, catching the 'milk' in little baskets of leaves. This extract was then washed in running water and pounded into long sausage-shaped rolls which the later Peruvian rubber traders termed '*chorizos*'.

In the early stages of contact between the traders and the Indians, this rubber had been exchanged for trade goods like machetes, powder, and caps for the few guns which the Indians possessed. Other articles of trade included beads, mirrors, tin bowls, basins, fish hooks and tins of sardines and potted meats. Those Indians who engaged in this initial friendly exchange quickly found themselves subject to increased and unending demands for rubber and the performance of varied tasks. The 'subjugation' of the Putumayo Indians was made possible by the superior coercive technology of the white invaders for the Indians' blowpipes and spears were no match for the rifles of the '*blancos*'. The area under the control of the rubber traders was extended from the banks of the two tributaries of the Putumayo to the interior. The pattern of expansion, which involved the appropriation of the rubber trees and an Indian labour force, was described by Casement in this way:

> These subduers formed themselves into bands and parties, dubbed commercial associations, and, having overcome the resistance of the Indians, they appropriated them to their own exclusive use along with the rubber trees that might be in the region they inhabited. Henceforth to the chief of the band they became 'my Indians', and any attempt by one of his civilised neighbours to steal, wheedle, or entice away his Indians became a capital offence.[12]

By the time of Casement's visit to the Putumayo in 1910, the commercial network (by that date controlled by the Peruvian Amazon Company) which linked rubber extraction in the rain forests to the export market was clearly established. The pre-capitalist system of organizing labour in the rubber industry resembled, in important respects, forms of forced labour (like the Peruvian *mita*) which were widely used in colonial Spanish America.[13] In the Putumayo region, as in New Spain, 'every part of the economic structure depended in the end upon the labour of the Indians' (Simpson 1941: 103). The principal rubber depot of the company was located at La Chorrera and controlled ten dependent stations which were responsible for the initial collection of the rubber which the indigenous population were coerced into producing. Male adult Indians were required, in each district, to bring in fixed quantities of rubber at regular intervals. At the time of a '*puesta*' (which meant literally a setting down of the rubber) the employees of the station were sent to provide an armed escort for the Indians as they deposited their rubber. The rubber collected from these *puestas* (which occurred at intervals of between fifteen and twenty days depending on the locality) were later transported to the depot at La Chorrera by Indian men, women, and children or to the nearest point on the River Igaraparaná, for shipment to that station. This general collection of rubber known as the '*fabrico*' took place after five or more *puestas*.[14]

The Indians were paid for their rubber on the completion of the *fabrico* which occurred every seventy-five to one hundred days. However, these payments were termed 'advances', which were understood to be advances for the rubber delivered at the next *fabrico*. By this arrangement, the company had unilaterally introduced a system of debt peonage in which the Indians had to work off their debts by continuing to produce rubber. The scale of payments for the rubber delivered was arbitrary and 'bore no true relation to the value of the produce forced from the Indian and but little to his needs or wishes'.[15] One Barbadian migrant interviewed by Casement on his 1910 visit to the Putumayo region reported that he had seen 'an Indian receive a tin bowl as payment for an entire *fabrico* (which might be put at possibly 80 kg.), which he had thrown on the ground and left behind him in disgust'.[16]

This system of forced labour was maintained by the threat of violence and violence administered gratuitously. Physical coercion, in the form of flogging, torture and mutilation, often culminating in murder, was necessary to sustain the output of rubber from an indigenous population which resisted the attempts to convert them to the discipline of commercial production. Although the Putumayo Indians were, as we have suggested, outgunned, they continued to resist their enslavement by running away. Indians ran away not only from the immediate neighbourhood where they had lived but to distant regions where they hoped to escape from the onerous duties they were required to perform. This long-distance flight was undoubtedly a response to the pressures exerted by the chiefs of the outlying stations (who were paid a percentage of the produce collected) to increase the output of rubber.[17]

The Barbadian migrants' role in this economic structure, which was based on involuntary servitude, was to police the indigenous population at different stages of the collection of the rubber produced. This policing function was not new to Barbadians outside their homeland for they were seen as the West Indian counterparts of the 'martial races' of India and had, for that reason, been recruited to the police forces of Trinidad, British Honduras and the Bahamas in the late nineteenth century (Johnson 1991: 71–91). The first party of Barbadian labourers which landed at La Chorrera in November 1904 numbered thirty men, accompanied by five of their wives. These men armed with Winchester rifles and provided with a large supply of cartridges were sent on a long trek through the forest to establish 'trade relations' with the Andokes Indians – a mission more accurately described as a process of enslavement. This mission involved raids on the Indians who, once captured, were compelled to produce rubber for the organizers of this foray. Barbadian migrants were also used on 'punitive expeditions' which were intended to capture or kill Indians who had earlier killed some Colombian traders who had settled in the Andokes' country to enslave that tribe and coerce them into producing rubber for them. The routine duties of the Barbadians most often involved 'guarding or coercing, or . . . actively maltreating Indians to force them to work and bring in india-rubber to the various sections'.[18] There were Barbadians who complained to Casement, during his visit, that they had reluctantly complied with the orders of their employers but he was convinced of the complicity of some migrants in this coercive labour system: 'In this system of armed extortion, which can only rightly be termed brigandage, the Barbados men were active agents. This part, no doubt, the men themselves were sometimes willing enough to perform.'[19] Michael Taussig (1984: 467–97) has argued that the level of 'dissension, hatred, and mistrust' among the company's employees was so high that their effectiveness as a social unit was maintained only by 'their group ritualization of torturing Indians'.

An integral part of a system for the subjugation and control of an Indian labour force, the Barbadian migrants were themselves victims of a system of debt peonage whose effect was to keep them at their jobs. Casement pointed out in his report of 1911 that Indians, Barbadians and even some of the early rubber traders were caught up in this web of indebtedness. He indicated that J. C. Arana y Hermanos had gradually assumed control of the rubber trade from men whom they had previously supplied with their necessities and transportation facilities by extending credit to them:

> Throughout the greater part of the Amazon region, where the rubber trade flourishes, a system of dealing prevails which is not tolerated in civilised communities. In so far as it affects a labouring man or an individual who sells his labour, it is termed 'peonage', and is repressed by drastic measures in some parts of the New World. It consists in getting the person working for you into your debt and keeping him there; and in lieu of other means of discharging this obligation he is forced to work for his creditor upon what are practically the latter's terms, and under varying forms of bodily constraint. In the Amazon valley this method of dealing has been expanded until it embraces not only the Indian workman, but is often made to apply to those who are themselves the employers of this kind of labour. By accumulated obligations contracted in this way one trader will pledge his business until it and himself become practically the property of the creditor. His business is merged, and he himself becomes an employee, and often finds it hard to escape from the responsibilities he has thus contracted.[20]

In 1910, Casement discovered that most of the twenty Barbadians whom he encountered in the service of the Peruvian Amazon Company were indebted to their employers. This indebtedness resulted from a combination of circumstances. In the Putumayo district, the company had not honoured the terms of the migrants' contracts which had stipulated that they would be provided with meals and medical attention. In the early years of their engagement, no doctor resided in the region. Although a physician had eventually been appointed by the company, he was based at the La Chorrera station where he was inaccessible to most of the employees. This meant that medicines needed by the migrants were not available or had to be purchased from their wages. As a result, large sums were deducted from their account with the company store for products which should have been supplied free by the terms of their contracts. The Barbadians had also run up debts in order to maintain their Indian wives and children. On their arrival, they had usually been assigned Indian women, by the agent of the company, to be their temporary wives. Some of these debts were incurred for basic needs like food and clothing which were sold at prices, Casement asserted, '1,000 per cent over their cost prices or prime value'.[21] Since migrants were located in remote districts, they had no alternative to the company's store for which they provided a captive market. The effect of these grossly inflated prices for necessities was to reduce the migrants' real wages below their nominal wages. Wages were paid essentially in truck. Thus Casement observed: 'Nominally, the men were well paid with from 5l. to 6l. per month, but this pay given with one hand was generally taken back with the other, for the prices at which the men were forced to satisfy their necessities from the company's stores ate up each month's and even several months of their earnings before they came due.'[22]

Another source of Barbadian indebtedness was gambling, which was a major leisure-time activity. In the outlying stations, the Barbadian employees passed the time, when they were not hunting or guarding the Indians, by gambling or lying in their hammocks. Since there was no money in circulation, debts were paid by writing an IOU which was debited from the loser's accounts in the company's books at the La Chorrera agency. This was an activity which was encouraged by the company. It was thus not unusual for the chief agent of a station to gamble 'with even his most subordinate employees'.[23]

The company deliberately encouraged migrant indebtedness for several reasons. First, they profited from inflated prices for medicines and basic needs at the company's store. Since no money passed hands, the employees were paid in truck which served to reduce the company's costs for the supervision of their servile labour force. Second, employee indebtedness was a strategy for lengthening the labour cycle for the individual was not allowed to leave until he had cleared his debts. To achieve this end, the company practised creative bookkeeping. As Casement pointed out: 'A man in debt anywhere in the Amazon rubber districts is not allowed to leave until the debt is paid, and as the creditor makes out the account and keeps the books, the debtor frequently does not know how much he owes, and, even if he had the means, might not always be able to satisfy the claim. Accounts are falsified, and men are kept in what becomes a state of bondage, partly through their own thriftlessness (which is encouraged) and partly by deliberate dishonesty.'[24] The company did not stand to lose from the employees' mounting indebtedness for debts were automatically deducted from the workers' future wages. It is likely that the Peruvian company applied to the rubber industry the techniques of debt peonage – in particular the *enganche* system – which was already used in the Peruvian sugar industry.[25] In 1910, after serving terms of five and six years in the Putumayo district, Barbadian migrants had little to show for their labour. As Casement reported: 'The man Dyall, who had completed nearly six years' service when I met him at Chorrera on the 24th September, appeared to be in debt to the company to the sum of 440 soles (say, 44l.) for goods nominally purchased from its stores.'[26] Another migrant, Stanley S. Lewis, also told Casement a similar story of his work experience in the Putumayo district. After five years of labour in that area, Lewis 'had only 3l. balance of wages due to him; all the rest of his pay had gone in various expenses and in buying things at the company's store'.[27]

The Peruvian Amazon Company's successful operation of these multi-layered systems of labour coercion was made possible by the autonomy which it exercised in an area remote from the centres of government and accessible only by company-owned steamers. As Casement explained: 'In a region so remote, where no civilised jurisdiction existed or Government authority was exercised, the agents of the so-called trading bodies had and have supreme control.'[28] In this period, a similar situation of coercive productive relations had also developed in King Leopold's Congo in the exploitation of natural rubber resources. The enslavement and exploitation of the Indian population indicates the continuity of white perceptions of the role of the indigenous peoples from the colonial into the national period. The persistence of these attitudes was remarked on by Casement: 'Custom sanctioned by long traditions, and an evil usage whose maxim is that "the Indian has no rights", are far stronger than a distant law that rarely emerges into practice.'[29]

In the literature on labour migration in the British Caribbean in the nineteenth and early twentieth centuries, scholars have routinely represented this outward movement as an ultramarine version of the post-Emancipation 'flight from the estates' argument. For British West Indians, they have argued, labour migration involved not only a flight from the plantation with its association with slavery but also an escape from 'the systems of domination' which were features of post-Emancipation societies. Typical of this approach are Velma Newton's (1984: 7) observations on British West Indian emigration: 'Whatever the factors which influenced the decision to emigrate, many British West Indians conceived of the move as a means of freeing themselves – even if temporarily – from plantation labour and the stigma of slavery attached to it; as a means of shedding the seemingly permanent lower class status to which the West Indian social structure condemned them.'[30] While acknowledging the existence of migrants who failed in the quest for self-improvement, the recent literature on labour migration in the British Caribbean, notably Bonham C. Richardson's, *Panama Money in Barbados, 1900–1920*, has emphasized the transformative effects of remittances on island societies and economies.[31]

The case of Barbadian migrants in the Putumayo district provides evidence that migrant experience did not always result in the greater independence or material rewards that they anticipated. It was for them a continuation of the coercion which they had experienced in their homeland where laws, enacted by a planter-dominated legislature, attempted to immobilize members of the black working class. The essential difference between the two experiences was in the degree of coercion and, in the Barbadian context, the existence of the rule of law though clearly weighted in the interests of the dominant class.

NOTES

1 See, for example, the biographies of Sir Roger Casement: Reid (1976); Sawyer (1984); Inglis (1974); Taussig (1984: 467–97, 1987).
2 For a discussion of Barbadian socio-economic conditions see Richardson (1985) chapters 2 and 3; Beckles (1990) chapter 6.
3 The classic account of early Barbadian emigration to neighbouring Caribbean colonies is Roberts (1955: 245–88). For the later period see Johnson (1973: 5–30).
4 In 1908, the word 'rubber' was dropped from the new company's title.

5 For an example of the service contract see Papers of the British and Foreign Anti-Slavery and Aborigines Protection Society (Rhodes House Library, Oxford). Mss.Brit.Emp. S.22. G3449 Peru-Putumayo Casement Dossier, f.103.

6 See Foreign Office to Consul-General Casement, 21 July 1910 in *Correspondence Respecting the Treatment of British Colonial Subjects and Native Indians Employed in the Collection of Rubber in the Putumayo District*, Parl. Papers 1912 (Cd. 6266), p.1. Casement had as British Consul at Boma, capital of the Congo Free State, investigated and reported on allegations of slavery in its rubber industry.

7 See *Correspondence Respecting the Treatment of British Colonial Subjects*, p. 1.

8 Consul-General Casement to Sir Edward Grey, 31 January 1911 in *Correspondence Respecting the Treatment of British Colonial Subjects*, p. 7.

9 Ibid., p. 9.

10 Ibid., p. 11.

11 Consul-General Casement to Sir Edward Grey, 17 March 1911 in *Correspondence Respecting the Treatment of British Colonial Subjects* p. 27.

12 Consul-General Casement to Sir Edward Grey, 31 January 1911 in *Correspondence Respecting the Treatment of British Colonial Subjects*, p. 10.

13 For an excellent discussion of coercive labour systems in Latin America, see Knight (1988: 107–17).

14 Consul-General Casement to Sir Edward Grey, 17 March 1911 in *Correspondence Respecting the Treatment of British Colonial Subjects*, p. 49.

15 Ibid., p. 50.

16 Ibid.

17 Consul-General Casement to Sir Edward Grey 17 March 1911 in *Correspondence Respecting the Treatment of British Colonial Subjects*, p. 35.

18 Consul-General Casement to Sir Edward Grey, 31 January 1911 in *Correspondence Respecting the Treatment of British Colonial Subjects*, p. 12.

19 Ibid., p. 9.

20 Consul-General Casement to Sir Edward Grey, 31 January 1911 in *Correspondence Respecting the Treatment of British Colonial Subjects*, pp. 10–11.

21 Ibid., p. 6.

22 Ibid., p. 18.

23 Ibid., p. 17.

24 Ibid., p. 18.

25 For discussion of the *enganche* system, see Gonzales (1985); Klarén (1977: 229–52).

26 Consul-General Casement to Sir Edward Grey, 31 January 1911 in *Correspondence Respecting the Treatment of British Colonial Subjects*, p. 16.

27 'Précis of the Statement of Stanley S. Lewis, a native of Barbados, made to His Majesty's Consul-General on board the "Liberal" on September 20 and 22, 1910, and on subsequent occasions' in *Correspondence Respecting the Treatment of British Colonial Subjects*, p. 65.

28 Consul-General Casement to Sir Edward Grey, 31 January 1911 in *Correspondence Respecting the Treatment of British Colonial Subjects*, p. 9.

29 Consul-General Casement to Sir Edward Grey, 17 March 1911 in *Correspondence Respecting the Treatment of British Colonial Subjects*, p. 28.

30 See also Newton (1984: 169) and Thomas-Hope (1978: 66).

31 See also Myers (1976).

REFERENCES

Beckles, Hilary McD. (1990) *A History of Barbados: From Amerindian Settlement to Nation-State*, Cambridge.

Chamberlain, Mary (1997) *Narratives of Exile and Return*, London and Basingstoke.

Conniff, Michael L. (1985) *Black Labor in a White Canal, Panama, 1904–1981*, Pittsburgh.
Foner, Nancy (1978) *Jamaica Farewell: Jamaican Migrants in London*, Berkeley.
Gonzales, Michael J. (1985) *Plantation Agriculture and Social Control in Northern Peru, 1875–1933*, Austin.
Greenfield, Sidney M. (1983) 'Barbadians in the Brazilian Amazon', *Luso-Brazilian Review*, 20.
Inglis, Brian (1974) *Roger Casement*, New York.
Johnson, Howard (1973) 'Barbadian immigrants in Trinidad 1870–1897,' *Caribbean Studies*, 13.
—— (1991) 'Patterns of policing in the post-Emancipation British Caribbean, 1835–95', in David M. Anderson and David Killingray (eds) *Policing the Empire: Government, Authority and Control, 1830–1940*, Manchester.
Klarén, Peter F. (1977) 'The social and economic consequences of modernization in the Peruvian sugar industry, 1870–1930', in Kenneth Duncan and Ian Rutledge (eds) *Land and Labour in Latin America: Essays on the Development of Agrarian Capitalism in the Nineteenth and Twentieth Centuries*, Cambridge.
Knight, Alan (1988) 'Debt Bondage in Latin America', in Léonie J. Archer (ed.) *Slavery and Other Forms of Unfree Labour*, London.
Lewis, Lancelot S. (1980) *The West Indian in Panama: Black Labor in Panama, 1850–1914*, Washington, DC.
Myers, Robert A. (1976) '"I love my home bad, but . . . . "': the historical and contemporary context of migration on Dominica, West Indies', Ph.D. dissertation, University of North Carolina.
Newton, Velma (1984) *The Silver Men: West Indian Labour Migration to Panama 1850–1914*, Jamaica.
Peach, Ceri (1968) *West Indian Migration to Britain*, Oxford.
Petras, Elizabeth McLean (1988) *Jamaican Labor Migration: White Capital and Black Labor, 1850–1930*, Boulder, CO.
Purcell, Trevor W. (1993) *Banana Fallout: Class, Color, and Culture among West Indians in Costa Rica*, Los Angeles.
Reid, B. L. (1976) *The Lives of Roger Casement*, New Haven.
Richardson, Bonham C. (1985) *Panama Money in Barbados, 1900–1920*, Knoxville.
Roberts, George W. (1955) 'Emigration From the island of Barbados', *Social and Economic Studies*, 4.
Sawyer, Roger (1984) *Casement: The Flawed Hero*, London.
Simpson, Lesley Byrd (1941) *Many Mexicos*, New York.
Taussig, Michael (1984) 'Culture of terror – space of death. Roger Casement's Putumayo Report and the explanation of torture', *Comparative Studies in Society and History*, 26(3).
—— (1987) *Shamanism, A Study in Colonialism, and Terror and the Wild Man Healing*, Chicago.
Thomas-Hope, Elizabeth M. (1978) 'The establishment of a migration tradition: British West Indian movements to the Hispanic Caribbean in the century after Emancipation' in Colin G. Clarke, (ed.) *Caribbean Social Relations*, Liverpool: Centre for Latin-American Studies, University of Liverpool.
Weinstein, Barbara (1983) *The Amazon Rubber Boom 1850–1920*, Stanford.

12 Globalization and the development of a Caribbean migration culture

Elizabeth Thomas-Hope

From the outset, Caribbean colonies were part of the wider global political economy. This globalization was based first on mercantilism, the trans-Atlantic slave trade and the plantation. Later, new forms of investment were developed within the framework of various types of European and North American colonial and neo-colonial relationships. The movement of people was an integral part of these global systems and migration became an important means of adaptation to the societal changes which were induced locally.

The first profound changes were those produced by the social and economic upheavals which followed the emancipation of slaves. These had far-reaching implications for the ex-slaves in terms of their quest for an identity based upon personhood, for the freedom to move and, related to this, their incorporation into the new globalized labour markets. Migration became so important a part of the processes of adaptation to new and evolving circumstances that, ultimately, the significance of the trans-national linkages at the level of political economies was matched by that of trans-national linkages at the levels of families, households and individuals. Such globalized lives and livelihoods influenced all aspects of material culture, goals and frames of reference which characterize the identity of the contemporary Caribbean.

EMANCIPATION, FREEDOM AND MIGRATION

The former slaves from the British colonies began to emigrate immediately after Emancipation (1834) and the abolition of the apprenticeship regulations (1834–38), and from the French islands after 1848. The ex-slaves, the first emigrants, inhabited lands in which they had no traditional ties or emotional attachment, quite the reverse. Ancestral attachment lay elsewhere and the disruptive and destructive system of slavery left the black population deeply alienated not only from their immediate past, but also from their present environments and, even more seriously, from themselves. Furthermore, the plantation created a single set of national criteria for social status and political power and these criteria were based on European norms. Therefore, by definition, status and power were outside the scope of the population of African descent. On grounds of race, culture, material possessions, occupation and employment, the overwhelming majority of the population in the Caribbean colonies occupied only a marginalized position.

The lack of freedom inherent in slavery meant not only an alienation of self and of identity but also a lack of those symbols with which freedom was associated. These included material possessions, especially ownership of land, and access to power. It also included freedom of movement. The migration from plantation to interior hill lands and the establishment of free villages provided a degree of independence, but only a poor economic base. Nor was there any potential for gaining the symbols of status or power which would be accepted nationally.

The pursuit of independence from the plantation and from the entire societal system on which it was based led to the movement of workers not only away from the plantations but, in many cases, away from the islands altogether to return later having gained some measure of economic advantage (Thomas-Hope 1995). This made the former slaves highly responsive to new and changing opportunities associated with the international division of labour. The identities of the emerging societies were shaped within the context of movement, absenteeism and return.

Many of the Caribbean territories, for example the Netherlands Antilles, never truly constituted plantation colonies. In others, the impact of the plantation was less all-embracing of the entire economic, political and social structure because of its later development in the twentieth century under United States' dominance. Therefore, the plantation alone could not provide an adequate explanation for the evolving process of migration. But what it did explain was the early occurrence and the particular characteristics of migration in the sugar colonies. Later on and in the non-sugar colonies (too), migration was influenced by the local social and economic structures which were, in all cases, fundamentally conditioned by the nature of metropolitan political economies and the associated implications for individual Caribbean territories.

TRANSFORMATIONS IN CLASS STRUCTURE AND MIGRATION

The first voluntary migrations from Caribbean colonies in the nineteenth century occurred at a time of major social ferment and economic uncertainty. The adjustment to the new societal freedoms demanded major adaptations on the part of all groups in a situation where the preoccupation of the plantocracy was the preservation of their access to labour supplies, and that of the former slaves the consolidation and putting into practical effect the theoretical achievement of freedom.

With the breakdown in the formal institutions of slavery and the emergence of a new social order, social divisions and social relations, previously determined by law, were then maintained by the accepted criteria of status and power – namely, race and economic wealth. The social distinctions of the plantation in the earlier period became the symbols of class in subsequent years.

The divisions between masters and other white colonists, freemen of colour and slaves evolved within the new economic order to produce counterparts in class terms. Internally differentiated by occupation and economic wealth, the three groups, distinct from each other principally on the basis of colour and political power, formed an upper, middle and lower class. Evidence of change in this pattern was minimal until the 1930s, though periodic challenges to the status quo (as in the Morant Bay rebellion in Jamaica in 1865 and the Federation Riots in Barbados in the 1870s) demonstrated that the society was by no means static. Nevertheless, the system was maintained around the prevailing economic structures still fundamentally based on the plantation.

The major post-war economic changes in the Caribbean were decreased dependence on agricultural monoculture and increased industrial activity. In those few Caribbean countries where resources permitted, industrialization included the development of extractive industries, but in most states it has been based on some measure of tourism and manufacturing. The first stages of industrialization, and in many Caribbean territories the only stage, has been manufacturing for import substitution or the formation of enclaves oriented towards the parent companies overseas. Elsewhere, the diversification of the economy has given the opportunity to former land-owning families, as well as others already prospering from commerce, to invest in and/or manage the new enterprises. As a consequence, the national capitalist class has increased in size as foreign, absentee control declined. Migration was one of the few means open to the masses to improve their material circumstances and thereby also enhance their social status.

The narrowly based, three-tiered class structure which characterized the period before the Second World War became more complex. It reflected the more varied and intricate pattern of economic relations based on a transformed and greatly reduced reliance on agriculture, alongside the expanded set of capitalist and semi-capitalist relations of the increasingly urbanized structures. A heterogeneous urban working class emerged from the former rural lower classes and urban lower service sectors; the expansion of educational opportunities facilitated the upward mobility of the children of the black lower class to fill a range of professional and urban white-collar workers, both in the private sector and in the growing civil service, as well as technical jobs in the industrial sector.

For all this class mobility and the broadening of the parameters of racial and cultural status with which class was associated, it was not accompanied by a corresponding increase in relative income levels of the upwardly mobile. The necessary economic base for sustaining such expectations simply did not exist. The reduction in the hierarchy of deference and the associated pattern of patronage and support shown towards those of lower status was not accompanied by incomes adequate to support the new aspirations for independence. Minimum wages rose beyond the reach of lower middle-class employers and thus the level of service employment declined. Social relations became less closely aligned to the former racial and cultural distinctions and much more to the capitalist commodity relations (Gordon 1987: 3).

These changes were partly due to the economic transformations and the increase in capitalist activity in the islands and thus the increasing opportunities for wage labour in the non-manual and non-agricultural sectors. At the same time, the channel for obtaining such opportunities was mostly through the expanded educational facilities which came with the period of post-war capitalist expansion. By the early decades of the twentieth century, education was beginning to play a greater role in class mobility, compensating for and, at the same time, starting the process of breaking down the rigid association of class and colour. Education became a critical factor in the acquisition of professional occupations and thus middle-class status. In addition to this was the special value accorded a foreign education, a direct legacy of the ascendant role of metropolitan frames of reference in the region.

There were limited opportunities for secondary education and vocational training, chiefly in the teaching profession, for children of the black working class. In this regard, though with difficulty, hard work and dedication, migration was beginning to play a role in providing the capital from which to start the accumulation of sufficient finance directly or indirectly to assist in the education of children. This was the means whereby the inter-generational upward mobility of an increasing number of black, working-class people was achieved by the end of the Second World War. This tendency increased in the following decades. Even where formal qualifications were not acquired, work experience or in-service skill training were important to the migrant's success and perceived migration achievement. Furthermore, it has been usual for migrants to appreciate a wide variety of migration experiences as contributing to their general educational improvement. Cultural symbols such as standard grammatical speech, public behaviour deemed 'socially respectable' and evidence that the horizons of the mind have been extended beyond the confines of insular parochialism are all highly valued. Migration takes on a special significance in this context.

The paradoxical association since the 1950s in most Caribbean countries of increased opportunities for social mobility on the one hand, and widening income disparities on the other, have reinforced the earlier role and significance of migration. As the middle class expanded, so expectations of bourgeois notions of status and living standards, based on North American norms, increased. At the same time, there was no commensurate distribution of capital to sustain these expectations. Transient flows to North America or Caribbean off-shore locations of American dollar influence, as well as longer-term circulation to North America, has ensued.

Likewise, the new urbanized working class in both formal and informal economic sectors have expectations of material acquisitiveness which cannot be readily met locally by most people. The former greater level of contentedness under conditions of rural self-sufficiency have been overtaken by much more widespread urban poverty and, at the same time, increased exposure to American television culture. Visits abroad for even very brief periods of time are perceived by the working class to provide the certain means of achieving ambitions of improved living standards.

Post-war changes in economic structures, social relations and educational opportunities were accompanied by increased not decreased migration. Where the level of industrialization was greatest, as in Puerto Rico, Jamaica and the Dominican Republic in the 1950s and 1960s, the increased available capital together with the changing pattern of class relations fuelled the migration process. For urban populations, the employment opportunities generated by the new capital intensive industries fell far short of the demand and the expectations for obtaining work. At the same time, for the agricultural smallholder, land was more valuable as a commodity for sale to the industrial and tourist enterprises than for agricultural production. This crisis in the internal development of most Caribbean territories led to worsening urban problems and to the further decline in agriculture. Migration rates increased as opportunities within the new economic order failed to meet rising expectations. Meanwhile, the growing disparities of wealth in the societies which accompanied the localization of resources heightened the potential for migration.

Capital in the hands of some was a facilitating factor in migration, while the widening gap in income, as well as in the ability of the economy to meet the new demands for urban employment, contributed to sustaining the high potential for migration for the majority. Yet again, as in the early post-Emancipation period, migration was fundamentally a means of adjusting to the changing economic and associated social stresses within society as well as providing a response to its opportunities.

Even where resources came under state control, as in Guyana in the 1960s, or state shares in the economy were extended, as in Jamaica in the 1970s, emigration did not slacken but increased. The fact that the state itself was seen to be taking over the role of entrepreneur alienated the upper strata of the society, accustomed as it was to such a role being played by either foreign corporations or local families. While manifestations of this alienation were translated into racial terms, particularly in the case of Guyana, the altered class relations and political tensions were basic to the migrations. Nationalization or localization of assets have been among the major transforming agents in the post-war era.

A second factor which occurred simultaneously in most Caribbean countries was the increased priority given to the education of the masses. Changing economic and ownership patterns with the demise of agriculture and the rise of industrialization, coupled with the expansion of secondary education, had profound influences upon the class structure and the subsequent new pattern of class relations in Caribbean societies. Despite all the new opportunities in the Caribbean and the more attainable symbols of status and power, migration was still an integral part of the society. It remained deeply embedded in social institutions and, above all, became incorporated into the new channels of social mobility.

MIGRATION AND PERSONAL ADVANCEMENT

In a situation where opportunities in the home country were perceived to be minimal or non-existent, the migrant and high potential migrant in the Caribbean was conditioned to expect upward mobility as an outcome of migration. Migration facilitated an extension of work opportunities beyond the limitations of the local or national economic environment. Thus the role of migration in this context was closely linked to the role it played in the achievement of one or more of the objectives of work. For the majority of migrants and those who desired to migrate, it was believed that their activity or intended activity abroad would produce the additional capital which would raise their standard of living in terms of material comforts, as well as provide the assets on which independence, security and status were based. Land and a house were the principal items in this category and migration to work abroad is known to make possible the accumulation of capital for purchasing them.

Status was enhanced partly through material assets acquired and also through the fact of having lived and worked abroad. The nature of the actual work undertaken overseas was not always readily disclosed, since it was invariably of an equally low or even lower status than the work available locally. Nevertheless, there was a general view that the work done in a foreign country was automatically of higher value by the very fact of its location, whatever the work actually entailed. Furthermore, in that work commanded higher financial returns elsewhere, its value, and thus its status, was also enhanced. This was a factor of prime importance in the migration process, for what it indicated was that location, more than type of work, determined its status.

This explains why work in a neighbouring Caribbean island has been regarded as being more desirable, even though the job was essentially of the same status. Likewise, in the metropolitan centres of North America or Europe the status of the same occupation in the Caribbean is multiplied several-fold. For example, there was seen to be no comparison between agricultural work in St Vincent and the same work done on contract by Vincentians in Barbados; and definitely no comparison in the choice between Barbados and the United States or Canada whether or not the work was the same.

The international historical framework within which Caribbean societies were established and the mechanisms whereby they were structured and class relations emerged combined to produce the underlying political economy conducive to population transfers on the one hand and a *raison d'être* of those populations for moving on the other. This combination of factors has been consistently manifest in the role that Caribbean people have played in response to European and North American demands for labour in the expansion of capital both within the Caribbean region and outside the region, in the metropolises themselves.

GLOBALIZATION OF LABOUR AND MIGRATION

Emancipation had created surplus populations, though not in numerical terms, since labour for the plantations always continued to be very much in demand, necessitating in many colonies the importation of other indentured workers. But surplus labour existed to the extent that the ex-slaves withdrew their labour from the plantations. As Caribbean societies became increasingly part of the metropolitan trans-national labour force, so each generation became socialized in a way of life and livelihood conditioned by migration. To these were added the non-labour migrants: landlords were traditionally absentee and Western Europe was always regarded as a normal extension of the Caribbean for the upper and professional classes. However, the great majority of migrants comprised workers; thus the location of different types of investment in the region was especially important in determining the direction of movement. At the same time, national legislation articulated the demands and the restraints of those same metropolitan societies concerning the immigration of Caribbean people, thus controlling the timing and volume of the migrations.

Three major periods may be identified in terms of the directions of migrant flow: the period from the mid-nineteenth century to the Second World War, the post-war years until the early 1960s and the period from the mid-1960s to the present. In the mid-nineteenth century, movements were predominantly to plantations of the sugar-producing islands, especially with the expansion of sugar into the former Spanish colonies, first Puerto Rico and then the Dominican Republic and Cuba by the early twentieth century (Thomas-Hope 1978 and 1986). At the end of the nineteenth century, industrial operations employed even larger numbers of migrants within the region. The cutting of the Panama Canal and railway construction in Central America, later oil drilling and refining in Venezuela and the Netherlands Antilles of Curaçao and Aruba were among the first of West European and North American industrial operations employing migrant labour in the region.

The later expansion of North American activities was associated with military bases, aluminium plants, tourism, banking, insurance and other 'off-shore' industries. Like the earlier operations, these have employed large numbers of seasonal or more permanent migrants coming in from neighbouring islands. Indeed, the labour force of some islands, like the Bahamas and the Virgin Islands, is comprised of a high proportion of migrants, renewed on an almost continual basis (Marshall 1979, 1984). Where industry was non-labour intensive or was located in territories where populations were very large, then no migration flows occurred – as in the case of Jamaican or Guyanese bauxite, Trinidadian oil, Puerto Rican manufacturing. Likewise, no additional labour was required where development initiatives were endogenous, as in the range of import substitution industries in most Caribbean states.

The mobility of labour within the Caribbean and circum-Caribbean countries continued while the movements outside the region were occurring from the early twentieth century and with increased momentum from the mid-twentieth century. West European and North American requirements for labour and manpower for the armed forces both in the First and Second World Wars led to the recruitment of workers from the Caribbean colonies (Colonial Office Report, cited in Senior and Manley 1955: 5; Proudfoot 1950: 23).

The post-war reconstruction in Western Europe also required labour, much of which was obtained from the Caribbean colonies. From the mid-1950s the hitherto small numbers of 'colonial subjects' going to their respective 'mother country' increased to flows of massive proportions. Large numbers of skilled, semi-skilled and unskilled workers were employed chiefly in industry, transport and hospital services.

Legislation in the United Kingdom in 1962 and 1965 brought that country's Caribbean migrant inflow to a virtual end. This merely resulted in a shift in the movement away from Britain and towards Canada and the United States. There, changing labour demands had led to alterations in their immigration legislation in precisely the same years – 1962 and 1965 respectively. These changes favoured Caribbean migrants, especially those falling within the professional and skilled labour categories.

The movements to France have continued to the present time because of the special departmental status which the Antilles maintain (Domenach and Picouet 1992). In the case of the Netherlands, policies were geared towards integrating the Caribbean migrants into Dutch society rather than restricting entry (Amersfoort 1982). In the course of time, the numbers of new arrivals dwindled without legislative intervention. As in the movement of the Netherlands Antilleans to Holland, the net migration of Puerto Ricans to the United States declined as the circulation of migrants established a balance between outward and return flows.

The migration fields have changed over time, largely determined by the changing demands for labour by West European or North American capital developments either within or outside the Caribbean region itself. The Second World War brought about a shift in the focus of migrations from a predominantly regional movement to one dominated by flows to Western Europe. In the 1960s, immigration legislation induced further changes in the direction of Caribbean migrations and the pattern became dominated by movements to the USA and Canada. Intra-regional mobility continued virtually throughout the entire period.

TRANSNATIONAL LIVES OF CARIBBEAN PEOPLES

The complexity of Caribbean migration is due not only to the varying types of migration which occur, but also to the wide range of movements incorporated into the overall process. Return or counter-flows have always been an integral part of Caribbean migration. As the migrations themselves have differed in purpose so, not surprisingly, have the migrants varied in regard to their intention to return and the extent to which these intentions were subsequently realized.

The volume of counter-flow has been consistently underestimated, chiefly due to the difficulty of recording them for official statistics. Nevertheless, empirical studies have shown that not only have they been highly prevalent throughout the history of Caribbean migration but also, in various ways, they have been an integral part of the migration process. (Philpott 1973; Thomas-Hope 1985; Basch *et al.* 1987, Gmelch 1987). Indeed, the linkages maintained by the migrants between their households at source and destination are not only significant in perpetuating migration, but are deeply rooted in the culture. Migrants, even *in absentia*, are part of the ceremonial and sometimes the decision-making of the household in the Caribbean.

Transnational linkages are also essential for the economic support of the migrants' households in the Caribbean. The sending of remittances involves the movement of money as well as a wide range of goods sometimes transmitted by the migrants themselves or at other times by intermediaries, usually members of the immediate family or wider kinship network (Frucht 1968; Dirks 1972; Philpott 1973; Hill 1977; Brana-Shute and Brana-Shute 1982; Pessar 1982; Richardson 1983; Georges 1990). The migrants themselves return with varying degrees of regularity, for differing periods of time and, whether or not they ever return permanently, the transnational connections are maintained by their migration orientation or the return mentality (Rubenstein 1983; Thomas-Hope 1985 and 1992). Even during a protracted absence from the home country most Caribbean migrants remain, in various ways, part of their Caribbean household and thus part of a family, household and personal transnational network. In this way, Caribbean households remain structurally linked to their absent members through the support system established. In return, migrants can, if necessary, or should they so wish, retain their places in the household with the option to return and obtain the benefits of that household and its inheritance for an indefinite period, sometimes the rest of their lives.

During the process of transnational interaction, whatever the specific time-span in any particular case, the displacement of the migrant is only partial, though the degree and nature of displacement varies throughout the migration cycle and from one migrant to another. The displacement of the work place invariably occurs in the case of transient movements without the displacement of any other aspect of the migrant's activity. A major home base is maintained simultaneously with a secondary base, and either the one or the other may be located in the Caribbean.

The pattern of displacement is dynamic and changes as the migrant's activities alter and either he or she increases the emphasis on the home country or reduces the commitments there allowing an increase in the commitments at the destination. The balance between the two alters throughout the migration cycle and though the precise nature of the transition is not clear and varies with innumerable factors in the process, it maintains the source and destination places in a network of transnational interaction. This is a very important and hitherto little recognized aspect of the process which is significant for the perpetuation of the process through the continuing, though ever-altering nature of feedback (Thomas-Hope 1988). Depending on the purpose and duration of the absence abroad, the displacement of the individual's work activities, domestic, social and leisure activities may occur to varying extent in either the country of migration source or destination. The interaction between place of origin and destination thus remains linked in a dynamic set of relationships changing both throughout the individual's migration cycle and extended beyond, to have implications for the future pattern of migration in the household.

Overall, the greatest impact of migration upon the household or wider family is in its ability to extend the parameters of opportunity beyond national limitations. The transnational dimension of the household and the family has permitted society to preserve its viability despite continued, sometimes large-scale, migration and possibly even because of it. Thus, households, families and individual lives are fundamentally transnational in character, giving rise to a Caribbean identity which is intrinsically global.

CONCLUSION

The term 'migrant' includes a wide variety of persons, and 'migration' a wide range of spatial behaviour. Nor is the system static. Within the life-cycle of a household a number of migration types may occur involving one or more members of that household. It is difficult to ascertain the nature of the pattern of change from one type of mobility to another, but a transition in migration types certainly does occur and the influence is undoubtedly carried on to subsequent generations. Thus to refer to migration as though it were a single type of phenomenon, and to regard a migrant as a stereotype of the worker in search of a job, is to so oversimplify the situation as to conceptualize the process as constituting merely the displacement of people and ignore the institutional framework and the culture surrounding it.

The pattern of international relations with its inherent inequalities had been set from the establishment of Caribbean societies. All developments subsequently have simply reiterated the underlying objective in the minds of all classes alike to aspire to the international lifestyles of which Caribbean society is continually reminded in a number of different ways.

The continuities in the pattern and process of Caribbean migration, despite dramatic changes in both international and national contexts, reflect the deeply rooted significance of migration to the society. The value of migration to the expansion of capital is in the labour it has provided metropolitan interests; the value of migration to Caribbean peoples themselves is in the adjustments which it has facilitated in the face of constitutional, economic and social change. So successful were these strategies of adjustment that they became institutionalized to form an important part of Caribbean lives and livelihoods. The fact that so many are perceived to do so well from migration continues to endorse its value.

Freedom of movement took on special meaning to Caribbean peoples and the migration tradition never permitted island social and economic systems to totally determine the parameters of opportunity. In a number of ways, the island opportunities were extended to incorporate a wider world conditioned by historical circumstances, with its legacies of colonialism and slavery, the later distribution of capital and the pattern of labour markets.

It was in this context that the various sectors of the society ultimately became emigrant: the white colonists when their economic power base was undermined; the Creole whites and coloureds and also Asian and Middle Eastern minorities, when economic wealth and social status were perceived to be threatened. For the majority in most Caribbean countries – black or mulatto – the situation was different. Emigration was never a response to the threat of losing wealth or status, but rather the means of achieving it. Because of this, the process was seen by the majority not as permanent escape but of temporary withdrawal, with the intention of returning later to an improved material and social situation back home. Thus not only the initial immigrations but also the subsequent emigrations were to have a major impact upon the formation of society, and the structure of society in turn stimulated a complex pattern of emigration. It is not surprising, therefore, that an entire culture should have emerged in which migration was an integral part.

REFERENCES

Amersfoort, J.M.M. van (1982) *Immigration and the Formation of Minority Groups: The Dutch Experience, 1945–1975*, London: Cambridge University Press.

Basch, L., Wiltshire-Brodber, R., Wiltshire, W. and Toney, J. (1987) 'Caribbean regional and international migration: transnational dimensions', unpublished paper.

Brana-Shute, G. and Brana-Shute, R. (1982) 'The magnitude and impact of remittances in the Eastern Caribbean: a research note', in W.F. Stinner, K. de Albuquerque and R.S. Bryce-Laporte (eds) *Return Migration and Remittances: Developing a Caribbean Perspective*, Washington DC: Research Institute on Immigration and Ethnic Studies, Smithsonian Institution.

Domenach, H. and Picouet, M. (1992) *La Dimension Migratoire des Antilles*, Paris: Economica.

Dirks, R. (1972) 'Network groups and adaptation in an Afro-Caribbean community', *Man* 7: 565– 85.

Frucht, R. (1968) 'Emigration, remittances and social change: aspects of the social field in Nevis, West Indies', *Anthropologica* 10: 193–208.

Georges, E. (1990) *The Making of a Transnational Community: Migration, Development and Cultural Change in the Dominican Republic*, New York: Columbia University Press.

Gmelch, G. (1987) 'Work, innovation, and investment: the impact of return migrants in Barbados', *Human Organization* 46, 2: 131–40.

Gordon, D. (1987) *Class, Status and Social Mobility in Jamaica*, Kingston, Jamaica: Institute of Social and Economic Research, University of the West Indies.

Griffith, D.C. (1983) 'The promise of a country: the impact of seasonal US migration on the Jamaican peasantry', unpublished Ph.D. thesis, University of Florida.

Hill, D.R. (1977) 'The impact of migration on the metropolitan and folk society of Carriacou, Grenada', *Anthropological Papers of the American Museum of Natural History, New York* 54, 2.

Marshall, D. I. (1979) *The Haitian Problem: Illegal Migration to the Bahamas*, Kingston, Jamaica: Institute of Social and Economic Research, University of the West Indies.

—— (1984) 'Vincentian contract labour migration to Barbados: the satisfaction of mutual needs?', *Social and Economic Studies* 33: 63–92.

Pessar, P. (1982) 'Kinship relations of production in the migration process: the case of the Dominican emigration to the United States', New York Research Program in Inter-American Affairs at New York University, Occasional Paper, no. 32.

Philpott, S.B. (1973) *West Indian Migration: the Montserrat Case*, London: Athlone Press.

Proudfoot, M. (1950) *Population Movements in the Caribbean*, Port of Spain, Trinidad: Caribbean Commission Central Secretariat.

Richardson, B. C. (1983) *Caribbean Migrants: Environment and Human Survival on St Kitts and Nevis*, Knoxville: University of Tennessee Press.

Rubenstein, H. (1983) 'Remittances and rural development in the English-speaking Caribbean', *Human Organization* 42(4): 295–306.

Senior, C. and Manley, D. (1955) *A Report on Jamaican Migration to Great Britain*, Kingston, Jamaica: Government Printing Office.

Thomas-Hope, E.M. (1978) 'The establishment of a migration tradition: British West Indian movements to the Hispanic Caribbean in the century after Emancipation', in Colin G. Clarke (ed.) *Caribbean Social Relations*, Liverpool: Centre for Latin American Studies Monograph Series No. 8, 66–81.

—— (1985) 'Return migration and its implications for Caribbean development' in R. Pastor (ed.) *Migration and Development in the Caribbean*, Boulder, CO: Westview Press.

—— (1986) 'Caribbean diaspora – the inheritance of slavery: migration from the Commonwealth Caribbean', in Colin Brock (ed.) *The Caribbean in Europe: Aspects of the West Indian Experience in Britain, France and the Netherlands*, London: Frank Cass.

—— (1988) 'Caribbean skilled international migration and the transnational household', *Geoforum* 19(4): 423–32.

—— (1992) *Explanation in Caribbean Migration*, London: Macmillan.

—— (1995) 'Island systems and the paradox of freedom: migration in the post-Emancipation Leeward Islands', in Karen Fog Olwig (ed.) *Small Islands, Large Questions: Society, Culture and Resistance in the Post-Emancipation Caribbean*, London: Frank Cass, pp. 161–75.

Part VI

Gender, socialisation and survival in Caribbean communities

13 Trends in levels of Caribbean Segregation, Great Britain, 1961–91

Ceri Peach

INTRODUCTION

One of the issues regularly produced by the Press is the fear of American-style ghettos developing in Britain (Smith, 1989; Peach, 1968; 1996a). The 1991 Census was the first to include an ethnic question and it allows us to measure the levels of segregation for different ethnic groups. By using birthplace data, we can also measure change over time. This chapter reviews the settlement pattern of the Caribbean population in Britain. It shows the high concentration in the inner areas of large urban areas, particularly London and Birmingham. It examines the change in tenure pattern over time from private rental to owner occupation and council housing. It shows that despite the enormous structural barriers, high levels of unemployment and other sources of disadvantage, Caribbean segregation is not only much lower than African American levels in the USA, but also that in so far as data exist, these levels have shown a continuous downward trend since 1961.

BACKGROUND

Between 1951 and 1991, the Caribbean ethnic population of Great Britain grew from about 30,000 to 500,000 (see Table 13.1). The period of most rapid growth was from 1955 to 1962 and by 1974 the whole cycle of primary immigration was over. Between 1974 and 1994, although small scale immigration has continued, there has been rather more emigration than immigration (see Figure 13.1). The growth of the Caribbean population since the early 1970s has been due more to births in Britain than to immigration and since about 1984, there has been a larger Caribbean ethnic population born in Britain than born abroad (see Table 13.1). Not only is this the case, but there has been a net decrease of nearly 100,000 in the Caribbean-born population of Britain between the censuses of 1966 and 1991 (Peach, 1996b, 26).

During the period of mass migration, between 1955 and 1974, immigration from the Caribbean to Britain was very highly correlated with demand for labour in Britain. Put differently, there was a high inverse correlation (r=−0.65) between unemployment in Britain and net immigration from the Caribbean;

Table 13.1   Caribbean ethnic population of Great Britain 1951–91

Year	Caribbean Birthplace	UK-born children of WI born (est.)	Best estimate Caribbean ethnic population
1951	17,218	10,000	28,000
1961	173,659	35,000	209,000
1966	269,300	133,000	402,000
1971	304,070	163,210	467,000
1981a	295,179	250,565	546,000
1981b	268,000	244,000	519,000
1984	242,000	281,000	529,000
1986–88	233,000	262,000	495,000
1991	264,591	268,318	499,964
		to 326,424	to 558,070

Source: Peach, 1996b, Table 1.1

Note: The 1991 figure of 499,964 is the official census figure for the Black-Caribbean population. However, 58,106 persons wrote into their census form 'Black British'. If these are assumed to be Caribbean in origin, the best estimate of the Caribbean ethnic population would rise to 558,070. A similar adjustment to the UK-born Black Caribbean population would increase the total to 326,424. The Caribbean birthplace column refers to birthplace and not to ethnicity. The ethnic Black-Caribbean population born in the Caribbean is 224,126. The row figures for 1991 do not sum to the best estimate figure because some of the ethnic Black-Caribbean population was born in places other than the Caribbean and the UK.

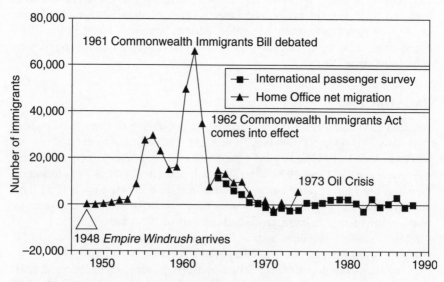

Figure 13.1 Caribbean net immigration to Britain, 1948–88

Note: The *Empire Windrush* was the first Caribbean migrant ship to arrive in Britain after the Second World War. The beginning of West Indian post-war immigration is generally reckoned from its date of arrival.

Source: Peach 1991

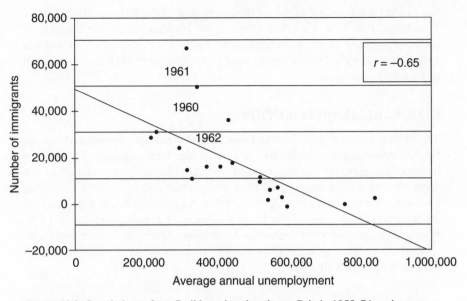

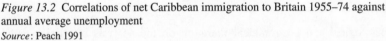

Figure 13.2 Correlations of net Caribbean immigration to Britain 1955–74 against annual average unemployment
Source: Peach 1991

when unemployment was high, net immigration was low and vice versa. The attempts to place political controls on the migration, through the imposition of the Commonwealth Immigrants Act, had the paradoxical effect of increasing the flow in the rush to beat the ban (Peach, 1968). Figure 13.2 shows clearly how the inflow in 1960, 1961 and 1962 during the period of debate leading up to the enforcement of the legislation in 1962 rises strongly above the line of overall correlation between unemployment and net immigration (but see also Thomas-Hope, 1992: 16–17).

The demand for labour was essentially in the lower end of the manual occupations for men and the service occupations for women. London Transport and British Rail figured significantly in the direct recruitment of male labour in Barbados and Jamaica. National Health hospitals featured particularly in the recruitment of women (Patterson, 1963), but often at the State Enrolled rather than the better-paid State Registered nursing level (Davison, 1962; Glass, 1960).

This demand for labour was essentially a replacement demand to compensate for the upward mobility of thc local labour force. In other words, it was moving into the jobs that the white population was abandoning, but for which there was still a demand. The reasons that the local population was abandoning such employment was that it was badly paid, dirty or involved unsocial hours.

In exactly the same way that the local white population was abandoning such employment, they were also abandoning the large urban areas in which such employment was concentrated. The British conurbations have shown a continuous decrease in population since the 1930s. Suburbanization and counter-urbanization has exerted a centrifugal effect on the population of the London, Birmingham, Manchester and West Yorkshire urban areas. In other words, the decrease in population of these large urban centres preceded the Caribbean settlement and was not precipitated by it. The Caribbean was a geographical as well as an occupational replacement population.

GEOGRAHICAL DISTRIBUTION

The Black-Caribbean population of Great Britain is heavily concentrated into the English conurbations. Nearly 80 per cent of the total is found in four main metropolitan clusters: Greater London and the Metropolitan counties of the West Midlands (Birmingham), Greater Manchester and West Yorkshire. This compares with less than a quarter of the White population. Greater London alone accounts for 58 per cent of the Black-Caribbean population (see Table 13.2). Within these metropolitan areas, the Caribbean population has an inner city concentration, although it does not exhibit the ghetto-scale of concentration of the North American cities.

Segregation levels

The sociological and geographical literature on the analysis of ethnic spatial patterning is underlain by the theory that there is a close relationship between spatial segregation of ethnic groups and their mutual acceptance. Low levels of segregation between ethnic groups indicate high levels of social interaction; high levels of segregation indicate high levels of social separation (Peach, 1975).

Table 13.2 Relative concentration of ethnic groups in large metropolitan areas of Great Britain, 1991

	White	Black Caribbean	Total
Great Britain	51,873,794	499,964	54,888,844
Greater London	5,333,580	290,968	6,679,699
West Midlands Met. County (B'ham) .	2,178,149	72,183	2,551,671
Greater Manchester Metropolitan County			
West Yorkshire Metropolitan County	2,351,239	17,095	2,499,441
(Leeds/Bradford)	1,849,562	14,795	2,013,693
Percentage group in named areas	22.58	79.01	25.04

Source: 1991 Census of Great Britain, *Ethnic Group and Country of Birth Great Britain*, Volume 2, London, Office of Population Censuses and Surveys, 1993, Table 6

Segregation is generally represented in the sociological and geographical literature by the index of dissimilarity (ID) or the index of segregation (IS) (Peach, 1975). Both indexes are very similar. The ID represents the percentage of the population which would have to shift from its area of residence in order to replicate the distribution of the total population in the city. The IS is the same except it measures the target group against the total population minus the target. IS and ID are broadly interchangeable except for very large target populations. Both have a range from 0 (no segregation) to 100 (total segregation).

Black-Caribbean levels of segregation show some variability between the South-East and Midlands on the one hand and northern towns on the other. Greater London and Birmingham, which contain over two-thirds of the Caribbean population, have indices of dissimilarity of 47 and 46 respectively at enumeration district level (see Table 13.3). To put these values into perspective, the average IS or ID for African Americans in cities in the United States is about 80 (Massey and Denton, 1993).

The level of segregation is not only moderate, but is decreasing (see Table 13.4). The London value of 49 seems to represent a significant decrease in levels of concentration compared with earlier studies. We do not have measures

Table 13.3 Indices of segregation of the Caribbean ethnic population at enumeration district level in selected cities, 1991

City	Caribbean Index of Segregation at ED Level	Caribbean total population
Leicester	43	4,070
Oxford	46	1,732
Birmingham	48	42,431
Greater London	49	289,712
Bradford	56	3,223
Greater Manchester	56	10,390
Liverpool	68	1,479
Leeds	72	5,102

Source: Calculated from 1991 Census, Small Area Statistics

Table 13.4 Comparison of Caribbean-born indices of dissimilarity in Greater London, 1961–91

Year	Borough level ID	Ward level ID	Enumeration district ID	
1961		56.2		Lee(1973)
1971	37.7	49.1	64.5	Woods (1976)
1981	36.5	46	53	Peach
1991	34	41	50	Peach

Source: Peach, 1996a

Table 13.5 Birmingham, ward level indices of segregation, 1961–91

Year	Index of segregation
1961	53.8
1971	49.8
1981	45.0
1991	40.0

Source: 1961 and 1971 from Woods, 1976; 1981 author's calculation; 1991 Peach, 1996a

of segregation for ethnicity in the past, but only birthplace. Taking the birthplace group, for which direct comparisons can be made, the ID at enumeration district level was 50 for Greater London. Comparison for Greater London, at a variety of scales from 1961 to 1991, shows a progressive decrease in the levels of segregation at all available scales (borough, ward and enumeration district). Given that the initial levels of segregation were not high by US standards and that the trend in segregation is downwards, this might suggest significant differences in terms of ethnic tolerance between Great Britain and the USA.

We do not have comparable data for Birmingham at borough and enumeration district level. However, at ward level, for which we have longitudinal data, there is a similar regular decrease in segregation for the Caribbean-born from an IS of 54 in 1961 to one of 40 in 1991 (see Table 13.5).

Coupled with this decrease in the levels of segregation of the Caribbean-born population, there is evidence of progressive outward diffusion. The map (Figure 13.3) shows the absolute change in the Caribbean-born population of Greater London between 1981 and 1991. It is clear that substantial decreases have taken place in areas of inner concentration while the major areas of increase are further away from the centre. Running a regression of absolute change in the Caribbean-born population against absolute numbers of that population shows a very high inverse relationship: the higher the numbers in 1981, the greater the decrease in 1991.

The highest proportion that Black-Caribbeans form of any ward in Great Britain is 30.1 per cent in Roundwood in Brent in London (see Table 13.5). Nine out of the top ten such wards are in London (Moss Side in Manchester is ranked 9). Even if the Black-Other and Black African populations are added, the highest proportion is still less than 50 per cent (see Table 13.6).

Even when all minorities are taken together there is only one ward in England and Wales where the proportion of minorities exceeds 90 per cent and only two between 80 and 90 per cent (see Table 13.7). These very high proportion wards are mainly associated with South Asian settlement (Peach, 1996a).

Micro-scale segregation

Within London and the other urban centres, the concentration was in the inner city areas. In London, the main railway stations were particular nodes of early

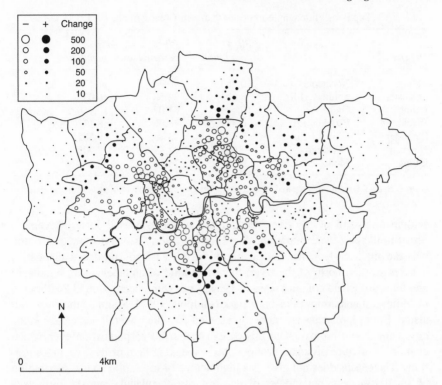

Figure 13.3 Change in Caribbean-born population in Greater London, 1981–91
Absolute change by ward

Source: 1981 and 1991, Small Area Statistics. Ward boundary changes in Borough of Enfield
courtesy of London Research Centre

Table 13.6 Top ranking wards in terms of Caribbean percentage of total population,
Great Britain, 1991

Local Authority	Ward	Black Carib per cent	Black Carib total	Ward total
Brent	Roundwood	30.12	2,043	6,783
Brent	St Raphael	25.95	2,768	10,667
Brent	Stonebridge	24.14	1,387	5,746
Lambeth	Tulse Hill	23.25	2,643	11,367
Brent	Carlton	22.25	1,370	6,156
Lambeth	Ferndale	21.68	2,706	12,479
Brent	Kensal Rise	21.07	1,273	6,042
Brent	Harlesden	20.52	1,216	5,927
Manchester	Moss Side	20.29	2,659	13,106
Haringey	Bruce Grove	20.25	2,124	10,488

Source: 1991 Census, Small Area Statistics; Peach, 1996b, Table 1.8

Table 13.7 Top non-White ethnic minority wards in Great Britain, 1991

District	Ward	Black population	Black percentage	Total population
Ealing	Northcote	10,083	90.21	11,177
Leicester	Spinney Hill	8,281	82.52	10,035
Ealing	Glebe	10,424	81.07	12,858
Blackburn	Brookhouse	6,339	78.06	8,121
Leicester	Crown Hills	7,261	75.75	9,585
Newham	Kensington	5,910	74.79	7,902
Ealing	Mount Pleasant	9,307	74.16	12,550

Source: Special tabulations prepared from ESRC 1991 Census archive at Manchester University

settlement. North of the river, Paddington in the west and Euston/Liverpool Street in the east were important. South of the river, Clapham Junction/Brixton was the main early node. Chain migration from islands produced distinctive clusters so that, north of the river, there is a kind of archipelago of Windward and Leeward island colonies (Peach, 1984) from Dominicans around Paddington to Montseratians around Finsbury Park (Philpott, 1977). South of the river, but also in Brent, Jamaicans are more represented than their overall percentage in the city. One should not overstate this case. The Caribbean population everywhere contains a mixture of island groups; one is speaking here of relative concentrations. The census does not give us a high degree of resolution on the distribution of small islanders, but indices of dissimilarity calculated from the birthplace tables indicate that a degree of segregation of islanders from one another still existed in 1991 (see Table 13.8).

Housing and tenure

Although the migration from the Caribbean was dominated by demand for blue-collar labour, the Caribbean population was initially effectively barred from

Table 13.8 Greater London 1991, indices of dissimilarity for selected Caribbean birthplaces, ward level

Birthplace	Ba	Ja	Tr	OI	Cd	WI	Gu	ID	IS	N
Barbados (Ba)	0	–	–	–	–	–	–	15	16	13,451
Jamaica (Ja)	22	0	–	–	–	–	–	13	26	76,529
Trinidad (Tr)	27	33	0	–	–	–	–	25	27	10,204
Oth ind states (OI)	26	34	32	0	–	–	–	23	29	27,675
Caribbean dependent territories (CD)	46	50	44	39	0	–	–	43	44	2,847
West Indies (WI)	30	36	35	24	42	0	–	28	29	5,136
Guyana (Gu)	26	26	25	35	50	39	0	21	24	14,752

Source: Local Base Statistics, 1991 Census, Table 7

Table 13.9 Caribbean household tenure, 1961–91(per cent). Figures for the White or total population are shown in brackets

Year of survey	Area and group	Owner– occupier		Rented from local authority		Other rented	
1961	England and Wales (conurbations)	27	(42)	2	(24)	69	(28)
1966	England and Wales	41	(47)	7	(26)	52	(23)
1971	England and Wales	44	(52)	21	(28)	35	(15)
1977	England and Wales	45	(54)	45	(30)	14	(14)
1981(a)	Great Britain	43	(56)	45	(31)	12	(13)
1981(b)	England and Wales	43	(58)	45	(29)	12	(13)
1981(c)	England and Wales	37	(55)	46	(32)	16	(13)
1982	England and Wales (ethnic)	41	(59)	46	(30)	14	(10)
1983–85	Great Britain (ethnic)	39	(59)	47	(28)	13	(12)
1986–89	Great Britain (ethnic)	44	(64)	44	(26)	12	(10)
1991	Great Britain	48	(67)	45	(24)	6	(7.8)

Source: 1961–89, Peach and Byron, 1993. 1991 data from OPCS, 1993

the most significant single source of working class accommodation, council housing (Burney, 1967; CRE, 1984; Cullingworth, 1969; Flett, 1977, 1979; Henderson and Karn, 1984, 1987; Parker and Dugmore, 1976, 1977; Peach and Shah, 1980; Sarre *et al.* 1989). The proportion of the housing stock controlled by local authorities was about 20 to 25 per cent in the 1950s and early 1960s and rose to about 33 per cent by the end of the 1980s before dropping back to about 25 per cent at the beginning of the 1990s. Table 13.9 shows that the proportion of Caribbean heads of household in council housing was a derisory 2 per cent in 1961 and 7 per cent in 1966, but by 1971 had tripled to 21 per cent and doubled again to 45 per cent by 1977. It stabilized around this figure until the mid-1980s, when council house sales produced a gentle decrease (Peach and Byron, 1993; Peach and Byron, 1994) (see Table 13.9).

Gaining admission to council housing did not, however, produce geographical dispersal. Most people are housed in local authorities where they have established their residential entitlements. The effect, at least in London, was a reshuffling *in situ* rather than suburbanization (Peach and Shah, 1980). There was, in addition, a considerable degree of discrimination in the allocation of local authority housing (Parker and Dugmore, 1977; Henderson and Karn 1984) and in housing investment (Mullings, 1991). In particular, Caribbean households were dis-proportionately allocated to flats rather than semi-detached or terraced housing (see Figure 13.4).

Not only was this the case, but within the flatted sector, they were allocated particularly to high-rise apartments. Nearly half were in 'ordinary' flats or maisonettes compared with one-third of the White population and a further one-fifth were in tower blocks, compared with 7 per cent of the White population (Peach and Byron, 1994). Whereas 40 per cent of White households in council

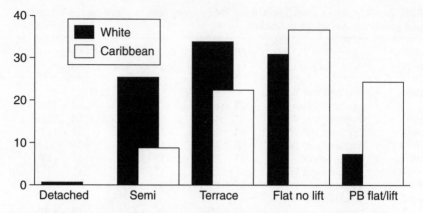

Figure 13.4 Comparison of Caribbean and White council house types, 1986–89
Note: PB FLAT/LIFT, purpose built flat with lift
Source: Peach and Byron, 1993

flats lived on the ground floor, less than 10 per cent of Caribbean households did so. On the other hand, over 20 per cent of Caribbean council flat dwellers lived on the ninth floor or higher compared with less than 5 per cent of White-headed households.

Part of the reason for this distribution was the large proportion of lone female-headed households with dependent children. These households are among the most vulnerable. High-level apartments in tower blocks are difficult to let and this group of clients is least able to argue with the housing choices offered to them.

Some factors favouring dispersal

All of these factors so far have pointed to conditions favouring a high degree of residential segregation of the Caribbean population in Britain. There were, however, countervailing developments. In the first place, there was a substantial growth in the degree of owner occupation of housing as well as in council housing. Owner occupation increased from about a quarter in 1961 to nearly half in 1991 (see Table 13.9). The establishment of families and the movement out of the multi-occupied bedsits and shared accommodation of the early years of settlement was also accompanied by increasing suburbanization (Lee, 1973). In London, the Paddington concentration moved outwards in a north-westerly direction into Brent; south of the river, the Wandsworth–Lambeth–Southwark concentration moved southwards into Croydon while the Liverpool Street concentration in the east extended north into Hackney and Haringey and east into Newham.

In addition, outside the London boroughs, council housing probably had a greater impact on dispersal. The scale of a city like Birmingham, for example, was much greater than that of a single London borough. Thus, while council housing in a London borough produced the *in situ* shuffling referred to above, in cities like Birmingham, there was greater scope for suburbanization. In cities like Oxford, for example, the main council house concentration of Caribbean population was in suburban estates like Blackbird Leys.

Ethnically mixed households

A further and perhaps surprising factor discouraging segregation is the degree of ethnic mixing in households. The British 1991 Census was the first in this country to include an ethnic question (Peach, 1996b). The 1991 Census was also the first to offer what in the USA is referred to as the Public Use Sample. The British equivalent is the Sample of Anonymized Records (SARs). The SARs allow us to gain a little insight into mixed households and indicate a significant proportion of Black Caribbean and White households.

Of the households in which either the head or partner gave their ethnic group as Black-Caribbean, in 10.1 per cent of cases there was a Black-Caribbean male with a White female partner while the obverse case obtained only half as frequently (4.8 per cent of cases). There were very few cases of other ethnicities being partners in Black Caribbean households, although, given the relative sizes of the different ethnic populations, this is to be expected statistically.

CONCLUSION

Putting all of this together, Caribbean segregation levels in Britain are about half the levels typically found for African Americans in the USA and falling. The highest percentage that Black Caribbeans form of a single ward in Great Britain is 30.1 per cent in Roundwood in Brent in London. The highest level of Black Caribbean concentration in any London enumeration district was 62 per cent (in Brent). These figures do not achieve the sustained 100 per cent levels common for block and tract data for African Americans in United States cities.

To put this in perspective, we can examine this table of ghettoization in Chicago in the 1930s at the end of the great era of European immigration to the USA. Although it was fashionable at that time to refer to the 'Irish ghetto' or the 'Italian ghetto', in effect, the Black ghetto was a reality. Only 3 per cent of the Irish lived in 'Irish' areas of the city and they formed only one-third of the population of those areas. Only the Poles formed a majority of Polish areas and just about half of Poles and Italians lived in the areas that were supposed to be their exclusive turfs. However, for the Black population, the situation was different in kind. Over 90 per cent of the African American population lived in Black areas and over 80 per cent of the population of the Black areas was Black (see Table 13.10).

Not only is this the case, but the level of African American segregation, instead of decreasing seems to have arrived at a saturated level of hyper-segregation (Massey and Denton, 1993). If we produce a comparable table to the Philpott Chicago table for London in 1991, we find that the levels of segregation and

Table 13.10 'Ghettoization' of ethnic groups, Chicago, 1930

Group	Group's city population	Group's 'ghetto' population	Percentage of group 'ghettoized'	Group's percentage of 'ghetto' population	Total 'ghetto' population
Irish	169,568	4,993	2.9	33.8	14,595
German	377,975	53,821	14.2	31.7	169,649
Swedish	140,913	21,581	15.3	24.3	88,749
Russian	169,736	63,416	37.4	42.5	149,208
Czech	122,089	53,301	43.7	31.4	169,550
Italian	181,861	90,407	49.7	46.2	195,736
Polish	401,316	248,024	61.8	54.3	457,146
Negro	233,903	216,846	92.7	81.5	266,051

Source: Philpott, 1978: 141, Table 7

Table 13.11 'Ghettoization' of ethnic groups at enumeration district level in Greater London: 30 per cent cut-off

Group	Group's city population	Group's 'ghetto' population	Percentage of group 'ghettoized'	Group's percentage of 'ghetto' population	Total 'ghetto' population
Black Caribbean	290,968	7,755	2.7	34.4	22,545
Black African	163,635	3,176	1.9	5.7	8,899
Black Other	80,613	–	–	–	–
Indian	347,091	88,887	25.6	44.0	202,135
Pakistani	87,816	1,182	1.3	35.2	3,359
Bangladeshi	85,738	28,280	33.0	51.0	55,500
Chinese	56,579	38	0.1	34.2	111
Other Asian	112,807	176	0.2	30.8	572
Other Other	120,872	209	0.2	39.4	530
Irish born	256,470	1,023	0.4	39.7	2,574
Non-White	1,346,119	721,873	53.6	45.4	1,589,476

Source: Special tabulations prepared from ESRC 1991 Census archive at Manchester University

concentration are like the Irish in Chicago rather than the African American. Only 3 per cent of the Black Caribbean population of London in 1991 lived in enumeration districts (the smallest census unit of about 700 people) in which they formed 30 per cent or more of the population (see Table 13.11).

The picture presented by these findings is more optimistic than that generally presented, although there are other optimistic findings, such as those of Western on Barbadian settlers (Western, 1992). Part of the explanation lies in the large-scale entry into council housing. Indeed, the housing tenure structure for the male Caribbean population is close to what its class or occupational structure would predict (Peach and Byron, 1993).

Although the structural constraints of the British labour market and the British housing market might have suggested that ghettoization of the Caribbean population might be taking place, the opposite seems to be occurring. Despite concentration in manual work (as far as the mean are concerned) and despite exceptionally high levels of unemployment, levels of segregation are about half the level of African Americans in the United States. Not only is this the case, but the levels show a gentle monotonic decrease for both London and Birmingham. London and Birmingham hold nearly 73 per cent of the Caribbean population of Britain. Not only this, but the map also shows a clear outward movement of the Caribbean-born population living in London and a decrease of Caribbean population in the areas of original concentration. Households containing Caribbean heads or partners show a significant level of ethnic mixing with White partners. If one equates levels of social interaction with levels of spatial segregation then the picture is much more reassuring than that for other minority ethnic populations like the Bangladeshis in this country or African Americans in the United States.

ACKNOWLEDGEMENTS

The author gratefully acknowledges the computational assistance of Dr David Rossiter of the Oxford University Computing Service.

The work was carried out with assistance from the OPCS and from the ESRC Research Grant R45126412793.

The research draws on material made available through the ESRC 1991 census database at the University of Manchester Computing Centre and the University of Manchester Department of Economics Microdata Unit, JISC/DENI and CMU. Crown Copyright is acknowledged.

REFERENCES

Burney, Elizabeth (1967) *Housing on Trial: A Study of Immigrants and Local Government*, London: Oxford University Press.

Byron, Margaret (1994) *Post-War Caribbean Migration to Britain: The Unfinished Cycle*, Aldershot: Avebury.

CRE (Commission for Racial Equality) (1984) *Hackney Housing Investigated*, Summary of a Formal Investigation Report, London: Commission for Racial Equality.

Cullingworth Committee (1969) *Council Housing: Purposes, Procedures and Priorities.* London: HMSO.

Davison, R.B. (1962) *West Indian Migrants*, London: Oxford University Press.

Flett, Heather (1977) *Council Housing and Location of Ethnic Minorities*, Working Papers on Ethnic Relations, 5, Bristol: SSRC Research Unit on Ethnic Relations.

—— (1979) *Black Council Tenants in Birmingham*. Working Papers on Ethnic Relations, 12, Bristol: SSRC Research Unit on Ethnic Relations.

Glass, Ruth (1960) (assisted by Harold Pollins) *Newcomers: The West Indians in London*, London: George Allen and Unwin.

Henderson, J. and Karn, V. (1984) 'Race, class and the allocation of state housing in Britain', *Urban Studies*, 21: 115–28.

—— (1987) *Race, Class and State Housing: Inequality and the Allocation of Public Housing in Britain*, Aldershot: Gower.

Lee, T.R. (1973) *Race and Residence: The Concentration and Dispersal of Immigrants in London*, Oxford: Clarendon Press.

Massey, D. and Denton, N.A. (1993) *American Apartheid: Segregation and the Making of the Underclass*, Cambridge, MA: Harvard University Press.

Mullings, Beverley (1991) *The Colour of Money*, London: London Race and Housing Research Unit, c/o The Runnymede Trust.

Office of Population Censuses and Surveys (1993) 1991 Census, *Ethnic Group and Country of Birth. Great Britain*, 2 volumes, London: HMSO.

Parker, J. and Dugmore, K. (1976) *Colour and the Allocation of GLC Housing*, the report of the GLC Lettings survey, 1974–75, Research Report 21, London: GLC.

—— (1977) 'Race and the allocation of public housing: A GLC survey', *New Community*, 6: 1–2, 27–40.

Patterson, Sheila (1963) *Dark Strangers*, London: Tavistock Publications.

Peach, Ceri (1968) *West Indian Miration to Britain: A Social Geography*, London: Oxford University Press.

—— (ed.) (1975) *Urban Social Segregation*, London: Longman.

—— (1984) 'The force of West Indian Island identity in Britain', in (eds) David Ley, Colin Clarke and Ceri Peach, *Geography and Ethnic Pluralism*, London: Allen and Unwin, pp. 214–29.

—— (1991) *The Caribbean in Europe; Contrasting Pattern of Migration and Settlement in Britain, France and the Netherlands*, Research Paper in Ethnic Relations 15, Centre for Research in Ethnic Relations, University of Warwick.

—— (1996a) 'Does Britain have ghettos?', *Transactions of the Institute of British Geographers*, 22, 1: 216–35.

—— (1996b) *The Ethnic Minority Population of Great Britain*, Volume 2 of *Ethnicity in the 1991 Census*, Office for National Statistics: London, HMSO.

Peach, Ceri and Byron, Margaret (1993) 'Caribbean tenants in council housing: "Race" class and gender', *New Community*, 19 (3): 407–23.

—— (1994) 'Council house sales, residualisation and Afro Caribbean tenants', *Journal of Social Policy*, 23 (3): 363–83.

Peach, Ceri and Samir Shah (1980) 'The contribution of council house allocation to West Indian desegregation in London, 1961–1971', *Urban Studies*, 17: 333–41.

Peach, G.C.K. (1967) 'West Indians as a Replacement Population in England and Wales', *Social and Economic Studies*, 16(3): 259–94.

Philpott, Stuart B. (1977) 'The Montserratians: Migration dependency and the maintenance of island ties in England' in James L. Watson (ed.) *Between Two Cultures: Migrants and Minorities in Britain*. Oxford: Basil Blackwell.

Philpott T. L. (1978) *The Slum and the Ghetto: Neighborhood Deterioration and Middle Class Reform. Chicago, 1880–1930*, New York: Oxford University Press.

Sarre, Philip, Phillips, Deborah and Skellington, Richard (1989) *Ethnic Minority Housing: Explanations and Policies*, Aldershot: Avebury.

Smith, Susan J. (1989) *The Politics of 'Race' and Residence*, Cambridge: Polity Press.

Thomas-Hope, Elizabeth (1986) 'Transients and settlers: Varieties of Caribbean migrants and the socio-economic implication of their return', *International Migration*, 24, (3): 559–571.

—— (1992) *Explanation in Caribbean Migration*, London: Macmillan.

Western, John (1992) *A Passage to England*, London: University College London Press.

Woods, Robert I. (1976) 'Aspects of the scale problem in the calculation of segregation indices: London and Birmingham, 1961 and 1971', *Tijdschrift voor Economische en Sociale Geografie*, 67(3): 169–74.

14 Migration, work and gender

The case of post-war labour migration from the Caribbean to Britain

Margaret Byron

INTRODUCTION

The relationship between migration and work in the experience of Caribbean migrants is the focus of this chapter and it is argued that this is very much a gendered issue. Studies of transitions in occupational patterns occurring during the migration process have often lacked reference to gender dynamics (Smith, 1977; Heath and Ridge, 1983; Robinson, 1990). This reflects the absence of gender as an explicit issue in the study of labour migration until relatively recently. In Britain, the results of the 1991 Census and Labour Force surveys of the late 1980s (Department of Employment, 1990; Office of Population Censuses and Surveys, 1993) have revealed the extent of the difference in the occupational experiences of migrant men and women. Here I use evidence of women's active role in the post-war labour migration to Britain to challenge the traditional view of women as the 'passive movers'. I then draw on UK labour force statistics further to support the argument for gendering the study of labour migration. Adjacent, and contingent upon the migrants' occupational situations in the public sphere, is the division of labour and linked access to power in the household. The domestic environment is included in this examination of migration-induced changes as alterations in the gender division of labour in the public sphere could be conveyed in some form into migrants' domestic lives. In conclusion, the interaction between the gender-work dynamics and the issue of return migration is raised as a further research area.

This chapter is based on current research on the socio-economic organization of the circular migration from the Caribbean to Britain. Census and labour force survey statistics are used to illustrate major trends in the employment situation of Caribbean people in Britain while case studies of migrant households from the Caribbean islands of St Kitts/Nevis residing in the city of Leicester provide ethnographic detail on the migration and work experience of Caribbean men and women.

GENDER AND WORK IN THE CARIBBEAN: THE PRE-MIGRATION SITUATION

The difficulty of defining 'women's' has been the starting point of several recent articles on women and work in the Caribbean (Massiah, 1990; Senior, 1991). A central issue in this debate is the fact that work has been equated with economic activity which, in turn, has been measured in terms of receipt of a wage, salary or profit. However, as Massiah states clearly:

> In sum, conventional definitions that limit women's work to paid employment (including self-employment) represent only a partial aspect of work as perceived by women themselves. At its most rudimentary level, women in the WICP consider work to be anything that is functionally necessary to maintain themselves and their households.[1]

(Massiah, 1990: 229)

The conception of work as perceived by the women themselves is crucial to understanding their position in Caribbean society and their strategies of survival. While women would in general argue that most of their waking hours are spent working, few would deny the importance of paid employment. Caribbean women's rate of participation in the labour force is high relative to other under-developed economies. Senior (1991: 123) gives rates of participation for women of 18–55 per cent across the region in 1960 (just before the peak in migration to Britain) and compares this with 15 per cent, 24 per cent and 29 per cent for Latin America, Africa and Asia respectively.

The historical position of Caribbean women in the economy is an essential reference in understanding the relatively high level of female participation in the labour force. During slavery, women were full-time members of the labour force as were the additional migrant women who came to the Caribbean from the Indian sub-continent as indentured labour in the post-Emancipation period. Although the post-Emancipation period brought a certain degree of female withdrawal from the estate labour force, a large proportion of women remained. As Senior (1991: 107) notes: 'In very few cases were black males economically able to become sole breadwinners and providers for their families.'

Although women occupied the same positions as men in the estate labour force, the introduction of paid labour in the post-Emancipation period was accompanied by wage differentials for identical tasks. Hence the establishment of a structurally inferior position for women in the economy. (It is notable that the direct descendants of the slave population were the black working classes of the post-slavery society and that Caribbean migration to Britain was largely from this source.) Despite this economic disadvantage, black working-class women in the Caribbean became established as providers for their family needs and, consequently, an aura of independence surrounded them. This position was reinforced by the fact that previous post-Emancipation migrations from the territories were largely movements of male labour which left women to run the household and do the farming (Byron, 1994; Senior, 1991) Although the intermittent visits and remittances from male migrants made extremely valuable contributions to the household economy, women devised a variety of additional strategies of survival, only some of which included participation in the formal economy. The post-war labour requirements of the British economy provided an additional survival strategy for Caribbean working-class women.

Independence

There are several important points to be made about the economic independence of women in the Caribbean. In the first instance, given the high proportion of female-headed households, 50 per cent for St Kitts/Nevis (Momsen, 1987), the woman's ability to sustain her family, with intermittent or no support from visiting or casual partners, was a practical necessity (Massiah, 1990). Second, even in the cases of women with permanent partners, women preferred to have an independent source of income as this was directly related to the degree of control over the children and resources in the household. Research done by the WICP (Barrow, 1986; Massiah, 1990) revealed that the man's authority in the relationship depended on the extent to which his partner was economically dependent on him. Recent work on Mexican experiences of migration argues that the much higher participation in the waged labour force by Mexican women after migration has increased their authority and independence in the household, challenging pre-migration patriarchal gender relations (Hondagneu-Sotelo, 1994). This female 'independence' is undermined by the inferior position of women in the 'recognized' labour force in the Caribbean, both structurally and in terms of unequal wages for similar tasks (Rogers 1980; Senior 1991), and the failure to identify much female activity as 'work'. The result is a situation which, while demanding a very independent contribution from the female component of the population, simultaneously undermines this by the gender inequalities which have been integral to the Caribbean economy.

MIGRATION TO BRITAIN FROM NEVIS: PAID EMPLOYMENT FOR WOMEN

The data from my work on post-war migration from the island of Nevis illustrate well this position of Caribbean women in the labour force. Two-thirds of the sample of fifty-four women were in some form of waged activity before leaving Nevis (Figure 14.1). The remaining third of the migrant women in this sample stated 'unemployed' as their status prior to migrating, twice the unemployment figure for the sample of male migrants. These women were young, the modal age group of the migrants in this sample was 19–24. They were still resident in the family home and were important contributors to the small farm economy of the household. Nonetheless, as they did not 'earn their own money' on a regular basis, they considered themselves unemployed. Momsen observes this feature in the following comment:

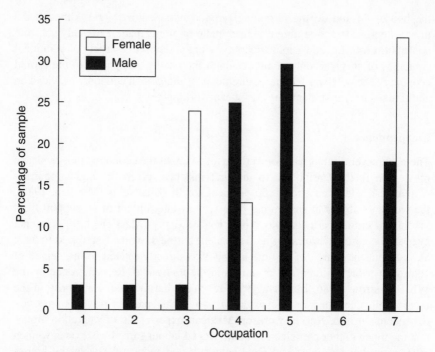

Figure 14.1 Pre-migration occupation types: samples of Leicester Nevisians. Occupations are coded as follows: 1, professional, managerial, artistic; 2, clerical, sales; 3, services (personal and private security); 4, farming, fishing and related; 5, materials processing and related industry; 6, construction and transport; 7, unemployed (so stated) or school-child

Source: Fieldwork 1988–90

> Women appear to view the farm as an extension of their household responsi-
> bilities, concentrating on subsistence production of food crops and small stock
> rearing rather than on the export crops and cattle preferred by men.
>
> (Momsen, 1987: 345)

The highest proportion of women in gainful employment (23 per cent) were employed in service sector occupations, which almost always meant domestic service in the Nevis context. This was the most poorly paid and exploited employment position in the region (Senior, 1991: 119–21). Between 12 and 13 per cent were employed in each of the categories of farming and vending farm produce, dressmaking and clerical/sales. The remaining 6 per cent were nurses and teachers, the classic female professional jobs, prior to moving to Britain.

The move to Britain promised the opportunity for employment *per se* for a third of the sample of Nevisian women, and for more regular and higher wages for the others. Above all, it must be stressed that women migrated primarily to work as opposed to moving as dependants, contrary to popular opinion as noted here:

It was often unquestioningly thought that labour migration was overwhelm-ingly a male phenomenon, with females either staying back home or arriving somewhat later as dependants.

(Cohen, 1987: 115)

The migration to Britain was the first labour movement in which women migrated in almost equal proportions to men. In earlier movements, within and outside the region, those women who did migrate did so mainly as auxiliary workers to perform household tasks for managers and supervisors or to provide various services ranging from laundry to prostitution for the male migrants themselves (Richardson, 1983; Byron, 1994). The move to Britain therefore offered women the opportunity to appropriate what had been a male-dominated activity and to participate in the wage generation in Britain *independently* of the male migrants. For this migration, in addition to and sometimes instead of men, women were mobilized to form the migrant labour force:

One day my mother said that she was going to send me to England to help the family, I am the eldest of her children. She had a brother in Leicester so I came here to him. He helped my mother to get me here, it was his way of helping out his sister after he came to England. I then got a job and helped bring Mother and the younger kids over.

(Rena, a Nevisian woman in Leicester)

This is an important observation, particularly in the light of the following statement by Phizaclea:

wherever a woman comes from, wherever she migrates to, whether or not she is married, or has children, her primary role in life will be defined, not as a waged worker, but as a mother and a domestic labourer. It is this definition which is replicated and reinforced through the creation of whole sectors of low paid 'women's work' and which provides the basis for the much broader sexual division of labour which is characteristic of all societies.

(Phizaclea, 1983: 2)

Whereas Phizaclea rightly emphasizes the unequal position of migrant women in both the household and the labour market structure, she is in danger of ignoring the role that migration played in altering the position of migrant women in the household and in the wider social structure. There is an absence of the relevant women's 'definitions of their situation' (Jackson, 1988). In this work I aim to include Caribbean migrant women's views on the impact of labour migration on their lives in the public work and domestic spheres. The following quotations from interviews with Caribbean women in Leicester illustrate that women saw themselves as migrating to participate in earning the household income.

No work was there for us except work in the ground. Everyone was coming and I knew that I would get some money if I came.

(Single woman with one child at the time)

Although 38 per cent of the sample of women did come to Britain to join their male partners, most of these promptly found jobs. Many of these women still gave work as the reason for migrating.

> We came to make a few pennies and go back. We didn't think it would take long so we left the children as we thought we would soon return to them.
>> (Married woman with seven children at time of migration)

> Things were very hard. Money wasn't coming in. No work, no money.
>> (Married woman who joined her husband in Britain)

These responses were very similar to male responses.

> Not much work doing there so I came away to make some money.
>> (Single man)

> Left to make a better life for myself and family.
>> (Single man)

> Not much work doing there – came away to make some money.
>> (Single man)

> No work unless you liked the 'land business'. Had kids to support.
>> (Married man)

> I came because of financial reasons.
>> (Married man)

This research reveals that, like male migrants, women perceived their migration as an opportunity to obtain paid employment. In general, this objective did not vary with their marital condition. Those women who were engaged in paid work in the Caribbean prior to the migration saw the move as a chance to increase their income. For many, however, it was the first time that they would work for wages.

BRITAIN: CARIBBEAN WOMEN IN THE FORMAL LABOUR FORCE

In the previous section it was observed that within the 'Third World' context a relatively high proportion of Caribbean women are in the labour force. In Britain, the economic activity rates for the Caribbean female population are also relatively high. In a study of motherhood and waged work in Britain, Stone (1983) noted that Caribbean mothers were the most likely to be in full-time employment at all stages of the working-age cycle. Studies of ethnic origins and the labour market in the late 1980s and in the 1990s provide further evidence that Caribbean women have remained heavily represented in the labour force. The average of the Labour Force Surveys for 1987–89 revealed that economic activity rates for women of working age were highest for Caribbean women: 73 per cent (DOE, 1990) and 76 per cent (DOE, 1991) compared to 69 per cent and 70 per cent for the white population and 20 per cent and 21 per cent for women of Pakistani/ Bangladeshi origin. The 1991 census of Great Britain gives economic activity rates of 73 per cent for Caribbean women of working age. This figure compares with 63 per cent for the white female population, 58 per cent for the Indian female population, 28 per cent for the Pakistani female population and 22 per cent for the Bangladeshi female population (Office of Population Censuses and Surveys, 1993). These considerable inter-group differences are explained partly by the different proportions of the groups which are in full-time education and, more importantly, by the proportion of women whose domestic and family commitments rendered them unavailable for work outside the home environment. For Caribbean women the lowest rate, 69 per cent, occurs in the 16–24 age group, mainly due to the larger proportion of this group in full-time education. Economic activity rises to 77 per cent in the 25–44 age range and peaks at 81 per cent in the 45–64 age group which includes the post-child-rearing phase (Office of Population Censuses and Surveys, 1993). The high proportion of economically active women in all three age groups indicates that many mothers work.

MOTHERHOOD AND WAGED WORK

Given this high labour force participation rate, the reproductive role of Caribbean women presents an interesting topic. As stated earlier, the modal age group of the migrants in this sample on arrival was 19–24 years. While agreeing that Phizacklea's comment (1983: 2), quoted above, is pertinent, this case study of Caribbean migrants challenges Phizacklea's relegation of the female migrant's labour role to a secondary position. It fails to prioritize the work intention in the migration goal of Caribbean women and also to recognize the role which migrant male partners played in the organization and operation of childcare and other domestic activities. The work strategies devised by women usually accommo-dated precise childcare arrangements. Male partners played a very active role in these plans contrasting with their absence, in general, from childcare situations in the Caribbean.

Three main forms of child care were identified during interviews with Nevisians: public nurseries, child minders and the rich kinship network in Britain and the Caribbean. Some families employed all of these strategies while others only made use of child minders. In addition, parents often devised alternate shift systems of working which enabled one parent to be with the children at all times. Generally, private nurseries exceeded the costs payable by migrants. Public nursery provision was even more limited then than it is now and was regarded as a preventative service to avoid admission into care for high-risk children (Curtis, 1989). Child minders were preferred as women felt that they were more sympathetic to their work needs than were the nursery staff.

If your child got sick, no matter how simple, even if it cut a finger, the nursery staff would ring you at work and you would have to go and collect the child and lose at least that day from work. A child minder would keep the child until you finished work and went to collect it. They could understand your position.

(Nevisian woman, interview, 1989)

CHANGES OVER TIME FOR MIGRANTS IN BRITAIN

This study of Nevisian migrants supports the evidence of larger labour force studies which indicate that changes in the industrial distribution of migrant workers have accompanied economic restructuring in Britain (Brown, 1984; Robinson, 1989). There were shifts from the manufacturing to the service and professional/management sectors for both male and female migrants. The shift was more extensive in the case of women, however (Figure 14.2). It is notable that a relatively high proportion of both groups remained in the manufacturing sector and were consequently vulnerable to the current and subsequent redundancies that were affecting workers in British industry. Caribbean men have been particularly affected by this. Table 14.1 compares the unemployment rates for the Caribbean and white populations by gender from the 1991 Census of Great Britain. The 45–64 age group is highlighted as it contains the vast majority of the Caribbean migrant population.

A comparison of the employed Caribbean population with the employed white population reveals distinct differences (Department of Employment, 1991). Overall, a higher proportion of the Caribbean population was employed in manual occupations than the general population, 54 per cent and 45 per cent respectively. Of these manual workers, the craft worker to other manual worker ratio was noticeably higher for the general population than for the Caribbean group. When gender is included as a variable, interesting differences emerge. For the total male working population, the ratio of percentage non-manual to manual occupations is 47 : 53; for the Caribbean population it is 29 : 71. This contrasts vividly with the data for total female non-manual to manual ratio of 67 : 33 versus the Caribbean female ratio of 63 : 37. For Caribbean female workers the picture is almost identical to that of the general female population. The initial over-representation of Caribbean women in the manufacturing sector has gradually been reduced as women moved into increasingly available positions in the service sector. This was aided by the high demand for women in the health service and related welfare services. While male Caribbeans also shifted sectors, they did so in smaller numbers and women as a whole were five times as likely as men to work in the clerical and related sub-category of the service sector.

All nursing jobs are categorized as professional even when they are relatively low grade jobs. There is evidence that a disproportionately high number of Caribbean women were channelled into the State Enrolled Nurse (SEN) nursing category (Harris, 1987). However, within the health and social welfare category there is greater opportunity for training and promotion than in those sections of the manufacturing industry and service sector where most Caribbean men were employed. Evidence from the Nevisian sample suggests that this has indeed been

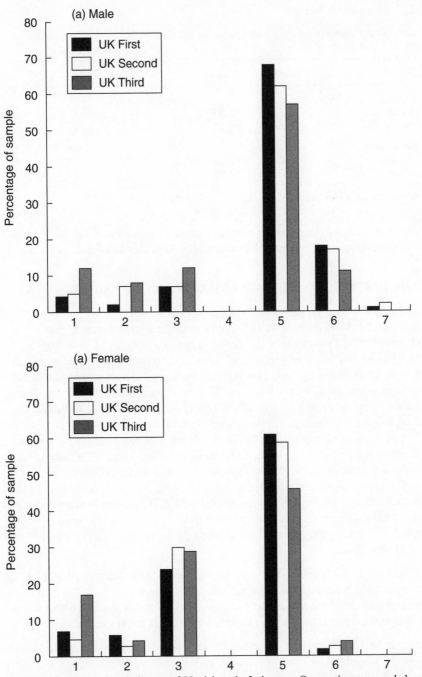

Figure 14.2 Occupational change of Nevisians in Leicester. Occupations are coded as follows: 1, professional, managerial, artistic; 2, clerical, sales; 3, services (personal and private security); 4, farming, fishing and related; 5, materials processing and related industry; 6, construction and transport; 7, unemployed (so stated) or schoolchild

Source: Fieldwork, 1988–90

Table 14.1 Unemployment rates by gender for the Caribbean and white population in Britain, 1991

	Male	*Female*
Total aged over 16		
Caribbean	23.84	13.53
White	10.68	6.33
Aged 45–64		
Caribbean	18.28	13.47
White	9.23	4.64

Source: Office of Population Censuses and Surveys (1993)

the case. Not only have more women than men moved into the professional/managerial category, but men have succumbed in higher numbers to redundancy.

THE HOUSEHOLD: GENDER AND DIVISION OF LABOUR

In the 1970s Nancy Foner noted that the status of female Jamaican migrants in the household had risen while in Britain due to their greater earning power there (Foner, 1977). Twenty years on, gender dynamics are critical to understanding the distribution of power, work and responsibility in the domestic arena. The following discussion is based on information gained during interviews in 1995 with migrants from Nevis who now live in Leicester. Thirty migrant householders from a variety of household types were interviewed. These included female-headed households, male-headed households and jointly-run households. Although most of the households in the sample included a migrant couple, a minority were headed by single, divorced or widowed women. The interviewees defined the role of the head of household and stated who headed their household.

The were seven female-headed households in the sample, twelve male-headed households and thirteen jointly-run households. Where a couple were present in the household each partner was asked to define the role of the 'head of household'. Otherwise, the present adult defined the term. These definitions fell into two categories:

- economic (the person who was the dominant financial contributor to the household economy) for example, 'the breadwinner';
- management of the household's affairs (decision maker, the one who holds the home together) for example, 'everyday running of the home, decision-maker'.

Just under half of the interviewees gave an 'economic' definition while the rest saw the household head as the manager and/or carer. Although there was a fairly even distribution of the categories throughout the sample of responses, women had a broader interpretation of the role.

- 'Someone who does everything, runs the home',
- 'Person of all trades',

- 'Takes responsibility for the household and home',
- 'Keeps family together'.

Given the dominance of male or joint household heads, interviewees were asked if there were cases in which the female partner would head the household. These responses also fall into economic and management categories. Economically, a women would qualify as head if she makes the greatest financial contribution to the household, or if she holds the house in her own name. The importance of access to financial resources was emphasized when a woman responded:

The majority of responses to this question focused on decision making, organizing and planning for the household.

- 'She may be the better manager',
- 'Some women are more forward going or better educated',
- ''The woman may be the one who makes all the decisions',
- 'Sometimes the men sit down and the woman does everything so she is the head',
- 'Women often play a leading role in the household',
- 'Man may be sick, or lazy or may not like responsibility'.

Several women explicitly noted that it should be the man but if he failed to live up to expectations, then the woman would have to do this:

- 'Not right for this to happen, but it could happen if the man not capable',
- 'The man should be in charge, but some men do not pull their weight',
- 'Should be the man, but she may . . . for financial reasons, say',
- 'Man should be head, but if he is not, then she has to be'.

None of the men interviewed explicitly objected to women heading households. The general assumption was that men or both adults should be in charge of the home and that the position of a woman as head when a man was present had to be justified. 'If she was head before the man came into the household then she would continue in this role.'

Men were clearly conscious of changes wrought by the migration and, unlike women, remarked on this.

- 'She may have the money and may buy the house. England bring in this equal rights thing you see.'
- 'Person who pays the bills and owns the house. England it's half and half.'

Differences in responses by age group were expected, but in fact there was little evidence of this. Three men in the sample had come to Britain in their teens to join their parents and were now in their early forties. There was a fifteen-year difference between their age and the average age of postwar Caribbean migrants in Britain (Byron, 1994). Their responses on the questions about head of household differed from each other significantly. The first of these men defined the head of household as 'the breadwinner'. He had always fulfilled this role. He left the housework entirely to his female partner but paid all the bills himself. He felt that the head of household could be a woman if she was the major earner of if the man proved a useless manager. The second man saw the role of the head of household as the every day running of the home and making decisions. 'Women play a leading role in the household.' He jointly headed the house with his wife and they shared all the housework. His wife's responses supported this picture. The third in this group saw the head of household as the provider and decision maker. He saw this as his role. None the less he helped with some housework, particularly cleaning, since his wife started an advanced nursing course, and played an important role in raising the children. Similar variation was observed in the older age groups although, in general, the division of labour in the home was heavily weighted towards the women. In a breakdown of household duties, 80 per cent of the men in the sample only helped with gardening and household repairs. During their early years in Britain men took on new responsibilities of child care while their partners worked. However the young families have now matured and in many cases the situation has reverted to that which existed in the Caribbean where the woman undertook full responsibility for housework. In the British context, she worked full or part-time outside the home as well. 'He did more when the kids were young. Now I do everything.' 'I used to help when they were small.

Although women earned less than their partners, their income was a vital element of the household budget. In an earlier research project many couples stressed how only the proof that they were both earning enabled them to arrange home loans during their early search for adequate accommodation (Byron, 1994). Interviewees in this sample were asked if women should contribute financially to the household. Here there was a clear difference in the responses of men and women. Men saw women's contribution as marginal and optional. Their major role was that of carer. 'Women have an option. Men don't. Also, they care for the kids.' 'Only if she has no young kids.'

Women also saw child care as a very important element of their responsibility but all worked outside the home. Most felt that the male should be the major contributor financially, either due to the woman's caring role or due to his greater income. 'Men earn more either because she has the kids and can only do part-time or because she is lower paid. So her working should be optional if he earns enough.' 'Depends on who earns most money and usually he does.' However, a woman's independence hinged on her ability to work outside the home and earn her own income. 'Yes, because everyone should be independent.' Both should work.' 'To enable you to have a joint say in what happens in the home.' 'Also you have family back home (in the Caribbean) and if you don't earn your own you cannot send something for them and it was them who helped you to come to England in the first place.' Clearly, it was considered essential to contribute financially if the woman was to make decisions on resource allocation in the home and to make independent decisions on assistance to her extended family.

As an indication of migration induced change or continuity in the position of women, the members of the sample were asked to compare their lives with those of their mothers. All responses stressed that materially they were better off. More than half then discussed the complexity of their lives compared with their parents and several women concluded, in this respect, that their mothers had an easier life.

• There are greater opportunities here but it gives much more responsibility.'
• 'There, women did not have to go out to work eight hours in the land like we do in the factory. Their farm work was suited to their household activities. We have more pressure here.'
• 'Women have more money here and we have less children. I don't think it is a much easier life though.'
• 'We have greater responsibility here'.
• 'Role same as mother, same responsibility. Slightly easier life, more money available. Not necessarily happier though.'

The majority of the men in the sample stressed the greater material well-being of the migrants. However, three men said that life was easier for their wives than their mothers due to the greater assistance with domestic chores given by their male partners. It is notable that each of these men were part of jointly-headed households in which both partners shared the household duties.

A major development which could affect household power structure is redundancy. Growing numbers of women are the sole or major earner within households as men working in manufacturing industry become redundant. I encountered evidence of this in more recent research, between 1990 and 1992, on 'sales of council housing' in Birmingham and London (Peach and Byron, 1994). In several households the woman was the sole earner in the household and had taken the recent purchase option in her own name. Given the definitions of head of household and the conditions under which the female partner would be head, it is conceivable that some shifting of position would result. In my Leicester sample, three men had been made redundant in the engineering industries. Two had found other jobs and one took early retirement. In these cases there was little evidence of change in the power structure and distribution of work in the home.

CONCLUSIONS: CHANGE AND CONTINUITY FOR CARIBBEAN MIGRANTS

Gendering the study of migration and work makes evident the extent of the changes which migrants experience. In the case of the post-war movement to Britain, paid employment *per se* increased for women while rates of pay rose considerably for both men and women. Structural shifts in the British economy have impacted on the employment trajectories of Caribbean migrants. Again, the extent and complexity of this effect is revealed when the data are broken down by gender. Whereas the shifts have tended to accommodate migrant women, Caribbean men have become increasingly economically, and by extension socially, marginalized.

During the early years in Britain, it can be argued that women achieved greater equality in both public and domestic spheres. Young children combined with the need for two incomes to force greater male contribution to duties within the home. This did not remain the case in most households though. The pattern alluded to by Foner in the 1970s (1977), of a withdrawal of men's assistance as the children became older, was evident in this case study. Women became independent earners and, despite earning less than men, contributed financially to the household and consequently exercised greater power in decision making. None the less, despite contributing financially, in general they still carry the burden of housework. While vigorously defensive of their economic independence, many Caribbean female migrants face the contradictory reality of lives which may be more difficult than those of their mothers in the Caribbean.

NOTE

1 WICP refers to the Women in the Caribbean project undertaken between 1979 and 1982 by the Institute of Social and Economic Research at the University of the West Indies with funding from regional and international agencies.

REFERENCES

Barrow, C. (1986) 'Male images of women in Barbados', *Social Economic Studies*, 35 (2).

Brown, C. (1984) *Black and White Britain: the Third PSO Survey*, London, Gower, for the Policy Studies Institute.

Byron, M. (1994) *Post-War Caribbean Migration to Britain: the Unfinished Cycle*, Aldershot, Avebury.

Cohen, R. (1987) *The New Helots: Migrants in the International Division of Labour*, Aldershot, Gower.

Curtis, S. (1989) *The Geography of Public Welfare Provision*, London, HMSO.

DOE (Department of Employment) (1990) 'Ethnic origins and the labour market', *Employment Gazette*, March: 125–37.

—— (1991) 'Ethnic origins and the labour market', *Employment Gazette*, February: 59–72.

Foner, N. (1977) 'The Jamaicans', in J. Watson (ed.) *Between Two Cultures: Migrants and Minorities in Britain*, Oxford, Basil Blackwell.

Harris, C. (1987) 'British Capitalism, migration and relative surplus population: a synopsis', *Migration*, 1(1): 47–90.

Heath, A. and Ridge, J. (1983) 'Social mobility of ethnic minorities', *Journal of Biosocial Sciences*, 8 (Supplement): 169–84.

Hondagneu-Sotelo, P. (1994) *Gendered Transitions: Mexican Experiences of Migration*, Berkeley, University of California Press.

Jackson, P. (1988) 'Definitions of the situation: neigbourhood change and local politics in Chicago', in J. Eyles and D. Smith (eds) *Qualitative Methods in Human Geography*, Cambridge, Polity Press, pp. 49–74.

Massiah, J. (1990) 'Defining women's work in the Commonwealth Caribbean' in I. Tinker (ed.) *Persistent Inequalities: Women and World Development*, Oxford, Oxford University Press, pp. 223–38.

Momsen, J. (1987) 'Land settlement as an imposed solution', in J. Momsen and J. Besson (eds) *Land and Development in the Caribbean*, Macmillan, London, pp. 46–69.

Office of Population Censuses and Surveys (1993) *1991 Census of Great Britain, Ethnic Group and Country of Birth, Volume 2*, London: HMSO.

Peach, C. and Byron, M. (1994) 'Council house sales, residualisation and Afro-Caribbean tenants', *Journal of Social Policy*, 23(3): 363–83.

Phizaclea, A. (ed.) 1983) *One Way Ticket: Migration and Female Labour*, London, Routledge and Kegan Paul.

Richardson, B. (1983) *Caribbean Migrants: Environment and Human Survival on St. Kitts and Nevis*, Knoxville, University of Tennessee Press.

Robinson, V. (1989) 'Economic restructuring: the urban crisis and Britain's black population', in D. Herbert and D.M. Smith (eds) *Social Problems and the City*, Oxford: Oxford University Press.

—— (1990) 'Roots to mobility: the social mobility of Britain's black population, 1971–1987', *Ethnic and Racial Studies*, 13(2): 274–86.

Rogers, B. (1980) *The Domestication of Women: Discrimination in Developing Societies*, London: Tavistock.

Senior, O. (1991) *Working Miracles: Women's lives in the English Speaking Caribbean*, Barbados, ISER, UWI, and London, James Currey.

Smith, D. (1977) *Racial Disadvantage in Britain, the PEP Report*, Harmondsworth: Penguin.

Stone, K. (1983) 'Motherhood and waged work: West Indian, Asian and white mothers compared', in A. Phizaclea, (ed.) *One Way Ticket: Migration and Female Labour*, London, Routledge and Kegan Paul.

15 Compromise and coping strategies
Gender issues and Caribbean migration to France

Stephanie Condon

INTRODUCTION

Over recent years, gender relations and gender issues have begun to establish a place in migration research. However, progress has been relatively slow (Lean Lim, 1993) despite debate initiated in the 1970s (Boserup, 1970; Morokvasic, 1975, 1983; Phizaclea, 1983) and many subsequent studies have served to reinforce images of passive women trapped in a confrontation between 'traditional' and 'modern' societies, and this analytical paradigm is used to measure the supposed one-way process of 'adaptation' or 'integration' (see Kadioglu, 1994). Although gender-conscious approaches in the study of migration remain in the minority and while there has been some confusion between studying 'women migrants' and 'gender relations' during migration and settlement (cf. Guillaumin, 1992: 236–8), women are increasingly recognized as being actors in the migration process and many aspects of their experience (labour market, housing, social activities, etc.) are seen as being influenced by gender relations (Chant, 1992; Hine, 1991; Walter, 1989).

Literature relating to women's place in past and present Caribbean societies is extremely rich. While some earlier works, notably in the sphere of fertility, unfortunately strengthened negative stereotypes of Caribbean women, much has been done since to deepen our understanding of gender relations in the Caribbean, be this literature of an academic nature (see for the French Caribbean: Alibar and Lembeye-Boy, 1981; Daguenais, 1993; Gautier, 1985) or creative (see Mordecai and Wilson, 1989; Nasha and also Liley in Buck, 1992; O'Callaghan, 1993). Since the pioneering work of Nancy Foner (1975, 1979), research into Caribbean migration has become more gender-conscious (Byron, 1994; Momsen, 1992; Olwig, 1993; Petras, 1989; Shepherd, 1995). Although migration from the French Caribbean has attracted little research until recently, a number of detailed and useful studies (not all published) relating to the history of this migration and the experiences of migrants focus on women and gender relations (Beauvue-Fougeyrollas, 1979; Darius, 1986; Ega, 1978; Goossen, 1976; Pierre-Evrard, 1983). This chapter intends to bring together issues raised in these works and pursued using various data sources.

Approaches to Caribbean migration to France essentially have been of a structural nature (Anselin, 1979; Edmond-Smith, 1972/74; Cirba, 1977; Constant, 1987; Condon and Ogden, 1991a, 1991b; Domenach and Picouet, 1992). While such studies have revealed much about the social relations and the politically determined strategies determining the migration, as well as many of its demographic and socio-demographic characteristics, the individual approach has been largely absent (see however Darius, 1986; Condon and Ogden 1996). Thus it has been impossible to evaluate the extent to which individual motivation has been operative in the history of this migration. This very concept was refuted by Leeds (1976) and led to considerable debate (see Morokvasic in Phizaclea, 1983; Babb, 1990). Yet while migratory processes and their determinants cannot be satisfactorily explained in terms of individual motivation, neither can totally structural approaches fully explain them; for example, how can we attempt to understand why some migrants leave and others stay? An individual approach must go some way to elucidating such processes. The second part of this chapter will be based on the results of a semi-structured interview survey carried out between 1990 and 1993.[1] This survey has revealed that while personal networks, kin groups or large-scale institutions have been important in decision-making processes (emigration, employment, housing and so on), individual motivation has often been crucial. Its importance varies from person to person or from one event to another during the life course. Only by such an approach can we begin to gauge the extent of individual motivation in such decisions and – importantly – how far the individual sees her/himself as having a major say in a decision or in a response to changing circumstances and whether he or she sees the decision as having been articulated through some personal or kin network or some wider set of relations.

The term *strategies* used in the title of this chapter must be interpreted loosely. Over recent years, researchers have often used the concept to explore some set of long-term plans, a notable example being the study of residential and housing strategies (e.g. Bonvalet and Fribourg, 1988). Migration strategies also have been much referred to, although numerous examples of the vulnerability of such long-term plans have been given (as in studies of the return migration decision). Plans for the future would seem to be made up rather of successive or parallel short-term plans, decisions or adjustments, including a number of contingency plans to allow for changing or unforeseen circumstances. Furthermore, recent literature has refuted the concept of such rational thinking by individuals, because of the more likely vague, unstable view people have of themselves, of their attitudes and desires, owing to multiple attachments and dynamic identities (Harvey, 1989: 53–4; Chambers, 1994). In this chapter, a few examples of such short-term – and evidently fragile – strategies are explored, their fragility being expressed in the words *coping* and *compromise*: strategies as a way of coping with new situations or problems and often including a degree of compromise. Women's – and men's – lives are full of moments of compromise and 'having to cope'. The various roles assigned to women by society, often difficult to articulate, mean that many forms of compromising and coping are specific to women, this form clearly varying according to social-economic circumstances. Migration is a life event giving rise to a set of new situations and difficulties to deal with.

Before exploring the way in which social and gender relations influence the life experiences of French Caribbean women migrants, it is helpful to know something of the context in which decisions have been made. Using various source materials, archival, contemporary literature, census and survey data, an historical overview of the migration will be given, focusing on a number of questions relating to gender.

CARIBBEAN MIGRATION TO FRANCE

During the 1950s and 1960s, increasing numbers of young women and men born in the French overseas departments (*départements*) of Guadeloupe or Martinique migrated to France. The state-organized migration, which began officially in 1963, principally concerned men for most of this period, be it through recruitment into public service employment, via training schemes or recruitment into private sector jobs, under the auspices of the specifically created state agency, the BUMIDOM, or, from 1960, through incorporation into the armed forces for national service (Constant, 1987; Condon and Ogden, 1991a). At this time, women migrated to France largely through informal channels, many responding to job offers for domestic employees or nannies (Ega, 1978). By the beginning of the 1960s, recruitment of Caribbean women by public hospitals in metropolitan France was underway, but the state was to play a crucial role in amplifying the movement, notably with the opening of training courses for female hospital sector workers. Yet the majority of women migrated with only a vague idea of the work they might find after arrival in France. Furthermore, those who migrated with their partner or came to join him formed a minority, even from the early days of the migratory movement.[2] Then, as the size of the Caribbean-born population in France grew, more and more women migrated to join siblings, female cousins, aunts or schoolfriends.

The government working party which prepared the Caribbean migration policy specifically made reference to women migrants (CGP, 1959). The intention was that large numbers of young adults, both male and female, should migrate and settle permanently in France. Women migrants were regarded by the policy both as workers and as mothers. For as well as hoping to solve the problem of high unemployment in the islands, thus avoiding social and political unrest (during a politically explosive period internationally), and providing much needed labour for the metropole, the policy's aim was to remove potential mothers from the Caribbean, where the problem of severe population pressure was seen as the result of 'rampant demographic increase'. From the early 1960s, then, an intensive campaign of information began to inform the inhabitants of Martinique and Guadeloupe of the problems facing the islands and of the opportunities awaiting them in metropolitan France (Condon and Ogden, 1991a; Condon, 1995).

An estimation of the proportion of migrants travelling to France under the auspices of the BUMIDOM suggested that it varied between half to two-thirds throughout the 1963–81 period (Anselin, 1979). Although many women were sponsored by migrants who had travelled via the BUMIDOM, the majority did not travel directly through the agency (INSEE survey analysis). In the case of those women who said that their passage had been paid by someone other than themselves, it was generally (in around 70 per cent of cases) a parent or other relative. For those women who did choose to migrate under the auspices of the state agency, schemes had been initiated for direct recruitment into public and private hospitals and other specialized clinics or nursing homes for elderly or handicapped persons. The BUMIDOM also arranged formal one-year contracts for domestic service posts, with the aim of protecting the women from exploitation (BUMIDOM, 1968). Arrangements were made with certain training colleges, notably the Dieppe college, to receive young Caribbean women. Then in 1967, the Crouy-sur-Ourcq centre, east of Paris, was set up by the BUMIDOM. The paternalistic nature of state attitudes to Caribbean migration is reflected in the responsibilities and activities of the state agency. The migrants were seen as needing a supervised adaptation period before working in metropolitan France. For women, the Crouy centre offered a 'pretraining' course before they took up domestic posts or followed other training courses. This pretraining consisted in 'introducing' women to metropolitan French culture, to modern household equipment, to French cooking, talks were given on city life and the Paris transport system and on health and personal hygiene.

The agency thus directed men to various heavy industrial sectors or into construction and women to domestic service or to the 'caring professions', notably the hospital sector. Public service employers oriented their recruitment policies according to their own conception of gender roles; for example, the recruitment of women into canteen or cleaning jobs, as well as into low-skilled office work. From the early days, the effects of the state organization and of public service recruitment were apparent. The 1968 census[3] shows that almost one-third of economically active women worked in the health and social service sector, a further quarter in office employment, 17.5 per cent as unskilled workers in other administrations and 5 per cent were teaching personnel. Using the socio-economic classification, for Guadeloupean migrants the category 'service personnel' accounted for 38 per cent of women workers (with only 6.2 per cent of the total being live-in domestic employees) and for 5.8 per cent of male workers. In the 'workers' category were 18 per cent of women, but almost half the men, with one-fifth of men and 29 per cent of women classed as 'employees' (non-industrial or non-manual workers). Thus around three-quarters of both men and women were in the bottom three socio-economic groups. These patterns were to become entrenched. The 1990 census,[4] which used a different classification system, published tables in less detail by island of origin than at the 1968 census, but reveals that 93 per cent of active women worked in service sectors. Moreover, detailed analysis of the results of the 1982 census for the Paris Region showed that 22 per cent of all active Caribbean-born women worked in the two lowest levels of the health sector, as either auxiliary nurses or ward orderlies and other hospital domestics (Condon and Ogden, 1991b: 446). The 1990 socio-economic classification gave 83.5 per cent of women and 79 per cent of men as classed in the bottom two groups (service personnel being classed with 'employees'). No upward social mobility within the Caribbean migrant population – cross-sectionally speaking – is apparent, suggesting though that perhaps on the individual level too, opportunities may not have improved since the early 1980s (Lucas, 1983).

Thus, the usual ghettoization of female employment, be it in Western societies (Perrot, 1978; Marchand, 1993), in French Caribbean society (Daguenais, 1993) or among migrant populations (e.g. Walter, 1989) is found again. For over and above the concentration of all Caribbean migrants in low-skilled occupations, Caribbean women are limited to a very narrow section of the labour market. On the one hand, most women work in typical women's occupations and, on the other, the range of occupations is concentrated in a smaller number of sectors than those of male migrants. Limited to using INSEE categories, we find that while 70 per cent of male migrants were grouped in ten occupational sectors in 1968 (building, metallurgical and mechanical industries, electricity, armed forces and emergency services, HGV or taxi drivers, public transport, as well as in various public services and in office work), only three sectors (health and social services, office employment and transport/communications) accounted for the same proportion of women workers.

As intended by the migration policy, Caribbean women's economic activity rates have always been high. In 1968, 57 per cent of Caribbean women were active, a substantially lower rate than that for men (73 per cent), but higher than that of metropolitan French women and far higher than for most foreign immigrant women. By 1990, their activity rate had increased considerably, to 73.5 per cent (the male rate was 81.5 per cent). However, at the same time, unemployment rates had more than doubled. This could be expected owing to the severe economic crisis in France, but the difference between female and male rates (13 per cent and 10 per cent respectively) is harder to explain. Moreover, when one compares those migrants having arrived in France since the previous census (1982) and those already resident in France at that time, unemployment rates are far higher among recent migrants and particularly among women, for whom the rate is just over 24 per cent compared with just under 15 per cent for men. While these higher rates reflect the youth of the recent migrant population (two-thirds are aged between 15 and 29 years, the non-active student population having been excluded), the gender difference must be explored, particularly since these recent women migrants are as a whole more qualified than the men (see below; and cf. Walter, 1991, for similar results among the Irish in London). Further analysis according to age group, qualification and period of arrival is necessary, as well as collecting information on what sort of networks are used to seek jobs.

Census data for the level of school qualifications for Caribbean migrants in 1968 revealed a majority of persons with no school qualifications. For women the proportion was 41 per cent, for men, over one-third. Few migrants had been able to pursue their studies and obtain secondary school certificates (18 per cent of both women and men). Data revealed however that an increasing number of women migrants had left school with their primary school certificate: one-third of migrants since 1962 as compared to only 25 per cent of those already present at the 1962 census. This is indicative of the general improvement in the level of schooling following the political integration of the islands into the French state in 1946.

Following on from this statement, it is surprising to find then that at the 1990 census, the proportion of Caribbean migrants, both women and men, declaring no formal qualifications remains high, at one-third, even though the proportion has fallen since the 1960s. Comparison with census data for the islands and a generational approach is clearly necessary. Nonetheless, when one looks at the data for the migrants having arrived between 1982 and 1990, in the majority young adults, the proportion of men without a primary school certificate is still a third, the proportion for women being somewhat less (28 per cent). Moreover, recent female migrants are generally more qualified than the male, with 31.5 per cent having the *Baccalauréat* or higher education qualifications, as against 24.6 per cent of men, the greatest difference being for those having left school after obtaining their *Baccalauréat* (19 per cent of women and 14 per cent of men). This is a recent evolution since for the population resident at the 1982 census, the main gender difference was between the higher proportion of men with secondary-level technical qualifications and that of women with the general secondary-level certificate (obtained around the age of 16 years).

Over the last four decades, secondary education has become more widely available in the French Caribbean. However, in the 1940s and 1950s, when the migrants who came to France in the 1960s and 1970s were of school age, secondary education was only to be found in the main towns. Families who wished for their children to have the chance of a better education sometimes moved to the main towns (Zobel, 1974) or sent a child there to live with a relative or as a paying guest while s/he attended secondary school. Thus, moves were made to the main town to further one's schooling or to attend certain training colleges (of which admittedly there were few). A reason for many women moving to the towns was the type of job opportunities available there, notably domestic work, whereas industrial jobs linked to agriculture or agricultural labouring jobs (predominantly male) were located in small towns or rural areas.

Questions relating to gender are raised by numerous aspects of findings to date. Most are of course very wide issues, beyond the scope of the present chapter. What intended here is, from currently available evidence,[5] to delve more deeply into some of the processes at work behind these statistical descriptions of the population at particular moments in time.

THE INDIVIDUAL EXPERIENCE

The question posed now is how individuals made decisions within this general changing structure. The state organization influenced the circumstances of departure and settlement in metropolitan France of hundreds of Caribbean migrants, but other influences, including individual motivation, came into play.

A full exploration of the issues raised throughout the migrants' biographies of course is a very lengthy task. Further papers and research will be devoted to other aspects. Here, a few themes have been selected to investigate various processes, at the same time as demonstrating the utility of such an approach. First, how prepared were women for seeking work, how did they find jobs and what ambitions did they have? Second, what or who influenced their decision to migrate? Third, how did they find work after their arrival and what or who influenced their decisions?

Three case studies will be used here. Some aspects of their biographies contrast, some are very similar. They arrived in the first decade of the mass migration, at similar ages; Cécile, born in a village in northern Martinique in 1935 arrived in 1958; Simone, born in Marie Galante, Guadeloupe in 1939 emigrated in 1963; and Lucette, born in St Joseph, a village east of Fort-de-France; in 1944 arrived in Paris in 1969. Cécile's mother was a sugar-cane field worker, her father a carpenter and she had one brother, seven years her junior. Simone's mother was a dressmaker and had four daughters and a son. Simone is the eldest; she did not know her father but knew the father of her siblings before he left Simone's mother in 1950, soon after which her mother left with the children for Pointe-à-Pitre. Lucette's mother was a cleaner at the local primary school and her father, a gardener; she has three brothers and an elder sister. Lucette managed to obtain her primary school certificate and her general school certificate, whereas neither Simone nor Cécile obtained their primary certificate. Each of them has children and met her partner at home, but their family circumstances differ. Cécile is married with five children (the first conceived with a different father); Simone has four children (the last three have the same father). Her partner left her in 1969, she has not settled down with another partner, and since the mid-1980s, she has being fostering a young girl. Lucette is married with five children and her elder sister came to France to live with the family in 1973. Cécile, after several years' domestic service and then a job in a printing works, gave up working in 1970; Simone works as a ward orderly in a private clinic; Lucette is a nursing auxiliary in a local public hospital. Cécile lives in a ground floor public housing flat in the northern suburbs; Simone and Lucette live in the same south-east Paris suburb, Simone in high-rise public housing, Lucette in a modern owner-occupied terraced house.

Schooling and preparation for the labour market

Most migrants wished to express their feelings on this topic. Thus several sets of social relations influencing the level of schooling achieved became apparent. Those who talked most about the chances offered to them seemed to be those who, at least in retrospect, would have preferred to stay on at school. Opportunities were determined principally by the degree of financial hardship experienced by the family. Other factors then linked into this major determinant, notably birth order and place of residence. Gender relations seemed to play a lesser role, especially in comparison with that played subsequently in vocational training choice and in the labour market.

Cécile had to leave school at the age of 14. Her mother sent her 'to learn how to sew with a white lady in the village', where she also did some housework and looking after the lady's seven children. Her mother took charge of her small wage, buying clothes and other small needs for Cécile, the rest of the wage contributing to the family's income. It was thus that Cécile helped enable her brother to stay on at school until the age of 18, obtain his *Baccalauréat* and become a primary school teacher. This seemed quite natural to Cécile, who did not express any regrets at not having had the same opportunity.

The sacrifice thus made by the eldest child in terms of education was a common finding in the interview survey, some interviewees clearly stating that their younger siblings had been fortunate. Lucette was given encouragement and financial support by her elder sister. She had had problems keeping up at primary school, was kept back on several occasions, but finally managed to obtain her primary certificate at the age of 15. Her sister meanwhile worked as a house-cleaner to assist with the family's finances, also helping her mother to bring up the children. When Lucette was 18, her sister paid for her to attend a private school in Fort-de-France run by a priest, where she was a live-in pupil. 'My sister wanted me to be a primary school teacher. She didn't want me to have to do the sort of work she did, but I only got as far as the *brevet* . . . but I did get it eventually.' Then she followed a course in accounting at evening school, which she paid for by working as a live-in maid, but after falling out with her employer, she had to give up the course. This she still regrets enormously: 'I adored accounting, but I could not continue paying for the course, as well as lodgings. Yes – I could have gone further and found a good job. But since at the catering college they gave us board and lodgings I went there.' The training was for waiters and waitresses, and this she did not enjoy very much, but she wanted to train to do something and financially this was the only feasible option. Being already in Fort-de-France, she had heard about the course and the advantages from people she knew from the private school.

Simone had to leave school at 13, around the time her mother left for Pointe-à-Pitre.

> I was doing well at school. At 12, I should have gone to secondary school, but since there wasn't one near our village, I would have had to go elsewhere. When your parents are poor, it's difficult to find the money for transport. And in town you need to find someone who will lodge you. As it was, I ended up going nowhere, because, after my mother took us to Pointe-à-Pitre, she said that she wanted me to stay on at school, but there weren't many places available and we did not have any contacts there.

She continues listing the barriers to her staying on at school. One feels that she is ashamed, wants to show that she could have done better but does not hold her mother responsible. Her brother went to a technical secondary school, her two youngest sisters stayed on until their secondary school certificate and now have jobs in an administration. Simone also adds that these two sisters are light-skinned, not like her and the other sister. She feels that she was deprived of a proper chance from the outset.

First work experience in the islands

Unlike records of rejection of domestic work in one's place of origin, as in Spain (Arondo, 1975) or in Ireland (Walter, 1989), such employment was one of the principal options open to women who left school with few or no qualifications in the French Caribbean. Domestic workers and cleaning staff were and are still almost all female (Daguenais, 1993: 90–1). The status of work varies from live-in posts, long-term day work with a single employer to more unstable, short-term jobs sometimes with more than one employer and often in the informal sector (implying the absence of health insurance cover). Several of the women interviewed had worked in this sector before emigrating and preliminary analysis of the INSEE survey (amongst migrants of all ages) showed that just over one-fifth of women who had been in regular or continuous employment before emigrating had been domestic employees at the time of departure. Each of the women whose cases are analysed here worked at some time in this sector.

After having worked as housemaid and nanny for about six years during her 'sewing apprenticeship' with 'the white lady' in her village, Cécile left to work in Fort-de-France. But this was not before long discussions with her parents. Cécile had a friend who had gone to the main town to work as a maid. On return visits to the village, she talked to Cécile about her job, about life in the town and how you could earn twice as much for the same work here. Cécile asked her parents on several occasions if she too could go to look for work, but they were wary. Cécile was then aged 20, so had not yet 'come of age'. Finally, they concurred. She agreed to send half her pay to her parents. Shortly after arriving at her friend's lodgings in Fort-de-France, she found a job as a live-in maid with a couple from France. Looking back, she was very happy about her working conditions with this couple and relations with her employers were healthy (she wrote to them for several years after emigrating). Her friend was instrumental in this move to find better work. Since her parents knew her friend, they were able to enquire about the work conditions and be assured that she would be correctly housed by her employers. Cécile was thus able to free herself from the direct control of her parents. Domestic work was available to her through her social network. At no point did she express an ambition for any specific career; she simply desired some independence from the family.

Having left the village of St Joseph for Fort-de-France to finish her secondary education, Lucette found a job as a live-in domestic in order to afford to go to evening classes in accounting.

> That sort of work was very easy to find. And it was with a primary school teacher who I knew. She gave me lodgings and I did her housework during the day and looked after her mother, who lived with her, and in the evenings went to the Chamber of Commerce. But that came to a stop because I started to have problems with the lady, so I gave up my classes and went to catering college, since they gave us lodgings there. . . . But the work we found, that we got through the college, you know, it doesn't pay at all and we worked really hard. And it was a classy hotel, there were lots of American tourists and given

what they made in the restaurant, when you see what they paid us . . . I just had to leave.

In terms of ambitions, Lucette had shown interest in accounting, then later in the interview, she talks of having thought of becoming an army nurse – women's work, but a job that would have enabled her to travel. For Lucette, domestic work was a means to another end to that sought by Cécile: she needed the money to continue her education, and then it became a means of surviving while she awaited her next move.

Simone's mother found a family for whom she could go and work as a maid, in exchange for a small wage and some needlework training. Thereupon began a series of jobs of a similar nature, where the acquisition of dressmaking skills was promised but where Simone felt she was simply being exploited. Over and above this, she abandoned her first job because her employer's husband continually made sexual advances – Simone was only 14 at the time, but told no one of the real reason for leaving the job, not even her mother. The second job she left because she frequently heard the husband and wife quarrelling and then realized that he was beating his wife. Then her mother found her a job with a Syrian dressmaking firm, where she really started to learn the trade, as well as how to use electrical machines, and had health insurance cover for the first time. Unfortunately, through competition, the firm had to make her redundant. She then went through two more domestic posts, without health insurance, where she felt she was being exploited again, before finally going to work for a young couple 'who were really lovely and treated me with respect. And when later I said I was going to France, the lady was really upset and cried.' For Simone, domestic work seemed to be the only option open. Her mother had found the first posts for her, then she continued in the same sector, despite numerous humiliations. She appears to have been isolated from networks informing her of better opportunities and the good conditions of her last job before emigrating were found by pure chance.

Emigration

Individuals were exposed to state propaganda to varying degrees. People heard about opportunities in France at school, on the radio or through relatives and friends. As the years went by, the whole of the island's population became aware of the different channels to emigration. Individual attitudes and responses to such opportunities varied for a whole host of personal and other reasons.

When Cécile recalls her departure from Martinique, she places her own motivation in primary position. Yet as in her move to Fort-de-France, the instigation or the pretext was provided by another person. For parental control over her decisions was still strong. Cécile had been corresponding with a female cousin who had gone to Paris a few years previously.

I had been thinking about going, because I wasn't very happy. Several times I asked my mother. But she didn't want me to go. And my father was worried

about a girl going off so far away alone. In the meantime, I'd had a boyfriend
. . . because you see my eldest daughter is not my husband's child . . . I found
out that I was pregnant . . . and after a month and a half, I hadn't said any-
thing to my parents. I said, 'Heavens, if my mother finds out she'll kill me.
What am I going to do?' I wrote to my cousin in Paris and she wrote back
'Come over here then, there's work to be found, we'll manage' and so I went.
My mother agreed because I told her that my cousin had invited me to stay
and I said that I was just going for a year, to see Paris. Then the day after
I left, my boyfriend went round to see my mother and told her I was pregnant.
She was not at all pleased. She wrote and said that if she had known, she
would never have let me go. In fact it was that which made me leave – fear.

Yet one feels that the pregnancy was the pretext for escape; she thus had an
urgent reason for her cousin to invite her over and a need to avoid the reaction
of her parents. Moreover she felt no real attachment to the boyfriend and if her
mother had found out about the pregnancy, Cécile would have been forced to
stay and marry him. The chance to escape would have been lost for ever.

Lucette was disappointed at having had to give up her accounts training.
During her work at the restaurant, she had met people from abroad:

and I had a Canadian friend. I would have liked to go to Canada. But my
brother was against it. He said he knew someone who'd emigrated there and
it was too cold. So I said too bad, I'll go to France. And since my boyfriend
at the time, he had to go to France for national service, we got married and
he arranged for me to follow after his service.

When Lucette talked about wanting to go to Canada, she stressed her 'spirit of
adventure', her 'need to move, to see places'. In the end, the decisions are made
for her by others. Her brother prevented her from going to Canada and her
husband arranged for her to go to France, a compromise which she accepted.

Simone, as she expresses it, emigrated 'for love'. She continues:

I had never thought of going to France. But when my fiancé went to France
to look for work, he promised to send me a boat ticket to join him. I didn't
hesitate, I just wanted to join him. I didn't know how long I'd be going for or
where we would live, so I left my two children with my mother.

It was thus that she left the first stable and good job she had found.

What these three cases reveal is an absence of long-term plans. Rather than
being planned as such, emigration had been, at the most, 'thought about' and
plans for the period after arrival in France were virtually non-existent.

Settling in the city

The three women arrived in Paris. Cécile went to stay briefly in the maid's room
her cousin occupied with her husband; Lucette and Simone went to join their
partners in the furnished rooms in which the men were lodging. Immediately,

each set about looking for work. Simone proceeded as she would have done at home: she walked along one of the main shopping streets in central Paris, asking in the shops whether they needed a cleaner. It was thus that she found her first job. She recounts:

> I needed to find something, to pay my way and to be able to send money home to my mother to feed and clothe the two children I had had to leave behind. I looked for cleaning work because that's the work I knew.

Cécile's cousin, herself a domestic employee, bought a newspaper and showed her domestic work advertisements. Within a few days, Cécile had been to two interviews and had accepted the job as a live-in domestic employee in which she was to remain for several years. 'I didn't know how long I'd be staying,' she recalled. 'I needed to be independent but to have somewhere comfortable to live while I was waiting for the baby to come. Mme J. was kind to me and my cousin was living not far away.' Then she continued, 'And after I'd had my baby, I was happy working with Mme J., she taught me lots of things and looked after me. So I stayed.' Neither of these two women talked of work-related ambitions. They spoke rather of independence. They sought jobs in the type of work they knew, the only type they thought available to them, at a time when such jobs were abundant in Paris.

For Lucette, the public service work network was operative. Her husband had been taken on by the Post Office after his national service and her sister worked in a public hospital. The process was very simple, as all the migrants interviewed who worked for the public services stated. 'So I wrote two letters, one to the Post Office and one to the central hospital administration, and since the hospital wrote back accepting my application first, I went to work in the hospital.' Lucette was ambivalent about the type of work. Even though she talks later on in the interview about having once thought of being a nurse in the army, this rather vague ambition was no longer an influence in her choice of work in Paris. She needed to find work and used the means readily available to her to find it. The migrant network gave her assurances about the many advantages of public service employment, stable jobs, access to public housing, possibilities of promotion, and favourable conditions for return visits to the Caribbean. Within the sector, choice of the type of job was a lesser priority, especially as most jobs available to these migrants were of an unskilled nature. Lucette was to discover that employment in the hospital sector differed from that in other parts of the public service in so far as it involved frequent night shifts. She was also to discover that hopes of promotion above the level of auxiliary nurse were rapidly abandoned by Caribbean migrant women: with children to bring up, often long journeys to work and domestic chores, most could not find the time or energy to study for nursing or administration diplomas. Twenty-two years after entering the hospital service, Lucette had passed the auxiliary nursing certificate but had not managed to gain any further promotion.

CONCLUSION

Over the last forty years, Caribbean women in metropolitan France have played a vital role in many branches of the economy and particularly within the public services. Their labour has been concentrated in a limited number of sectors, frequently in occupations often considered by society to be 'women's work' by their nature or their skill level: domestic employees, hospital domestics, auxiliary nurses, and low-skilled office jobs in both the public and private sectors. An analysis of the individual experience of migrants was conducted in an attempt to understand the links between schooling, work related expectations and the desire to emigrate to metropolitan France.

A common theme throughout these experiences is financial constraints. These partly determined educational opportunities and consequently employment possibilities. Yet other factors came into play, such as the extensiveness of one's social network, number of siblings and one's birth order. Gender relations particularly influence women's perceptions of what employment is open to them and play a role in higher levels of education, linked to career choice. Low-skilled young women – or their mothers on their behalf – looked for employment in a limited number of occupations, especially in domestic work. Similarly, after emigration, women sought work in the sector in which they already had experience, unless they were tied into a social network enabling their access to other sectors. However, access to public service employment, although accompanied by various financial advantages, was often access to similar work, of a domestic nature. Census data give statistical evidence of the perpetuation of such processes.

To understand the emigration decision, this part of an individual's history has to be returned to at various moments of the biographical interview. For the way it is recounted may vary by association with different events or relationships that the individual is recalling. Yet the brief insight given here does suggest one finding: long-term 'strategies' are rare. Decisions are based on much vaguer plans, thought of in parallel to a number of other desires or hopes. Decisions often occur when an opportunity arises, making the individual take one path rather than another. Sometimes this opportunity takes the form of an influential person in the individual's life, or of a particular set of social relations, be they gender, economic, generational and so on. Only a small number of themes could be explored here, focusing on the time around emigration. Future papers will investigate how women and men manage their lives throughout their stay in France, how their relationship with the Caribbean evolves, including the pivotal position of migrants between their family and friends in the metropole and those in the Caribbean and how gender relations influence the opportunities open to women and men and decisions they make.

NOTES

1 Thirty-two interviews were conducted from 1990–93 with Caribbean-born migrants, mainly women (access to male migrants then being more difficult; see note 5), living in the Paris region. Interviewees were contacted using the snowball method, from five sources. Most interviews were taped and fulyl transcribed. (All names used are pseudonyms.)

2 Preliminary findings from analysis by the author of data from the INSEE survey 'Migrations des personnes nées ou orginaires des DOM' (1991–92) on migrations between the overseas departments and metropolitan France.

3 Analyses of the 1968 census data are drawn from the 1970 INSEE published tables. All percentages are calculated by the author.

4 The 1990 census data is taken from the tables drawn up by Marie (1993).

5 At the time of the study, women were most easily contacted. This was for a number of reasons, one being that most key informants and interviewees seemed reticent to put me in contact with men. Thus the number of men so far interviewed (four) does not allow any in-depth analysis of the effect of gender relations on the issues explored here. Here the analysis is limited to gaining an understanding of women's ambitions in relation to work and emigration, how they perceived their opportunities, and the compromises and coping involved.

REFERENCES

Alibar, F. and Lembeye-Boy P. (1981) *Le Couteau seul. La condition féminine aux Antilles*, (2 vols), Paris, Editions Caraïbéennes/Agence de Cooperation Culturelle et Technique.

Anselin, A. (1979) *L'Emigration antillaise en France*, Paris, Anthropos.

Arondo, M. (1975) *Moi la bonne*, Paris, Editions Stock.

Babb, F. (1990) 'Women's work: engendering economic anthropology', *Urban Anthropology* 19(3): 276–302.

Beauvue-Fougeyrollas, C. (1979), *Les Femmes antillaises*, Paris, L'Harmattan.

Bonvalet, C. and Fribourg, A. (eds) (1988) *Stratégies résidentielles*, Congrès et colloques n°2, Paris, Editions de l'INED.

Boserup, E. (1970) *Women's Role in Economic Development*, New York, Earthscan.

Buck, C. (ed.) (1992) *A Guide to Women's Literature*, London, Bloomsbury.

BUMIDOM, (1968) 'Compte-rendu d'activités de 1967', Paris (unpublished).

Byron, M. (1994) *The Uncompleted Cycle: Post-war Caribbean Migration to Britain*, Aldershot, Avebury Press.

CGP (Commissariat Général du Plan) (1959) *Troisième Plan, 1958–61. Rapport général de la Commission de Modernisation et d'Equipement des DOM*, Paris, Imprimerie Nationale.

Chambers, I. (1994) *Migrancy, Culture, Identity*, London, Routledge.

Chant, S. (ed.) (1992) *Gender and Migration in Developing Countries*, London, Belhaven Press.

Cirba L, (1977) 'L'émigration antillaise vers la France', unpublished doctoral thesis, Université Paris V.

Condon, S.A. (1993) *L'Accès au logement: filières et blocages. Le cas des Antillais en France et en Grande-Bretagne*, Report to the Ministère de l'Equipement, Paris. Published April 1995 by the Plan Construction et Architecture, Paris as n°55.

—— (1995) 'Migration, assimilation and identity: Caribbean migration to France'. Paper presented to the 27th conference of the Association of Caribbean Historians, Georgetown, Guyana, 2–6th April 1995.

Condon, S.A. and Ogden, P.E. (1991a) 'Emigration from the French Caribbean: the origins of an organised migration', *International Journal of Urban and Regional Research* 15(4): 505–23.

—— (1991b) 'Afro-Caribbean migrants in France: employment, state policy and the migration process', *Transactions of the Institute of British Geographers* 16(4): 440–57.

—— (1993) 'The state, housing policy and Afro-Caribbean migration to France', *Ethnic and Racial Studies* 16(2): 254–93, plus appendix.

—— (1996) 'Questions of emigration, circulation and return: mobility between the French Caribbean and France', *International Journal of Population Geography* 2(1): 35–50.

Constant, F. (1987) 'La politique française de l'immigration antillaise de 1946 à 1987', *Revue Européenne des Migrations Internationales* 3(3): 9–29.

Daguenais, H. (1993) 'Women in Guadeloupe: the paradoxes of reality', in J.H. Momsen (ed.) *Women and Change in the Caribbean: a Pan-Caribbean Perspective*, London, James Currey.

Darius, F. (1986) 'Femmes antillaises en France: de l'oppression à l'immigration', unpublished doctoral thesis in Anthropology, Université Paris V.

Domenach, H. and Picouet, M. (1992) *La Dimension migratoire des Antilles*, Paris, Economica.

Edmond-Smith, J. (1972–3) 'West Indian workers in France', *New Community* 1(1): 444–50, II(2): 74–79 II(3): 306–14.

Ega, F. (1978) *Lettres à une noire*, Paris, L'Harmattan.

Foner, N. (1975) 'Women, work and migration: Jamaicans in London', *Urban Anthropology* 4(3): 229–49.

—— (1979) *Jamaica Farewell*, London, Routledge and Kegan Paul.

—— (1986) 'Sex roles and sensibilities: Jamaican women in New York and London', in R.J. Simon and C.B. Brettell (eds) *International Migration: the Female Experience*, NJ, Rowman and Allenheld.

Gautier, A. (1985) 'Politique familiale et familles monoparentales dans les DOM depuis 1946', *Nouvelles questions féministes* 9–10: 8–33.

Goossen, J. (1976) 'The migration of French West Indian Women to metropolitan France', *Anthropological Quarterly* 49(1) special issue 'Women and Migration', pp. 45–52.

Guillaumin, C. (1992) *Sexe, race et pratique du pouvoir. L'idée de nature*, Paris, Côté Femmes Editions.

Harvey, D. (1989) *The Condition of Post-Modernity*, Oxford, Blackwell.

Hine, D.C. (1991) 'Black migration to the urban midwest: the gender dimension, 1915–1945', in J.W. Trotter, (ed.) *The Great Migration in Historical Perspective. New Dimensions of Race, Class and Gender*, Bloomington, Indiana University Press.

INSEE (1970) *Population née dans un département ou territoire d'outre-mer et résidant en métropole. Recensement de 1968*, Paris, INSEE.

Kadioglu, A. (1994) 'The impact of migration on gender roles: findings of field research in Turkey', *International Migration* 32(4): 533–60.

Lean Lim, L. (1993) 'Effects of women's position on their migration', in N. Federici *et al.* (eds) *Women's Position and Demographic Change*, Oxford, Clarendon Press.

Leeds, A. (1976) ' "Women in the migratory process": a reductionist outlook', *Anthropological Quarterly* 49(1): 69–76.

Lucus. M. (1983) 'Rapport du groupe de travail sur l'insertion des ressortissants des départements d'outre-mer', unpublished report to Ministère des DOM-TOM.

Marchand, O. (1993) 'Les emplois féminins restent très concentrés', *La Société française, Données Sociales*, Paris, INSEE.

Marie, C.V. (1993) *Les Populations des DOM-TOM, nées et originaires, résidant en France métropolitaine* (sondage au quart), Paris, INSEE (série Démographie et Société).

Momsen, J.H. (1992) 'Gender selectivity in Caribbean migration', in S. Chant (ed.) *Gender and Migration in Developing Countries*, London, Belhaven Press, pp. 73–90.

Mordecai, P. and Wilson, B. (1989) *Her True-true Name*, Oxford, Heinemann.

Morokvasic, M. (1975) 'L'immigration féminine en France: état de la question', *Année Sociologique* 26: 563–75.

—— (1983) 'Why do women migrate? Towards an understanding of the sex selectivity of migration', *Studi Emigrazioni* 70 (special issue on women and migration): 132–40.

O'Callaghan, E. (1993) *Woman Version: Theoretical Approaches to West Indian Fiction by Women*, Warwick University Caribbean Studies, London, Macmillan Press.

Olwig, K.F. (1993) 'The migration experience: Nevisian women at home and abroad', in J.H. Momsen (ed.) *Women and Change in the Caribbean: a Pan-Caribbean Perspective*, London, James Currey.

Perrot, M. (1978) 'De la nourrice à l'employée . . . Travaux de femmes dans la France du XIXe siècle', *Le Mouvement Social* 105: 3–10.

Petras, E.M. (1989) 'Jamaican women in the US health industry: caring, cooking and cleaning', *International Journal of Urban and Regional Research* 13(2): 305–23.

Phizaclea, A. (ed.) (1983) *One Way Ticket: Migration and Female Labour*, London, Routledge and Kegan Paul.

Pierre-Evrard C. (1983) 'L'intégration des infirmières antillaises dans les équipes soignantes des hôpitaux de Paris', (unpublished master's dissertation) Université Lyon II.

Shepherd, V.A. (1995) 'Women, migration and indentureship: the case of Indians in Jamaica, 1845–1921', paper presented to the 27th conference of the Association of Caribbean Historians, Georgetown, Guyana, 2–6 April 1995.

Walter, B. (1989) 'Gender and recent Irish Migration to Britain', in R. King (ed.) *Contemporary Irish Migration*, Geographical Society of Ireland Special Publications, no.6.

Zobel, J. (1974) *Rue cases-nègres*, Paris, Présence Africaine.

16 Strategies and strategizing

The struggle for upward mobility among university-educated Black Caribbean-born men in Canada

Dwaine Plaza

There was no sense of permanence to Canada . . . five years tops . . . We had the notion we were going up there to kick-ass exploit the place and then go back . . . in essence to sell our labour to the highest bidder . . . Since the Caribbean could not offer the kinds of wages or the sort of lifestyle that we dreamed possible we were going to leave in search of better opportunities.

(Ruben)[1]

This notion of going to Canada and working hard for your children does not work the same with Caribbeans . . . Yes, we want our children to do well, but we also want ourselves to do well . . . We want to be the Prime Minister of Canada too . . . I did not leave Jamaica with the notion that I am going to Canada to sweep floors . . . that's the kind of model that most people have of the immigrant and this was very different for the mind-set of Caribbean immigrants arriving in Canada.

(Basil)

INTRODUCTION

Since 1967 Caribbean immigration to Canada has been completely transformed by the 'Points System'. Over the period 1967 to 1992 approximately 300,000 immigrants from the Caribbean entered Canada. This cohort accounted for 7.8 per cent of the overall Canadian immigration total. Most Caribbean immigrants settled in Toronto because family, kin and friends were already living there. The early pioneer migrants were likely to be between the ages of 20 and 45 years, skilled and have few dependents. Like most immigrants arriving in Canada, Caribbeans had the expectation that they would experience the 'mobility dream'. In Canada the mobility dream is directly linked to the American ethos of being 'the land of opportunity', where any person willing to work hard can 'make it' regardless of colour, ethnicity, or place of birth. The central tenet of the mobility dream, which made it especially appealing to Caribbean migrants, was that every immigrant was the architect of his or her own fortune, because equal opportunity was available to all. The reality of life for most immigrants to Canada, however, has rarely matched these ideals. The opportunity to be upwardly mobile in

Canada has never been evenly distributed among all the talented or ambitious in the population.

This chapter examines the ways in which the social mobility strategies of Black Caribbean-born men living in Canada are shaped both by the cultural values of their home region, and by their responses to specific structures of opportunity and discrimination. In order to cope with bleak opportunities for mobility at home Black Caribbean-born men have devised unique socio-economic mobility strategies. The fundamental set of strategies involves a combination of emigration and the attainment of university or professional training. These strategies are rooted in Caribbean regional history and culture. Racism and other barriers to immigrant mobility in Canada, however, limit the success of this strategy.

The analysis which follows is divided into four parts. The first section provides a broad overview of the characteristics of the men interviewed in the sample. The second section uses the narratives provided by the interviewees to examine their revised mobility strategies in Canada. The third section discusses these revised mobility strategies and comments on their long-term implications *vis-à-vis* a transnational reality most of these men live in Canada. The final section of the chapter comments on the similarity between the current mobility strategies and the ones which emerged during the historical development of the Caribbean *circa* 1834.

CHARACTERISTICS OF THE MEN IN THE SAMPLE

All twenty of the men in the sample were born in the Caribbean, only two arrived in Canada under the age of 15 years. The rest arrived in Canada in their mid-twenties or early thirties. The oldest man interviewed was 69 years old while the youngest was 30 years old. The average age of the men was 49 years. Nine of the men were born in Jamaica, three were from Barbados, two were from Guyana, St Lucia and Trinidad respectively, and one each from Grenada and St Kitts.

Fifteen of the men migrated directly to Canada from the Caribbean. The other five came to Canada as 'double lap' migrants – that is via the United States or Britain. All of the men settled in Toronto because family, kin or friends were already living there. With respect to the period of arrival, most of the men (eleven out of the twenty) arrived before 1975 while seven arrived between 1976 and 1986. Only two arrived in the period between 1986 and the present.

The social origins of the men in the Caribbean were fairly similar with most being concentrated in the middle and lower middle classes. Fifteen of the men identified their social class to be either from the 'lower middle' or the 'middle class'. Four men identified their family social origin as being from a 'working class' background. Only one man felt that he was from an 'upper class' house-hold prior to migrating to the Canada.

With respect to current occupations a significant proportion of the men in the sample, seven, were in the education field: this included secondary school teachers, university instructors, and an education consultant. Another group of four men were professionals. This group consisted of a doctor, a lawyer, an engineer, and an accountant. A third cluster, three men, were in business: this included a real estate agent and two entrepreneurs. The final group was a miscellaneous cluster of three men consisting of a film maker, a writer and a social worker. Only one man in the sample had a blue collar job in Toronto. Although he had completed a geography degree at the University of the West Indies in Jamaica, this individual had only recently arrived from Jamaica and as a result took the only job he could find, dispatching for a tow truck company.

Thirteen of the men interviewed were married, five were officially separated or divorced. The remaining two were single. Not all of the men who were married lived with their wives. Four men who indicated that they were married at the beginning of the interview, revealed during later conversation that they were no longer living with their wives. In the case of those men living with a spouse, their partners were all in stable employment at the time of the interview.

All but three of the men had children. Nine of the men had three or more children in Canada, eight had either one or two children in Canada. Five had children from previous relationships who were still living in the Caribbean. Although the men talked of these 'outside' children and were in occasional contact with them, most did not provide regular monetary support.

With respect to the highest level of schooling, thirteen of the men had completed a bachelor's degree, four had completed a master's degree, and three had completed a doctorate. Half of the men finished their first degree outside of Canada. These foreign qualifications were completed in the Caribbean, Britain, and the United States. Of the ten men who completed their first degree in Canada, most had worked full-time before going back to school. Only two of the men arrived in Canada at an age young enough to attend high school before going on to university.

Some two-thirds of the men (thirteen out of the twenty) make frequent return visits back to the Caribbean. This suggests the continued importance of maintaining a link to family and kin still living in the region. With respect to their aspirations for one day permanently returning to the Caribbean to live, eight of the men were not quite sure what they wanted to do, seven were adamant that they would 'return tomorrow' if given the right opportunities. Three men were quite positive that they never wanted to return because close family and kin were mostly living in Canada, Britain or the United States and hence there was 'no one left to visit or stay with'. Two men who were close to retirement age indicated that they wanted to live the life of a 'snow bird', spending their winters in the Caribbean and their summers in Canada.

From the above socio-demographic profile of the twenty men in the sample, it is apparent that this is quite a heterogenous mixture of individuals, who nevertheless had a common Caribbean background, high levels of educational attainment and had migrated to Canada. As a consequence of the sample size being small and non-randomly selected it is inconceivable to make strong claims of validity or representativeness in the findings that follow. The life experiences of these men can, however, give us a general picture of the way Black Caribbean-born men with university level schooling in Canada make sense of and act in relation to their position. In the analysis which follows it must be remembered that the men are identified by fictitious pseudonyms as are the place and organization names which appear.

REVISED MOBILITY STRATEGIES IN CANADA

In this section we thematically explore the mobility strategies Black Caribbean-born men put in place once in Canada. These strategies were devised to cope with the barriers preventing the men's aspirations for the 'mobility dream'. The strategies are interesting because many involve negotiating a transnational balance between doing well in Canada by reflecting back to the Caribbean. The revised strategies allow the men to respond, manage, manipulate, and control their circumstances in Canada so that they are able to derive some sense of accomplishment and satisfaction about their decision to migrate.

'You have to admit that this is a racist society'

One of the realities that all the men needed a strategy for dealing with was the discrimination and racism they encountered in their workplace and their day-to-day activities. Although the men had come from societies where distinctions of colour, social behaviour, speech, and education played an important part in determining status, in Canada none of these fine distinctions were of much significance in relation to the more dominant issue of colour. Learning to deal with the colour issue was difficult because it went against the men's constructed notion about the 'mobility dream', where everyone is suppose to be treated equally and what matters most is a man's educational achievements and work ethic. Individuals seemed to respond either by ignoring or actively confronting the incidents of discrimination and racism when they encountered them in Canada. Those men who ignored the incidents were likely to be individuals who had confidence in their abilities or themselves. On the other hand, those who openly challenged discrimination tended to believe that people who discriminate are ignorant and disrespectful. There was no clear pattern as to which men ignored the incidents or which reacted to them.

Everton's reaction to discrimination and racism characterizes the overall sentiments of the passive group of men in this study. He says:

> I never lost my cool when I confronted a situation where racism was involved . . . I never let the oppressor get any reaction from me because that's what he wanted . . . I made sure that what ever he was saying or doing did not penetrate, I just deflected it and tried to move on. It took a lot of courage for me to carry on in those situations but I was determined not to let him see me perturbed by his actions.

Basil's philosophy, on the other hand, characterizes the active group's response to incidents of discrimination. These men openly challenged the situation as soon as they encountered it because as many indicated they were 'afraid that it might grow if left unchecked'. Basil said:

> My approach was that when I saw or heard racism I confronted it right away . . . This shit is not going to go on . . . I am part of this society and I am not on the periphery . . . I adopted the stance that I am not going to get worried or depressed. I am not going to allow this racist society to kill me. I know it exists . . . I am going to work in it and I am going to survive.

In general, the men seemed cautious about 'blowing the race whistle' in Canada. Most felt proud of their achievements in Canada and as a result they were apprehensive about blaming all of their woes on the fact they were Black and their employers were White. Overall, the men resisted labelling events racist unless they were absolutely sure they were being subjected to differential treatment because of colour prejudice. There was also a strong feeling for wanting to take the time 'to sort out a racially charged situation' rather than seeking external help from official bodies like the Human Rights Commission. The overwhelming sentiment was that they wanted to fit in and, therefore, regarded 'making waves' in their workplace as a last resort. Some like Ruben wanted to handle discrimination or racism in the workplace 'in the quietest way possible' because as he said 'one would still have to go on working in the same place regardless of what happened'.

'Being mentally strong in this society is important'

In coping with racism and discrimination in Canada the men also had to find additional strategies. One strategy which was repeated in a number of interviews was the importance of being 'mentally strong'. Being mentally strong requires that individuals have 'confidence in themselves and their ability'. They also needed a certain kind of 'drive' that not only pushed them along but also helped them to maintain a 'level mental perspective' as Simon noted. In developing a mental coping strategy to deal with their unequal employment situation in Canada some of the men described how they used the conditions of their slave ancestors as a reference point. By casting slavery as the ultimate state of inequality a Black person can experience, individuals could then see their own circumstance in Canada as 'less to complain about', and hence they derived strength from this to carry on.

Pierre's reflection typifies the optimism that was derived by juxtaposing the plight of his ancestors with the situation he found in Canada. He says:

> I had an attitude that said I know who I am . . . I know that I am the descendant of slaves . . . my ancestors paid the ultimate price . . . they survived slavery by coming up with creative solutions . . . I am not going to let what ever they dish out get the better of me or stop me here . . . you need to have that kind of drive and determination to cope in this system

'Education gives you many more options'

More education was unanimously seen as being the most important strategy for coping with barriers to mobility in Canada. The men strongly believed that education provided them with 'options', and built up some 'security'. When faced with institutional and systemic barriers in Canada the men tended to see more schooling and qualifications as the way to handle the situation. Both Edmond and Patrick are prime examples of how education was used in Canada as a safety-net to fall back upon when they encountered barriers to mobility.

Edmond, on the one hand, continued to collect more qualifications after his first university degree because he felt that eventually his superiors would find it impossible to deny him the position of school principal. His desire to collect more 'certificates and credentials' is a response undoubtedly influenced from being socialized in the Caribbean where historically the more education one had the more mobility one could expect to achieve. In Canada however, mobility depended on more than just high education qualifications. A lack of networks, colour prejudice, and insufficient 'Canadian' work experience were also among the many factors which prevented the mobility aspirations of the men. By constantly striving to 'better himself on paper' and being 'one up on his White competition' Edmond was hoping to compensate for what he described as a 'colour barrier in the promotion game'. According to Edmond:

> The more schooling and qualifications that I accumulated the better I felt . . . As long as I could trick myself into believing that I was making some forward progress in Canada then I could continue to do more courses and to live in a fantasy world were everything was alright . . . All of my additional qualifications became accolades for my own fulfilment since my employer did not acknowledge or reward my efforts.

Patrick's situation, on the other hand, was typical of the men who arrived with a university degree already completed. Although he was a qualified engineer, he still faced barriers in trying to practise his profession in Canada.[2] As a result of not finding employment in his field Patrick had to 'shift his thinking' to another occupation which required that he return to school for new qualifications. By maintaining an open mind and a willingness for more education Patrick was able to experience some success in Canada despite the barriers that he faced.

'I have to be twice as good and work twice as hard'

The men also felt that they worked harder than Whites in the process of getting higher status jobs in Canada. They further acknowledged that even with hard work it was often the case that they would still be overlooked for promotions. Despite this frustrating situation, however, most continued to believe that the best way for responding to the barriers and discrimination they faced was to 'work even harder' and to 'get more qualifications'. The men see and understand that compared to Whites, being Black is a disadvantage, and therefore to be able to overcome their disadvantages and 'beat' their White counterparts they have to be 'twice as good'.

Donovan's rationale for working harder in Canada makes the point quite clearly. He says:

> What I have to do is work twice as hard here in Canada . . . I figure there is a perception that I don't cut it . . . what you have to do is your speech and presence have to be cantankerous . . . you have to show very forcefully that you are compatible . . . I make sure that whatever I do I am prepared because there is a whole lot riding on who I am. I am not just the lawyer, I am the Black lawyer . . . I have to be strong do my research, make sure I am ready that is the attitude that I take . . . its a constant struggle . . . you don't allow it to get you down.

Working twice as hard also meant for some men simultaneously holding down more than one job in order to compensate for lower annual income. Leroy's situation exemplifies this: he worked as a real estate agent but he also went door to door selling vacuum cleaners. By having a 'regular job' and a 'side line job', Leroy commented that this gave him the extra income he needed to 'maintain a certain lifestyle'. This lifestyle included being able to have such items as 'a nice car, a cellular phone, decent clothing, and good accommodation'. Undoubtedly, another unspoken reason for wanting some of these luxury commodities was that Leroy needed to have symbols which conveyed to others that he had 'made it' in Canada. By possessing certain conspicuous items Leroy was able to get affirmation from friends and family in Canada that he was achieving the 'mobility dream'.

'Learning how the real hiring and promotion game worked'

It took some men a long time to become aware of how the 'real hiring and promotion game' in Canada was played. Once they learned, however, some were able to be relatively successful at playing it. In Patrick's case, learning to play the game included realizing that he needed to 'water down' his resumé so that he was not perceived as a threat by potential White employers. For Donovan, on the other hand, it included developing a 'dual accent'. In the early period of his arrival to Canada, Donovan realized that being 'bilingual' – speaking Jamaican and Canadian – was advantageous. He learned to imitate the Canadian accent when he was in the company of White people, because this made him more 'accepted'. Later on in practising law, Donovan continued to use his 'bilingual' abilities because he found that White lawyers and judges treated him differently if he spoke to them with a Jamaican accent.

Canadian 'mannerisms and dress' were also adopted by some individuals as a way to fit into the predominately White networks in Canada. By 'looking and acting' in a certain 'Canadian way' John found that he was 'more readily accepted'. He also found that being accepted was 'essential for penetrating into the Canadian networks'. John's reflection on how he became part of the writer's network in Toronto makes this point. He says:

A lot of things in Canada had to do with networking . . . I have a gift of being able to network through my ability to communicate . . . I know how to do that very well . . . I was very fortunate about my background in Barbados as a newspaper reporter . . . In Toronto I went to social functions with my partner and we networked, she with the women and me with the men . . . Once people got to know us and saw we were just like them, then we were 'accepted' . . . These contacts have been very important in me becoming a published writer.

In dealing with employment discrimination in Canada, some men described how they used a network of Caribbean friends to help locate work. The 'grape-vine' worked especially well for those individuals arriving in Canada with just secondary schooling. The 'grape-vine' did not, however, work the same way for men arriving with university level qualifications completed. Qualified men who aspired to immediately enter occupations commensurate with their qualifications typically did not have the benefit of family, kin, or friends to introduce them to potential employers. As a consequence, many had to use 'head hunting' agencies or their own ingenuity to find relevant employment. A difficulty arose using 'head hunting' agencies because many were racist in their treatment of non-Whites. Some agencies acted as 'gate keepers' for companies to filter out people of colour. According to Patrick this was subtly done by the agencies 'only referring qualified Black clients to certain types of jobs and not telling them about others'.

Other strategies used to avoid discrimination involved looking for work within the Canadian government. A number of men recalled their fear of working in the private sector because of its reputation as a place where Blacks stood little chance of breaking in. Like Eugene, some men remembered an initial desire to work for the Municipal, Provincial or Federal governments because this would mean 'stability, prestige, promotion, and a good future pension'. Many of these ideas about the stability of government employment undoubtedly came from the interviewees' socialization in the Caribbean where civil service appointments have historically been prestigious and long term. Arriving in Canada it is little surprise that many men would initially desire jobs in this sector, above the private sector.

Some individuals who did get government jobs in Canada found that contrary to their constructed notions about 'fairness and stability' in the government sector there were certain unwritten rules for hiring and promotion. Roland, an accountant who works for Health and Employment Canada, highlights the point that promotion and hiring in the government sector was as much dependent on networks as it was on qualifications. He says:

My experiences in the office at Health and Employment Canada has been quite an eye opener. I work in an environment where my co-workers are divided into ethnic cliques, there is the East Indian group, a Chinese group and a White group . . . the White group are the ones on the top. All the other groups look out for their own in the office . . . Me, I only have one other Black person in the office and she is a secretary . . . The other ethnic groups are struggling to bring in more of their own friends . . . its like they are trying to get rid of me so that it will be easier to bring in one of their own.

'Getting into business for myself was emancipation'

Although only four men in the sample had a private business, more than half of the men indicated a keen desire to become entrepreneurs in Canada. Most men who wanted to go into business for themselves in Canada were interestingly enough individuals who arrived with a university degree already completed. The sentiment of these men was that they were frustrated with their mobility in Canada and because of this they had constructed the idea that by having their 'own' business this would mean 'freedom'. The freedom that they desired was also thought of in terms of avoiding the pain and disappointment of dealing with discrimination and racism in the workplace. Having a business did seem to allow individuals to avoid some workplace discrimination but it also exposed them to new types of discrimination which included difficulties trying to negotiate loans with White bank managers who had very little experience with Black clients. Patrick's reflection on his becoming an entrepreneur captures the overall sentiment of why some men wanted to get into business. He said:

> My business was emancipation from the routine of working long hours with very little recognition or the chance at promotion . . . At least if I am working in my own business for long hours, at the end of the day I have my fair share of the rewards and I don't have to face the same tensions or politics in the office from me being Black and the majority being White.

The small number of men in the sample who are in business for themselves is not surprising since Caribbean culture is one that does not overly emphasize entrepreneurship as a mobility strategy. Individuals raised in the Caribbean are more likely to find encouragement to become 'good civil servants or to work for someone else rather than being independent and taking the chance to own their own business' according to Ruben. This cultural characteristic might partially explain why in the 1991 Census of Canada there were so few businesses being run by Blacks. The Census showed that 'Black' (which included people of Caribbean origin as well as other groups) are among the three lowest ethno-cultural communities participating in self-employment with less than fifty per 1,000 for men and even fewer for women.

A new type of small business which seems to be increasingly more prevalent in the Caribbean community in Toronto is the forming of transnational family businesses. Anton and his brother in Jamaica are a good example of these inter-national business ventures. The two brothers have a partnership which involves exporting used Volkswagen engines from Canada to Jamaica. In his off-time from work, Anton travels around to scrap yards in Toronto looking for cars with good engines. He purchases the engines and has them exported to Jamaica. His brother in Jamaica, who is an auto mechanic, uses the engines either to fix customers' cars or he sells them to other mechanics. This 'side line venture', as Anton put it, has helped him to put up a 'nice retirement home in Jamaica'.

Raymond, on the other hand, sent down an industrial size ice-making machine to his brother in St Kitts. Raymond's brother has been able to start up a business from under the family house supplying the village with bags of fresh ice. Each month Raymond's brother sends him money to pay for the ice machine. Eventually, when the ice machine is paid off, Raymond says 'he will then begin to see some of the profit'.

Both Anton and Raymond's international business ventures are interesting because they demonstrate the cross-system negotiation which some men are using to measure their upwardly mobility. The international partnerships might also be interpreted as an attempt by some men to transfer part of their wealth they have accumulated back into the Caribbean where as an investment it can do more direct good for family members still living there. By broadening their perspective from just doing well in Canada to include the Caribbean, both Anton and Raymond have been able to derive an enhanced sense of their progress.

'Getting back into the Caribbean is important to me'

For some men seeking affirmation of their success in Canada also involves making many return visits back to the Caribbean. By making these visits individuals are in a sense able to validate that although they might not be getting to the more prestigious occupations in Canada they have indeed 'progressed' more than their family, kin, and friends who are still in the Caribbean. John's observation about his friends from the newspaper in Barbados makes this point quite well. He says:

> When I go back to Barbados I know that if I go to 'Peppers' at 5:00 pm on any weekday I will see all of my old friends from the newspaper liming. They will be in the exact same seats we use to be in 15 years ago. In many ways these guys have not progressed. Many are still stuck in the same laid back mode as when I left them . . . Although my life in Canada is at times madness, it is still more exciting and fulfilling than what I see back in Barbados . . . Had I stayed in Barbados, I am sure that I would have been one of the fellas in the bar come 5:00 pm.

In struggling with their circumstance of blocked mobility in Canada most men used their eventual return 'home' to the Caribbean as a means of coping. 'Home' is often constructed as a sunshine paradise, a place where life is simple and issues like discrimination and racism do not exist. By having the dreams of returning to an idyllic 'home' to enjoy the economic benefits of their years of sacrifice and toil in Canada many men seemed to derive strength and courage to carry on.

Five men in the sample already owned land in the Caribbean which they intended to use for building a retirement home. Owning property in their place of birth was important for these men because it showed family, kin, and friends, who were living both in the Caribbean and abroad, that they intended to return 'home' in the future. Returning 'home' and putting up a house was important because it showed others that the individual was indeed successful in his migration. The act of migrating and then returning to put up a house in the Caribbean can be traced back historically to the post-Emancipation period. According to Conway (1989: 7) one of the most important rites of passage for a man to complete was to return to the Caribbean after having worked abroad and then to be able to put up a 'walled' house. The permanent house became a monument for others in the village to know that the individual had been successful in his adventures abroad.

'Leaving Canada will give me better employment opportunities'

Moving to the United States or back to the Caribbean was considered by five men in the sample as a way for them to have better employment prospects. The group who were considering remigrating to other countries were mainly younger men (under 45 years) with professional qualifications. Most of these men had completed doctorates and were in the process of seeking full-time employment.

These highly educated men generally felt dissatisfied with their future prospects if they remained in Canada. The common sentiment within this group was that the existing employment equity legislation in Canada only was benefiting White women. According to Raymond 'the current legislation is implemented to fill quotas with White women'. Black males are rarely considered in the Canadian legislation especially if there is a woman candidate around. In contrast, Raymond notes that 'in the United States, being Black and male is recognized in the Affirmative Action policies, therefore we might get treated better if we go there'.

Basil's optimism about the United States being a place where he will seek future employment was typical of the hopes that this group of young professionals held onto. He says:

> I know in the United States the jobs will be there when I am finished this degree . . . I know two other Black friends who defended three years ago. At first they refused to look outside of Canada for work. Unemployment and not making any short-lists caused them to widen their job search to include the States. Within a few months each man had job offers from colleges in Florida and New York. Although they were not university jobs, at least they were stepping stones . . . you know progress, that sure beats unemployment.

'Measuring mobility in other ways'

For some men, they came to define their mobility not only in terms of their own progress but in terms of their ability to help others achieve. The men who tied their own improvement to others seemed to be individuals who had encountered considerable barriers in their own aspirations for mobility. The most common avenues through which these men projected their accomplishments were their children's success, their involvement with Caribbean-based organizations, and their ability to continue to help out family and kin remaining behind in the Caribbean.

The achievements of their children in Canada was an important yardstick for some of the older men to measure their own success. The sacrifices that these men had made in Canada was seen to be worth it so long as their children were able to have access to better opportunities. A common sentiment heard was that although 'I am not able to make it to the top, I'm going to make sure that I open up as many doors as I can for my children'. By passing on their own wealth of experience and encouraging their children to take up study in certain areas, many men were optimistic about their children's future in Canada. Martin's reflection exemplifies this optimism. Although he initially came to Canada in 1985 for his 'own benefit', this focus soon changed to his children. He says:

> When I arrived in Toronto it was for me and my own betterment. As time passed I began to realize that I was not going very far in this country as an engineer. It's funny, I refocused my attention to my children and them doing well . . . I tried to give them the benefit of my experience here in making choices for school and what kinds of careers they should be pursuing . . . My sentiment became that if I was not going to be able to make it I was going to make damn sure that they might.

By working within organizations that were doing fundraising and charity work for the improvement of hospitals, schools, and old-age homes back in the Caribbean some men were able to derive a sense of importance and the feeling that they were helping out those still left behind. Making a positive contribution to 'home' for many was seen as important because they regarded the Caribbean like themselves as 'under dogs', whereas they saw Canada as a more well-off place where it would not make much difference if they contributed to it or not. Making a positive contribution to 'back home' by working with the Jamaican/Canadian Association was important to Patrick because it relieved him of his guilt for having left Jamaica 'especially after the country and its people had invested so much into his education and training'.

These transnational practices provide another vehicle for migrants to obtain and reinforce their social position. Joining, and even more significantly leading, such transnational organizations provide individuals with a chance for public validation and recognition both within Canada and their country of origin. Such status validation becomes a high priority for many men who through migration to Canada have achieved a higher standard of living but only by accepting lower status positions.

Being in a position to send money, clothing, and small household items to family and friends in the Caribbean was also important to the men because this gave them affirmation of their success in Canada. Some men like Simon, felt better about themselves because over the years they had consistently been able to put aside something to help relatives still living in the Caribbean. The ritual of sending money and goods 'back home' can also be traced historically to the earlier periods, when it was important for individuals who departed to use remittances as a sign that they were successful in their new location, and that they were now in a better position than those left behind (Marshall 1982).

DISCUSSION

From the mobility strategies discussed there is some overlap and continuity with respect to the strategies which exist in the Caribbean. Although many of the mobility strategies which emerged in the Caribbean came about because of particular historical circumstances, it seems that migrants arrived in Canada and tried to put variations of these strategies into place notwithstanding that the conditions were markedly different. This is not surprising given the years of socialization that these individuals received growing up in the Caribbean and the transnational manner in which these men conduct their lives.

Undoubtedly the most important avenue for achieving upward mobility in the Caribbean since the post-Emancipation period is through education. When Caribbean-born men in Canada are confronted with racism, discrimination, and differential incorporation it is little wonder that many respond to these situations by obtaining more credentials and qualifications. By doing this, there is a hope that more education will compensate for the other ascribed factors which the men cannot change – skin-colour and ethnicity. The idea of obtaining more education to become mobile also fits the men's constructed ideas about the 'mobility dream' which promises that through good qualifications and hard work anyone can make it to the top in Canada regardless of his ethnicity or colour.

Migration also continues to be an important avenue through which Caribbeans circumvent the constraints of a stratified social system and limited opportunities. What seems apparent from the findings in this study is that the 'migration culture' still continues to influence the way individuals in Canada think when confronted with seemingly difficult circumstances. The option of remigration continues to be very much part of the way Caribbean men think about their opportunities in Canada.

In the Caribbean one of the most important elements for becoming upwardly mobile is through the networks that one has access to. Caribbean men and women are socialized from a very young age to develop multiple layers of these networks. Some of these affiliations are established through the church, politics, marriage or strategic friendships. Attending the 'right' schools, having a 'good' family name, or having the 'right' colour are also elements important in accessing particular networks and opening up doors for future employment or mobility. Arriving in Canada, Caribbean-born men soon found themselves at a disadvantage when it came to having access to important networks which serve the same purpose. Contrary to the promise of the 'mobility dream' where everyone is suppose to stand an equal chance at employment based on qualifications and work ethic, the reality in Canada is that networks are important in 'getting one's foot in the door' as Raymond puts it. For men who arrived with their university qualifications or professional credentials already completed outside of

Canada the situation was especially difficult. These men did not have the right contacts which could help them obtain employment commensurate with their qualifications. Most had to be willing to take a 'step down' in occupations in order to be employed and then hope through dedication, hard work, recognition and good qualifications to move up.

Other values which have been transplanted from the Caribbean to Canada are seeking employment in the public sector and the importance of keeping up appearances. Being in a position to build a large home, drive the latest model car, or being able to make many overseas shopping excursions are among the many ways in which individuals keep up the appearance of being successful to family, friends and acquaintances in the Caribbean. Living in Canada it is little surprise that Caribbeans are also concerned with keeping up the appearance of success for family, friends and neighbours. This is especially difficult in Canada because Caribbean migrants tend to be in occupations which are low paying and below their qualifications. To keep up appearances, therefore, individuals often must go to extremes.

In terms of strategies and strategizing in Canada, the men interviewed have also developed a new set of coping mechanisms to deal with the racism, discrimination and differential incorporation they experience. What is interesting about these new strategies is that many individuals continue to rely on the Caribbean in order to cope with circumstances in the Canadian system. Although these individuals physically live in Canada many will think back to the Caribbean in order to locate themselves and to measure how successful they have been. Being able to think and act in this transnational manner, Caribbean-born men seem to derive strength to cope with their circumstances which at times can seem daunting.

One of most important coping strategies the men had to develop in Canada was learning to understand and deal with the pain of racism and discrimination. When confronted with these realities, some men used the approach of passive resistance. Typically, this involved not acknowledging the racist person or the incident that was taking place around them. Other men adopted a more direct 'in your face' approach to dealing with racism or discrimination. These men confronted the incidents immediately as they happened. For other men, maintaining composure and confidence to carry on under these circumstances required that they use the historical reference point of their ancestors who had endured and survived slavery. By thinking in these transnational terms, whatever was taking place in Canada in terms of racism and discrimination could be rationalized as not being nearly as significant as what their ancestors endured.

Another coping mechanism which the men developed in Canada was learning to deal with earning lower incomes relative to the Canadian-born and having to take jobs which were below their ability and skills. For some men learning to deal with this demeaning situation meant that they looked for affirmation of their own success through other means. One of the most important ways the men accomplished this was through the success of their children within the school system. The other way was through their transnational charity work in Canada and the Caribbean. By measuring their success from these other two factors some men were able to feel a certain sense of affirmation about their decision to migrate.

For others seeking affirmation about their own success in Canada involved making numerous return visits to the Caribbean. By making these excursions back 'home', individuals were able to validate first hand that they had indeed 'progressed' more than family, kin, or friends who had remained behind. Getting back to the Caribbean also meant for some having a long-term plan for returning 'home' to live permanently. Part of this long-term dream was also to put up a 'dream home' as a symbol to others that they had indeed migrated and were now able to return as a success.

The final strategy which emerged from this sample of men was the setting up of private businesses in Canada. The men who are pursing this strategy tended to be individuals who arrived in Canada with university level schooling already completed. These men indicated feeling frustrated with their progress in the Canadian workplace. As a consequence, these individuals felt that they could do better for themselves by starting up a private business venture where they were the ones solely responsible for their future and they could avoid issues of racism and discrimination.

From the strategies which the men put in place in Canada, one can see that many overlapped historically with those that emerged in the Caribbean. The strategies which have emerged in Canada seem to be ones specifically devised to deal with the racism and discrimination that the men faced. For Black Caribbean-born men with university level schooling, surviving and maintaining composure in Canada has been a challenge. Since their arrival into Canadian society, these men have been constantly confronted with new predicaments and challenges to their credentials and positions.

CONCLUSION

This chapter has concentrated on identifying how university educated Black Caribbean-born men perceive, interpret and react to their circumstances in Canada. The mobility that individuals desired and dreamed about before arriving in Canada has not always manifested itself because of the combination of racism, discrimination, differential incorporation, and a lack of networks. As a consequence of not getting to where they had hoped, many Caribbean-born men have experienced status strain in Canada. This strain has caused some to rethink their original desires and others to lower their aspirations in an attempt to avoid disappointment and realize some sense of betterment.

The loss of status that almost all Caribbean-born men experienced when they migrated to Canada caused many to build and maintain transnational social and family networks that connected them to the Caribbean. Although they physically moved away from the Caribbean many felt compelled to produce and maintain multiple layers of social connections. These connections acted as an insurance policy to cushion the realities of racism and exclusion from mainstream Canadian society. A pattern which seemed to emerge among the interviewees in this study was that the longer they had lived in Canada the more nostalgic and ardent they were about maintaining and building up connections with family, kin and friends left behind.

The mobility strategies which the men put in place are interesting because many involve negotiating between doing well in Canada by reflecting back on the Caribbean. Some strategies have a historical foundation and were transplanted as part of the culture from the Caribbean. Other strategies involve seeking affirmation about individual success by measuring it in terms of others. Overall, the revised strategies allowed the men to respond, manage, manipulate, and control their circumstances in Canada so that they have been able to derive a sense of accomplishment and satisfaction about their decision to migrate.

The extent to which the men felt satisfied in retrospect with the decision to migrate to Canada seems to be reflected not surprisingly in the degree to which their migration aims have been fulfilled. Those interviewees who seemed to show the most regret for having migrated were men who arrived with professional qualifications or university schooling already completed. This group initially had high aspirations and expectations for themselves but after being hit by differential incorporation, institutional discrimination, and the lack of networks they had to devise new strategies to give themselves some sense of achievement. Those individuals who arrived without a university level of schooling and subsequently completed their qualification in Canada seem to be happier about their migration decision. Although these men also experienced systemic and institutional barriers in their quest for high status employment, most felt that they had better opportunities in Canada which they would not have had living in the Caribbean.

APPENDIX

Table 16.1 Summary profile of Black Caribbean-origin men interviewed

Alias	Age	Occupation	Place of birth	Year of arrival in Canada	Social class in Caribbean	Marital status	No. of children	Highest level of schooling	Year completed first degree	Return visits Carib.	Hope to return Carib.
Everton	42	Part-time lecturer	Barbados	1983	Lower Middle	Married	2	PhD Geography	1980 UWI	Rarely	Maybe
Roland	34	Accountant	Jamaica	1975	Lower Middle	Single	None	BA Economics	1988 York U	Never	No
Horace	43	Consultant	Jamaica	1982	Working Class	Married	3	PhD Sociology	1978 Guelph	Often	Yes
John	40	Writer	Barbados	1979	Working Class	Married	3	BAS Admin-Studies	1978 UWI	Often	Yes
Edmond	65	High/Sch teach	St Lucia	1957	Lower Working	Married	2	BA Philosophy	1962 Acadia	Often	Yes
Raymond	42	Part-time lecturer	St Kitts	1966	Upper Middle	Married	1	PhD History	1986 York U	Often	Maybe
Anton	69	High/Sch teach	Jamaica	1969	Lower Middle	Married	3	BSC Math/Physics	1952 UWI	Often	Snow-bird*
Philbert	53	High/Sch teach	Guyana	1962	Upper Class	Separated	2	MES Environmental	1969 Ryerson	Often	Not Sure
Leroy	49	Real estate agent	Jamaica	1971	Middle Class	Separated	5	BA Sociology	1994 York U	Often	Yes
Freddy	30	Dispatcher	Jamaica	1994	Working Class	Married	2	BA Geography	1990 UWI	Never	Yes
Donovan	37	Lawyer	Jamaica	1981	Working Class	Divorced	None	BA Law	1992 York U	Often	Not Sure
Pierre	67	Social worker	St Lucia	1958	Lower Middle	Married	2	MA Social Work	1965 Acadia	Never	No
Eugene	61	High/Sch teach	Jamaica	1975	Middle Class	Married	3	MED Education	1959 UWI	Often	Not Sure
George	63	High/Sch teach	Barbados	1954	Lower Middle	Married	5	BA Sociology	1974 Concordia	Often	Not Sure
Martin	58	Engineer	Jamaica	1985	Middle Class	Married	3	BE Engineering	1955 UWI	Often	Not Sure
Ruben	42	Entrepreneur	Trinidad	1987	Middle Class	Married	3	BA Psychology	1983 SUNY	Never	Not Sure
Basil	34	PhD student	Guyana	1978	Middle Class	Single	None	MA Political Science	1987 MAC	Rarely	Yes
Patrick	51	Entrepreneur	Jamaica	1980	Middle Class	Separated	1	BA Engineering	1974 London	Often	Yes
Albert	57	Physician	Grenada	1967	Lower Middle	Married	3	BA Medicine	1963 UWI	Often	Snow-bird*
Simon	51	Film Maker	Trinidad	1970	Middle Class	Divorced	1	BA Film Studies	1979 Ryerson	Never	No

Note: * Term used by respondents to describe someone who spends winters in the Caribbean and summers in Canada.

NOTES

1 In the analysis which follows the men are identified by pseudonyms as are the place and organization names which appear. Table 16.1. in the appendix summarizes some of the characteristics of the men interviewed for this study.
2 Many immigrants, like Caribbeans arriving in Canada, had to undertake further education, to re-qualify in such fields as medicine, nursing, teaching, social work, engineering, architecture etc (Cummins *et al.*: 1988)

REFERENCES

Abella, Rosalie (1984) *Equity in Employment: Royal Commission Report General Summary*, Toronto: Commission on Equity in Employment.

Anderson, Wolsley (1993) *Caribbean Immigrants: A Socio-Demographic Profile*, Toronto: Canadian Scholars Press.

Beaujot, Roderick, K. G. Basavarajappa and Ravi Verma (1988) *Income of Immigrants in Canada*, Ottawa: Statistics Canada.

Blau, Peter and Otis Duncan (1967) *The American Occupational Structure*, New York: Wiley.

Blishen, Bernard (1970) 'Social Class and Opportunity in Canada', *Canadian Review of Sociology and Anthropology*, 24: 465–88.

Bolaria, Singh and Peter Li (1985) *Racial Oppression in Canada*, Toronto: Garamond Press.

Conway, Dennis (1988) 'Conceptualizing Contemporary Patterns of Caribbean International Mobility', *Caribbean Geography*, 2, 3: 145–63.

Cummins, J. and T. Skutuabb-Kangas (1988) *Minority Education: From Shame to Struggle*, Clevedon: Multilingual Matters.

Darroch, Gordon (1979) 'Another Look at Ethnicity Stratification and Social Mobility in Canada', *Canadian Journal of Sociology*, 4: 1–25.

Gibelman, Margaret (1993) 'The Glass Ceiling in Social Work: Is it Shatterproof?' *Affilia*, 8, 4, Winter: 442–5.

Head, Wilson and Enid Lee (1980) *The Black Presence in the Canadian Mosaic: A Study of Perceptions and the Practice of Discrimination Against Blacks in Metropolitan Toronto*, Toronto: Ontario Human Rights Commission.

Henry, Frances (1994) *The Caribbean Diaspora in Toronto: Learning to Live with Racism*, Toronto: University of Toronto Press.

Henry, Frances and A. Ginzberg (1985) *Who Gets the Work? A Test of Racial Discrimination in Employment*, Toronto: Urban Alliance on Race Relations.

Henry, Frances *et al.* (1995) *The Colour of Democracy: Racism in Canadian Society*, Toronto: Harcourt Brace & Co, Canada.

James, Carl (1993) 'Getting There and Staying There: Blacks' Employment Experience', in Paul Anisef and Paul Axelrod (eds) *Transitions: Schooling and Employment in Canada*, Toronto: Thompson Educational Publishing, pp. 3–20.

Marshall, Dawn (1982) 'The History of Caribbean Migrations', *Caribbean Review*, 11, 1: 6-9.

Ornstein, Michael (1982) *The Work Experience of Immigrants to Canada, 1969–76*, Toronto: Institute for Behavioral Research, York University.

Ornstein, Michael and Raghubar Sharma (1983) *Adjustment and Economic Experience of Immigrants in Canada: An Analysis of the 1976 Longitudinal Survey of Immigrants*, Ottawa: Department of Employment and Immigration.

Porter, John (1965) *The Vertical Mosaic*, Toronto: University of Toronto Press.

Rajagopal, Indhu (1990) 'The Glass Ceiling in the Vertical Mosaic: Indian Immigrants in Canada', *Canadian Ethnic Studies*, XXII: 96–105.

Ramcharan, Subhas (1976) 'The Economic Adaptation of West Indians in Toronto, Canada', *The Canadian Review of Sociology and Anthropology*, 13, 3: 180–215.
—— (1982) *Racism: Non-Whites in Canada*, Toronto: Butterworth and Co (Canada).
Richmond, Anthony (1964) 'The Social Mobility of Immigrants in Canada', *Population Studies*, 18: 53–69.
—— (1982) *Comparative Studies in the Economic Adaptation of Immigrants in Canada*, Downsview: Institute for Behavioral Research, York University.
—— (1989) *Current Demographic Analysis: Caribbean Immigrants*, Ottawa: Statistics Canada and the Minister of Supply and Services.
—— (1990a) 'The Income of Caribbean Immigrants in Canada', in S. Halli (ed.) *Ethnic Demography*, Ottawa: Carlton University Press.
Satzewich, Victor (1987) 'Immigrant Labour in Canada: The Cost and Benefit of Ethnic Origin in the Job Market', *Canadian Journal of Sociology*, 12: 229–41.
—— (1989) 'Racism and Canadian Immigration Policy', *Canadian Ethnic Studies*, 21: 77–97.
Simmons, Alan, and Dwaine Plaza (1992) 'International Migration and Schooling in the Eastern Caribbean', *La Educación*, XXXIV, 107: 187–213.
—— (1995) 'Breaking Through the Glass Ceiling: The Pursuit of University Training Among Afro-Caribbean Migrants and their Children in Toronto', unpublished paper presented at the Learned Society Conference, University of Quebec, Montreal, 31 May 1995.

Index